Next-Year Country

Voices of Prairie People

Barry Broadfoot

M&S

⟦A DOUGLAS GIBSON BOOK⟧

To my mother,
Sylvia (Scoular) Broadfoot,
... a pioneer's daughter

Canadian Cataloguing in Publication Data
Broadfoot, Barry, 1926–
    Next-year country : voices of prairie people

New ed.
"A Douglas Gibson book".

ISBN 0-7710-1680-6

1. Prairie Provinces–History.   2. Prairie
Provinces–Social conditions.   3. Prairie
Provinces–Biography.   I. Title.

FC3237.B76 1994   971.2   C94-930617-7
F1060.B76 1994

Design by Linda Gustafson
Printed and bound in Canada on acid-free paper

A Douglas Gibson Book
McClelland & Stewart Inc.
The Canadian Publishers
481 University Avenue
Toronto, Ontario
M5G 2E9

Contents

❧

Introduction to 1994 Edition

❧

When I finished this book in 1987 it was not just the result of months spent criss-crossing the Prairies, it was also the sum total of many years of writing oral history books on this fascinating land. From compiling true stories for *Ten Lost Years* (published in 1974) and its successors I learned the skills of where to go, who to see and, most important, what questions to ask. And the most rewarding interviews were always on the Prairies.

The West indeed had problems back in 1987, although in those days the mark of prosperity remained on the land. There were new homes, $140,000 combines, and bustling towns, although the villages showed more and more that they were becoming "old folks' homes" as they are described in the book. Yet, even then, farm bankruptcies were numerous and farmers were deep in debt, hoping against all probability that the days of eight-dollars-a-bushel wheat would return. In fact, only the keenest of observers might have ventured that wheat itself could some day become irrelevant – in a land known for ages as The Bread Basket Of The World.

In those days Canada itself had yet to go through the awful realization that its annual deficits mounting into enormous national debt were becoming a threat to its very nationhood.

In the years since then, things have got worse. Hard times, bitter winters, no rain when it was needed and too much at harvest times, when it was a curse. Low and then lower prices for wheat, thanks to the loss of traditional overseas markets, high oil prices briefly because of the Gulf War and now low prices to diminish the memories of the great boom days. Alberta, the strongest financially and the most populated of the three Prairie provinces, has seen its fabled oil fields being drained away, and its Heritage Fund squandered, with no industrial strategy in place. Manitoba, with no boom and no bust, has always had its own peculiar strength. Half of its population is to be found in the metro area of Winnipeg, my old home town: it is able to survive, despite what the pundits said, because although it has supposedly been in a downward spiral since the Second World War, it's still there.

Like Winnipeg, the rest of the Prairie cities will continue to experience the influx of Natives, mostly young, flooding in off the reserves in search of something better. My chapter in this book "Indians" is a dark and gloomy one, and things have not got better in the years since those voices spoke. I wish I could be optimistic that this problem will solve itself in the near future.

The other gloomy chapter, "Trouble On The Family Farm", has been proved sadly accurate, all over the Prairies, with things getting worse for the little guys. Saskatchewan, for example, saw fewer farmers and bigger farms. Meanwhile its youth, happily, realized that education was all-important, and government money flowed into higher education, what money there was. The population decreased slowly but steadily. The price of wheat remained rock-bottom low.

In the East, the West – despite the heavy crop of Western Tories in Brian Mulroney's Government – was often referred to as irrelevant. Anger against the Ottawa and provincial politicians mounted – and as a result Preston Manning's Reform Party became a real force to be reckoned with in the 1993 election. He vowed that with the aid of a large contingent of MPs from British Columbia, the West would be heard, and served.

The late 1980s and the 1990s have been depressing but not depression years. Recession, yes. The large cities may have maintained their vigour, but as Alf Bryan, who farms 32,000 acres with his brother and nephew, said, "Take away the government and all they employ and there's not much work in Saskatchewan." Lack of small and productive secondary industry has always been the curse of the Prairie economy. In fact, agriculture in Saskatchewan now accounts for only 6.72 per cent of the Gross Provincial Product. Believe it or not, it's in fourth place, behind manufacturing, transportation and trade.

But as in a siege, if you hold out long enough a feeling of optimism arises. It could be a change in the national economic climate, but more likely in the global climate. Gary Fairburn, editor of *The Western Producer*, the weekly which is the farmers' "Bible", sees hope. He is still very cautious, but he sees better crops and bigger ones and predicts benefits from diversification by farmers, from wheat into lentils, sunflowers, plots of "pick-'em-yourself" berries and, especially, canola, once called rapeseed. He sees the day when canola production will surpass wheat in value. Twenty years ago that would have been unthinkable.

He speaks carefully: "We are at the bottom. Now I see optimism. But it is too early to be more than the beginning of hope."

It will take time, a long time, for the West to rise again. Not the way it was, full of boisterous and muscled enthusiasm. Those days are probably gone for ever. But it will survive, mainly because it always has survived. The people, usually descended from immigrants who came much less than a century ago, put together a wonderful inland empire through guts and work and know-how and determination, and with their sons and daughters following. To say, "I'm from the Prairies," was to say, "I'm proud my roots are in the Prairies."

Yes, the West will rise again. It never was down for the count; just groggy from too many blows not caused by its own mistakes. It will be the people, through their sense of community and their commitment to, let's face it, a unique and rewarding way of life, who will save the West. Take a look at the final story in the book, and at the final line: "People will never know." I wrote this book so that people will know, and will understand, the people of the Prairies.

Barry Broadfoot
Nanaimo, B.C.
March 1994

One

The Prairies Are Always With You

🕊 ══════════════════════════════════

Next-Year Country . . . Food Basket of the World . . . The Miracle . . .
Looking for Damyen . . . Those Women Who Made the West . . . Look,
a Red Blanket . . . Coal from the Train . . . Depression Whoopee . . . Off
the Farm . . . Driller . . . Wonderful People . . . The First Team . . . Trust
. . . An Indian-Hater . . . Our Old Home Towns . . . The Smart Money
Boys . . . Honour Our Pioneers . . . The Prairies Are Always With You

══════════════════════════════════

This chapter will give you an idea of the range of people I met and talked with
as I criss-crossed the Prairies. The stories they told me were sometimes happy
and sometimes very sad, dealing with the distant past, or the present, or talking
about the way the future seems to be shaping up. Some stories are very personal,
some very general. In every case I hope the tape-recorded voices ring out from
the page as clearly as they rang out for me.

🕊 Next-Year Country

"It's hail that breaks your heart. Not drought. Not grasshoppers.
None of these things like rain and bugs and grasshoppers. Hail.
It was like this. When you had a drought, this happened. You
planted and then the wheat came up, and it got higher and higher,
and with good rains you knew it was going to be a good crop.
Then no rain. This would be about early in June and then it got
hot and hotter and no rain. For days, weeks. Three weeks. No rain
and the hot, hot sun and the hot, hot wind. Especially the wind,
that did most of the damage. And the crop stopped growing and
you knew you were in a drought and there would be no crop.
Then there was no crop. But you could see it coming. Your heart,
it would pray for rain, but you knew, somehow, that it would be
a drought. So you were ready.
With the grasshoppers, it was like this. They would come, just a
few at first. They always moved in from the south. You'd know
they were twenty or fifteen miles from you and there was nothing

to do. It was impossible to spray everything. You could do just a little bit but after some years you knew that spray and chemicals wasn't going to do the trick. Then they would come. A few at first, then lots, and then millions, and you could see them in a field. You'd walk through it and they'd be jumping by the thousands all around you. All the fields. The gardens. The roadsides. Everything. That was when you knew it was over. But you knew they were coming, so your mind was ready.

But the hail. It would be a good crop, maybe one of the best. Our biggest field was ninety-four acres. That was a big field. And one time I remember it was all in wheat. My dad said it was going to be his best crop in history. We'd go out after the dinner chores and just look at it. Dad would say, at least fifty bushels to the acre. That was something, you know. There was our wealth in the field and we'd be starting with the binder in two days.

And then this afternoon my father came running in from the machinery shed and said to get the blankets nailed on the windows. He pointed, and off to the west there was this big cloud. Oh, it was so big. 'Hail,' he said. 'That's hail.' It was black and kind of greenish and we could see flashes of lightning through it. We knew. We'd seen that before. 'Get the chickens in,' Mom said, but they knew. They were already cowering around the door. There was thunder and the air suddenly got very cold. All this was happening in about four minutes. Dad was cursing, saying, 'Damn it, damn it.'

It was coming straight for us and Dujik's farm and Bailey's farm and us and there was a roaring sound in the air. It came then. The sky was black and the hail came down, just came down by the millions of hailstones. You couldn't see, almost. This went on for about four or five minutes and then it stopped, and the thunder was over us and going towards the Fosters' and the Christopher-sons' and over to the east. There was another rush of rain and then it was quiet.

Ten minutes before, we had about ninety-four acres of wheat we were ready to cut and another two fields, both smaller, and some rye and barley and oats. When we went outside there was nothing. All you could see was the wonderful wheat smashed flat into the mud. Hail everywhere. Mud everywhere. And the wheat smashed flat. You didn't even have a bushel to keep as a souvenir.

That was the way it was. But a mile to the north and two miles to the south the sun kept on shining. They could see our storm going over and it didn't touch them. They had their crop. Not a bushel lost, and we didn't have a bushel to harvest.

That's hail for you. Hail will break a farmer's heart. It is like God is picking on him, saying, 'I'm going to teach you a lesson.' No reason for it. Everyone is happy and we're feeling rich and somebody feels the air getting colder and you see that cloud coming, and what happens? Ten minutes later you're right back to where you started from in the spring, no crop, but you're also an awful lot poorer. And you're sadder. You're maybe wiser too. You say, how can anybody make a living in this country? Drought and hoppers were bad, but hail, there was no accounting for it, and that's what made it Tomorrow Country. Next-Year Country."

❧ Food Basket of the World

"All of us, you know, we really have been living in a fool's paradise. I mean, when did you first hear that the Prairies was the Food Basket of the World? I'll tell you. It was in your geography books, or your history books, when you were in grade school. Canadians thought the world was depending on our wheat. It couldn't do without our wheat. The world would starve, or that's what we were told.

It was never true, and it isn't true today. I mean, when the world's wheat production is about 510 million tons and Canada produces about 27 million tons, we're pretty small potatoes, whichever way you look at it. And I think a lot of people haven't got it into their heads yet that we're pretty small in the overall picture.

You're looking at a lot of very high-powered competition out there. I can tell you that France – and that country grows more wheat than Canada – when it subsidizes its farmers up to sixty-five per cent of their costs in growing and selling their wheat, hey boy, we're in trouble. The same with the Americans, and they produce more than double the wheat we grow, and they're in the subsidy game up to their noses, too.

Trying to sell, that's that problem, with the other large nations cutting prices right and left, and here's something that might shake you. Take Britain. Little old Britain, and that is only England, mostly. All those small fields. How England can grow about 15 million tons of wheat, well, to me, it just boggles my bloody mind. But they do. Or China, once one of our major buyers, they now produce nearly three times as much wheat as we do. Bloody Turkey. You thought it was all mountains, didn't you? About 18 million tons. India, and all those starving millions, they double our production, almost. And Russia, and think of the vast wheat sales we've made to them through the Canadian Wheat Board, the Russkies pull in about 80 million tons a year.

The whole picture makes us look pretty small, and yet what is Canada known for throughout the world? Well, Eskimos and Mounties and wheat.

There's nothing we can do about it, naturally. There is no more agricultural land left in Canada, so we can't increase our wheat harvests. But what we can do is change our thinking. That we're not one of the saviours of the world. I'd say the world is doing pretty damn well in wheat without us. We're just one of the boys now."

❧ *The Miracle*

"Around the first of August is always the best time. One morning around that time I'll get in my car and drive out Number One to the Drumheller turn-off and turn left and drive until I come to a view that pleases me. On top of a rise, where I can see the fields all around me, all dark green of wheat growing, but over it all there is this film of yellow, the wheat just starting to turn the slightest bit gold, and that means the ripening has started.

I walk about a hundred yards down a side road and then you're surrounded by the tall wheat and there is always a slight breeze and you've heard of waving wheat. That is exactly the right expression.

It is quiet, no traffic sound, no man sound, and the wheat is growing heavy. The kernels are getting fat and there is no sound but the quiet rustling, and you can see the little currents of wind bending it, in swirls. You can almost feel it, each stalk of wheat pulling up the last moisture and richness of the soil, and the grains are swelling and fattening and soon they will be hardening, and in three weeks it will be ready for the harvest.

When the harvest is done, there will be a huge mountain of this beautiful wheat. There will be enough to fill hundreds of elevators

all over the Prairies and thousands of grain cars and it will make
our daily bread.

It really is a miracle, you know."

❧ *Looking for Damyen*

"When I got to Edmonton I walked north to Barrhead. I had this
piece of paper with my cousin's name on it and the name of
Barrhead, and people I met, I'd show them the paper and they kept
pointing up the road.

We had bad roads in the province where I lived in Russia, but
nothing like this one. This road was mud. It was spring and it had
rained and rained, and people were driving their buggies and
wagons in the ditches. The road just pointed to where they wanted
to go, the real road was the ditches, which were harder. I thought,
this doesn't look to me like much of a civilized country.

Two days it took me to get to Barrhead, and one night I slept in
a haystack in a hole that the cattle had eaten out. I had only some
cheese and a loaf of bread and that was all, and when I got to
Barrhead nobody had heard of my cousin. I found this man who
spoke Russian and he said no, but if you go to the store there,
that's a post office and they'll tell you if this man gets mail
there. I know he did because I had written him and he'd written
me. The man in the post office spoke some Ukrainian and he said
yes, there was a man with that name, Damyen Kwasnica, but he
didn't know where he lived, and he said it would be crazy for
me to start wandering around the countryside trying to find
my cousin.

I said, yes, you are right, but what do I do? He said, if you are
smart, you will get a job right in town here and so I'll know where
you are. Well, that's what I did. If my cousin came in to get his
mail, he would tell him where I was working.

That was okay, and I was ready to do what he said, because he
was the first man to be kind to me since I had got to Montreal on
the boat. He said, go over to the livery barn with this note, and
he wrote a letter for me, and the livery-barn man gave me a job. It
was looking after the horses of people who brought them in, feeding them. I also would drive the doctor around the district when
babies were being born and things like that. Each place, I would

show them the paper the boss had written for me, asking if they knew Damyen. Nobody ever did.

This went on until summer came and I wasn't getting any money. I slept in the harness room of the barn on a cot, so if anybody came to the door late at night I would be there. I used to have to go outside to smoke my pipe. I ate at the Chinese man's café and I don't know how much I spent because the boss paid it, but he didn't pay me.

One day the grocery-store man came to me and said, 'You have been here for maybe four months now and you know, this cousin of yours, he hasn't been in once. I think this fellow has left the country and maybe there is a letter waiting for you in the Ukraine which says so.' I said, 'Well, I am not going back there to try to find it,' and that's when I told him I had no money and I wanted to go away and the man who owned the livery stable, he hadn't paid me. 'Just my meals,' I said, and he asked me what I was supposed to get. I said I didn't know. I just went to work for him. He didn't speak my language and I could speak some English now, you bet, but I was afraid that he would kick me out. Something like that. I was only seventeen and I guess I was kind of dumb.

This man, he said something like, 'Well, we'll see about this.' He took me over to the owner and they're talking away and then he says to me that the deal was that I would get four dollars a week and my meals, and I would live at the stable and look after it at night. I asked him, 'But where is my money?' The man said, 'He says you didn't ask for it. He thought you wanted him to keep it like in a savings account. You can have it any time you want. He says you have fifty-two dollars coming to you.'

Well, I just jumped up in the air with a yell. Fifty-two dollars was an awful lot of money, and I had come with a little more than nine dollars and spent it on tobacco and socks and a straw hat and candy, and all the time I had money I didn't know I had.

This was so good, you see, because all that time I really hadn't talked to my boss. He had pointed and made motions and we got along just fine that way. I knew what to do, everything, currying, harnessing, and driving the doctor around, and looking for my cousin who would give me a job on his farm, and then when I was eighteen he would show me how I would get a farm of my own. And all the time I was learning some English – and now this grocery-store man tells me I have fifty-two dollars.

So I tried talking to the boss and he said, 'Sure, I understand you.

I just don't know why you wouldn't talk before.' That's another thing I learned in Canada. You got to look all the time after yourself. I said I would work two more weeks and then I would go to Edmonton for a job. He said, 'That is fine, you have been a good worker and your money will be ready.'

Then, when two weeks was up, I bought a new shirt and pants and got my good shoes out of my suitcase and had a haircut and a bath and there was a stage going to Clyde. The stagecoach was run by a man named Marshall and he charged me two dollars. That was a lot, half a week's work, but I didn't want to walk all that way in my new shoes I hadn't worn since I bought them new in my own village. Then we came to Clyde and I got the train down to Edmonton and a woman and her two children were near me on the train. They had a big basket of lunch and they gave me sandwiches and pie. That made me happy.

At Edmonton I got off at the station and the woman said she had heard that the Alberta Hotel was a nice place to stay until I found a room. She said to buy the *Bulletin* paper and it would have places for rent, so I bought a paper on Jasper Avenue, and I saw the sign that said it was the Alberta Hotel, by 97th Street. I went in and I have my suitcase in one hand and the paper in the other and I'm wondering what to do because I'd never been in a wonderful big hotel like this before and then I hear a voice in Ukrainian and it says,'Deszie Kindrachuk, is this really you?' and this guy who is sitting in a a chair in the lobby, he comes running over to me.

You know who that was? Well, I'll tell you. It was my cousin Damyen. He was the guy I had spent all the time looking for. This cousin of mine, the guy who had written me the letter saying to come. I can't believe it. He keeps looking at me and saying, 'Damn, damn, this gotta be the craziest thing. You supposed to be in the Russian army.'

Well, that is something, isn't it? Just like that. In ten minutes I find him. We talk and he tells me he doesn't get my letter saying I'm coming. And he thinks farming is no business for him, so he just leaves, sells his two horses to a neighbour and just leaves. I tell him there is mail waiting for him in Barrhead and he says, 'Damn it all, I'll have to get that. Maybe somebody is dead or something.'

Anyway, this is crazy. It was raining for two or three days and there is no harvesting and he's working for a Scotchman on a farm at Leduc and so he comes in to Edmonton for two days to get drunk. He asks me if I want a job there. Sure, I says, so I sleep with him that night and next morning we go. Two dollars a day is what I get for two weeks, and that is hard work. This farmer knows how to make a man work.

When it is finished, we go into Edmonton again and Damyen and me, we both get jobs in a brickyard, and that's how I spend the winter in Edmonton, and that's how I meet my cousin."

✎ *Those Women Who Made the West*

"I was born in my mother's bed in a farmhouse about eighteen miles north of Melfort at 4 a.m., so they tell me, on a snowy day, a morning, on February 19 in the year 1908. My father wasn't at the bedside holding her hand or gawking away, the way it's done these days. Dad was probably out in the barn getting a two-hour head start on his chores, and the only people that were there were two midwives. That was the way it was done. There weren't many doctors around, and a doctor couldn't be spared to drive by horse and cutter all that way from the hospital and his patients just for a baby to be born. My two older brothers had been born at home when the family lived up near Carrot River in the wilds, and there were no doctors or hospitals, and besides, everybody did it. I think only a few women in the town would have gone in for their babies. In those days hospitals were for serious cases like pneumonia and a heart attack and operations and the like. Women having babies, they're not sick or hurt. They're just having a baby.

One midwife would come about five or six days before the baby was due and she took over. She walked in with her bag and she ordered the husband and the mother and the kids around. Do this, do that. Make this, put that there. She made sure the mother rested a lot for three or four days before her time was due, and she kept the kids out of the way and the husband too, and saw that everybody ate and everything.

She checked everything, the clothes, the scissors for cutting the cord, the natal patch for putting around the baby's tummy, the little clothes, that everthing was sterilized, and that there was good food and supplies ready. And then it was just waiting and washing the mother and the other things you do to her and waiting.

Babies do a lot of arriving between two and five in the morning. Did you know that? I don't know why, and there was none of this forcing the baby or delaying it a few hours so the doctor could get in his golf game. None of that. The patient came first in those days.

Then the baby would come, after the labour, and the widwife was in there helping. The first midwife, she looked after the mother, who needed it most. The other midwife or 'baby-ketcher', she'd have come over quite a few hours before, and she looked after the baby, tied the cord, washed it, and got it all warm and in its warm clothes, and if the mother was okay, they put it to the breast. That was it. Another baby was born and lived. Everybody was happy, and when the doctor saw it a few days or a month later, he'd check it out and say that it was a good job. Not many babies in our neck of the woods were named after the doctor, but a few were named after the midwife. Kind of a tribute, you might say.

Things were different in those days. I don't think any young woman had any teaching of what marriage and sex and babies were all about. Oh, a mother might tell her daughter on the day before the wedding some things, but a farm daughter, seeing birth all around her, she might have a good idea. But if she saw a stallion covering a mare, all that fury and squealing, she might have a poor idea of it.

With the boys it was different. There were always one or two girls around in any district who, well, you know. But the girls knew nothing about birth control. Seven, eight, or nine children, that was normal. Every two years, just about. It was the wife's duty, along with getting the meals, cleaning the house, feeding the chickens, collecting the eggs, sometimes milking, feeding the pigs, doing the wash, ironing, making clothes, teaching the kids their manners and trying to make every penny last to the very end, and having babies one after the other. That was her duty.

The midwives, they were wonderful women. They knew what it was all about, the life of a woman on a prairie farm in Saskatchewan in those days. I often wonder, did they think, 'Well, here is another girl born, safe and sound – and what kind of a lousy life it really is.' I suspect they did. They saw so much misery during one year, like the mothers who cried when they were finally free of the baby, not crying because the pain was gone, but crying because they knew the girl baby would face the same misery as they had to.

That is why, I think, that the women's rights movement and the early feminists were so strong in the West. They knew that a woman's life was pure hell most of the time, and miserable the rest of the time. The men could go off and shoot and fish and drink whiskey and play ball and raise a bit of hell at times, but the woman, no. There she was, tied with a big iron chain to that big black kitchen stove, and there she stayed and stayed and stayed, and did her duty to her husband and children. Nobody dares say these things, but it wasn't the men who built the West. No sir, believe me, it was those women in those lonely farmhouses far from everything and the women in the tiny villages and the towns.

I honestly don't think the person of today, say my granddaughter, can ever hope to understand or appreciate what she owes to that little grandmother of hers, my mother, and all those other grandmothers who lie in the cemeteries everywhere. That's where the real pioneers lie, those women who made the West what it is today. I hate to preach and that's what I'm doing, but let's show some recognition. I don't know what the solution is. Maybe just talking to you about it, that's maybe the answer."

✎ *Look, a Red Blanket*

"The day before Thanksgiving I drove down to Red Deer and we had lunch and then the gathering was to be at 2.30. It seemed like the whole school was there, maybe three hundred children. I'd never talked before but I had a good strong voice and I knew if I got talking on one good story first, then the rest would just follow along.

I told them my name, Mrs. Jamieson, and I told them I was seventy-two and I told them I had been born near Tofield when Alberta wasn't even a province. I said I was five years old when Alberta stopped being the Northwest Territories and became a province. I was just setting the scene. It seemed the right thing to do.

Oh, I told them about what it was like to go to school when I was their age. The little schoolhouse and walking two miles, winter and summer, and the big stove which tried to keep the children warm, and the Christmas concert, and all the things you've heard a thousand times.

Then I branched out, of course, and told about farm life and how little advantages we had, and the great blizzards in winter. And I told them about our neighbours who were mostly of foreign extraction, and the desperate, desperate struggle they had to just survive.

Then I told them one story, about when I was about eleven or twelve and my father was taking me to town in the cutter. It was cold and we were on a trail, no roads then, and we came to this soddie, this soil shack, and there was no smoke coming out of the window. My father noticed this, the smoke not coming out, and then he said, 'Look, a red blanket,' and he turned in.

A red blanket or a quilted blanket hanging on the clothesline meant a cry for help in those days. So we pulled in and went in and there was a woman lying on a bed. She'd had a miscarriage, and she was very, very weak. There were two children with her, about six and four, and the woman said her husband had gone up north to cut logs in a bush camp.

My father saw everything at once. He told me to get going, to get in the cutter and push Belle as fast as I could to town and get the doctor, and to tell the doctor that a woman was dying. I was to come back with Belle but let the doctor take his own horse. I ran out and soon we were flying down the road. It was about eight miles but we never stopped once. I got the doctor and he was on his way in ten minutes. We had good doctors in those days – they made house calls.

When I got back the house was warm. My father had got the stove blazing and he'd made a hot meat gruel for the woman and bathed her and fixed her up as well as he could, making her comfortable. The doctor said my dad had done well. By that time I was feeding the children and my dad and the doctor, and we sat around, and the woman seemed to be better. She got better in a few days but the doctor said she'd have died in that cold house, burning up with fever. A neighbour woman stayed with her for a couple of weeks, and she was all right by spring.

That's what I ended my little talk with. The story of the woman. There was a lot of applause and I think they really enjoyed it all.

As these were polite children and everything is done by the book these days, it seems, except educating them, one girl about ten had been chosen to thank me. She did it very nicely, but at the end she said, 'There's one thing I don't think I understand. Why would that woman ask her child to put a red blanket on the clothesline

so somebody would come and help her? Why didn't she just phone
the doctor?'
You know, I wonder. I really wonder."

❧ *Coal from the Train*

"I never suffered in the Depression because I was on the railroad, but I knew times were tough. There was a place just outside
of Saskatoon and there would be kids waiting and they'd stick their
tongues out at us or thumb their noses, just kid stuff, you understand, but we'd pretend it would make us sore. I'd grab the shovel,
and I'd throw two huge shovelfuls out onto the grade. Of course
I wouldn't be within fifty or a hundred feet of them.

I'd look back and see those kids scurrying around picking up
those pieces of coal. It was good coal – can't say the CN ever stinted
on quality. And if it helped to warm some squatter's shack that
night, then that was okay with me.

All over our division, all over Canada, and I guess all over the
North American continent, I bet firemen were throwing out a
couple of good big ones to kids in the ditches."

❧ *Depression Whoopee*

"Girls became very good seamstresses just making over and making
do. You'd take your cousin's dress and make it over for you and
she'd take your skirt and make it over for herself. If it was a dance
or party, you would swap clothes so you wouldn't seem to be
wearing the same things twice in a row.

Oh, we had our vanity even then in the hard times. The one
thing we could always get money for, by hook or by crook, was
to buy cosmetics in Woolworth's across from the Marquis Hotel
there in Lethbridge. They were absolutely essential, so we thought.
They just made you feel like another person, and I think the
manufacturers realized this because they didn't price them too
high. And you had to have silk stockings. You'd kill for those,
but the synthetic ones, they were coming in, so a lot of us used
them. They painted their legs during the war, you know, to look

like they had stockings on, but that was pretty old hat around Lethbridge. The girls did that, and my, did we ever get frowns from our mothers. But dances and house parties were very important to us. Our mothers knew it, so I think they frowned just for show. If there was a dance, and some towns had them every Saturday night, you'd see all the young people. That's where I met my husband, at Pincher Creek, and that is a long, long way from fourteen miles north of Lethbridge, so you can see we travelled around the country for these dances. Gas was next to nothing, maybe twenty cents a gallon, and everybody would chip in and buy the gas for the owner, and there always was a couple of mickeys of rye whiskey, so if you stuck six into a car it would be a merry bunch who unloaded for the dance. There was probably more drinking then than a lot of people realize. Whoopee! That was what we'd yell. It was called Drinking From The Flask. And you'd dance to two in the morning and then home. In the summer, you'd get home at dawn and change into other clothes and help Mother in the kitchen, the milking, the separating, and then she'd let you lie down for a couple of hours to sleep."

🕊 *Off the Farm*

"When Hunter brought in Leduc Number One in '47 the whole thing just exploded. They'd discovered oil, big oil, in Alberta. Remember those days? J. H. Christ. I'm sixty now and I can still remember that first day I signed on with Imperial. The rigs then were nothing like the big ones they have today, all mechanical and computer and the works, and that was some day. I was free of stooking and pitching and one-waying and seeding and slopping pigs and getting a cow's god-damned tail slashing into my face at six in the morning. I was off the farm. No more 5 a.m. stuff for me.

And it kind of worked out that way. First, Imperial. Then Shell, and then a spell at Gulf and with an independent as tool-push. I was on the rigs until '72, making good money all the time. Lots of it. Saving it was hard, the wife always wanting the house in Calgary and me on the site, and kids growing up and needing education and loans, and there I was out in the rain and the snow and the cold. Then in '72 I fell off a platform. Just a slip, but that did it. This bad back of mine.

The company brought me in to Calgary to headquarters and here I'm a nobody, but I like it. I can push these figures around on this desk and know what they mean in half a second, and when I've done that for two hours, well, that's just about my day. I don't let on. I just keep sending the completed reports back during the day, timing them, noon, two, three, four, and they think I'm working my butt off. Hell, they're all done by eleven or so.

The rest of the time I sort of sit and think and daydream, and more and more I think of the old home place, I don't know why, but I just miss the old place. I'll be at my desk and looking out on a clear day I can see the fields green and then they get yellow and then I know they're cutting out there, and I think, what am I doing here?"

🐌 *Driller*

"Working for one outfit, I lasted six hours once. I went on this shift with a Home outfit and we're pulling pipe so I walk about a hundred yards away for a smoke. I'm smoking away and this pickup comes up the trail and a guy stops and says, 'What are you supposed to be doing?'

I didn't like the look on his face because I knew he was the super, and he was a snake. A lousy shit of a guy and everybody knew it, and I don't know why I had hired on that rig knowing he was around, but I did. And I said back to him, 'I'm supposed to be working.'

He threw the pickup into gear and a few minutes later the driller says to me when I walk up, he says, 'Brad, I've got to fire you. The super doesn't like you.'

I said I'd never met the bastard before, but I like this driller, a friend of mine, and I say okay, give me a lift to town, because he was going in for some gear. A mile down the road Regal is drilling a farm-out, and I say for him to stop and wait a minute. Their shack is right by the road and I knock and walk in, and three minutes later I walk out and I got a job working for Regal. That's the way it went."

👐 *Wonderful People*

"I can tell you when we came to Regina in 1948 we had nothing. I mean nothing. And we didn't have a place to live.

There was kindness, I can say that. This woman and her husband, their names were Mr. and Mrs. Williams, were kind to us and to our children. They didn't have to take us in and let us sleep and live in these two rooms they had in their basement. They had never had people living with them, but they saw this piece in the paper that people from Estonia had no place to stay, and Mrs. Williams went down to the office and said they would take a family. They did everything for us, for my husband and me and our three children who had come over on the refugee boat. They got clothes from their neighbours. They got furniture and beds and other things from their friends, stuff they could have sold, but they gave them to us for nothing. They had us for Christmas and they had presents for my husband, for me, for our children. They took us around in their car to see the Christmas lights and they took me and the kids to see Santa Claus.

Mr. and Mrs. Williams didn't have to do this for us. We were strangers and foreigners. The word they called us was DPs. That meant Displaced Persons. People in Canada thought, 'Oh, DPs are just useless dumb people who used to be farm slaves on a big shot's place.' But we weren't, we were middle class, as you call it. My husband had been a teacher in Estonia, and he spoke English quite well. I had been a teacher's aide before my first baby came and I know that teacher's aides did not come along in Canada until years later. You see, Estonia was not a poor country. It was just in the wrong place in Europe.

Mrs. Williams had a few friends over this Christmas and my husband and I met them, and I could see them thinking, these people aren't serfs, these people are like us. They just don't have any money and are living in the Williams' basement.

Mrs. Williams had a piano and she had let me play it, and she asked me if I would play for her friends. I did, three pieces, the most difficult ones I knew. I wanted to impress them. Oh, I was good that night. I even impressed myself and my husband. I could see these six or eight neighbours thinking, 'These aren't the kind of people I've read about, these people are like us.' I'm sure that's what they were thinking.

I remember someone asking my husband what had happened to us, and he talked and talked, about leaving our country, getting to Sweden and then to England, and then sailing on the *Empress of Canada* up the St. Lawrence River, and how we all felt, without any Canadian money at all. How the government put us on trains and fed us and let us off in Regina with a few others, and how we liked Regina and the people, and how we hoped to make this our home.

It was a wonderful party, and through it my husband got a good job. He'd been working outdoors in the cold for the city on a work crew and one of the men at the party, Mr. Albert, came around to see him just after Christmas. He said he could give him a job in his business, as a book-keeper. That was fine, because that was what John taught in the school in our own country. He made more money, and that's when we started to pay money to the Williams. We felt better about that, although my husband had been doing all the work around the house.

Then when spring came my husband said to Mr. Williams that we would have to go to a farm to work because he had signed a one-year contract. The government made us sign these, because after the war the soldiers who were supposed to have gone back to the farms didn't. They went to school and university and to the cities. That is what they told us. We were needed on the farms. Mr. Williams said he would see about that. He did some phoning and then he told us we didn't have to worry.

So that was fine, and we were saving money and Mrs. Williams was getting me housework jobs with her friends and every day I worked that was two dollars, and we saved. In the spring, my husband told Mr. Williams we would find an apartment, and I guess they felt that was fine. They had looked after us long enough and they were wonderful people, the most wonderful people we have ever met in Canada. So we moved to an apartment and my husband got a chance to work in a furniture store, and the money was better and I did housework and did sewing for some women, and we had lots of money.

We stayed in Regina and in 1950 we bought a house for $6,000 and my husband spent a lot of time to fix it up. He became a manager in the furniture store on Broad Street, and then in 1959 we thought we would like to see Vancouver and we had this car so we drove. The two boys loved it and we both did, and so we sold the house in Regina and moved to Burnaby.

Mr. Williams, he retired a few years later, and they moved to Vancouver, and we are still friends. They still are our best friends, and my son named his first son and first daughter after them."

❧ The First Team

"Times come when I sit in my rocking-chair and I look at the old photographs in the books. There they are. The first team of horses, Dolly and Mike. Heeeyup! Mike! Hey there! Ho! Heeuppp! The first combine. That was in 1946. A Cockshutt. Not much of a machine, but the best they had then. New house. The new car and our trip to Victoria, British Columbia. All the ones of the kids and their kids. Hundreds of them. They all turned out good. Not the pictures. I mean the kids."

❧ Trust

"My wife and I came out from Poland in 1963 and her uncle sponsored us for five years, meaning he would see we didn't go on welfare for five years. And my uncle he said, 'You'll stay with us on the farm this fall and winter, and in the spring I've arranged that you rent a quarter section.'

That fall I worked on the farm learning everything I could, and I did the same that winter, and learning English and reading all the government papers on farming. I'd go with my uncle when he went visiting, talking to farmers and people in Portage and Winnipeg, and that helped my English, too. I could speak it pretty good in six or seven months.

My uncle said he'd loan me the money for the seed and he'd rent me his equipment and keep me going until there was a crop. He was a businessman. Family didn't mean that much to him. He would help me, but he wouldn't give me money.

That was okay with me, and in the spring I got the land ready and seeded and did the farm work I had to, and I worked for farmers around, on their tractors for good money, and when it was time to take off the wheat crop my uncle came with his combine and truck and we did that, and I got a big crop of thirty-four bushels to the acre, and that was very good.

What I liked about it was this. My uncle and I went into Portage and saw this businessman I was renting the land from and he said, 'How much did you get into the bins?' I told him and he said, 'Then you owe me so much.' It was a third of the crop. One-third to him. I got the rest.

Then he said, 'There's all this business of the quotas and the wheat board, and you won't be able to sell it, so I'll find out what the grade is selling for, and I'll buy your share for ten cents less a bushel.' I asked my uncle and he said, 'That's good. The man is being very fair.'

So that's the way I did it, and when I'd paid off my debts to my uncle I had about $4,000 for us off those 143 acres and I thought, 'Oh boy, you'd never be able to make that much money in just one year in Poland.'

That was fine, but what I liked ... I always remember. That businessman trusted me to tell him how much wheat I'd got. He didn't come around snooping during the summer looking at it, and he didn't send somebody to check the bins. He just took my word for it. Dear mother, I thought, this is going to be such a fine country to live in.''

An Indian-Hater

"Last winter I'm driving into town and she's one bitch of a cold day. There's three kids walking along the highway, busy as hell, and I think, 'God, if they're going into Macleod they ain't going to make it. Freeze to death.' They look as if they're wanting a ride, which they do, and I slow down and look 'em over. About fourteen years old. Christ knows how far they've walked. I roll down the window and tell 'em to hop in the back of the pickup. It's still as cold as Billy-be-damned back there and it's warm in the cab and two of them could have got in with me, other in the back, but no, I tell 'em to hop in behind. At least they'll get into town. That's what I did, and I'm ashamed of myself. But there it is.

You know what that is? I'm thinking like a white man, just like everybody does. You don't have anything to do with them. Why?

I'm damned if I know. And then we pull into town and they get off and a friend, he walks over and says, 'Joe, why did you pick up them Injuns?'

Jesus H. Christ, man! There it is. I'm no better than the rest of them around here. I talk a lot, but when it comes down to doing some kindly act, something to help them, it just shows off my prejudice as much as if I'd gone by them at 60 m.p.h. See what I mean? You're looking at an Indian-hater, even though I don't know I am. Worse, I don't understand that I am. But, damn it all, I am.

So don't ask me for solutions. We got to go back two hundred years and start all over again, and that isn't going to happen."

❧ Our Old Home Towns

"When I drive into one of these little villages along some of the railway lines and where the highway has been shifted a mile east or north, if I see a young fellow hanging around, I think he's either shiftless and doesn't have any ambition, or he's visiting his folks.

No place for the young people. Who is going to stay in a ghost town? Nothing doing there. A couple of businesses, a little store run by an old lady and her husband, and sometimes a hotel that's only a beer parlour now.

The big event is when the beer truck comes in once a week and drops off a couple of kegs and a few dozen beer.

You never in your life saw such places. I never thought I'd see them, but there they are, all through southern Saskatchewan, in the middle and some up north too. Maybe fifty or sixty people left, who make going to the store for a loaf of bread the big deal of the day, and you could remember when they were busy little places. Might even have a butcher shop, a stationery shop with notions and such, and two or three stores. And now there's only one store, an itty-bitty thing, and it might take in ten bucks a day and why they keep open I just don't know.

But that's it, and remember, all these little dead or dying villages, they were all our old home towns. The places we left to go off to war, or off to the city and succeed. And now they are just a lot of memories. Good ones, and now they're all gone with what they call progress."

👐 *The Smart Money Boys*

"Retailing was not where the money was. That was litty-bitty money. The money was in industrial land, real estate for business and industry, and you could go out way out in the country, way out where the West Edmonton Mall is, and pick up scrub land for nothing an acre. Fifty bucks. Fifty acres. It wouldn't support a crop or cows, but the buildings didn't care what kind of land they were sitting on. Land is land. Put in servicing and fifty bucks an acre becomes a thousand dollars the day the last pipe was laid. Two thousand, in the right location, no worry.

That's the way I made money. Look at St. Albert in '51. A village, out in the farming country. Sherwood Park. They built that out of nothing. Bonnie Doon, right in the city, and you could have had it for a song. Out by the refineries along the river valley, that's where it was moving in those early days. Just follow the smart boys who could get highways and roads and intersections and bridges put in, tickling the belly of the politicians with bribes and gifts, and that was the way it was done.

I just followed the smart money boys. Picking up ten acres here and there they didn't want. By '70 I had more money than I'd ever want for the rest of my life."

👐 *Honour Our Pioneers*

"We retired about 1965 and Mr. Horvath died and then after a while I sold my house and went into an old folks' home. That was fine, but after my two best friends died, I said to the supervisor that I wanted to take a trip. She took me to the trust company which was looking after my money and the man said I had lots of money. I could go anywhere in the world I wanted. I told him I wanted to visit the farm where I grew up and he said where, and I said it was near Winnipeg and I had a nephew in Winnipeg and he'd look after me. That was fine.

They got me the ticket on Air Canada and I flew there and my brother's boy, this nephew Jerry, he was waiting. After a day we drove up to the farm, three hours, and he was saying, 'Sure you know where it is?' Of course, it was sixty years ago and everything was changed, but I found it. There was nothing the same. Nothing. A beautiful bungalow and nothing like the old log house I remembered. All these steel white bins, about ten or twelve, and a big lawn, and you know what? When we drove in, there was some kind of a picnic on the lawn there. It was a party for the people who owned it. I told my nephew to just say we had made a mistake, but he wasn't going to do that.

He got out and a young man came over. The owner. The farmer. I could see Jerry explaining and the young farmer, about forty or so, he came right over to the car and he said to come in, get out, please come in, and so I did. He took me over and introduced me to everyone and they got a chair out of the house for me and we sat down at their picnic. A big picnic, about twenty-six people, I guess, and there was lemonade and beer and sandwiches and cake, and we all talked and he told me about his farm. I said I hadn't really been on a farm for seventy years and so he pointed out all the machinery he had around. I said I couldn't believe it.

One of the little boys asked what it was like when I lived on this farm and I said, well, first it was all bush. You should have seen their eyes go big. 'Trees here? Is that right, Dad?' He said he guessed so, and I said the trees, every one, all poplar, first they had to be cut down with an axe by my father and then hauled into big piles and dried. In the winter we burned these piles. Then the stumps had to be pulled out by the two oxen we had, with a chain and my dad chopping at the roots while my bigger brother made the oxen pull the stumps. Hundreds, thousands, of stumps and trees, I said. Then I told them, and boy, were they ever listening, I told them my father used a single plough to break the earth up, and then it had to dry up, and in the fall he harrowed it smooth. Then he'd get on the train and go to Moose Jaw and work for the railroad and come back at Christmas and bring us money and food, and then he'd go away for two more months.

In the spring, I told them, this was our first crop and my dad got the wheat seed and threw it out, you know. Broadcast it. Like in the old pictures. Then he got the oxen and harrowed it again and this covered the seed with dirt, and then, well, we just waited. Then my dad and my brother used scythes. What's a scythe, they wanted to know? I tried to describe it, and then I asked them, do you know those pictures of Father Time at New Year's? That big knife, the curved knife on a kind of stick? Oh, yes. Ooooh. Aaaah. He cut the ripe wheat with that and we only had maybe ten acres, and then came our turn. My mother and me and my other brother, we gathered up this wheat into bundles. Then we took long stems of the wheat and made them into a rope and we tied up the wheat into a sheaf.

Same thing again. What's a sheaf? Their father explained that to them and then I told them that my mother used to make a special sheaf and save it. We'd put it in the corner at Christmas and pray at it, like a shrine. That meant we prayed for a good harvest next year. More oohs and aaahs. Big eyes.

I told them that then we put all these sheaves into these stooks and the sun riped them all up and when they were ready we piled them carefully on a stone-boat and hauled them to the barn. What's a stone-boat? More oohs and aaahs. You see, these kids didn't know anything about all this. I guess it's not interesting enough to teach them.

Then I told them, what happened next was that one of the Scottish farmers near Gladstone would come. He'd have a big thresher and he'd come into the yard one morning, usually in December because we were so small and way out of the way, and they'd do our piles of stooks in one morning. So all that work – planting, scything, taking the sheaves and making stooks and moving the stooks and waiting – was all done for that morning. That was our crop. Our harvest, after cutting down the trees and clearing the land and burning the trees and everything.

I said that's the way it was done when you didn't speak English and had no money and didn't know much about anything, like farming in Manitoba.

I was just telling all this from memory. In my normal voice. And then that little boy, one of the bunch there, he said, 'My dad can do 120 acres in one day with his combine and he doesn't have to chop trees or burn them or make a little rope to tie up the grain or any of that stuff. He just goes out and that's all he does, and in about two weeks everything is done and then it's time for us to go back to school.' He said, and I remember, 'I think the way in the old days was a lot harder.'

Well, I had to agree with them, and we all laughed and the young farmer said that they had learned something today that they would never learn in school. Wasn't that right? All those children nodded their heads, oh yes, it was true. All big-eyed and looking at this old lady like she was something out of a history book.

That was that part of it, and then this farmer's wife stood up. It turned out she also taught school in some town near, and she told the children that they had had an experience this afternoon that they would never have got anywhere else. She said all the people who had done this were dead now. Excepting me, of course, and everybody laughed. She said we should honour our pioneers. Think good thoughts about us, how we worked so hard, and some did fine and some did not do so well. She said we should be honoured and then she thanked me and I thanked her for having us, and then she said she had learned more about what had happened a long time ago than she had learned in school. Her husband called out, 'Me too,' and we all laughed.

Then it was time to go. It was a wonderful time that afternoon, the picnic and seeing the place so rich and neat and clean and such a nice family living on it. And when I got back to Vancouver, why, a few days later a package came in the mail and it was a picture, taken from an airplane, of the farm and the house, and everybody in that family, even the littlest, had signed it and wished me luck. That was a very, very nice thing for them to do."

❧ The Prairies Are Always With You

"If we don't love or at least like the Prairies, why the hell when we go to a party or just sit around the clubhouse after a round, why do we always talk about the place?

Victoria, as I see it, is populated by people from the three prairie provinces. There are old codgers like myself who decided one day we just weren't going to take another Manitoba winter. There are others, fairly young, maybe forty-five or so, who came out here on a holiday or for some other reason and said, well, this is it, and went back to Saskatoon or Winnipeg or wherever and told the boss he was packing it up, sold the house, and came out here. In this town everybody comes from somewhere else, and that's the Prairies. We subscribe to the *Western Producer* or the local newspaper, Calgary or Regina or wherever, and so we keep track of our roots and we talk about them, what is doing and who's doing what to whom, and about the crops and the Stampede and the football games and this, that, and everything.

I'm always amazed. At these parties, the talk is always about where we come from, not where we are. There's nothing, and I mean nothing, nothing at all doing in Victoria. Everything we are interested in is over the last range of mountains, way off there. It isn't that we are unhappy with living in Victoria. I don't see people walking around with long faces wishing they were back looking out the kitchen window and saying, 'Pa, come over here and take a look at this beautiful blizzard.'

Everyone's happy here, I'm sure of that. Miss the kids, sure. Miss the sunsets on the Prairies, I guess, although I personally can't remember one sunset I'd choose over another. Miss the friends, sure, but the same kinds of friends are living right down the street or on the floor below. Miss being their own boss, 1,400 acres and not knowing what the hell is going to hit you tomorrow, that's for sure, but I'm sure they miss the excitement waiting for it. Miss deer-hunting in the fall, I guess, but it was just the hunting part of it, not the venison – as far as I was concerned, one feed of venison a year was enough. Now moose meat, that was another matter. They, and me, we all miss a lot of things, but I guess the big thing they don't miss is the climate. Our bones get old and our step gets slower and we can't do the things we used to do and there's the time when it is best just to say goodbye to it all.

But we sure talk about it, and what amazes me is this. The Prairies, you know, it's like a small town. Now take us. We came out from Russell, had this big farm there and my boy runs it now, and we'll go to a party or get talking to somebody, say from Alberta. Pick a town. Okay, Wetaskiwin. He's from Wetaskiwin, and the more you talk, you find that he knows somebody you know, maybe a cousin. Or his niece married a boy whose dad farmed north of Russell, or you knew his brother from curling at the same bonspiels. Same with the women. It is uncanny, and I mean it. All these wheels spinning apart from each other and then, there you are, two of them start spinning together.

But I guess it's all because the Prairies are where your roots are. It is where you married, bought the first quarter, maybe came back to after the war with new ideas. That kind of thing. Where your kids were born and brought up, went to school, went off and became successes. Or where you failed, or where you won. These things. Not big things, not little ones. But all a part of you. After all, you can't whack sixty or so years of living out of your body and your mind. So, the Prairies are always with you, always will be. City folk, town folk, farm people. It's always there, the good and bad times, the way it was, and it was just a big, big part of you that you don't want to part with.

That's okay with me. That's just fine. And I think we're better people for it, born and living out most of our lives on the Prairies, and nobody is going to say to me that that's not a good thing to have in your life and in your background, because it is."

Pioneers

🐦

Those unsung heroes, the surveyors, were there first, working for decades to bring order to the vast spaces, taming them on paper and leaving careful markers on the open grassland. Then the railway, the CPR, came clanging through, opening up those vast tracts of prairie land.

The land rush was on, free land, a homestead, and they came in from around the world. The New World! Opportunity.

As always, the best land was claimed first – rich loam, deep and fertile, often along the slow-moving rivers and streams. Then they moved north and southwest, even into the massive Palliser Triangle which the CPR Exploratory Map of 1876 had called "Extensive Plains More or Less Barren". North, there was very good soil, in the parkland or bush, and that first day a homesteader would select the longest and straightest tree and say, "This will be the ridgepole for the house" – if he knew how to build a house, which he probably didn't.

No one will ever know how many of the immigrants were totally unsuited for the heavy toil of pioneer farming. Did they ever think of the years of labour facing them, for rewards that could only be meagre? Did they know the hazards of this country, the brutal winters, the blizzards lasting days, the searing heat, the hail?

Think of their isolation. The tiny village a day's journey away by horses hauling sixty bushels of wheat for sale or barter, over stumpy trails. The nearest neighbour five miles away through the bush. The long wait for a school until more homesteaders came in. The loneliness of the wife when the husband worked in the lumber camps north of the Saskatchewan River all winter. The thoughts of home. No matter how bad it was there, should we have left it?

They couldn't quit. Where would they go? Life was hard in the towns and cities, too. Besides, this was now their home. There was another factor. They had

guts. They wouldn't quit.
They survived, and virtually every Old Home Place in the West today is a
monument to their determination.

🪶 Sod-busters

"I have actually seen a strong man, a brawny Highlander, take a piece of sod about a foot by a foot and try to tear it in half, and the muscles in his arms bulged and he got red in the face but I'm damned if he could. That stuff was like carpeting. Yes, just like the stuff on that floor.

You see, that's where a lot of homesteaders went wrong. They thought prairie sod was like English sod, like Minnesota sod, like any sod. It sure as the devil wasn't. It had been there for generations, and it had millions of little roots in it, all entangled together, and it was tough, bloody tough. We were using the old double gang plough, and four horses were needed to make the thing work, or four oxen. But men who were used to ploughing deep with two horses had trouble. They couldn't crack that stuff when they went deep. The thing the old-timers learned was just to slice the sod the first year and harrow it, break it up as best they could. Hell, the soil would grow anything that first year. It was so rich they used to say you could plant and harvest buttons.

Ever hear the expression 'sod-busters'? That was us. Just break up the soil the first year. The next year, plough deep as you wanted.

I can still see that brawny Scotchman grunting and heaving and trying to tear that piece of sod, and all of us standing around laughing."

🪶 On the Scow

"My husband and I came to this country, Islay, before the railroad came through in 1905. And all the things the settlers needed, well, you take sugar, it had to come through Winnipeg on the CPR and then up to Edmonton on the railroad line and then it went into a warehouse and then it was loaded on a scow, to be floated down the Saskatchewan River.

The men on the scow were Indians, Cree, strong men who used

sweeps and poles, and the scows were not scows at all, not the one
I travelled on, but a raft made of big poles. All the freight was piled
up on boards put on top of those poles, and if you were a passenger
you found a spot as best you could. It would take three days to
float down that river when the water was good. When the river
was low, you got caught on the sandbars and you'd be there for
hours, maybe a couple of days, and oh, it was an awful mess. But
it still was the quickest way. The other way was to come in from
Saskatoon, and that was two or three weeks with oxen, and at Eagle
Creek the banks were steep and you never knew whether you were
going to make it or not.

When the raft got to Hewitt's Landing, Mr. Hewitt had a sawmill
and he unloaded the food and there were men ready to freight the
goods into Lloydminster on what we called the Fort Pitt Trail.
There was no Fort Pitt left, as I remember, but it had something
to do with the Riel Rebellion. And then Mr. Hewitt would take
the logs off the scow, or raft, or whatever you want to call it, and
he'd put them through his sawmill. My husband had been an
accountant in a London bank and efficiency was his God. This is
why he liked Mr. Hewitt. Using his boat or scow and then breaking
it up and selling the lumber to the settlers–now that to my husband
was something!

Then the flour and sugar and tea and turpentine and all the things
the settlers needed–stoves and axes and nails and harrow teeth and
all that – they would go on sale in the stores in town. I mean, a
fifty-pound sack of flour cost $6.50 or $7.00. That is far higher than
it is today. You must remember a dollar was worth a lot of money
in those days. A man would work for another man from six in the
morning until the other man told him it was time to quit and he'd
get a dollar. His board too, naturally, but there was very little cash
money in that country.

My husband was lucky. He had four lovely horses, great big lads
that he had gone back to Ontario for. He looked for days before
he finally found what he wanted. He wasn't like so many men who
came out knowing nothing. Clerks from London, draper's assist-
ants, iron-moulders, shipyard workers. No, he'd grown up on a
big farm in Shropshire and he knew horses and ploughing. Why,
do you know that some of the people who came out here didn't
know how to harness a horse after they'd been shown ten times?
They just couldn't get it through their silly heads. With these four
horses and a good sulky plough my husband could break three to

four acres a day if it was good moist land. I mean no brush or scrub
or willows. Furrows half a mile, twenty-four a day, and the homesteaders who were proving up their land, they would give him four
dollars an acre or three. I don't remember why he had two prices,
but I think it was that he felt sorry for some people. At any rate,
he did well and we were quite well off. Better than most. The
ploughing did it for us."

❧ *Not Your Ordinary Immigrants*

"About this time, about 1905 or so, the Americans started moving
into this part of the country, along the Soo Line, the railway that
came up from Minneapolis. They came from Minnesota, over in
Wisconsin, but mostly from North and South Dakota, Iowa,
Nebraska, places like that. There were these big land companies in
Canada then, and most of them were American outfits with the
money to buy up land, tens of thousands of acres of it. They bought
it from the Canadian government and from the CPR, which had
millions of acres of prairie land, and these American promoters,
they knew a darn good thing when they saw it. They might buy
land for seven bucks an acre and advertise it, 'Good land, come
one, come all,' and they'd sell it for fifteen bucks an acre. Double
their money.

There were plenty of good farmers down south and these advertisements caught their eye. They could get 160 acres, you know,
for a ten-buck filing fee. That would be the father. Then maybe
there were two sons over eighteen years old and they'd each get a
quarter for homesteading. Maybe a grandfather. Okay, so why
couldn't the grandpa take out a homesteader's filing? No reason at
all. Bring along a hired man. Sure, why not? Make a deal with him,
so he files too and then you buy it back from him, and why not?
Hired men never amounted to a hill of beans, anyway, they just
went along for the money part of it. So there, right off the bat,
this family, say from Minnesota, they're looking at five quarters,
800 acres, tied up right away. Bingo, just like that.

Now, five quarters was big stuff in those times, and, of course,
they had the money so they'd fill in the holes with more land they
bought off the big American land company, so they'd buy three
more quarters and that was two sections, and that was a real big

farm. I know, because I married into one of these families, the Grutmans, who were down there for many years, just east of Ceylon. But there were Americans right from the border north along the Soo up past Milestone. Look at any map and you'll see that takes in an awful lot of country.

Now, mind you, these weren't your ordinary immigrants. Not by a long shot. Their grandfathers would have been immigrants coming in to the Dakotas and Minnesota in the late fifties, I'd think, but these people were experienced farmers, and they knew all the tricks of the trade when it came to farming. You've got to remember that those American states were way ahead of us at that time. We were just starting out, a couple of generations behind, you know. Same sort of land and the climate a lot like up north, and they had figured out all the tricks. They had another thing going for them, too. These were educated people. Germans, Scandinavians, and Swedes, and they had cities and towns and colleges down there when all there was in Canada was miles and miles of nothing, with a few people dotted along the rivers. They had what you'd call a tradition of education, and I've yet to see an educated German who didn't make a good farmer. Education means you've got the intelligence behind you to back it up, and another thing, they were religious and God-fearing, and they had one special thing going for them. They spoke English.

Good farmers, like I said. And smart. They had these farms in the States, maybe started by their grandfather or at least their fathers. Big places, big barns, lots of cattle, and they certainly knew a lot about horses. So their land down there was worth a lot of money, and they could sell it to neighbours who didn't want to go high-tailing off to a new country. They would think, well, I'll sell out here in Minnesota and take my do-re-mi and the wife and kids and head north into Canada and start again where there's free land, cheap land. New land always means good land. You get your best crops ever the first few years, when she ain't mined out and worn out.

The Canadian government didn't want to put much in their way, natch. People like the Grutmans, Americans, they was the kind of immigrants they wanted. People that could start right in paying taxes, and buying in the town, and moving their grain on the railroad. It all fitted, like a hand in a glove. Speaking English, hard-working, smart, maybe a bit too much of know-it-all, but they were good citizens right off the bat. Not like those poor devils with the big moustaches and only five English words to their name who'd go up north into the tree country and build a log house and grub around with an axe and an ox and pull out two acres of stumps a year and my gosh, it took them years even to prove up their land.

But these Americans. Mary had this photo album. It showed a gang of workmen taking down their home on their farm southwest of Minneapolis. Each board was numbered. Each brick from the chimneys was counted. All packed. Doors, frames, windows, you name it, they crated her all up, and anything that wasn't nailed down, they took. Farm machinery. Wagons. Horses, about sixteen, and foals, all of them, that fall of 1907, in September, and milk pails, the blacksmith shop and, well, they took everything and shipped it to the railroad and it was put in box-cars, and because this was their settlers' effects, the Canadian government paid for the box-cars. So it cost nothing to move. Then to Minneapolis and then to the drop-off point nearest their farm and, bing, bang, off the stuff came, out came the horses and cows and pigs and chickens. They put the wagons back together and in a few days there they were, living in tents and having a high old time helping the gang put up their house and getting a barn and sheds built, and getting ready for winter.

In this case, the family scooted back to Minnesota, where others in the family lived, and they could stay for the winter there. Only the oldest boy, George, and the hired man, they stayed behind to look after the stock and, well, that was about it unless they got a big kick out of watching the snow pile up.

Then it was spring and they came back and finished the house and got on with the breaking, and that was a cinch. They had all the best equipment the Moline company in Minneapolis could make, and good strong horses, well fed over the winter, and they were all raring to go. They got a big crop in. I think it was about 250 acres, so you could see how hard they worked, breaking that prairie sod and discing and harrowing and seeding, and still getting a crop. I mean that was something. These people were farmers. You can bet your boots on that.

First year, new land, big crop. You know, wheat probably came in at sixty or seventy bushels to the acre and barley at a hundred, easily. Just one year, think of it! They'd more than paid for the land they bought and they'd proved up the other five quarters by breaking it and selling the crop at good prices and there they were, sitting on two sections. When the work was all done that fall, they had a lot more money in the bank than they'd started out with. I look back and I think, opportunity and reward beyond anybody's dreams.

And, natch, they went on and on. I think they wound up with five sections, spread around that south part of the country, and it was like manna from heaven. Then the war came along and the boys didn't have to go because they weren't Canadians then, and wheat prices just went higher and higher. That became a rich family, a rich family. Then hard times. The Dirty Thirties. The blizzards of dirt blowing, hoppers, everything. Russian Thistle Country, I called it. The only green on any farm in August, that was sure to be a patch of them thistles, and some people were even using them for feed. They mostly went busted, this family did, in the Depression. Couldn't hold out to the good years of the war and after and by jiminy, those were the big years, with combines and rubber-wheeled tractors and all.

That family's all gone now, but there's still an awful lot of folks in Saskatchewan who are Canadians through and through, but when you ask them where they first came from, they'll say Minnesota, Nebraska, those states in between. Some, I think, don't even know they were from south of the line. You know, a lot of people don't think of immigration like this, that a lot of it was south into the north and north into the south. Like all those folk not so lucky to have money who came up here in covered wagons. Yes, I've seen pictures of them in covered wagons just like the pioneers. I don't think they went through customs and immigration. They just crossed over a trail, and when they went to register their homestead, I guess that's where the business of immigration came in."

🐚 *Short of Horses*

"The whole country was short of good horses. Good strong pulling horses, but gentle. You see? Too many of these cayuses just off the range were coming in, and farmers, settlers, they wanted real work horses that would work all day.

I had a good crop that year and I went back to the States and I bought two carloads of horses and shipped them back here. I did that twice. I'd buy horses for $20 each and I'd sell them for $200 each. I did that until the price of horses fell and then I quit.

But I wasn't rooking anybody. I've seen the bid start at $500 for a team of horses not as good as the stuff I was bringing up from Iowa, and I was selling them at $200 each and my expenses, shipping, feed, into that. So anybody that bought offa me, they got a good deal. We both made money."

❧ *The Poor Immigrant*

"It worked this way. When you got to Winnipeg you got to see the immigration. They had people there they could talk to you in all sorts of language, and I don't think there was a language that couldn't be spoke. But before you went to the immigration you were in the station, all sorts of people standing around. You may be looking for somebody, a friend, some cousin, or you may just be standing around for someone to help you.

So these men would go through this crowd and here's a family. The old man, the old lady, the kids, and the bundles. Galician, maybe. Polack. English. It didn't matter. This man had this house and he'd go up to them and start talking official. Where are you from? Where are you going? What's your name? Come with me. I show you. Show them, sure they did. Show them right to the street and a horse and wagon, and the family goes down Higgins Street, up north on Main, to this guy's house. It's a boarding-house. He gives them shelter, he gives them food, he looks after them.

You say there is nothing wrong with this. He's making a dollar the best way he can. I agree with you. Oh, I agree. But the poor immigrant, he's not going to the immigration hall where everything is waiting for him. He's going to some guy's house where he has to pay, and finally he still has to go to the immigration hall when his money is running out.

That way it is a racket. Just a racket. I bet you there were fifty men in Winnipeg that did this, charged two or three dollars a day. Now, where will those people get that kind of money? That money is not for hanging around Winnipeg looking at city hall or the guys building Eaton's new store. That money is all they got, see, and it is going to help them when they get off at Kamsack or Weyburn or wherever they are going. These men who act and talk official like they are immigration, they take the money off the poor immigrants. It is a racket, on their own people."

🐦 *They Wanted Wood and Water*

"One day I was talking to an old man named Mike Michaluk, and I asked, 'Mike, how come all your people came up into the parkland around here to start up? Why not down south? No trees to cut, no brush to burn, not as many mosquitoes and flies. Not so far from town. Better and bigger towns, too.' That's the way I put it to him.

He said that when they came out from Poland there just wasn't much land for homesteading on the Prairies. All the good land had been taken up. Okay, I said I'd buy that. But they could have gone further west where there was land open in Alberta. No, he said, the word had got around that most of the south country there wasn't all that good for farming.

The clincher, he said, was two things. One was, they had to be together. If two or three immigrants took up land where it was just Anglo-Saxons, they would not feel right. They needed to be among their own people. Apparently this was important to them in the old country, where they came together to help each other, and, I guess, defend themselves in a way from the landlords. I understand a peasant in those days was really a serf, and had to kiss the hand of the landlord. The hand of the priest, too, for that matter, but I guess that was another matter too them. They're very religious.

And another thing. They knew what they were doing when they moved up into the parkland country, after the railway went through in 1905. It all boiled down to wood. And water. They'd choose a homestead, old Mike told me, that would have a lot of poplar on it. In fact, it might be all poplar trees and fir, with a slough here, and one over there, and maybe a spring. The government agent would point out a quarter which would have most of it open land and they'd say no. They wanted wood and water. Mostly wood.

You see, it was this way. Old Mike said in Poland with winters almost as cold as in Saskatchewan, the fight to find burnable material was a continual one. They had no money for coal, and there was no wood, no trees they were allowed to cut down. If a tenant farmer cut down one of the landlord's trees he'd be in deep trouble. Jail, maybe. Maybe kicked off his land.

So, what did they find here? Not only free land, 160 acres, but land covered with trees, and they knew they'd never be without firewood for the rest of their lives. They could cut it and stack it and dry it and burn it all their lives, and there always would be more down the road to use. I guess you could say they'd never be cold again.

I'm not sure that was the only reason they took over these homesteads that nobody else in their right minds would tackle. Poplar and fir trees, 50,000 of them, every one to be cut down for them to grow wheat or run cattle. But to them it made perfect sense, because they'd have firewood and poles to build their homes, and poles to build fences and barns and corrals.

One thing, too, you've got to remember. They were into this for the long haul. Years, generations, that's the way they thought of it. Old-country thinking. Build a soddy or a shack, have kids, and they grow up and you build a bigger house and clear more land and make more babies and have bigger crops and keep going. All the time, there they are, and they've got all the wood they can ever use and all the water they can ever use."

🐦 The Bumper Crop

"I once asked my grandfather what it was like in the old days when he and Grandma came to the Odessa area in 1908 when it was all new and they had no money and didn't speak English. He had this old cane and he waved it at me and he said, and this was in Ukrainian, of course, he said, 'The bumper crop!' He practically yelled it.

I had never heard of this event, but back in high school we were never taught anything about our own province or the people in it. History was still about the kings and queens of England and the Spanish Armada and stuff about Sir John A. and Confederation. I was always dying to know something about my own people and the province of Saskatchewan.

He said that in 1914 the war started and that year the crops were terrible. The next year, 1915, the government needed all the wheat it could get for the war effort, and they asked every farmer to plant more and more wheat and my grandfather did. This was the second year he had owned the two quarters he had bought. Before that, he and my mother had worked for Canadian farmers and then he had rented, but in 1913 he had enough money for a down payment on these two quarter sections. A house and barn and sheds, and it had a good well. Then, as I said, 1914 was a bust.

But not 1915. It was the bumper year. He seeded about two hundred acres in wheat, which was all the land that was good for wheat. The rains came just before seeding, and then when it dried up it got warm and they seeded, and after that they got more rain and then sunshine, and then the good rain they needed at the first of July, and then a lot of sunshine and then more rain, and everybody knew it would be a bumper crop. It was. Oh, I can just hear him now saying it when I was that little girl sitting beside him. It was very exciting to hear it.

The crop was phenomenal. In fact, it was so big it was very difficult to stook it, everybody was stooking. And then because there was so many farms getting the custom thresher and the crop was so heavy, that slowed down the custom thresher. But there was no snow, he said, and they finally got their crop threshed about the end of November.

It was the best wheat, that's how it graded out. And the yield – I can tell this story today to these farmers who dose up their fields with thousands of dollars of fertilizer and get about thirty-five bushels to the acre – my grandfather told me he got seventy bushels to the acre.

He got about $15,000 for his crop. Now, can you figure what that would be worth today in our money? It doesn't matter, but I think it would be worth maybe $250,000. A quarter of a million dollars.

Now you can see why that one crop stuck in his mind forever as the most important event in his life. So it should be. It was like finding a gold mine in the field.

That one year, that 1915 crop, it lifted him and Grandma out of the poor class, out of the peasant class they had been in in the Ukraine and what they had come to in Canada. In one summer they had suddenly become big people. Not rich, but they had money and their own land and they could look anybody in the eye."

❧ *The Fireguard*

"I was driving north of Swift Current one year, in about 1908 or so, and I came across this homestead and I stopped, asked for a drink. The woman said yes, she'd give me a drink, and I expected a dipperful of water, but you know what that woman did? She took a lemon. Lemons were precious in those days. You didn't see too many. She took that lemon and she made me lemonade. Now, I thought that real nice of her.

I said to myself, I got to do something for this woman out here on the bald prairie with nothing but two kiddies. She said her husband was sick in hospital in Calgary. I looked at her fireguard and I told her that wouldn't hold if she got a big fire coming down from the north, and she said the land agent who sold them the place said it would be fine. Well, I told her it wouldn't be. Five furrows wouldn't hold back a thing. Might just as well not have them, and it was fall, the grass was dry as old dead bones, and there she was alone.

There were two horses in the corral, a big gelding and a nice little bay mare, and I took them out and harnessed them up, cleaned off his dirty old plough, and whooshed those two back and forth along that fireguard until I had twenty more good furrows. That made twenty-five, as broad as a city street almost. It took me quite a while and she brought me out another lemonade when I was half way through and I thought, well, there goes your last lemon. No lemonade for the kiddies.

I was glad to help out, and when I finished I got in my buggy and rode on. I heard later that not long after, a big fire had gone through that part of the country. It sure was ready for it, I'll tell you that, and Jehoshephat, I think I may just have saved her house for her."

❧ *Miles and Miles of Nothing*

"We came right out to Regina and then we went on. Looked around and for miles saw miles and miles of nothing, and the women were crying and the men weren't feeling so chipper, either. But that didn't last too long.

Some had never been on farms in their life. Not even to visit. But they tried. There always was somebody to show them how to do what was needed, lend a hand. Some tried farming and knew they'd never catch on to it, and they'd go into the towns. There were towns springing up everywhere, you know. The towns needed carpenters and a butcher and a blacksmith, and, of course, a bartender. There always seemed to be someone with two wagon-loads of lumber and one of whiskey and ready to put up a hotel. The smallest places would have a hotel.

They dug in and said, 'We're going to lick this country.' And they did. And even some, those who'd gone home after a year or less, you'd look up one day and there would be Mrs. Beatty or Mrs. Chambers in the store and you'd ask what they were doing back, and they'd say something like they missed the country. The old country seemed different after Canada and they'd decided to come back.

I'm glad we came out. I've never wanted to go back. Oh, yes, I've wanted to go back, but just for a visit. Not to stay. After all, it is the land of my birth and I'd like to see the old places once again. But Canada, no, this is my home."

ꕤ *Grandpa George*

"Grandpa George, he was a shoemaker. His father was probably a shoemaker, and his grandfather too. He probably did okay in the Ukraine, but somebody who left the village for Canada wrote back and said it was wonderful. Of course, he was lying. It was not wonderful. It was terrible.

So George and Sophie packed up and sold their furniture and the shop and headed for Hamburg with their three kids, and after a long time, maybe a month, they were dumped off at Moosomin. That was in 1906. Just one year after Saskatchewan became a province. They had nothing, and they knew nothing about farming, and there they were. In March, 1906. All alone. Poor.

Now, you think about that some more. And their first few years, that is really the story of Western Canada. Everything complimentary we want to say about them is wrapped up in one word, and that is 'survival'.

They didn't take the easy way out. They took the sensible way out. They didn't file on a homestead right away. They hired out with a farmer named Miller, an American who had come up from Ohio and was opening up a big farm north of Moosomin about twenty miles. He was in town that day and he found Grandpa George and his brood sitting on the station platform waiting for something to happen. Well, it did. They somehow made a deal. Grandpa George would work on the farm for $325 a year. My grandmother would work in the kitchen and in his house, and they would live in a sod house that was on the property and they'd get their meat and milk and eggs from this farmer, and my grandmother would have her own garden and two baby pigs.

In other words, the whole family, with the kids about eight, six, and four, were working for about ninety cents a day. But this was 1906 and here was a wonderful chance to learn farming, learn Canadian ways, sleep, eat well, and be paid for doing it. I think this man Miller, I'd take off my hat to him any old day. I'd say the Frasz family was one of the lucky ones, in the long run. Not everybody was so lucky.

So, the way my mother tells it, they stayed for three years, and the whole family learned about Canadian farming and planting and the chores, and about the hot summers and the cold winters, and in three years they may have had five hundred dollars saved and that was enough to buy their own quarter section. That's 160 acres, and it had a sod house and a sod barn. There was a creek running through it, which today is a deficit mark but in those days was a very substantial plus. They were near the Miller farm and could get help when they needed it, and besides, my grandfather also worked for Miller when times were slow, so that was another plus. All in all, they were lucky.

But times were still tough. Terrible. They had early frost and the creek flooding and a drought every few years, but they kept going. By this time there were eight children. Two more had died. Dead at three weeks, dead at four months. That was the way it was, a very high mortality rate. But the years went on, the children grew up, and some went out in the district working and some went beyond the little white school two and a half miles away and went to Regina for business college, and two went to the Grey Nuns for nursing, and there was the war and that took two of my uncles for a while, but they came back.

All the time, here is this couple, getting old by now, but keeping that family together. And about five years ago at a family picnic at my Uncle Joe's farm the family started talking about chipping in and sending the old folks to the Ukraine to see their village. Lots of them were doing it and it was all arranged, with escorts.

My mother was the one chosen to put it to them, as she was the youngest and his favourite. When she'd finished her pitch, as it were, the old man just put out his hand to stop her and said, 'No. None of that. Nothing of that stuff.' And that was that.

That's what he was like. The family really didn't know very much about his days in Russia as a boy and what made him decide to come to Canada to a country he knew absolutely nothing about, and what he was thinking when they were here the first few years. One day when we were visiting I got all geared to ask him, but after my first question he knew what I was up to, and he just waved it off, nothing, stop, no more.

I always think of that little family standing on that station platform on a cold March day with just a couple of suitcases and bags of stuff and no money and no English and not even any idea of where they were."

🕊 *Come Right In*

"One day at dusk my sister said, 'Dad, the roof is on fire,' and it was. This was a log house with a sod roof, and the roof was made of poles, then a layer of hay, then two layers of sod. It was the hay that was smouldering, and all that night I carried big pails of snow up the ladder and my father peeled back the sod and dumped snow on the smouldering hay, all over that roof because the fire had spread. This was in bitter cold weather, and all night we fought that fire, and to his dying day my father carried the scars of the burns he received on his body from big sparks and pieces of burning hay and sod. By morning we had the fire out, but the house was no good for that winter.

He went to another farm and borrowed an ox team and a sleigh because we had nothing of our own then, and he drove us – me, my sister and a younger brother, and my mother – two and a half miles to the home of a family named Metherall. My father just told them what had happened and the Metheralls opened up their house. Come right in, stay with us. No questions asked. I don't think we even knew the Metherall family very well, but they had room and we needed a place to stay.

That's the way it was on the Prairies in those days."

🕊 *Grass Right Up to the Horse's Belly*

"There was this old guy, dead now, named Harry Pick and he was quite a talker, and he had every right to be. He'd done an awful lot of things since he came out to Saskatchewan about 1905 with the Barr Colonists. Quite a story there, a promotion dreamed up by a minister named Barr. All these Englishmen who'd never seen a horse and plough and maybe not even a herd of cattle, and they came out to farm in the Wild West. They fed them all sorts of stories in meetings in England about how you could have your own peach orchard, and beside your house there would be your own stream and bingo, throw in a line and a fat trout for breakfast.

Remember, they landed at Saskatoon, and that was the end of rail. He had this picture, showing a few houses, maybe seven or eight, and all these tents. That was the Barr Colonists at the end of track. Out there on the prairie and no place to go, and people flocking in from every point of the compass to cheat these green-horns. To sell them horses that were too old to pull their wagons across the couple of hundred miles they had to go, or Indian ponies just too damn mean and wild to ride. Mouldy flour and third-grade harness they didn't know how to use, and ploughs that were no good, and cattle that were on their last legs. They bought, though, because they didn't know any better. They didn't sell much whis-key, though, because it was set up to be a temperance settlement, but that didn't last long, according to Old Harry. Anyway, the government finally stepped in and got things in order, and they went on their way.

The West was surveyed by that time and Harry kept looking for a good piece of land and he found it, went back to Saskatoon and filed on a homestead. It was ten bucks then and he had a fair amount of money and he knew something about cattle, and he bought a bunch and moved them out to his homestead somewhere south along the Battle River. He survived the first winter and he had bought a bull, too, so he had a calf crop, and he just let that bull and the cattle roam. No fences, lots of water and grass. He said you never saw anything like it, for miles and miles to the horizon, and he used to hold up his hand and say, 'Grass right up to the horse's belly.'

There was nobody very much in that country because everybody was heading further west to greener pastures, when their wagons were rolling right over some of the best land you could ever find. Harry put up a shack, a bachelor's shack. A dirt floor, a stove, a bed, a small table and two chairs, boxes nailed to the walls for food and such, and a bookcase. He was a great reader. Could quote you anything. He had water from the river and plenty of driftwood and so that first winter he made out fine. The only visitors he had the first winter were a few Indians, and he'd give them tea and a biscuit and they'd take his mail into Battleford and bring it back if they came that way. Anyway, he always got his mail and his English magazines eventually.

That first summer he left the cattle and headed south and west on a saddle-horse with a pack-horse with grub and went looking around the country. I guess it took him a couple of months, but the further he got, the more he liked it. Vetch grass, he said, and pea vine and grass right up to the horse's belly and streams that ran clear and full of fish, and deer and birds and geese and ducks.

I don't think any man could have had a finer vacation. He just rode and rode and there wasn't a settler in that huge block, or he never saw one, and he rarely saw a human being except a traveller like himself, an Indian, maybe. There was the flowers, too, and he'd talk about the wildflowers by the millions.

I guess it was every settler's dream. The land, where no white man had ever been before. The buffalo were gone, but the rest was all the same.

No towns or villages, or railroads, naturally, because if there was no railroad there would be no towns. Why have a town in the middle of nothing? But to Harry it wasn't nothing. It was everything. The skies so high and blue, and the sun always shone and he said you could eat the air. He'd reach out and grab some air and pretend to eat it, just to show us kids how it was.

He shot prairie chickens and caught fish and made his bannock and boiled his tea and got on his horse the next morning and rode, crossing rivers and hills and just seeing the country. I'll tell you this, I would give everything I have today to be on that trip.

When he was gone about a month, he came upon a store where the farming country started east of Calgary and he stocked up and then he turned his horses around and started home. He made a wide loop, heading south and then up again, and just by counting the days and his time, he got back to his homestead. And, oh yes, when he got back, he found his cattle easily. They had gorged themselves all summer, just gorged, and he said they were like big square chunks of beef. Could hardly move they were so big. Just think.

That was an adventure nobody alive has ever experienced because he died quite a few years back, and he was ninety-five or so then. So Harry Pick may have been the last man to tell young people what the country was really like.

Then we look around us in this dump of a country now. Everything looks like a garbage pit. Pollution, smoke, crap everywhere, all run on diesel and gas, and when that runs out I guess we've all had it. I can't stand to go in to Edmonton any more. It's not even the city it was thirty years ago. One big concrete pile full of worried people scurrying around giving themselves ulcers and heart attacks. That's when I think of Harry in his old gas station in the Depression, making no money, not caring, and telling us young guys what it was like when there was something about the West you could care about. That you could really be proud of. Not any more. Harry, I'd say, had it the best of times."

🐾 *Pioneering in the Towns*

"Listen. I worked at Regina seventy-one years ago right now. Digging cellars. Forty cents a cubic yard. Imagine it. Forty cents a cubic yard with pick and shovel, and when you drove your pick into the clay, you just made a hole. You couldn't lean on your pick and bring out a chunk of dirt. Hardest work anyone ever did.

I was hardly making any wages, a dollar a day, if that, for ten hours a day, but I had to do it because it was the only work I could get. Man-killing work. There was somebody right there all the time to see that you worked, hard, and if you didn't, you were sent packing.

Pioneering on the prairie wasn't any harder than pioneering in the towns."

✿ *A Place Set Out for You*

"In those days, if you stopped at a place near night-time, then you stayed until daylight and nobody asked you a lot of questions. If you arrived near a meal, there was always a place set out for you. I stopped in at one place on the prairie about supper and the woman said her husband would be bringing meat home, and sure enough, after dark in comes her husband with a good-sized jack-rabbit. Said he walked miles to get him. So we all dug in and helped get that rabbit ready, and in about two hours' time we all sat down to rabbit stew. No bread or vegetables. Just rabbit and gravy. We finished it up for breakfast. I thanked them and they thanked me for staying and I went on my way."

✿ *A Decent Christmas*

"In the old days, my grandfather's times, everybody trapped in the winter. That brought in a few dollars, and then, you know, a few dollars would go a long, long way. You've no idea how much two hundred dollars would go then unless you could see an Eaton's catalogue of before the First World War. That two hundred dollars for lynx and wolf and maybe a couple of bear and mink and ermine, that two hundred dollars could be the difference in having a not bad time of it for necessities and a decent Christmas. The men went working for the B. and B. gang for the railroad in the summer, too, or went up around The Pas in winter and worked in the lumber camps. Just anything to bring in a few dollars."

✿ *My First Teacherage*

"Yes, I taught in one of those little one-room schoolhouses out in the homesteading country. I've always wondered where this business of the Little Red Schoolhouse came from. It must be American. The only schoolhouses I ever saw in those days were painted white, or plastered white, just like their houses. Of course, some weren't painted at all. They ran out of money, most likely. They were made of logs or lumber or both.

I'll never forget my first teacherage. I was seventeen, and I was all they could get, I suppose. I had Grade 11 and there was a month of a sort of normal school in Edmonton and then they sent me to this school east of Edna, which later became the village of Star. It was the start of January. The teacher who had been there the first term had just thrown up her hands and walked away. So they needed a teacher. Any kind of a teacher.

It was new country for homesteaders. Nearly all Ukrainian children, six to sixteen, about half boys, half girls, and when I first saw them they all looked the same. They all dressed the same. Their parents were terribly poor, but they had enough to eat and warm clothes and that was all they thought was necessary. Their fathers, all of them had Interim Homestead Receipts, meaning they'd paid their ten-dollar filing fee but they hadn't proved up their quarter sections yet. You could see by the looks on their faces that they certainly intended to.

There were about fifty children, and it was winter, and about half of them, I'd think, did not speak English. They spoke Ukrainian. Even those that spoke some English or understood it, as soon as they went out that door for recess or going home, they spoke Ukrainian again. That was all right, just as long as they learned English in my class.

There were nine grades, all in that one room. One row would be Grade 1, the second row Grade 2, and so on. There was no subject that you could teach to all of them at once, so you actually had nine classes going at once. I'm not sure I know how I did it. Remember, I was just out of school myself.

You kept attendance, and I think maybe fifty to sixty per cent of the children attended school. In other words, one week you might have only twenty-five or thirty children. For the others it maybe was too cold, or there was some reason they didn't come to school. Their parents were very, very anxious that they get an education, but if there were jobs that had to be done, then the bigger children would be kept home. Maybe it was helping take a load of wheat to town and the boy would have to go along. Maybe there was a new baby in the house and a bigger girl had to help her mother. Maybe a pig was being butchered that day – then all the kids in the family would stay home. You kept records, but you couldn't do anything about this, it was just a fact of life.

There was a blackboard, in four parts, across the front of the room and I'd put arithmetic exercises on one part, and if there were four children in Grade 6, say, they'd go up to the board and work on those. Then I'd be doing reading with Grades 3 and 5, setting them to work. You see, in Grade 3 reading, there usually was only one book, so the four or three in that grade would share it. I'd work with the Grade 1's with little lessons I'd done on paper, like the picture of a cat and the alphabet printed across the top and the letters c-a-t printed out. I'm not sure how they learned, but they managed. I know there were children of settlers who were speaking English at the end of Grade 1 and they hadn't spoken more than a word or two when they started. They just seemed to pick it up. When I think of it, maybe they were teaching each other and I was just there to see that everything went on an even track.

There was a stove at the back and a boy was paid to keep it full. He came an hour early before school opened to get the room warm. There was a screen over this stove and at eleven-thirty I'd let them put their lunches on this screen to heat them up. They usually brought a piece of meat, pork or beef, between two thick slices of bread. There was this cherry powder you could buy and on Fridays I'd dump a couple of packages into a big pot and make them a hot cherry drink. That was something! In those children's lives my little treat was something.

Once I felt that a pork sandwich and water was not enough to fill them up at noon, and I started making a stew in the pot. With my own money. I was just trying to help. Food was dirt-cheap and I'd been staying with an English family, the Caldwells, as a boarder, and I bought a couple of pounds of potatoes and a couple of carrots and turnips, and about five pounds of what we called fat belly. I cut them all up and put them in the pot with water and gravy powder and I let that simmer all morning. At noon I gave those kids a real feast. It cost me hardly anything, maybe fifty cents, and I was prepared to do it as a Friday noon treat, sort of.

That was the first and last time I got in trouble with the school trustees. On Sunday the father of the little Hawreliuk girl, the trustee, he drove over to the Caldwells and told me in half-English and half-Ukrainian and a lot of sign language that I was never to do that again. I promised I wouldn't. According to Mr. Caldwell, who also did some interpreting, I was insulting them, that they couldn't provide for their children. That was the last time. A very proud people, and they weren't going to have any snip of a seventeen-year-old child like myself come in and tell them they didn't know how to feed their own children. Too bad. I missed doing it and the children loved it.

They didn't mind their children getting the cod-liver oil, though. That was from The Doctor. He came from Chipman, I think, or maybe from Edmonton, once every term. Just checking. We had to give them these pills, one per child per day at noon out of this huge jar. The parents thought this was wonderful. They revered the doctor, and I think, feared their priest, but they paid them heed. If the doctor said their kids needed the cod-liver oil, then that was just fine.

They were good children. I never had to use the strap once. When I rang the big brass bell at noon and recess they came running back. I think, though, it might have been better if they had had a teacher who spoke Ukrainian, or was Ukrainian. But this was back in the 1900s and the country was so new, you know. Nobody, their daughters, I mean, none had trained yet as teachers. That came quite a few years later. I actually have the feeling that the Department of Education didn't want people of Ukrainian nationality to teach Ukrainian children. It seems very wrong now, but it wouldn't have seemed so wrong way back then. Remember, this was way back then when everything was different.

You cannot understand how different it was. Children walked three or four miles to school. In May and June and September they'd come in their bare feet. The rest of the time they wore those heavy felt slippers with rubbers over them. Their clothing was barely enough to keep them warm. Their parents had absolutely no money. A couple of horses or oxen and a walking-plough and a cow, a couple of pigs, chickens. A sod house. Everyone had a sod house for a few years. I visited one house once where there was a birthday party and you know what the parents were the proudest of? They had two windows, about the size of the cardboard thing that holds a record, and they had glass in them. Glass! That was an achievement in the new land.

I was the honoured guest. I think I was the first English person to step foot in their house and they were so proud. I remember this big Slavic and happy man gave me a drink. I didn't know what it was and it was the size of a good-sized wineglass. I'll never forget it. I still don't remember how I got home for supper that night. I must have staggered all over that trail through the bush.

I enjoyed that half-term. I mean I learned a lot, and I got an understanding of what lay ahead for those children. They were eager to learn, you see, and they certainly were not what you would call stupid. No, no. They picked up on things very quickly. I was seventeen and only a year out of school myself and maybe I could relate to them more easily. After all, the Bayduza and Osadchuck boys were almost as old as I was. If there was the slightest bit of trouble I would get one of those big fellows to stop it. They'd get up and cuff, cuff, and the two younger ones who were scrapping or horsing around, that was enough for them. I never used the strap. I wasn't one of these female teachers who got some sort of satisfaction in strapping the boys. Oh, yes, there were a few of them around.

It was a wonderful experience and my first school. I had another seven before I decided on the man I wanted to marry. That was one thing about a rural schoolteacher. She was the belle of the neighbourhood. Plenty of young and eager bachelors. Pick and choose. Take your time.

But I can still see the rows of those faces looking at me, and I wonder, where are they now?"

Three

The Twenties

🕊 ══════════════════════════

The Farm School Train . . . Comic English . . . The Hat . . . Just Indians . . . Bush Money . . . Nine Years Old . . . Not the Government's Business . . . This Nice Little Car . . . The Crash on a Bike

══════════════════════════

Gradually the farm took on the appearance of a "going concern". Paint on the house. A new barn. One of those new gang ploughs in the yard. More horses, or a better breed, after the slow and stubborn oxen had been sold off, or eaten. The milking herd was up to a dozen. A few more acres cleared - torn, ripped - from the bush.

Perhaps a branch line of the Canadian National Railways was only fifteen miles away, and Battleford - or Wainwright, or wherever - was booming and Saskatoon, or Edmonton, was going to be a major city. Goods became more available and cheaper.

The farmers had got together and petitioned the government in Regina or Edmonton for a school district; English, Scottish, German, Scandinavian, Ukrainians, Ontarians, all determined that their children would get an education. A work bee built the school and their grudgingly paid taxes and a government grant paid the schoolmarm her thirty dollars a month. Each family got half of that in board and room as they took turns boarding her month by month. It was their survival money – fifteen dollars.

There was always agitation for better transportation, for what good was wheat and barley on the farm if you couldn't get it to market? The trails became graded semblances of roads, the work done by the settlers to pay off their taxes. Rivers were bridged by ferries.

Few children were born in the isolated hospitals. They were for sick people. Midwives made their rounds. Because the children were the work force, and the future of the community, families were large.

The village grew. Soon there was a wide main street and a few secondary streets, and the population was made up of the tradesmen who dealt with the farmers, in money or barter, goods and services.

The grain company in Winnipeg had built an elevator. That was the focus, along with the general store with post office that was soon built, usually by a settler from Ontario or an American. A harness-maker followed. Then the livery

barn, and the thirsty and sociably inclined wished they had a hotel. A butcher.
*A lumber yard. A seamstress. Soon there was talk of getting a twelve-bed hospital.
A council was formed of prominent merchants. The lawyer, if they had one,
usually became the mayor. Wooden sidewalks were laid down. Now it could call
itself a town. Passenger trains ran twice a day, north in the morning, south to
the main line in the afternoon. A Chinese came by and opened a restaurant with
earnings from working on the railroad. It was suggested that it would be a good
idea to form a chapter of the Masons, and there was further thirsty talk about
the need for a hotel.*

*Well, it was only a few years later that folks got up a petition asking for a
waterworks system, and while you're at it, Mr. Mayor, why don't you buy a
generator so we can have electric lights in our homes?*

Progress, they called it. The town was on its way.

❧ The Farm School Train

"Believe it or not, I learned most about farming from a school on
wheels. This was back in the early twenties. We'd come out from
England, Manchester, the mills, that's where we worked. England
was in a mess in those days, and there were no jobs. My father, he
had a bit of money when his mother died and we decided to go to
Canada.

When we got to Saskatchewan it was the spring of '21. The idea
was to go farming. I was the oldest boy, only thirteen, and I had
two sisters and a brother, a baby. There was no money, and so we
went to work for a farmer. We hired out as a whole family, and
we were living in this little shed, no bigger than a garage today.

One day the farmer showed us a story in the *Saskatoon Phoenix*
that said that the farm school train was coming and it was going
to be at a station down the road for about five days. This was a
train of box-cars and coaches, and they were fitted with seats and
blackboards and the like. They had instructors and they taught
farmers and everybody how to farm.

Well, we didn't know a darn thing about farming, so the farmer
said to go and get in on this thing. The station, Melville, was about
fourteen miles away, so that meant sleeping out. He gave us a tent
and the loan of his buggy and we went there Sunday night and put
up the tent, got a fire going, and slept, and next morning we walked
over and signed up. My father, my mother, and me. It was free, of

course, because it was run by the government. They worked you hard, you had to be on the jump all the time, but at night it was good, too, because there were all these farmers from a long way around and they'd get together and talk. You'd learn a lot from just listening. All sorts of stories, and even though they were farmers, they were there to learn. Lots of joking, too.

It was a big thing, this train, maybe fifteen cars long, and the people just came by the hundreds. You learned about machinery and crops and how to look after your animals and what to feed them. What to give if a horse or cow was sick, how to raise chickens, and what to do for pigs. All day the classes went. The women, they had classes in these cars, about how to cook and can food and feed the family, all the new and important things that were coming out. The people who taught the classes, they knew what they were talking about. You see, they were all from the university in Saskatoon. Good people.

We stayed the whole five days, and worked hard listening, and when I got away from that, I think I knew a lot more about farming that I ever thought I would, in such a short time. It was a good experience. I can say that and nobody can say me wrong. Lots of good things you learned there. Friends, you made them there, too, and that was something, an immigrant not knowing anyone and then he knows a lot of people. Ball games, they had them, and a kind of little fair, you see, because there were lots of people at these school trains. Hundreds of people came. They were a big thing then, but you don't hear about them any more.

It was there that I got on for a winter job with a farmer, so that helped out my family that winter, and I was tired of regular school anyway, so that was the end of me going to school."

🐚 *Comic English*

"My father told me he arrived in Nipawin in the fall of 1927, and instead of rushing off to the land-titles office, he rushed off and looked for a job in town. It didn't matter how much he made, he said, he wanted a job where he'd learn English.

The first job he got was in a livery stable. He spent the winter there and he slept in the barn and looked after the horses, and he got his first English out of the *Free Press Prairie Farmer*, reading

the comics they had. He had an English-Ukrainian dictionary and
he'd decipher them out. He said that was the best way. Comics are
simple. Simple pictures, simple little jokes. Okay, a joke is a joke,
no matter what language. You could pick up a lot of words that
way. And talking to people who came in. Ever notice, when you're
talking to a person who has no English, really, you talk slowly?
They did that, and it helped. And when he could, he went to the
picture show. Talking around.

By spring he could get along. It must have been simply terrible
English. Oh, my God, I just can't imagine it. His English even up
until he died it wasn't so hot."

❧ *The Hat*

"My father tells this story. It was in 1923 and there he was just off
the train, and coming from Austria he knew nothing about Canadian winters. It was a cold snap and he says it was so cold, and he's
just off the train and walking down the main street in Saskatoon,
wearing a kind of velvet coat with a darker brown velvet collar
and pants, rather immigranty in a way, I guess, because he wasn't
from Vienna or some big city like that but from a farm. Anyway,
it was kind of a Sunday outfit and not warm and he was freezing
and he had only two dollars in his pocket. Imagine. Coming to a
new country and not speaking English – not one word – and wearing nothing for winter, and with only two dollars in his pocket.

Well, he knew that about one-third of your body heat escapes
out of your head, so the thing you had to do was get a good hat,
and he looked and he saw that men on the street were wearing a
kind of big fur hat, bushy-like. So he knew that was what he had
to have. With two dollars in his pocket and not knowing anybody.
Nobody to help him and he couldn't speak English.

God's little helper must have been perched on his shoulder.
That's what he said. You should have seen him. Then, I mean. He
was seventeen and about five foot four inches and slight. In Canada,
he told us, the first thing he noticed about the people he saw on
the train and in the streets, how big the men were.

So he sees this store where they sell clothes and he walks in.
There's nobody in the store, all dark, and then this little man comes
out of the back. You know, he says, this man is the only man he's

seen in Canada who is smaller than he is. A little Jewish man with one of those things on his head. He thinks he's about sixty and it turns out he is. Abe. For Abraham. It seems he was well known in Saskatoon about that time, with this store, and being not much over five feet tall.

This Jewish man, Dad says he didn't even speak to him in English, he spoke to him in German. He could tell my dad was an immigrant and, well, my dad thought that was very nice. The storekeeper asked him what he was doing and when he had come, and Dad had come that morning. Oh my, so he asks him if he'd like a bowl of soup. That's why he had been in the back, having his lunch. Okay, so far so good. My dad thinks he has made a friend. So that was nice. Then they eat and then my father asks about a hat. He tells about losing heat and yes, that is true, his new friend says, I've got just the hat for you. Just the hat. It's a big kind of Russian thing, or the kind that policemen used to wear.

He says it's three dollars, and he says it in marks, like twenty marks or whatever it was, so my dad would understand. Oh, says my father, I only have two dollars. When he tells him this, Abe cannot believe him. He can't believe anybody would come all the way from Europe, by a long ship journey and a long train trip, and only have two dollars.

My father said this kind old Jewish man just looked at him and said that was no good, no good at all. He said he would sell him the hat for two dollars and other clothes for winter for another eight dollars, and that my dad could work it off. 'How?' asked my dad. 'Well,' says this Abe, 'I need a caretaker and a boy to clean my store and keep things neat and go for the mail at the post office and tell me what the old country is like now and keep me company and eat with me when I have lunch and dinner here. And then there has to be somebody to stay at night and keep the fire in the basement going with coal. That's you,' he told my dad, and he said he would pay him five dollars a week and give him seven meal tickets to the Chinese restaurant.

Now, you should see my father tell this, but it was his first job and he hadn't asked for it. He had just seen this store and gone in, and in a minute he was talking his own language, German, with a man who gave him a job. Now, five dollars a week, I think, wasn't really good for all the work he did, but he had a home and free meals and he could pay off his debt for the clothes. But the most important thing was, first, he made a wonderful friend. But second, this wonderful old man Abe taught him English. Once my father said he would be glad to work for him, that's when he taught him English.

Look, think about it. There were lots of immigrants in town and all over the Prairies. Tens of thousands. There were Slavs and Polanders and Germans and Norwegians and Dutchmen and Frenchmen and Italians, everybody from Europe. Do you know how long it took for them to learn English? Years, before they were any good, and you had to be good to get a good job. My father said if you weren't good you were sure to go to the CN track gangs, to work for farmers, to work in the brickyards, or the lumber camps, or just doing the jobs nobody wanted. That was the way. If you had English, spoke it well, then it was a different story. A good job.

This is the way it happened. By spring my father was excellent in English. The old man wouldn't let him talk German. English, English, English, day and night. By spring he could wait on customers, fit them, sell them this, that, sell them things they didn't even want. Look, sir, this is a bargain. You'll never find a bargain like this again. Just look at the material. This is not cotton from the States, sir. This shirt is made from the finest cotton from India.

That's how you make your mark. A lucky break. Walking down the street thinking, I need a cap, a hat, one of those big fur things. Going into a store, meeting a wonderful old Jewish man who helps him and helps him for years until he dies, and they are the best of friends, play chess together, sip coffee for hours and talk, and that is my dad and Abe. Both little guys.

I never met this wonderful old man because he died when I was little, but I know him. If he walked in that door this minute I would know him."

🐦 *Just Indians*

"My grandfather and his brother made a lot of money when they bought the store in Lloydminster during World War One. All storekeepers then just gave their order to the salesman. Not my folks. They went right to the big boss in the warehouse in Edmonton and haggled for the wholesale stuff for their store, the Maple Leaf Store, and they could undercut other stores in town.

They also got a lot of the Indian trade, because they'd make friends with the Indians when they were clearing their land, hiring them when nobody else would. To the others they were just Indians. My grandfather made friends with them and learned some of their language. They'd even come down all the way from Onion Lake with their furs and trade at the store. Indians gossip a lot, you know, and the word spread around. But that's another story, how twice a winter he'd load up a huge sled pulled by four horses and go around to the Indians and trade for their furs and pelts so they wouldn't have to travel a long way to get to the other traders, and the Indians knew he wouldn't cheat them. He always loved the Indians.

The other traders didn't like to give money. They just wanted to trade and keep the Indians dependent on them. My grandfather would trade with goods if they wanted it, but if they wanted money, then that was okay. Mostly they seemed to spend the money on whiskey, but it wasn't Grandfather Connie who was giving them the whiskey. It was just his money that was buying it.

The store prospered, and they hired one of these big steam engines and they had twelve big gang ploughs with a chain affair and this would tear down the trees and plough the land deep. This way, they could do an awful lot of clearing, and soon the two quarters they had were cleared of all the trees that could be cleared. The Indians weren't doing anything after the muskratting was over and they'd sold them. So they'd come, a few families in their old wagons, and they'd pile the trees for a couple of weeks, and then they went off to do whatever they do. Then they came back in late August and burned them. The fires would go on for days, my grandfather said."

🕊 *Bush Money*

"You talk to a fellow, he tells you he made a living right off the start on his homestead, then you look at this fellow and you can tell he is lying to you. Nobody could make a living in that country, for a long time. Maybe on the Prairies, I don't know about that. Up in the tree country it couldn't be done.

This was in the twenties when quite a few families and fellows came into that country to the north of the Athabasca. It was all bush. Lots of spruce, lots of pine, lots of birch. You had to clear that. Maybe five acres the first year, the whole family. Dad, sometimes my mother, me, I was about thirteen, my brother, my sister, we're all working and maybe it was five acres the first year. No money coming in.

Homesteaders were kept alive by logging. You know, that's where the money came from. They paid off at the end of the logging season, you see, and that would be in March and you had maybe one hundred dollars. It was a lot of money. It was all we had. Just bush money, you know, from the logging.

This was tree country, but we used to have some guys from the Prairies working in the camps. If a guy brought his own team it would take him maybe five days to get to the camps in the time I'm talking about. The camps were where the big trees were, where lots of spruce were. You know, we didn't cut poplar or birch, because that stuff didn't float, and the logs had to be floated to a mill. A lot of logs went down the river in the spring.

The first year I went into the bush with my dad, I was thirteen. My father had made arrangements when he left, in March, could he bring his kid along next year. I was to work as a flunkey, in the cookshed. I wasn't old enough then but I was big enough, so this Mr. Rather, when he looked at me, he said if I was big enough I was old enough. That meant he was putting me down as sixteen years old so I could work.

That winter I helped the cooks. There were about one hundred men in this camp, so they had two cooks. Day cook, night cook. Night cook made pies and bread and cookies and did breakfast. Day cook, he was the best, he did lunch and supper. Lunch was kind of my job, as it wasn't as hard as breakfast or supper. Working for two cooks, you know, that meant I worked when these guys wanted me to. Five in the morning, eight at night. All the time. You peeled potatoes, you washed dishes, set tables and cleared them off, and ran, ran, ran. How could you run in a small cookhouse just so full of guys eating there was no room for nothing else? Well, you ran anyway. Pay was fifteen dollars a month. You work hard, the day cook told me, I'll see you get on as bull cook next year.

Next year I'm fourteen but nearly fifteen, and I worked as a bull cook. That's mostly daytime work. Cutting wood, keeping fires going, helping the cook a lot, and cutting meat and doing what the cook told you to do. I was boss too. I could boss around the flunkeys, two of them, and do some of my lessons. I was missing school. My dad didn't like that. My mother didn't like it worse, but there had to be money. Dad was earning about twenty-five bucks a month and I was making twenty and that was forty-five bucks. You add that up, multiply, five months, that comes to about two hundred bucks for us, for a season. That's about what we all had to live on for a year. There was no other way to make money. The next year, 1925 I guess, my father said he'd take me for his partner. It was working in pairs those days. They put up the camp in the middle of this big spruce forest, so there wasn't much walking to work and not far to haul the logs to the river.

You could cut as much as you wanted. No government guy said cut this, cut that, leave these alone because they're too small. A log that was too small at the butt, it wasn't worth cutting. Most of other trees were about two feet across. A big one would be three feet, and around the swamps that were there, they were even bigger. You cut trees down to about ten inches at the butt. That was okay.

My dad was good on the big saw. We went out on the timber claim and he'd look up, there's this big tree, going up and up. He'd say, we'll put it this way. Drop it to the northeast. He'd nick in the saw and we'd start. Back and forth. Easy. It takes a bit of learning. 'Don't force it,' he'd say. 'Let it come to you and I'll let it come to me. Don't ride it. Don't bind it. Let the saw do the work. That's the way you get it done.' About two inches from cutting through we'd stop and Dad would just lean against the tree and push, and over, over, over, down she'd go. Puuuttt! Just like that. That was a big one. The smaller ones were easy, but they were all the same.

They didn't tell you how many to cut. You knew. You made your mark on the butt in red or green or blue crayon, showing the tallyman that was you. You trimmed it, canted it over and trimmed the other side, and then bucked it. They'd tell you, we want eight- or sixteen-foot lengths. Then maybe around three o'clock you might have 100 logs down and bucked. If you had 100 you were doing average. If you had 115 logs, say, you were doing good. No bonus. You were just working to make sure you got a job next winter. If you had maybe 80, and that was the day the tallyman checked you, you better do better. You could be walking down the road. Guys were always looking for a job. It was only because my dad said I could work good that I got a job at my age. But I was big then, and strong.

The logs were hauled in bundles on sleds to the river, and all

over the ice you'd see these big bundles of logs. This place didn't
have the sawmill. They had a river drive in the spring and picked
up the bundles further down at the mill.

You worked hard, damn hard. But I liked it. Sometimes an hour
or more would go by and my dad and I would not say one word
to each other, unless it was about the work. It was nice in there.
You had your own patch to cut and it was like your own cozy
little house. No wind, you see, no wind at all.

At the camp, there was a triangle of iron, and the flunkey would
take a bar and hit around inside the triangle and that meant lunch.
It would take you maybe ten minutes, fifteen maybe, to walk to
camp, then lunch. Pretty good, I remember, pretty good. Not as
good as at night though, but good. Even if a guy needed the money,
if the food was terrible, they'd leave. Not enough to keep them
going, not with a winter to put in, and if they came out of it
scrawny in March they'd be in bad shape for the spring and summer
work. That was harder than this, and no pay for it then. Just hard
work, clearing, picking and pulling roots, picking rocks, burning
brush, working for neighbours. All that kind of thing. No fun
then.

The bunkhouse? Don't ask me how big it was. I remember a big
stove in the middle and around it on wires the guys had strung out
underwear and socks. I guess I'm going to my grave remembering
the smell. You know, sweat, man smell, body smell. Every kind of
damn smell there ever was. And tobacco smoke. That was blue,
about four feet off the floor. And guys spitting snoose. Pssst, a big
gob of spit, bang when it hit the stove. A lot of guys reading. Two
guys that winter, two Dutchies from over to the west, playing chess
every night. Night after night after night, just staring at that board.
Guys talking. Arguing. They threw one guy out into the snow
once, in his boots and underwear, and he had to sleep in the
cookshack that night. This guy was a trouble-maker, and next
morning he was down the road.

Some guys sleeping. Some guys going out to the toilets before
lights out, or just going out to rip off a few big farts before turning
in. Lights out at nine o'clock. That sounds like treating men like
little children, but no, it was good. Everybody was about ready
for it, so tired and the place was so warm. The flunkey would come
in and load the stove up with birch. Then the boss would stick his
head in and yell, 'Ten minutes for last smoke,' and be back at nine
and go around hooking down the lanterns and blowing them out,

and you know what? In five minutes that place, well, it sounded like a railroad station. You'd think there was ten big engines in there all groaning and hissing. Everybody was asleep, and if there was eighty or a hundred guys in these bunks, you can bet half of them were snoring. Boy, you had to go to sleep just for protection. Dad went home the first of December for one night. Walking eighteen miles, to see how Mom and the kids were. He brought back the two horses and a huge load of timothy hay, so we made more money that month because we could skid our logs. We had five days off at Christmas, going home, and brought the team back with another load of hay for January. Then, at the end of January Dad took the horses home again because he didn't want to wear them out for the spring work. Some guys kept their horses there all the time to earn more money. Besides, then you didn't have to work so hard. But they'd ruin their horses from too much hauling and they'd be in bad shape in the spring. If a guy had four or six horses he'd be rich and I guess wouldn't have to work in that bush all winter.

You could sign up for the drive down the river, but when the snow went, there would be no more logging and you might have to sit around a week or two, waiting for the ice to go out. You were wasting a lot of time. Besides, Dad said it was dangerous, too dangerous, and so he said no to it.

The company threw a big dinner for us the last day. We'd say what we wanted, like ordering in a café. If most of the guys wanted turkey, then that's what it was. If they wanted beef, okay, but that year everybody was so sick of beef and pork that they all said they wanted turkey. It was a big party and the company bought booze, quite a bit of it. Beer too. Guys were drinking half a bottle of beer and filling up the rest with whiskey. A lot of guys got drunk, but it was okay. Payday was tomorrow. Guys who wanted to take a swing at another guy all winter, that's when they did it. They just swung away, and I guess they were so drunk they couldn't hurt a fly. It was like the end of school in Holland, with a party. No troubles that night.

Next morning this company paid everybody off. Right to the last cent. Everybody knew how much they had coming. That's maybe what everyone was thinking of when they pulled that saw back to them five million times. What they would have coming and how they'd spend it.

I did. My dad did. We got about three hundred dollars with what we got for the horses. It was in cash, and you packed your sack of stuff and you walked down the trail and home.

Mom and the kids, they'd know just about what day you'd be coming. If you left after breakfast, say nine o'clock by the time you got away, then if you legged it pretty good you should be home by one o'clock. That's pretty well the way it worked. A big dinner was waiting for us that night after we came down the road. We had a big feast with a lot of Dutch things. This was a special day, you see.

We said our prayers and then we ate, and then Dad took all the money out, one-dollar bills, up to twenty-dollar bills, and he counted them out. He gave them all to Mother and he said, 'One winter's work. Make it go round the clock.' That was an expression he used. Make the money last until we had some more coming in.

But before that he took one five-dollar bill and he gave it to me. Now, you can say I worked just as hard as he did and I had earned my money, but that's not the way my father did things. It was like communism or something. Everybody worked at what they did best and they threw it all in the pot, and my mother and Wim and Louise, they had been working just keeping the farm going.

Next year we didn't go to the bush camp again. We couldn't make the farm work. It was just too much. We moved to Edmonton and got jobs. We worked for other people and were much better off."

🐦 *Nine Years Old*

"My father didn't believe much in education, although there was a school about a mile and a half away. When my two older sisters were twelve he hired them out to neighbours to work in their kitchens. They got maybe ten dollars a month in the twenties, and that was pretty good, and they'd come home on Saturday nights and Mom would do their washing. They'd give Dad the ten dollars and he'd give them fifty cents for spending-money.

He did the same with my four brothers. They worked in the bush in the camps when they became thirteen and fourteen. You know, first around the cookshack and doing odd jobs and they'd give the money to my father. One by one as they got older, the boys would work two years in the bush or for a neighbour, and giving Dad their money – and then they'd say, 'No, I won't.' So they'd go out on their own to some other district where Dad couldn't find them and there they would be all by themselves at fifteen. I don't think it was so bad for them.

But my story. One night, deep in winter, we hear a horse coming into the yard. And there's Mr. Hargachuk running up to the door and he says his wife is having a baby too soon, and my mother and father get in our cutter and my brother takes Mr. Hargachuk's horse, and he goes for the midwife in Odessa, and the cutter goes to the house where the baby is being born.

Everything works out fine. The midwife gets there in time, and the baby is born fine. Except it's not a baby. It's two of them. Two girls, and this is really something.

A few days later the midwife comes by, driven by one of the Hargachuk boys, and she talks to my father. Then she goes away and my father talks to my mother, and what they are talking about is this: I'm to go and work and look after the twins. I'm nine years old.

So I get some of my clothes and a couple of my toys and they say I can take my little dog with me, and I go. And that is when I started my working life, although I had been working pretty hard at home, too.

I liked it because I got ten dollars a month, and there were the babies to play with, but it meant the end of going to school. I worked for those people for a year and gave the money to my father and he'd give me a dollar back. And that was okay – a dollar was a lot of money for a kid in those days. Then Mrs. Hargachuk was having another baby, so I stayed longer, and I stayed with them for three years until I was twelve, and then the family moved away.

This was 1940 by now and the war had started and I didn't think I wanted to go back to school. I was thirteen and big for my age, and the other kids in my class would be nine years old, so I didn't go back. I worked around the district and when I was fifteen I got a job in a store in Odessa, doing everything, and made my own money. I mean I kept it.

In 1944, when I was seventeen, I went to Winnipeg, where I had an aunt, and I took a secretarial course, and nobody asked me about my education and I did as well as any of the girls. It was easy, in fact, and I could hold my own very well with all the city girls who had Grade 11. I got a job just as quickly as they did, in the Great-West Life, and I stayed there and then I got married.

That was the way it was in those days. You did what your parents told you, and it worked out for the best, always."

❧ *Not the Government's Business*

"There was this doctor, he was Jewish, an awfully nice man. He and his brother escaped from Russia after the Revolution, where his parents were wealthy, and where he had a very good education. Then he went to England and completed his medical education and then he and his brother came to Canada. The brother went to Ontario, and he came to Saskatchewan and went to this town and tried to start his practice there.

He was told this town could use another doctor, but the two doctors who were there then, they found out about him. Every time he tried to rent a building for an office, these two other doctors would go to the owner or the real estate man and would buy the building or pay twice the rent. So the poor young doctor, well, you can see he didn't stand much of a chance. That town, well, all I'll say is that it started with a 'W'.

He was wise to what was going on, so he went to this other town and all I'll say is that it started with a 'K', and he went in quietly and rented a big house down at the end and off the main street. Then he had a place to live and a place for his office, and when he was ready he put in a newspaper advertisement and put up a sign. But he didn't get much business. People were just suspicious, but then he started getting people because the word got around that he spoke Russian and Polish and a bit of Ukrainian, and there were sure a lot of farm people like that around the country.

Then when he was doing okay, something big happened. A young girl who worked as a maid in one of the hotels came to him and wanted an abortion. Now, you have to remember those days. In the twenties, a lot of women didn't want babies any more than they do today. And being pregnant and not getting married right away, that was a terrible thing. There were no birth-control pills, and these devices they had, maybe they weren't so good. Anyway, women would buy these pills that were advertised in the cheaper kind of magazine. They didn't say they were for abortions but usually something like it was for 'women's ailments'. Everybody knew. Then there were women like midwives who would do abortions, but they were the ones you feared the most, Backroom Butchers they called them.

So this doctor, whether he didn't know all this, or whether he felt sorry for the girl, anyways, he gave her an abortion. A good, clean one, apparently, and, of course, knowing it was illegal he told her not to tell anyone. Well, being a silly young girl, she told it to someone. And so the word got around.

Within a couple of years women were coming in from Regina and Saskatoon and Calgary and Winnipeg and points in between. This big house was famous. Women would get off the train and the station agent would know what they were there for. The town even had a taxi and that was his business, driving these women around. I think he must have had four or five women in his house all the time, and they'd come and go. Everybody knew what was going on, and, of course, he had his other patients from the town and farms, because people had confidence in him. He wasn't just a foreigner with a heavy accent. He was a kind and nice man and nobody thought what he was doing was so very wrong. They were more liberated fifty years ago than they are now. I think part of that is that it was a large farming district and the town depended on the farmers, and everybody had a more down-to-earth attitude about things like this.

So, it went on and on, and I left to go to Winnipeg in 1931 and he was still there, this doctor, and then I heard he'd left and gone to Calgary. I know he was never arrested by the police, so I guess he made a lot of money and maybe didn't like those Saskatchewan winters. I heard he charged up to eighty dollars for an operation to women who could afford it, ones with wealthy husbands, but the poor and those who were desperate, he charged half of that or less. He charged according to ability to pay, I guess.

He was well respected in the town and everybody liked him. It was the sort of a thing nobody talked about but everybody knew about, as if it was our business and not the police's business or the government's business. I knew most people thought he was a very generous and good doctor who loved people."

🐚 *This Nice Little Car*

"I'd been in France with the 149th Battalion, three years, in transport with mules and then trucks, and then they put us in the trenches. I thought, it was a tough time and now I'm back, so I'm going to have some fun. I was twenty-three at the time. Oh yes, I owned the farm. The way I got it was my dad died when I was seventeen, so he gave it to me, half, and the other half to my brother Luke, so we each had 320 acres. Free and clear. That was something in those days. You never had to look a bank manager in the eye and say, I need some money. To hell with them guys. The girls kind of looked at you different when they knew you owned half a section free and clear. You were a wealthy man, or they thought you were going to be wealthy.

So when I got back in the spring of 1919, Luke and me and some of the boys around, we did some early duck-hunting, and then I remember going into Brandon to the doctor. I wasn't out of the army yet, but if you got a doctor to examine you and you were okay, then you could kind of get your discharge and back pay by mail. You just sent in your medical certificate and they did it that way.

When I finished the doctor and I was fine, just fine, I walked around and I passed by this place on Rosser where they sold cars. There were some new shiny Fords in this agency and I looked at them through the window. I went on and had a cup of coffee in the hotel dining-room and I thought, that's a nice car. Then I thought, I'd like to have one. Then I thought, why can't I have one? I've got the money. So I walked back and there was a little man in the agency, wearing a Christy Stiff and smoking a big cigar, acting like a big shot. I didn't like him on sight and I didn't want to talk to him, so I just pointed to this nice little car and I said I'd take that one. I didn't ask how much, or anything. I just told him to push it out into the lane and I'd drive it home. You could say he was surprised. I was even kind of surprised with myself. I wasn't like that in those days. Still kind of shy.

I asked how much and he said it was $590. Okay with me. I just told him to wrap it up and I went down to the Bank of Montreal. I told them I wanted the money and they phoned the bank in my town and in ten minutes I had the money. Just like that. Went back, counted it out to the owner, the boss of the guy in the Christy Stiff, and a kid was putting gas into it, out in the lane, and the boss gave me five minutes of his valuable time after we filled out the papers and he showed me how to run it.

This was what they called the Model T. It became famous, you know. Books have been written about it. That was a fine little car. It was light and it got you over the mud roads in them days and it just spun along. If it broke down, you could fix it with wire and a pair of pliers. It wasn't like a watch. That car had about only ten moving parts and it was simple to fix up. The manual pretty well told you how.

Now, that was in 1919. Believe it or not, I was still running that car in 1937. That's a long time, and it was good as new, because if you took care of it, it took care of you. I did my courting in it, and I took my wife to hospital in it when we had our first boy. I hauled people around in it, to town on Saturday night and to weddings and funerals, and I went duck-hunting up at the Delta Marsh in it, and I did just about every damn thing a farmer could do in it. It just ran and ran, and about '30, when things started to get lean for us, I sawed off the back seat and put in a box, and I used that Model T for a truck and that's what she was. She ran in winter and in the mud and in spring break-up. I'd haul big loads in her, but by then I'd put heavy-duty springs in her. I put her into the ditch more times than I can think of, like hitting ice and boom, there you are looking at the sky. She never quit on me.

I think that was probably the best car Henry Ford ever made. It put a lot of people on the road. You know, getting them off the farms and out where the lights are bright. When a girl around the district would have a baby, not married, you know, but gone off to Winnipeg to visit an aunt for four months, like an aunt she didn't have, then we'd say she's gone visiting a Model T. That meant they figured she'd been knocked up in the back seat of a Model T. Might have been mine. I was always lending it out to the young bucks.

Like I said before, I had it till 1937, the Depression. There was this family who sold out, just couldn't make it. He was a poor farmer anyway, a drinker, a wife plumb worn out and four kids, and they wanted to start again in Peace River. Well, he had this quarter and a poor old house and barn, and it was half bush and he owed a thousand on it. Anyway, he'd done some work for me and he came over and said he was going, and I said okay and he asked if I would pass over on the fifty dollars he owed me from the winter before. I said okay. Knew I'd never see it anyway. Then I asks him what he's doing with the farm and he says just going to throw it on the bank's doorstep as they went through town. Then he asked, did I want to buy it? I said no, it wasn't worth nothing, and he said, 'Yes, but you give me your old truck and take over what's owing and it's yours.' I thought, 'Oh hell, why not?'

So he and I go into town and in an hour we've got the job done. I own the farm and the thousand in debt. Then we drive back to his wife and his kids and what they load on that truck is a pitiful sight to see. Practically nothing, and he's taking that family to the Peace River District, all bush, short growing-season, cold as Billy-be-damned by November first, and he hopes to make it. You know, I marvel all the time at the stupidity of some men. Reads a fancy article in the *Free Press* and there he is, heading into the bush with a poor wife and four kids under ten.

I drove them into Brandon, about forty miles away, and filled up the tank for them and wished them well and away they go, the kids piled up on top of this pile of furniture junk and boxes, eating ice-cream cones I'd bought them, happy as all get-out, and not knowing what was ahead.

There's another thing I mustn't forget. That place of theirs. I got a tree-swather in and a big breaking plough and got about forty more acres out of it, and it was good land. Big crops off it all through the war, big crops after, and I sold it for $130,000 just a few years ago when everybody went land-crazy. On the car business, I figure I'm pretty far ahead on the whole thing."

❧ *The Crash on a Bike*

"I got out of high school in '29, Winnipeg, and I was waiting for this office boy's job to open up in the Grain Exchange, and in the meantime I got a job pedalling a bike for the CPR, delivering telegrams. I had to. My old man was dead, so the only money coming in was my grandfather's pension. That was only twenty dollars a month, so you see that the thirty dollars I had coming in was really something pretty big.

This was in the summer of '29, pedalling from eight in the morning until nine at night, but we needed the money to hang in there until the Grain Exchange job came open and that would pay forty dollars. Then we'd be in clover. I didn't know beans from sausages but it was easy work, mostly downtown to the big companies, the warehouses and offices and those places.

Late that fall things picked up. It was go, go, go, and I mean that.

That bike was going full speed all the time. And you know why, although I didn't know why then? It was that all these telegrams were from broker houses in Toronto and New York, going to people who had bought these stocks on margin, and the bottom was just dropping out beneath their stocks. So, because they had bought on ten-per-cent margin, like ten bucks would buy you a hundred worth of a stock, and when it was going up, fine, you were making money. When the stock went down, you had to cover your position. So, when your stock went down, you stood to lose an awful lot. If you hung in and didn't pay up, then you'd be sold out and you were busted.

That's why all these telegrams, hundreds and then five hundreds, that's why they were keeping us hopping."

Four

The Dirty Thirties

❧

Will You Join Me, Please? . . . Living in a Cave . . . Equal . . . I Saw a Lot of Canada . . . Legal Work . . . The Stuff We Had To Burn . . . The Old General Store . . . Testing-Time . . . A Car for a Bike? . . . How the Prairie Can Come Back . . . Just Something You Talked About . . . I Remember Mr. Aberhart

The Great Depression, 1929–39. Those were the years Canada went belly-up. "Ten lost years" one man I talked to called them, giving me the name for my book – yet they were lost in another sense, too. They were not taught in any depth in the history classes of our schools. The War of 1812, yes, every skirmish, but 1929–39? I found just four paragraphs in one Grade 7 history book about the Depression on the Prairies. That, as much as anything, drove me to research and write Ten Lost Years.

Farmers are used to bad years, because "you can't lick nature", but when, year after year, hopes were high in May and, after weeks of searing sun, gone by mid-July, then what was the use of farming? On top of this assault, there had been the Wall Street Crash, the signal of the collapse of the North American and world economies.

Few were spared. Men in the cities lost their jobs by the hundreds of thousands. Everywhere. No city was spared the scene of long line-ups at soup kitchens, or of hundreds applying for three clerking jobs at seven dollars a week. Bankruptcies were countless. Money was virtually unknown in some families. Despair was everywhere.

But I learned that nowhere was it so bad as on the Prairies. Drought killed all the crops. Even if a farmer in a favoured area did get a crop one year, prices were so low it hardly paid his expenses. Thousands of farms were abandoned. A section of land seized by a bank was auctioned off north of Red Deer for $160, plus back taxes. One bidder. Farmers without fodder or pasturage sold their cattle at a cent a pound to the government. Families left for Ontario, some city, for the Peace River Country or Vancouver. Often they just slipped away silently in the night, ashamed that they couldn't make a go of it.

When the count had reached eight, in 1938, the rains began again, and in 1939 Hitler rolled his tanks into Poland. More rains followed, and in 1940, a year into the war, the West was reawakening. *The grim joke was that Hitler had ended the Depression, with a little help from the Lord. There was more than a measure of truth there.*

🐦 *Will You Join Me, Please?*

"Everyone was leaving. This neighbour, and then you'd hear that another was leaving, then another one, then another, and these weren't any Johnny-come-latelies. No, these were the sons of the first homesteaders, and in some cases the homesteaders themselves, and they saw they couldn't make a go of it in our district any more.

I remember so well. Sometimes there'd be a little going-away party for them in somebody's home, or maybe two or three families were leaving at one time and there would be something for them in the schoolhouse. They were just going, not really knowing where. Like the Alex Johnson family headed for the Peace River Country and we never heard of them again. They just disappeared up there, in a town, on a farm, God knows where. Some were going to the Okanagan Valley or the Coast. The Fraser Valley. The drought, the Depression, was on.

They'd take what they could, stuff from the house, stuff from the buildings and from the yard that they figured they would need. But they left everything else, house, barn, sheds, everything. They sold their stock for what they could, kept the best, and left the horses and the good stock with a neighbour or at the pound in town, and came back for them when they got settled.

My husband and me hung on. We were young and we thought we could make it. Jim's father had homesteaded the place, and he and Jim's mom were dead. Jim didn't think it was right to just give up on everything his dad and mom had worked so hard for. It was very sad. We put in three crops, '33 to '35, wheat and oats, and didn't take off enough to give us seed for the next year. The Saskatchewan government had a scheme where they gave you seed if you didn't have money to buy it. God knows, that was us.

We got nothing in the '35 crop. There was a fair amount of straw but no heads to the wheat, and that's what farming is all about.

That fall one day we sat around the kitchen table and talked, but there wasn't all that much to talk about. We had no crop, we had no money, and we just couldn't feed the horses and stock on straw another year. Jim said they just wouldn't pull through, and I could see that. They were not in good shape anyway. God knows what would have happened if we had got a crop next year and those horses had to pull a binder through it.

Though, we still had hope. I just don't remember what kind it was, and maybe it came out of the Eaton's catalogue. They were still advertising every nice thing in the world, and the models all had smiling faces, so maybe the city folk in Winnipeg thought things were going to get better. For us, we were only using the catalogue for what we'd always used it. There wouldn't be much of a Christmas that year.

Something else made up our minds for us. Sleeping sickness. It hit the whole area, about from west of Davidson right through to the Manitoba border, and I guess thousands of horses died. It was a terrible thing. We had ten horses and I watched ten of them die. You put big canvas straps under their bellies and hooked them to the beams, and this way you tried to keep the horse on its feet. But it was no use. They just died. Five died that way and the vet from town said the others were going too. Jim couldn't stand it and he took the others, one by one, he led them slowly out to a bluff in the pasture. I can still see him, leading that stumbling horse. A man on a farm gets awfully attached to his horses. He might not show it except by little ways you came to know, a pat, a way of talking to them, but you could tell. And then Jim would go out of sight and in a couple of minutes I'd hear a shot.

The day he shot the last one he told me we were going into Davidson and he harnessed up his driving mare, a little beauty called Flash. The sickness hadn't touched her. So we went into town and he dropped me off at my sister's house and he went off. I didn't ask him anything. I just chatted with my sister and had supper with them and chattered on as if nothing had happened. About nine o'clock, I guess, I heard Jim calling to me and I just threw on my coat and said goodbye and rushed out and got in the buggy, and when we got out to where you cross the highway going north to our place, Jim stopped the buggy.

I'll never forget it. It was dark and I couldn't see his face, but he told me he'd gone to the lawyer and told him to sell the farm. He said there was no use going on. Everything was against us. We had no kids, so God was against us. We had no crops, so God was against us there too. He took a long time to say all this, because

Jim was not a man whose words came easy, and besides, he was drunk. I had only seen him drunk once before, before our marriage. Even before I was going with him. At a dance, in what I called his wild days. But he was drunk now, but quiet-drunk, thoughtful-drunk.

I didn't blame him. I loved him more. It was just something. In those days a man was the head of the family and he made the decisions. If he had to shoot his horses, then he did it. If he couldn't see any blue sky above, then he would sell the farm, because, as he said it, we were still young and there was plenty of time for children and he wanted to bring up our children in a happy land. That's about the way he put it. I'll not forget that.

If he wanted to get drunk after signing the papers to sell it, then he had the right to go to the hotel and get drunk. He said he just sat alone and nobody came near him and he asked nobody to sit with him. He said he just did a pile of thinking. Remember, this was fifty years ago, but I still remember what he said. He said he had done a pile of thinking. Then when he'd told me everything, he handed the reins to me and said just to hold them, that Flash would take us home. He said, 'Flash will take us home.'

That did it. The word 'home'. In a few days or a few weeks it wouldn't be our home any more. It would belong to somebody else, or some bank or some company. It wouldn't be the Barnes place any more.

Jim just slumped down against me, little me, and he started to cry. Not really crying. Just sobs, sobbing as though his heart would break. Not loud sobs. Just soft ones, as if his heart was breaking. It was the saddest moment of his life, and the saddest moment of my life because I loved him so. I loved him with all my heart.

We finally got home. Flash took us home safely and Jim was all right by then and he unharnessed Flash and I heard him opening the gate and the slap when he slapped her, and her hooves running out into the pasture. He came back to where I was and we went into the house and I made us a cup of tea. Jim was all right by that time. It was all over.

He'd made his decision. He'd had his sorrow. He was my Big Jim again. He looked at me, and I can still see him, and he said, 'Kate, it's not the end of the world. I'm looking forward to tomorrow. Will you join me, please?'

When I say it again I still think it is very poetic, and coming from a man who probably never read a line of poetry in his life, I thought it was beautiful. Before I went up to bed that night I wrote it down and I still have it. Dated Friday, September 20, 1935.

I guess I should quit this story right then and there. Such a nice ending. But I won't. We did sell and we were gone by the middle of November, in a truck piled with everything we could carry. We sold everything else at auction and got nothing for it. Jim said we should have given it all away and felt better for it. A few dollars, I think about $200, for years of work. And $1,500 for the farm, to some businessman in Regina who had the money and knew times would get better and he'd make a big profit.

First, to Edmonton, and Jim got working in the packing-house, the hardest work he'd ever done then or before or since. Most men lasted a week wrestling those big sides of beef. Jim stuck it out till spring. Then we went to the Okanagan, Kelowna. We bought a small orchard, not for the fruit. Fruit was going for nothing. It was a place to live and Jim did odd jobs. Then to the Coast during the war, welding in a shipyard, and then to Victoria, and Jim went to work for the government and got the promotions and raises that came along, and when we retired we were fine and dandy.

You had to make the break some time. I'm glad we did when we did. That Depression lasted four more years. Four more years."

♨ *Living in a Cave*

"It was spring 1932 when I was let go and I tried for a month and there was no work in Winnipeg. Finally I said to hell with it, nothing can be worse than this is, and I got all my duds and stuff together. What I didn't want I sold to a second-hand dealer in Notre Dame Street and I headed out. I guess I had about fifty bucks.

I remembered that once I'd gone bird-hunting with a couple of guys to a little town called Melita. It was on the Souris River south of Brandon and the river was in a nice valley and there was just something about the place I liked and I thought, well, I'll see how I do.

I got talking to the town cop, a guy named Bannerman. A real nice guy who just wanted everybody to behave themselves so he didn't have to arrest them. I said I liked the place, even though there were no jobs, and I thought I'd go camping along the river for the summer and see what happened. He thought that was okay and told me that south of the town there were nice spots.

From then on everything sort of fell into its right place. I found a good place about five miles south of town on the river, with no farmhouses near it. So I went back to town and hired a guy for a dollar to drive his old truck out with my camping gear as close as we could get.

I lugged all my camping stuff down and I found a flat near the river on this bend and I set up my camp. It looked pretty darned good to me. I put up my tent and built a camp stove out of rocks and there was oodles of wood around, lots of wood piled up. There was plenty of water, naturally, and I thought I'd have a garden too. I got all set up and stayed there a couple of days just thinking and shooting a couple of partridges and catching pickerel in the river. There were lots of both of them.

I had about forty bucks left and I thought, this is going to be a good way to spend the summer and then I'll decide what to do. I had beans and salt and bacon, and the bacon and butter I kept in a pail in the river to keep cold, and I had sugar and a few other things and my .22 and a .410 shotgun and my fishing-lines, so I figured I'd do okay.

But in a couple of days I decided I'd have to go into town and get more grub and so I hiked in. I did some shopping, and on my way out with this gunny-sack of grub I stop in the Metropolitan Hotel for a beer. It's early afternoon and I get talking to this old guy and the owner, the only ones in there. They ask what I'm doing and this old guy, he says, you should build a soddy and stay for a while. I knew what a soddy was. A shack made of dirt. The other guy, the owner, he says a soddy was like living in a cave. That hit me. A cave!

There was this big bank on the river out there and I could dig in a tunnel up near the top and have a big room, and dig up a hole for a stovepipe. We got kicking this around, the three of us, and our thinking got better and better. Then the old guy said, 'I've got tools and shovels and a post-hole auger over at my place and I'll lend them to you. I'd like to see how all this turns out.'

I said that would be fine but I'd have to go back and see if the place I thought of was any good for a cave, and he said, 'Hell, of course it's good. Let's go.' And so we did. I lugged my stuff out to his truck and we got in and over to his house. He lived alone, his wife had died, and this was just something different for him to do that day. He had a whole shed full of stuff, and he gave me two round-nosed shovels and a rake and a potato fork and the post-hole auger and a great big chunk of canvas and nails and a couple of axes and a Swede saw and hammers and chisels and all sorts of stuff. You never saw the like of it. I said I'd pay him but he said everybody in town had more of this junk than he did and he couldn't get two bucks for it at an auction, so give him a buck and he'd be happy. Fine. Then I saw a wheelbarrow, and I said I'd like to buy that. Things were starting to form in my mind. He said okay, that would be another dollar. He had two days of drinking ahead of him, I could see that. Okay, and we put the stuff in his truck and he hauled it out to nearest to where my tent was and we said goodbye and I said for him to come out and visit me.

That night I sat by my fire, full of fish and bread and butter and fried spuds and coffee, and I thought, well, you've come this far, why not go all the way. Next morning I looked around and I figured this is a river that has to flood some time or another, so I poked around in those clay banks and found a spot about fifteen feet down from the top. That'd put her about twenty feet above the river, and no river in Manitoba I'd seen ever flooded that high. If they did, there wouldn't be any Manitoba. I started to dig a door.

All this comes back to me clear as a bell because I was sort of starting on a big adventure. I started to dig a door. Oh, maybe four feet wide and five feet high. I just kept digging, and by noon I was surprised how far I'd gone in. Maybe five feet. That was easy digging. Then I spent that afternoon looking around up and down the river. It wasn't so bad. There were fish in the river. There was plenty of trees, what some call cottonwood and others call poplar. There was a million tons of driftwood. Lots of birds. There were ducks on the river, and I figured there had to be a lot of wild creatures around, and there were. I found that out when a friend from town, Charlie Carels, gave me a bunch of traps.

I can tell you, I felt pretty peaceful that night with my fire going and eating bacon and beans and bakery bread smeared with Bee Hive syrup. In those days a ten-pound pail of that syrup cost seventy-five cents, and that would last a man half a year, and they let you keep the pail. You don't forget something like that.

To make a long story short, I worked hard every morning on the business end of that shovel and the earth was easy to move, and thank God something had told me to buy that wheelbarrow. Thanks, God. In about two weeks of tough work every morning

I had a big room, about seven feet high and twelve feet by sixteen, all hollowed out.

I went into town and got an extra lamp and kerosene, and then got the two lanterns going in the cave, and that way I could see to fix it up. I got old boards from abandoned farmyards for free. And for a dollar here, fifty cents there, I got a stove, a bed, a few chairs for maybe ten cents each, buckets, pails, some linoleum for the floor, shelves, dishes, cups, bowls, knives and forks, this kind of stuff. They were actually giving it away, you know. People even then, and this was 1932, and things really started to crumble about '34, they were saying it's no use and were moving out, taking their cattle north into the park country where there was feed and shelter, and what they left, why, anybody could have. You didn't even have to pay for it. Wait till they left and then just take it.

That summer I worked hard and I got everything pretty good. Real cozy. Bannerman, the policeman, he came out one day and he told me to keep in touch with him every time I came to town. Just so he'd know I wasn't lying dead on the floor. He was a good guy. When the RCMP came along later in Manitoba and he had to switch over to their uniform, then all the new regulations made him a bit cranky, but he was still a real nice guy.

About the middle of August I'm in town and having a beer in the Metro and old Weinstein, the owner, asks me if I'm going harvesting. I laugh and say no, the hoppers and the 95-degree temperature, they got it all. No, he says, a bunch of young bucks from around were going up around Foxwarren and Russell to harvest, where they always got good crops. He thought they'd take me along. The pay that year, and this is '32, was two bucks a day, all found, and you worked from dawn to dusk. Boy, those farmers sure knew how to work you. But these guys from Melita had been doing it up there since '30, and they knew the farmers, so we went up there and didn't have to compete with all the other guys from Saskatchewan and Manitoba for jobs. We worked seven days a week for seven weeks and I never spent a cent in town on beer and I came back with a lot of new muscles I didn't know I had, and about eighty bucks.

I'll tell you this right now. That eighty dollars, that got me through the winter. It bought me second-hand bush clothes. It bought me shells, and a few pints of bootleg whiskey when I went to parties and dances in town. It bought me my food and the movie shows at the Strand, and I'd stay overnight bedded down at the livery stable and go home the next morning. A big night on the town. I even bought two pounds of chocolates at Christmas for the ladies of the Women's Institute. They ran the Rest Room and had a library and I went through everything they had, maybe three or four books a week. When I left the gift for them, you'd have thought I had given them the world.

Then I guess I made about eighty dollars that year just trapping. There was a mink farmer across the line who'd pay ten cents a pound for rabbit meat for his mink. Rabbits were everywhere, thick as thieves. Just chop 'em up, boil 'em, and freeze 'em into blocks and he'd pick it up. You got ten cents a skin, too, to wrap wee baby bunting in. Fifteen, sometimes twenty cents for squirrels. I sold about half a dozen coyote pelts every year. Dozens, dozens of muskrats you got off the big sloughs in the spring. Weasel. Oh yes, plenty of them. Somebody would always pay for anything you caught, those days, and my friend Charlie Carels was the fur buyer, and he was fair. Three fox that first year. Big healthy buggers, what with all the rabbits around. I never went after beaver, but an old Indian named Eagle, he'd drop around for a meal once in a while, and he said he knew where they were easy to get.

I could always get some kind of an odd job, like helping with a big job at the station. That was if I was in town. I always seemed to pick up jobs. I don't think people were sorry for me, just that they knew I'd put in a day's work. Pay was usually $1.25 a day, but you could walk home with a good bag of meat for that, like some pork chops and five pounds of hamburger. In spring I worked for a couple of weeks in March cutting ice for the ice-houses. That was hard work. Wet too. Or digging a well. Once I went down, five feet wide, down sixty feet, and the farmer said to hell with it, come on up. No, I said, I'll go five more feet for you. For free. Two feet farther down I hit water. And I had a darn sight of trouble, I can tell you, getting up that ladder, when that water just came roaring in. He gave me fifty bucks for that.

I had my garden. With the sun, and the water running by my door, those vegetables never had had it so good. Potatoes, onions, radish, cukes, lettuce, peas, beans, you never saw such a crop. And I'd planted a lot of sweet peas around and I'd give fresh stuff to Mrs. Carels and I sold stuff to Weinstein for the dining-room at the hotel. I could have given every kid in town a pumpkin for Hallowe'en. Big ones. Up on the farms they may have had no gardens, but down there on the river I had a hundred. Oh, it was grand.

I was never cold in my house. In fact, I was so warm I could sleep without any blankets in winter because, you see, some process was going on, and the earth held the heat. I'd read and polish up my arrowheads and other Indian stuff I'd found. There was a lot of old Indian places around, and the wind just took away the soil and left these arrowheads and spearheads lying around. I put an ad in the *Winnipeg Free Press*, once, and a man came out from Winnipeg in his car one weekend and I sold the lot, just the ones I'd collected in about five times of going out. I sold them for fifty bucks, which was enough to buy a good car in those days. If you wanted one and could afford to run it.

That first year I got to know people in town, and a few would come out and see me at times. They'd get saskatoon jam on good bread and some coffee and we'd have a nice visit. I got to know a few families. Some people would say, oh, that Jimmy Hoover out there in the cutbank, he's gone Indian. Look at him, living like that in a cave, he's crazy or he's up to no good. Now, that just wasn't so. I had a good life and I had a fair bit of money, more money, I think, than a lot of the people in that town.

That was the first year. The second year was the same, except I made more money. I'd bet I made five hundred dollars or more that second year, and that didn't include the money for harvesting at Russell, because I didn't go. I just worked a bit around the district, a few days, and I could go home at night on my bicycle and look after things.

But then I got this letter from my brother in Kelowna and he said he could get me a job in a garage. I had to let him know soon. I waited and waited and didn't write, but then I decided, well, I said I could do it and I did. Living in a cave and doing okay. So I just nailed the door shut and took what I needed and I left, and when I got to Kelowna there wasn't any job left for me in the garage. That didn't matter. I could go back and be what I had been before. But it didn't happen. I got a job on an orchard, and next year I got a job in a garage in Kelowna, and the next year I got married. We had five kids and I'd tell them, I once lived in a cave and ate muskrats and sold their skins and did okay. They'd say, Dad, let's go and see that place. But I never did.

I told Bannerman the policeman that if he wanted to let somebody else live in it, just make sure you get the right people so they won't wreck it, because I might come back. But I never did."

🕊 *Equal*

"You see, with us, we didn't know we were poor. We knew the Ukrainian kids were poorer than we were, but they had always been, I guess. That was the way it was. But we had nothing. We had clothes, overalls for me, and my sisters wore them too, and my father and my mother, she never went out of the house. The point is, we didn't know we was poor. Not an idea. If an Eaton's catalogue came into that house, I guess I don't remember it, but it would have shown us that other people didn't dress in overalls and rags for dresses, and there was such a thing as new shoes you could buy.

All around us, the Dancy family, the Hoppers, the Carters, the Boyds, all these good pioneer names in the district, they were all as poor as we were. So, don't you see, everybody being poor, without a cent, that meant everybody was equal.

In Winnipeg it would be different. On a street you've got ten families living in a row and one would be a mechanic and one would be a teacher, one a salesman, one without a job, two without jobs. So on that Winnipeg street, some families would have more money than the others. Not so on the farm, everybody was broke so everybody was equal. All broke, all busted, and not knowing what it was like outside in the world, I suppose we were all pretty happy about life."

🕊 *I Saw a Lot of Canada*

"There was no point in my hanging around. By that time I was eighteen, and there wasn't enough work around and none in town. There was nothing for a kid just out of high school, that was me, so one day after we did the spring clean-up and got things in shape, I told my folks I was heading out. I didn't know where. Calgary, I thought. I had no plan in mind.

My mother made a fuss. You'd have thought I was going into Darkest Africa. I was just heading for Calgary. Next day I left. I remember what I had – a change of clothes in a cloth bag, a few things I needed like shaving stuff, and I think my old man gave me two dollars. He was going into town and he dropped me off at the station and the farmers were bringing in their cream cans. I helped throw about twenty of them aboard and the guy in the baggage car told me I could ride with them to Calgary. So long, farm. This was in '34, the spring.

Well, that was an education. I went into it as a first-grader, you could say, and two years later I came out a high school graduate. That works out to eleven grades in two years, and I saw a lot of Canada. I can't get too enthusiastic about it now, because I can see that something like it might just happen again.

Anyway, I'm in Calgary with two bucks in my pocket and I ain't going anywhere. Nobody's got a job, because there aren't any. I'd like to say some little old lady came up to me on the street and asked me if I wanted to be her chauffeur and wear a fancy uniform. Nothing. It was all ham and eggs, without the ham and without the eggs. I tried. I did try, but for every job which I never even got to hear about, there were fifteen guys after it. That's the way it was.

There was a shape-up outside the mission some guy and his wife ran. Not the Salvation Army, they wanted prayers, guys who'd pray and sing along with them, and I wasn't exactly fitted out for that. This place was run by this couple and they got donations and they gave it out until it was gone and then they said there was no more. Good, kind people. Like my mother. God must have looked down on them and smiled.

Oh, there was work. I've worked for ten cents an hour in a junk-yard, this iron scrap going to Japan. If you stopped more than two minutes for a piss you could expect to have no job when you finished that night. Somehow nobody wanted to work for that outfit. You know, it may be crazy, but maybe we had an idea what that scrap was going to be used for–I mean bullets to kill our boys at Hong Kong.

Then I went out to the yards with another guy named Scott Forsythe and we hopped a freight going west. There was a lot of talk about picking fruit in the Okanagan, and that shows you just how dumb we were. Here it was June and everybody is talking about picking fruit, and it doesn't ripen until August. But that's the way it went in those days. But you could sit in a nice box-car with a lot of other guys and listen to the craziest stories, just like the army.

Revelstoke, I went through there twice, back and forth. Full of bulls. They didn't want you to stay in the town, but they didn't want you to ride their train, which was empty anyway. That CPR. They talk about it building Canada. I wish they hadn't. Then no work for those guys, those railway cops. Besides, then B.C. would be part of the United States, and if I had my way, that's just the way it would be. They're crazy out there. I know, we've got some crazies running around loose here too. Look at that Jim Keegstra. If he'd seen what I seen when I was in the army overseas, he wouldn't be talking about that stuff.

Anyway, I was all over B.C., and in the end I went back to Alberta. Treat a man like a dog, he goes running home like a dog. I was never so glad to see the last of those damned mountains. I felt every one of them was talking to me and saying, 'Get the hell out of this country.'

I worked harvesting that year at Wetaskiwin and then there was Edmonton that winter. Finest people in the world. I worked steady and worked hard. They expected more than a dime's worth out of you for a dime's worth of pay.

There used to be a whorehouse on the hill below the Macdonald Hotel. I remember that. We'd get off work Saturday night and spruce up in the washroom of the Mac and have a meal at a Chinese café and then head for the girls. Just sitting around, talking politics with the big shots who'd come in. Go upstairs, come down, tip your hat, and there was no free whiskey drink when you went out. You got that when you went in.

I worked in the city all that winter and had good pay mostly. I think maybe thirty cents an hour. Good pay then. Lots of fun. Nobody had nothing, but everybody had a hell of a lot of fun.

Then I went home for harvest. My dad wrote and said he was going to have a crop that year, and he did. I was glad to be home. Mountains may be lousy for your health in B.C., but on the horizon they sure looked good. That was my place to be. As Alberta Slim used to sing, 'Back in Good Old Alberta'."

🕊 *Legal Work*

"Wilkie, Saskatchewan. Good farming country and good farmers, but this is the Depression, the drought, everything is bust, and this little town has four lawyers. None of them are making a living, so they go to their offices every morning and putter around doing nothing and eat lunch, and then they all meet in the lobby of the hotel and have a bridge game all afternoon. This went on for a long time, and one day one of the lawyers didn't show up, young fellow named Ney, who later became the judge up at North Battleford. The others sent the hotel flunkey over to his office and he came back and said, 'Mr. Ney can't be with you this afternoon. His client has come to see him.'

Lawyer's jokes usually aren't funny, because they usually have a punch line with some Latin in it that you have to figure out. But that one, that one I liked. A real Depression yarn."

🥀 *The Stuff We Had To Burn*

"It was terrible. It was the very worst of the times. No, we didn't starve. That was a Mennonite community around there and we look after each other, we always have. That is our religion.

It wasn't the drought. I can't say we had it. But we had the other. Rain, for one thing. You get too much rain and you get rust, and then you don't have any more of a crop than if you didn't have a bit of rain.

The grasshoppers. You wouldn't believe them. They'd just come one morning going north and by afternoon you had nothing. Just nothing. No crop. No garden. No pasture. You were finished.

But I remember worst the stuff we had to burn because we didn't have money for coal. We had to burn manure. Everybody had cows and horses and pigs, and they'd collect all the manure from them, all winter and spring and fall.

Here is what we did. You would take this manure and spread it around on the ground with your pitchfork, until it was about a foot high. Then you walked around on it, the whole family. In your bare feet. You led the horses over it and they packed it down too. Imagine walking around all the time in your bare feet, that squishy stuff. Then you hoped for a lot of hot sun so it would bake it, dry it. Then in August we'd cut this mess into squares and put them on end so they would dry some more. Then, before it rained in the fall you'd store this, and that was your winter's burning supply.

That's what I remember about the Depression in southern

Manitoba. Not rust. Not the grasshoppers. None of that. I just remember every winter until about 1937, every winter I'd think, this bread I'm eating, this meat I'm eating, everything is cooked by that awful stuff. That manure, you see. It just left a bad taste in my mouth.

The food was okay. Oh, it was good. But burning this stuff and eating the food this stuff cooked, it meant to me, poor, poor, poor. I guess it meant peasant to me. If there is one thing a Mennonite does not want to think himself to be, I can tell you it is being a peasant. Like in Russia.

The winter after things got better, I think maybe the coal and lumber yards in our towns sold a lot of coal that winter. People wanted to forget that manure coal."

❧ The Old General Store

"My uncle had a store, and it was just like every store. I guess within a thirty-mile radius of his store there would be maybe ten like it. They sold the same things and had the same kind of customers and gave the same credit, and during the Depression a lot of them went broke.

People used to think that my uncle had a lot of money. That's because he handled money, but they didn't know he was on credit too. He'd get his groceries and stock from the wholesalers in Winnipeg, and he'd have to pay up in thirty days. But a lot of his customers just paid when they could. Mostly in the fall. *If* there was a crop. *If* they could sell it. *If* they didn't have people they owed to who they thought were more important and had to be paid. *If* they didn't just pack up a wagon with their belongings and their kids and light out for greener pastures. *If* there wasn't another store in town where they'd go and deal if they had run up their limit of credit with my uncle.

That's why I am using all these 'ifs'. My uncle used to say storekeeping was an iffy business.

You wanted cash. You hoped the customer would buy with cash. But there was this credit system, and each customer on that would have a receipt book. When I clerked for him, I think just about three-quarters had a book. This kind of tied them to that one store, you see, I mean if they had a conscience. But as I remember, as the

Depression wore on, less and less people had a conscience. Quite a few became crooked in a small way. They'd try and cheat their neighbours, like petty stealing, and naturally they'd try and cheat the storekeeper.

Times were very hard, you know, in the Dirty Thirties. I'm talking here about whether they had even enough food to put on the table. I'm talking about whether there was enough gas in the car to take a kiddy to hospital in Brandon if she had a very bad fever or appendicitis. I mean, this is about whether children had shoes to go to school, and this was in Manitoba. We're not talking about Saskatchewan and the drought, where they had no crops at all. We're talking about farmers who had crops but couldn't sell them for what it cost them to grow them, and that, you know, didn't cost much. Some gas, some oil, binder twine. Where we lived, nineteen miles north of Brandon, it was good, but it was still bad.

If it hadn't been for Eaton's, I think the storekeepers would have done fine, but they took all the big money because they sold everything. Why, that catalogue was that thick. Maybe an inch and a half. It was marvellous, just to go through it. See all the things we couldn't stock. With Eaton's, you sent a money order to cover what you'd ordered. They didn't fool around, and that was fine.

But the guy in the general store, well, that was different. And people took advantage of him. He had to give credit, but he also had to pay his suppliers. So he couldn't let a family get too high a bill. But if he didn't, people would say he was a Scrooge. Then, if a couple of families who had big bills, if they skipped out in the night, people would laugh and say he was a sucker. If there was two or three other stores in town, he had to be real nice and give bargains to get customers, to keep his customers. So you'd have what would be like a price war sometimes. It was all so unfair, you see.

People were desperate, and the meanness and the blackness in our hearts comes out when we are desperate. Hard times, it may bring out the good and neighbourliness in a lot of people, but it brings out the very worst in a lot too. I saw it. I helped with my uncle's books for nearly three years. So I know.

No, I wouldn't have wanted to be a storekeeper then. That's for sure. You saw so much misery during the drought and hard times, and you didn't make any money. If you came out ahead by a thousand dollars at the end of a year after paying your bills, you were lucky. That's no way to make a living, working from seven in the morning until eight at night, and somebody waking you up at twelve o'clock at night and wanting something. They did it. They thought nothing of it. And they'd want it on credit, too. Maybe a gallon of kerosene. Twenty cents. I used to hate that."

❧ *Testing-Time*

"In June 1936, when we could see we weren't going to get a crop that year, we gave up our farm south of Shaunavon. We should have left two or three years before, because that country then just wasn't worth farming. If you had no money and no crop and you weren't really farmers anyway, you finally had to get out.

My husband, Alex, had a 1925 Durant that hadn't worked for a couple of years and he towed it into Shaunavon with his team and he told me and the kids to stay put. He'd be back. He took the eldest boy, Dick, along to steer the car and they were gone two days. Then he came back driving the car and no horses. He'd got the car fixed and sold the horses for fifty dollars and paid off a few small bills we had and that was the end of Saskatchewan for us.

I remember Alex drove into the yard with Dickie about eleven in the morning and nothing would do that we leave right away. After living in that shack for about seven years, he wanted to leave in an hour or two. He meant it. The man was dead determined. He didn't want to have anything to do with it for another day and night.

He had made a little trailer and that was hitched behind the car, piled with our things. The washing-machine, the sewing-machine, blankets, the tent, dishes, clothing, a couple of bedsprings, and I guess that was about it, and the food that Alex had bought in town with the fifty. I think we had about twenty dollars left.

I asked what about the machinery and the harness and all the tools and the chickens and everything around, and he said to leave it. He'd talked with a man in Shaunavon and he'd come out and take it all away and sell it at an auction. He'd send the money to us at my husband's brother's house. You see, he'd had it all planned. I thought, we'll never see a penny. But, funnily enough, we did. That man sent us about eighty-five dollars a few weeks later. That wouldn't happen today. People were more honest then.

In about three hours we were gone, and I can't say I looked back with tears in my eyes. That was what the Dirty Thirties did for you. There was no future in those days. Just day to day. You got by, but it wasn't living. No sir, not one bit.

We went to Winnipeg. Alex's brother worked in a garage there and played a bit of senior hockey. He got, I think, a dollar a game, and he wrote and said he thought he could get my husband on with the man who owned the hockey team, if he played hockey. Alex was a very good hockey player, but not good enough to play for Toronto. Besides, there had been this farming business in his mind since he was a kid, and when we were married we went farming. That was in 1925, and naturally that was a mistake.

I forget how long it took us to get to Winnipeg. Maybe ten days. We took the southern roads and did a lot of stopping. We'd come to a nice spot by a river and we'd pitch the tent, and the three boys would sleep under a lean-to and we'd have a little vacation. Swim. Fish. Plenty of fish. We bought vegetables and eggs and bacon at places along the road, and talked to farmers. They were getting rain and some crops, but there were patches where it was just as bad as we'd had it. But prices for wheat was so low that nobody could make a living.

I remember sitting around the bonfire at night and toasting marshmallows. Just that little family of ours. I'd think we've got no money. We've got no possessions worth anything. No furniture. No farm, no land, no livestock, no machinery, no bank account, all these things. But I would think, for the first time in years I was happy.

Well, we got into Winnipeg after spending two nights on the river at Headingly and swimming and cleaning up and phoning his brother. You came in those days on the narrow little highway and you could see the city in the distance, and you noticed the green trees and then the wide streets and the streetcars and people driving cars, and I thought, it's been a long time. I'd almost forgotten what a city looked like.

There was no job for my husband where his brother worked – no jobs anywhere, for that matter–but my husband was a go-getter. He got us into a boarding-house without the board on Langside and he went looking for work. There was none that summer, and he couldn't get on relief with the city because we had just arrived. But he kept looking and he did pick up the odd job. Just by walking and knocking on doors and asking if he could clean up trash or wash windows or do all these things that nobody thought of.

He was walking by the Winnipeg General Hospital on one afternoon and there had been no rain for a long time and in the parking lot marked off for doctors he noticed all their big cars were very dirty. He waited, and as every doctor came out to get into his car he'd ask him if he could wash and shine up his car. Well, doctors are busy men and they make good money and nine times out of ten they'd say yes, go ahead. My husband told them he'd be there bright and early next day. He borrowed a couple of brushes and soap and a couple of pails and some hose from our landlord. Then he got over to the hospital and went to work on these doctors' cars, and when they were finished their business in the hospital they'd have a car all freshly washed and polished up. That first day he made three dollars, and that was pretty good. So he did that the rest of the summer, right into September. By that time a job opened up in a garage at River and Osborne and he would be making two dollars a day there, which wasn't as much, but he knew it would be steady.

Then we put the kids in school, where they got a good education, and because I had typing and filing from Success Business College years before, I was able to get a job in Eaton's. The mail order. That was nine dollars a week and that paid for a little apartment, and we lived on Alex's wages and he got a dollar a night playing hockey at the old Olympic rink.

Alex and I and the kids got through the Depression. We never missed a meal, although we ate a lot of macaroni and cheese and liver and onions and second-hand bread. We had no future. You didn't think of it that way. It was just a time of putting in time and hoping. Not hoping for much. Just hoping.

There was never much in the papers about it all. I'd watch, thinking if we are so bad off, then people must be starving, but it was not so. Nothing in the papers. People just didn't live as they should have, but it was like this, I figure. When everybody's in the same boat, then it is all right. We were young. You can ignore a lot of things when you are young. It wasn't a good time, mind you, but it was a time that tested people and made them better."

🐦 *A Car for a Bike?*

"I was just about twenty-nine when I got my first car. This was in

'36 and I had no job, just picking up two bits here and fifty cents there doing odd jobs, around the neighbourhood or downtown. I'm downtown this day and I always rode my CCM bike around, a 22-20 drop. Grey. I remember that, and all shiny and new although it was four years old. I'd paid twenty-one dollars for that bike, all the money I'd got working for three months on a farm near Whitecourt.

But there I am this day, right in downtown Edmonton, and I'm passing this used-car lot and I saw this little grey Ford bug with red disc wheels sitting next to the sidewalk. I don't know why but I stopped and looked at it. That day I didn't have one red cent, but looking was free, and in a minute this salesman came over, all ready to make a big deal. He said it ran good and he started it up and it sounded good, and they only wanted fifteen dollars for it. I told him I had no money, and just as I was leaving he called me back and I told him again I had no money, and he said he would trade for the bike.

Well, the bug had no licence plates on it and the cops were tough, but finally I agreed to a trade if he'd tow it to my home. We made up the papers and I rode the bike home and, sure enough, just before supper they towed the Ford into the yard and I gave him the bike.

This was fine and dandy. Now I had a snazzy little bug but no licence, and it cost five dollars. What was I going to do? It was early May and there was a market gardener out at the end of our street, and I went to him and asked for a job. He had a lot of garden to put in and I worked about twelve hours a day for him for a whole week and I got five bucks for that hard work and I bought a licence with it.

Gas was only about twenty cents a gallon, and I could always scrape up that much or a pal would have it and he'd put in a couple of gallons, and this way we scooted around all summer and into the late autumn, me running around looking for odd jobs, and us going out spinning in the evening and on Saturday afternoons and Sunday. This little bug ran faithfully all the time. Never a bit of trouble.

Then, before it snowed I sold it to the gardener, who had liked it. He paid me thirteen dollars for it and that helped me get through the winter, and that was that.

I told this to my son, the dentist from Edmonton, just like I'm telling you, and I don't think he believed me. He said, 'Dad, a car

for a bike? And then you sold it to a farmer for thirteen dollars?'
Didn't believe me."

🕊 *How the Prairie Can Come Back*

"You go south of Nanton and then you go about five miles east.
In the Depression that was dry country, you better believe me.

We had the normal number of sloughs and, oh, I guess about
four or five acres was the size of each one. But then we had drought
for about five years and that land was like triple-strength concrete.
You could land a bomber on some of our fields, that's how thick
the crust was.

Then in 1938 we had a good winter with lots of snow, and not
much of it blowing over into Saskatchewan, and rain in the spring,
May. Lots of it. This was more like it. You'd feel it in town. The
storekeepers were opening up too. A little more credit. It looked
like a good year. We didn't care about what was going on in Europe.
All we cared about was what was happening for twenty miles on
each side of us.

This was something, believe me. We've got this land with nothing
growing on it, and then this spring there's water in the sloughs.
Ducks you've never seen in five years, there they are parading
around on it. There's no feed for them, but anyway some sort of
compass told them to fly in and look around before they went on
north. And then green things started around the water edges.
Shoots. Little plants. The start of bulrushes. This didn't happen all
at once, but if you went back in June and then in July, you'd see
the difference. The stuff was coming up. Like the desert, they say
it blooms after a rain. What about the old Canadian dryland prairie,
eh? Those seeds had to have been there for five years, just waiting,
biding their time. And flowers around the edges. Bluebells and the
like, some daisies, Black-eyed Susans. And here it all is starting over
again.

Now, you ain't gonna believe this. Frogs. Yep, frogs. They
showed up from somewhere. It's a hell of a long way to the river
for a frog but they made it, or they may have been in the ground
just hibernating. Shrimp too. Those little prairie shrimp. Thousands of them, but they were there and, well, it was just like
something out of them National Geographic films on the TV.

In one summer, there it was. Bulrushes, weeds, flowers, shrimps, the whole bit, and at night we'd hear a few frogs going away at it, like baying at the moon. By next year the whole countryside was a going concern and some of the ducks stayed, and I wouldn't have been a bit surprised to see a beaver family packing their camp over the trail and down to the slough.

When people ask me about the Depression I don't tell them about the hard times my mom and dad went through. What I tell them is how the prairie can come back. So damned quick, you couldn't believe it. That's why I say, good times will always follow bad times.

Oh, it was wonderful. People would go into town and they'd be happy. Lots of talking and laughing and then we'd get in the old truck and off we'd go home, and there'd be ducks sitting on the sloughs, and blackbirds and, well, it was like being given a chance again to do whatever you wanted to do. Like God saying, okay, you've suffered. Here's a new life."

❧ Just Something You Talked About

"I remember 1936, the year I got married, and how it was, the feeling we all had that as we'd gone for about five years in the Depression then, it soon had to end, because it was just crazy. The drought and the grasshoppers and the pain and the sorrow of it could not go on much longer. It didn't seem right that God should punish us that way, that farmers for miles and miles and miles around who were all God-fearing and honest men would be subject to such conditions – and their wives and their families.

Young people, we saw no hope. Young men thought they were a burden on their families and that's why so many left. Riding the rods, they called it. You know, travelling back and forth in box-cars across the country looking for work. There was nothing in the towns around, nothing, because the towns and villages, they all depended on the farmers for their money and living, and the farmers had no money. There was barter, too, of course. You'd take in a case of eggs or six pounds of butter and barter it for things you really needed. I mean really needed. There was no frivolity then.

At Christmas a child was lucky to get a fifty-cent toy and a bag of candy and an orange, and that was about it. It would be all right for a small child, say eight or nine, because they really hadn't known what it was like before the Depression.

So, we had no money. My husband and I knew that. We decided, we can't wait forever. When you're farming dryland, good times may never come, and so we decided to get married. May 23, 1936, smack dab right in the middle of the Depression. A Saturday, and it was a beautiful day. The wedding was in Coaldale and the reception at the farm, and everybody came. Even the local Hutterites, and that is something. Well, the elders, the bosses. Not the people themselves. My father was very popular. A big party, wedding, at ten in the morning, and then the party, and have you ever heard of anyone going on a honeymoon in a truck? Well, John and I did. A 1928 Ford with the back cut off and made into a truck, and about three we headed off to Waterton.

It was wonderful then, before the government stepped in with their big ideas and ruined it all for everybody. We had an army bell tent, the one we took when we went to work the sugar-beets in the fall around Raymond, very hard work, and not much money. We had blankets and pots and pans and dishes and a tin oven. And we had fishing-poles and food, the staples, and sixteen dollars, my poor pitiful savings, and have you ever seen a bride drive away on her honeymoon wearing breeks, a khaki shirt, and boots, with rice in her hair? That was me. We took books and a checker-board and, oh yes, two bottles of moonshine. That was from Steve, our hired man. I think he might have made more than my dad on the farm, just selling a few pints here, a few pints there. I always knew Steve would do well.

It took us a struggle to get up the tent, they're so big you know, and we had a wonderful time. About a week. We fished and caught trout in the creeks and one day John found a turtle, as big as a frying-pan. He skinned it or whatever you do to turtles and I did it in butter in our tin stove.

It had to end, of course, and we went back, because John was working in Number One Colliery and he'd got his seeding done at the right time and we got a fair crop that year. Prices were still low, we didn't get much for it, but we had four good cows and that gave us a small cream cheque, because I wouldn't let him go back to the coal, and we worked the beets, too. Well, scratching here and scrambling there, we did fine.

When nobody has any money you fall back on other things, like yourselves, your family, the neighbours, and I guess just the community spirit. You helped each other out. It was amazing how you could survive and eat well and feel good. I think we all knew things had to get better.

They did, of course. The rains came about 1938, at the right time. That year the district got a good crop. Then the war, of course. We didn't lose many of our boys, but a lot of them joined up. That was the end of the Depression. By 1941, I'd say, everybody was back on their feet and doing just fine. In a few years everybody had forgotten about the Dirty Thirties. It was just something you talked about, once in a while."

🕊 *I Remember Mr. Aberhart*

"I remember Mr. Aberhart very well. I never met him, but he was something else again. He really was. People of Alberta today, well, they just know him as a name, a religious fanatic. He wasn't that at all. He was a good man, a man who wanted to do the best he could for the poor farmers and all the poor people of Alberta.

The funny thing is, he never did anything real for the poor farmers and the poor people in the way of giving us more money, or a better way of life, or relief from the bankers in Toronto. That was what he was elected on in that exciting election of 1935, but he couldn't do it. One man even with his ideas couldn't fight the Depression, which was all over Alberta. People were literally starving in some places, and kids were not going to school because there was no shoes and warm clothing for them. That is a fact of life. I knew it personally.

But what Mr. Aberhart and his Social Credit did was give us hope. He said he'd get us out of this mess and we believed him. I guess we had to. What else was there to believe in? Crop failures, and burned out and rusted out and no money coming in, because a farmer couldn't get enough money when he sold his wheat or barley to pay for the cost of growing it. It was bad on the farms, and remember, oil hadn't been discovered yet in Alberta, so it was all farming, mostly, and people living in cities and towns and living off the farmer. If the farmer didn't make any money, well, it is easy to see that the people in the city wouldn't be doing any good at all.

Mr. Aberhart was a young man from Ontario who came to Alberta, and he was a very fine schoolteacher and was made a principal of a school. He was a religious man, too, and he preached on the radio every week. There were a lot of people in the province who had radios by that time. Mr. Aberhart's program was called 'Back to the Bible Hour' and it was broadcast over CFCN in Calgary, I think it was at three in the afternoon, and most people listened to him. It was a religious program, but after reading about Major Douglas and his Social Credit program, Mr. Aberhart took up his ideas and started mixing religion and how to run the country in the program. I don't think he asked for money, but somebody had to pay for the radio program, so people would send it in. My father would send in a dollar bill now and then. And then out of all this, there was more money than needed, and people in their letters would say that he was the leader to help us beat the Depression. Gradually it came clear to Mr. Aberhart that the people were sick and tired of the United Farmers of Alberta trying to run things, and the politicians in Eastern Canada, and we better do something about it. That's how it all started, and being religious they never called it a political party. They called it a movement. That was a much better word. It sounded more . . . well, more like it was a holy thing.

I think it was in '34 when Mr. Aberhart came to Taber to speak. There were a lot of United Church around there and a lot of Mormons and a few Catholics, but everybody showed up at this meeting. It was my fifteenth year and I didn't know squeak about politics, but I went with my mother and dad, being the oldest. My goodness, what a thing. There must have been five hundred people at his meeting that night. They knew that they'd never get that many in the hall, so that men started taking out the folding chairs so there would be more room for standing. And you know what? By the time it was meeting time there were about a thousand. In that little town, that little district.

Mr. Aberhart came down the road in a big car, and when he got out, a big man with a round face, a cheery man, everybody clapped and cheered and yelled. They almost roared. You never saw the likes of it. It was about fifteen minutes before he could get to the platform, because everybody, every blamed person, wanted to see him, touch his coat, you know.

When the meeting started, he could hardly talk for the cheering. He had a marvellous voice, a beautiful voice, and his speech just

rolled out, and everything he said made sense. That was Mr. Aberhart. Nobody there except a few, I guess, knew that what he was
saying was not going to work. We just wanted somebody to
say that he had a plan to make things better. That he could do it
and he needed our help. That was what he was saying. With
our help and God's help Mr. Aberhart could make Social Credit
work.

My father told me later he knew Mr. Aberhart's Social Credit
wouldn't work. Ottawa and the politicians wouldn't let him make
it work, but that wasn't why Dad voted for him. He said he'd even
vote for a talking telephone pole if he thought the pole would give
people hope. That it would give them some confidence in themselves and what they did best, growing wheat and giving themselves
and their families a good life and in a God-fearing way.

Well, in that country nobody understood much of what he was
talking about – the Social Credit money theory, what they called
'Funny Money' in the newspapers – and I'll say this, he didn't harp
on it too much. But even if people didn't understand, they understood the man behind all these words. He was telling us there was
hope. That it wouldn't always be like this. When he said he'd
realized that something had to change, he told us about the thing
that changed his mind completely, and he said that's why he was
up on the platform. He said one of his students a couple of years
before, in high school, had become so desperate about the way
things were going, with his life and his family, and the people in
his town, the hardship, the despair we all felt, that he saw no future
in his life, and he hanged himself. That shook everybody up. A
young man committing suicide, and that was the most terrible
thing to do in those days.

People came out of that meeting and they talked about Mr.
Aberhart for days and weeks. There was no doubt about how most
people would vote, and on voting day it showed up right there.
The Social Credit got what is called a landslide, and here was Mr.
Aberhart and now Mr. Premier, and he didn't know anything about
politics and government. He was just a good and kindly man, and
you know what? When his days were over, he didn't die rich. He
didn't even die wealthy. He died just like an ordinary school
principal and preacher like he was

Oh, they talk about him. They say he was a fool. You know, a
dreamer and a madman and a fool and a phoney, but he wasn't.
He went across the grain and he did a lot of things wrong, but in

my heart I know that everything he did, everything he did, was
in his heart for the good of the people. You, me, everybody. He
failed, of course. The Supreme Court in Ottawa, those Tories and
Liberals, they wouldn't let him put his money plans into use. But
a lot of us, in our seventies and on up, we carry Mr. Aberhart
around with us in our hearts."

Five

Pride and Prejudice

❧

The Flag Business ... The Racism of the Prairies ... Another Baby ... Passionate About Education ... Ukrainian Heritage ... The Game of the Name ... How Do You Spell That, Ma'am? ... "Polacks" ... Looking for an Honest Englishman ... French and English ... Chosen People ... Mormon or Otherwise ... The Old Hutterite Business

The federal government and the CPR wanted the Prairies populated, and launched widespread, expensive, and effective publicity campaigns to find possible immigrants. The CPR wanted to sell their large land grants, fill the quarter sections with settlers, bring the goods of Eastern Canada to the towns, and carry the grain and cattle back to Ontario. Their motive, their only motive, was profit.

The federal government wanted that vast land filled with homesteaders, because their presence would make the nation stronger, and the Americans would regard the 49th parallel with more respect.

It made simple sense to have the Great Lone Land filled.

First preference in the grand scheme of immigration in the old days was for Canadian settlers from the East, and then for British settlers. Massive publicity campaigns were carried on, so wide-ranging that one man I met came to the West with his parents from their rocky land on the Falkland Islands; publicity posters had even found their way into the deep South Atlantic. Next preference, voiced quietly, was for Americans. They were experienced farmers, from the Dakotas, Illinois, Iowa, Minnesota, Nebraska, and they could sell their family farms for top dollar. A large family, with a bit of manipulation, could file on six or more quarter sections, with a ten-dollar filing fee per quarter. They moved lock, stock, and barrel, at the expense of the Canadian government. No better deal existed, and they knew where to find the best land. After all, the border was just a series of stone markers. The land on either side was the same.

Then, the others, those celebrated in story and song. The Men in the Sheepskin Coats. Galicians, Ukrainians, Poles, Russians–from all the Slavic countries where life was hard and harsh. Their motive, I've always believed, was freedom. They sought a faraway land where they could live free, a land where their children would have a chance to prosper and grow. Studying the prairie mosaic today, one can only agree that they succeeded, in spades.

Obviously there were hundreds of individual motives for immigrating. Greed, yes. Opportunism, yes. The spirit of the frontier, yes. The chance to make a free life. The hope to break away from old ties. The hope of becoming rich. Who would immigrate to be poor?

But in the minds of these peasants – and we all have peasant instincts, because they are basic – Western Canada symbolized land, their own, the only constant factor, and with that land came freedom, to succeed or fail.

As this chapter shows, every group – Canadians, British, Americans, French Canadians, Europeans – they all found discrimination. Many disliked others because of race, colour, language, religion, standing in society. We still have all this today. Perhaps we always will. But this is a free country, and we are free to pass on the bad news about discrimination, past and present, and expose it to the light of day.

🐞 *The Flag Business*

"At Maidstone we had a lot of Yanks, and as you know their big day is July 4. Independence Day. Well, we got along with them all right. No real problems. A bit pushy, some of them. They came over from Washington and Oregon, Montana, south of there, but most from the Dakotas and Illinois, Iowa, and the first year they thought they had more push than we did, so one of them skinned up the flag-pole and cut the lines on the British flag and put up the Stars and Stripes. Their goddamned bloody flag. Just dropped our flag to the ground. This was for their dance that night.

Well, we outnumbered them in the district but not in the town, so I stepped right over to the telegraph office and told Joe Harris to send one down the line, telling every able-bodied man to get right up there. There was a train coming down, a way freight, and when it got to town there must have been a hundred fellows on it, and three-quarters must have been Orangemen who came out from Ontario

Well, did we clean up on that dance. It was like a night in an Irish saloon, and I'd seen many of them on Third Avenue when I worked as a sandhog in New York. I remember two big men, both Ulstermen, Wright and McGillivray. Most of them were Scots anyway, those Ulstermen, and they had this big Yankee farmer and one would knock him on the head and he'd go flying across the floor, and the other would stop him, twirl him around, and clout

him back. Like a tennis game. I finally had to stop it by diving in
and throwing this big Hoosier out of the line of fire.

When the twenty-five or so of them were all lying about the hall,
I made a speech. I said this country was British, and if they didn't
like it they could leave, go back to the States. I said if they wanted
to stay they could, and welcome, but we never wanted to see that
Yankee flag flying again in our town. Nothing ever happened like
that again.

It wasn't so much the flag business. It was just that they were so
goddamned pushy, coming up and thinking they could run the
show. They couldn't."

🐚 *The Racism of the Prairies*

"Being Ukrainian or Polish or Galician then was the same as being
black today. The racism of the Prairies, it was there to a very large
degree. It still is, of course. Today we think of racism as white
against black or the other way around, or Native Indian against
white. Well, East Indian too, of course, that's all you ever hear.
But the other racism, English, Scots, Irish, Swedish, against the
Slavic, oh, that was there to a very large degree back then, and still
is, but not as much.

In my day, teaching school, I knew this racism was wrong. I
really felt it was wrong, but I accepted it as just something natural,
the way it was."

🐚 *Another Baby*

"My parents came out west from Goderich in Ontario and took
over the general store, and my mother worked in the store. She
did the books, too, as she'd been a teacher back in Ontario before
she and Dad got married. This way, you see, for many years she
had a ringside seat on the comings and goings of the little village
and the district. You couldn't even call us a village, really. Just a
widening in the road about four miles south and east of Mallard
Lake, but it was a quiet life, and apparently my parents did make
enough to live on.

Now, about my mother. She was English and Ontarian to the

core and rather proper, and she should have had some difficulty, because maybe ninety-five per cent of the district was Ukrainian. This was back about 1910, I think, when they bought the store and that area was well settled. I believe the first immigration from the old country came in about 1890, somewhere around there. After the Northwest Rebellion. I know that because my father had come out from Ontario to fight in that, in 1885, and later he brought mother to the Territories – it wasn't even called Saskatchewan then – because he liked it from his army days here.

Anyway, back to Mother. The district was Ukrainian and so were all their customers, and when I was a little girl I can remember the English people in Wakaw telling what a hard life these people had. I should mention I was four years old when we came, so I sort of grew up with all this. Very impressionable. Very big-eyed, watching these Ukrainian people come into the store. Even then they were very poor. Not having much, naturally they didn't buy much.

But Mother's diary. She kept a diary that was a sort of chronicle of the district. Births, deaths, picnics, parties, things sold, things bought. She was always astonished at the size of their families. She'd write, and I'm making this up, but her diary would say, 'Mrs. Rybchuksy came in with another baby. This makes 18, I think.' Something like that. Or maybe, 'Joe Koslowski in, bought cotton, another baby. Thinks this is 16th.' To Mother this was incredible. A woman would be forty-five and have had sixteen or eighteen children, bing, bing, and they were still having them. It was as if they didn't know how babies were made. You can't believe that, but then, why did they just keep on having them, year and year and year forever? Well, you're right, they were Catholics. The Orthodox church and their priests were very, very hard on them. Oh, yes, they lived in fear of their priests. But to just go on and on, that baffled my mother.

Big families were fine in those days. Seven or eight, that was considered about right. That was for an English or Scandinavian family, mind you. But eighteen or twenty, and living in these small mud houses or even the sod ones that were still around for years, and how did they feed them? These farmers were poor. I mean poor. My mother's diaries always emphasized how poor these people were.

She was very concerned. Her diary would have notations, like wondering what they did about doctors. Well, you can figure that one out yourself. They didn't go to doctors. It was all midwives, and in winter, I suppose the oldest daughter and the father could deliver the baby. They were a tough people.

Another thing. Oh, yes, there were many notations like 'Waslynchuk baby died. Boy. Lived two days.' Things like that. These were the ones she knew about. But how many, she'd wonder, just died and were buried out in the bush. Maybe a little cemetery out there. It wasn't illegal to have a private cemetery. Many families had them.

But these babies, according to Mother, just kept coming and coming. All these little notes she made, you could just see her taking time off in the evening to make her notes, and then in some kind of exasperation she'd write, 'Why do they keep having all these babies, and what do they do with them when they are born?' Something like that. Very exasperated."

🕊 Passionate About Education

"My grandfather worked for a few Canadian farmers around for two years and then he got on with a Mennonite. I didn't know there were Mennonites around about 1910 but there were, and as they both spoke Russian, they got along fine. My grandfather told me that's where he first started to get a decent chance to start out. The others had been Canadian farmers, and Americans who had moved up from Iowa and South Dakota, and they treated the immigrants like dirt. The conditions they had to live under, well, you just would not believe them. Living and sleeping in a barn was one experience he had to go through one winter. Things like that.

Anyway, in 1910 he decided to strike out, because he had about one hundred dollars saved, and he walked to the Wakaw district, where a lot of foreigners lived, and he filed on a homestead there, because he was told there was talk of a school being built there. That is why he had not brought my grandmother out from the Ukraine before, because he knew his kids just wouldn't fit into the English schools where he had been working. My grandfather was so passionate about education, he would do without a wife and her love and the love of the children until he knew the kids would come out here and start right off with a good teacher and getting a good education.

Anyway, as he heard it, a rancher named Venne, Louis Venne,

was the one getting the homesteaders organized to get a school, and they got the approval about 1911 and then they waited for the government grant, which was a few hundred dollars, and the next year the settlers built a school. My grandfather was one of them, he was a homesteader now, working away on his little 160 acres out there in the bush. The men built the school themselves, and it was a bad summer and they worked mostly in the rain but they got this little one-room schoolhouse built. There were twelve students the first year, and my grandfather, Old Wasyl, as we called him, that's when he sent for his wife and kids.

This rancher Venne, the man who got things started, he thought he was running the show. But all but two of the kids were Ukrainian, and their parents wanted a Ukrainian teacher. Well, according to my grandfather, you never saw such a hullabaloo. Mr. Venne apparently was the only one who could write English, so he wrote letters to Regina to the Department of Education, and he wanted an English teacher. The Ukrainian people, and they were paying the taxes, of course, they wanted someone who could speak Ukrainian. Somehow they got the right message through to Regina and the message got through to the right person and the man hired to teach was named Washuk. So it worked out okay. The school was taught in English, because that was the law, but at least they had a Ukrainian-speaking teacher who would be able to help the little immigrant kids over the jumps easier.

Now I'll tell you something. That almost never happened. The teachers were almost always English. Young teachers from Ontario, mostly, but some from Western Canada, but in those days they were almost always English. So it goes to show you the determination of Old Wasyl and his neighbours to get through the red tape in Regina and get a Ukrainian-speaking teacher.

Oh, sure, he insisted that everything be taught in English. That was the law. Even if there had been a law that said kids could have been taught in Russian or Ukrainian or Chinese, even, he would have made darn sure it was in English. This was an English country. If you didn't have English, couldn't talk in it, write in it, even spit in it, you were nothing. Without education you were nothing.

You know, I'll tell you something else. Ukrainians and Polanders, they called them Ukes or Hunyaks and Polacks, they were not thought of very highly in the West in those days. Oh, they are just dumb peasants, people in the town would say. Strong of back and weak of mind. What do their kids need an education for, because they're never going to get off the farm. That sort of thing. Canada is for the English. Okay, for the Americans too, because they were once English, and besides, they look like us and talk like us and think like us. That sort of thing. It wasn't even called racism or discrimination. It was just the way things were then.

That's why education was so important. A kid didn't have to go to school after fourteen, I think. In fact, a lot quit earlier to work at home or go into the bush or down to Estevan and Bienfait and Lethbridge, that's where the coal mines were, or in Crowsnest Pass. But if they had some education, they could go to Saskatoon and take a commercial course or learn a trade like welding or carpentry, or they could even go further, like the university.

But they had to have the three R's first, you see, and good English. Some of these old immigrants, you know, still don't speak English well at all. Not their fault. Too busy trying to make a homestead into a living. But their kids, my mom and uncles and so, they had the chance to get out. They took the first big step and they didn't do all that okay, but they weren't too bad off. Then me, degree, Arts, U. of S., and my four kids, three are out of university now and the youngest, he's a mechanic and that's all he ever wanted to do, fool around with motors, so fine, that's what he's doing. Doing well, married and a little girl and a house, and they're happy."

Ukrainian Heritage

"I have lost my Ukrainian heritage, that of my grandparents and my parents. There is not much left of it for me now, even though when I was a kid it was still pretty strong. We were pretty isolated then but, you know, we made our own isolation. I mean, we didn't get out and mix.

Seven or eight families came from the Ukraine with my grandparents to around the Chipman district. This was in 1903, and the men had elected my grandfather to be what you'd call a wagon boss if you were talking about the Wild West. He didn't have much more education than the others, but they knew a leader when they saw one. They all had done their three years' service in the army, so they weren't just farm hicks. They had been around, you might say.

These old boys and their wives, they all got homesteads around

Chipman, which I believe was quite a busy little place. Homesteading had been going on in that district for about eight years before, and it was mostly Ukrainian and Polish and German, all foreigners, and some people used to call our district the Solid Ukraine. But I've heard my grandfather talk of neighbours named Paige and Bowsfield, Robertson, Harris, Tyler, so there were some English scattered through there. But it was probably ninety-five per cent foreign then.

They worked terribly hard. I think the only thing that kept them going was that they had this dream for their children. That's why they were so eager to have schools. Can you imagine a bunch of fifteen or so Bohunk homesteaders – and not one with more than a lick and a promise of English – getting together and forming a school district? Well, they did it. Maybe one of these men, Paige or Bowsfield I mentioned, they headed them up, but it was the old boys from the old country who got the show going. That is a pattern I know was everywhere in this country. The desire, no, the demand, that the kids be educated. To make something of them. They knew their own lives were going to be toil, hard work, Churchill's blood, sweat, and tears. So they did it.

Nobody could make a living on a homestead. Just 160 acres and ten, twenty, twenty-five acres cleared, so the men went to the bush to cut wood or went to work in the coal mines or worked on the railroad. Came home, did more clearing and burning and root-picking, and off they'd go again, more work for dollars, and home again. The old 'baptchi', my grandmother, she held the family together. Some of these women trapped, you know. A few muskrats and weasel and mink, a few dollars. Looking after the kids, and they had big families. Ten in our family, and that was not huge. Just average. They kept the thing going, year after year, and the kids growing up, becoming Canadians. I don't think too many of the old people really became Canadians in the sense that we know the word.

So many of that family married into the other Ukrainian families in the district. I'm not sure that was a good thing. Nine times out of ten, a Ukrainian boy would marry a Ukrainian girl. Many of the marriages were arranged, you know, right up into the 1920s. Two fathers would get together and decide his son would marry his daughter. It was accepted, and the girl might be only fifteen. If they're big enough, then they're old enough. That sort of thing. But remarkably, they worked out. Naturally, divorce was out of the question. The church was very, very strong. In one way, it was about all the people had. The priests, they'd come around every month or two, and they made sure those old homesteaders absolutely toed the line. Not an inch off. Believe me, the priest called the shots.

My generation, well, it all changed so much. After the war, which is my time, it was so much freer and easier and we all went off to the cities and towns and to colleges and down to Ontario, out to B.C., and the ties that bound us got looser and looser, and after the war there began to be intermarriage, and that's something I don't think happened much before. Our boys marrying into German families, the Norwegians up near and around Neerlandia, French, English, all Canadian families. It just seemed to happen. The system was breaking down, and with higher education, more teachers, more professors, more professional men, and more stores and businesses owned by our people, it took place rather quickly, as a matter of fact. About the only thing that keeps us together is weddings and funerals."

❧ The Game of the Name

"You know, you have to be pretty careful about talking about things like this. My baptchi, that's my dear old grandmother, she's dead, passed away about fifteen years ago at a very old age, but my parents are still alive and there are dozens of us around. They look down on me a bit, not understanding why I changed my name.

Oh, it is fine if you live in Edmonton or Lamont or Chipman or Bruderheim, Vegreville, where there are plenty of Ukrainian people on every street, but, well, when you're in Calgary and working with people like Americans from Texas and Oklahoma and Canadians with English and Scots names, well, it is just easier if you don't have an old-country name.

I can see why they want to be proud of having a professional with an old-country name. I could say, you're here in this small town, or you're on the farm, and you've never been in business or at the university, so you don't know exactly why I made that decision. I could say it was important to me. I didn't think it would be when I left the farm and went to university. I found out there that it was. I was not asked to join in any of the clubs, but maybe

I was just shy. I didn't get into any of the select circles. If I had wanted to show my family's bank balance against theirs, I'm quite sure ours would come out on top by a very healthy margin, but that is just not the way the game is played. Anything I did at U. of A. was the result of my being more than a little bit pushy. Good training for a lawyer.

Then out of Edmonton and get on with a law firm in Calgary, and I had no trouble there because it didn't seem to matter too much down there. Or so I thought. Being a woman lawyer was not too common, and I thought that was why I was still doing Joe jobs after five years while the men were moving up. We dealt a lot with legal work in oil leases and the million and one other things that go with it, and Calgary was booming in the sixties. But I found out from one of my colleagues that if anything was holding me back it was because I had this name with all the c's and z's in it. Merit didn't count for much when it would be a decision on whether a woman with my name or a man with a name like McDonald got a promotion.

So I changed. I changed my name quietly, and one day I walked into the office manager and I told him what my new name was. You know, he just sort of smiled and he picked up the phone and he phoned personnel and told them that all documents, the pay cheque and everything to do with me, should be changed to my new name. Right away. He smiled at me. He knew what was going on. They really didn't need anyone with a name like mine to attract new business in those oil-crazy days. They wanted good old Anglo-Saxon names. Well, they got one.

It was funny the way it came about. We were closing some big deal with I think it was Delhi Oil. Texas money. I was in on it as the assembler of all the documents. A very important job, they had to be just right, in order. Just like signing a peace treaty, you might say. There was this fellow on the other side of the table and he kept looking at me, and I got a few good looks at him and I kept thinking, his name isn't Richardson or Richards or whatever it was. No, I thought, there is something else there. But this was all very, very, very high-level stuff with millions riding on it on both sides, so I couldn't think too much on it. But there was something about this very assured young man of thirty, about my age.

Later it struck me. His name wasn't Richardson. There are ten thousand Ukrainian names and he used to have one of them. I was sure of it. Something about him.

About two days after the signing there was a cocktail party of the principals of both companies and the lawyers of the firms that had taken care of it all. He was there, and maybe after two drinks I went up to him and in a low voice I asked if he missed his mother's kolach. That's braided bread. We call it the Bread of Life and it is important to us, on special occasions. Without batting an eye he said yes, he did, and he also missed his mother's paska. That's bread made at Easter. Then we both laughed and he said something like you can fool a lot of other people, but you can't fool one of your own. Sure he was Ukrainian. In fact, he came from Vegreville, the Solid Ukraine.

We talked for a while, as long as it was wise in a gathering like that where everyone is watching everyone else. You know the intrigue that goes on in the oil industry, and add that which goes on in law offices, and, well, together you've got something. So we talked for about five minutes and then he said he'd phone me and we'd have dinner. He wanted to talk to me about something.

A few days later he did and we met and we did have dinner and that's all we did. A few drinks and dinner. But what he wanted to talk to me about was this. To tell me, 'Look, Helen, you're not going to get any place in this Anglo-Saxon and American town with a name like that.' He said he was living proof, and he could name a dozen other people who were doing very well, because they had changed their names.

I thought, this is awful. I was insulted. Then I thought of university and the great career I was not, repeat not, carving out in my own firm, and that's what we talked about for two hours. He told me to think it over and I did, and then I phoned him back. I told him if he wanted to have some good food I'd make him some kolach and paska, and that was the last I'd ever make. I said I agreed with him. The deed would be done as soon as I could.

I'm not telling this right. I sound very mercenary. Giving up my heritage and all that. That may be so, but it doesn't seem that way to me. I was a woman in the toughest of all worlds, the legal world, and I need more than all my looks and personality and skills to survive, which I had not been doing too well. The last thing I needed was a handicap like my name. Without that, everything would be okay. I could handle everything after that.

So all I was doing was putting myself ahead of all other things, which anyone upon reflection will do in ninety-nine out of a hundred circumstances, regardless of whatever.

Oh yes, you're right. There is a little grain of doubt in there. Like a grain of sand in an oyster. I think of it, but there is nothing I can do. Except this. Don't laugh. When I am retired, wealthy and secure and a bit famous, then maybe, possibly, perhaps, I could always go back to my old name. I can still spell it. I can still pronounce it. It might be fun to see how it is just living with it."

✪ *How Do You Spell That, Ma'am?*

"There may be twenty or thirty times a year when you have to give your name, for a card or a delivery from a store or, well, you know what I mean. They ask you for your name and you give it.

Every time they ask me to spell it, I always give them a good look to see if they're trying to put me down. What's so difficult with the name 'Balanuk'? There's only one way to spell it. Just as I sound it. But no, every time and I guess I'm just getting sensitive enough to think they've caught the 'uk' of it and they think, oh, a foreigner.

Okay, Balanuk. We've been here since 1899 and the name was Pewincza and then it became Siprowstz and I married a Balanuk. My daughter married a McPherson. How do you like that? I'd have preferred she carried on with the tradition.

But they do this, you know. How do you spell that, ma'am? They know, I'm sure. I just get the feeling they think this person is, well, a foreigner and I'll put her down a bit. How stupid and small can you get? But it happens. Maybe they're hard of hearing, or maybe I'm too sensitive, but it gripes me. This kind of thing really does."

✪ *"Polacks"*

"I didn't have a hard life, but I had a strange one. We lived in the Virbank district. Would you believe we lived in a sod house, and this was in the thirties? There was nothing wrong with them if they were built right, and this one was twenty feet by twenty-six feet and it was warm in winter and nice in hot weather. My family lived in it for about twelve years and it was built by an old pioneer and was kind of a curiosity around the district, but we just thought it was home. It was a good home. In 1941 after a tremendous crop my father had a wooden house built and it was never as warm as the old soddy. You couldn't beat them.

Anyway, it was kind of a tourist attraction. People would drive by and look at this house and take pictures. And the people who had brought them, they probably told their visitors, 'Oh, it's all right to take pictures. The people in there are 'Polacks'.''

✤ *Looking for an Honest Englishman*

"My grandfather Konstantin owned a store in Nipawin and had somebody run it for him. He said he looked and looked for an honest Englishman, figuring one of them would be the best because they spoke English, but he said they were either too stupid, too lazy, or drank too much. He finally hired a young Austrian with not much English but a lot of common sense, and the store prospered for years."

✤ *French and English*

"There was this small town in Manitoba. South of Winnipeg and just a bit west. I won't tell you the name of it, I've got a few relatives around there still. Half the town was French-Canadian, and all the families, they shared about three names. Half the town was English, Scotch, a couple of Swedes and Icelanders. Some Mennonites.

The French and the English, why, they fought all the time. Not fists. Just because they were French and English. They never did get along, even over in Europe. They'd even fight over whether to gravel the main street. That's why it was still dirt. Yep, the main street was mud, and when it rained, well, think of it. Up to here in Red River gumbo.

The general store was owned by a little Frenchman, French from Quebec, named Goulet. Naturally it had the post office. He had this beautiful niece from St. Boniface, she came down and was the postmaster, and you know what she did? She wouldn't speak English. If you wanted a money order you had to speak in French. But she'd speak English for the Mennonites, and when she was clerking in old Goulet's store she'd speak English to the English. It was nuts, but nobody could do anything about it.

At field days, it was French against English in the tug of war, and the Mennonites going about their business as usual. Every other town had one ball team. We had two. One French, the other the others. Two this, two that, two of everything.

Nobody in that town from one side ever married a girl from the other. You'd've been killed. Or she would. Not that bad, but you see what I mean. Anyway, I got sweet on this French girl. Madeleine. It was tough, but we managed to meet.

I mind this night we met and I was going to ask her to marry me. I had it figured out. We'd go to Winnipeg to my aunt's place and get married. Before I could ask her, she says she's got something to tell me. She'd told her cousin about us, and the cousin had told her mother, and the mother had told Madeleine's father, and that was it. She told me they were sending her to the convent at St. Norbert.

I couldn't believe it. She was to become a virgin daughter of God, or some such fool thing. Well, she was still a virgin, I knew that, but what was going on? I told her I loved her and I knew she loved me and we'd get married right away. I had it figured out. She cried a lot but she said no, she had to become a nun. It was all arranged, and there was nothing I could do. Or she could do.

I was very bitter about that. I was only nineteen then and she was eighteen and there was the situation. Two lives being buggered up. She didn't want to be a nun. Too much of the devil in her. I didn't want her to be a nun, and I wanted to marry her. Too late. The thing was arranged, and that's the way they handled their kids in those days.

That was the town, or call it a village. I went back there about fifteen years ago, and the main street was gravelled. They hadn't brought a paving outfit to that part of the country yet.

The French were still there, but not as many. The English, still there, but not as many. The town looked a bit brighter, like there was some money circulating. But the French and the English were still fighting their old wars. The Mennonites, there were a lot more of them, and they seemed still to be standing on the sidelines, but from what I could see they were making all the money. Like they had been waiting for the two other sides to fight and argue themselves into exhaustion, and then they moved in. The Mennonites, they'd won out at last."

❧ Chosen People

"The Mennonites, say, over in Manitoba, they knew how to stick together. Of course, the best example was the Hutterites, but they overdid it so much they made everybody so mad at them they'd sometimes try to burn them out. It happened. Don't kid yourself.

Southern Alberta had the Mormons, coming up from Utah in the early days, and look how they almost took over some parts of the country, lock, stock, and barrel. Cardston, a Mormon town. Stirling, Taber, a dozen others. Solid Mormon. From what I've heard they weren't such good neighbours at first, and I figure it was because of their religion and they figured themselves to be God's Chosen People. That didn't help things. They were thought of in those days like Hutterites are now. Land-grabbers. Money-grubbers. People it was best not to deal with if you wanted to come out with a full skin."

❧ Mormon or Otherwise

"Now, in this district we've got an awful lot of Mormons. They came into this country as homesteaders a long time ago, and they've done well, better than any other group. They are good Canadians, no doubt of that, and they believe in education for their children more than any bunch I know of, and their religion, why it's as much a part of their lives as television is for you and me.

But what puts a lot of people off is, well, they are smug. You look at them and you see well-satisfied faces. Smug. As if they've got it all. They've got the secret. Nobody else has, and unless you join the church you aren't going to learn that secret. Successful at what they do, and smug about it and their religion, and that should make them real successful and I guess they are, but it puts a lot of people off, including me. I'd like to see a few great big failures among them around here, just so I'd know it isn't all that rosy.

I could have married an L.D.S. girl before I married my wife, but the thought of being kind of drowned in all that religion and goodness just put me off. I still could, you know. My wife's been dead quite a while, and there is this Mormon widow who I figure has been giving me the glad eye. Don't think it would be any problem to get hitched again. It would be good for business. Turning Mormon wouldn't hurt me with my other customers and it might bring in a lot of L.D.S. business.

But that's something I'd have to give an awful lot of thought to. One thing, you can't go out and get a bit drunk with the boys after a shoot or a bonspiel. Got to toe the line. No beer, no wine, no liquor, no Coke, no tea, no coffee. But you can drink all the Seven-Up you want. Now that's one I can't figure out. I mean, I can get pretty browned off sometimes, like when I'm at a wedding reception and I'm having a drink and a Mormon neighbour walks up and he looks at my drink and he smiles that little smile of his and nods sympathetically. Like I'm going straight to hell. I'm not going to hell, Mormon or otherwise. I'm just having a drink."

🕊 *The Old Hutterite Business*

"When I left the colony fifteen years ago, I just did it one day. I just left and walked down the road. People saw me and they thought, oh, she's finished her chores and is going for a walk, maybe to think about marrying a boy from another colony. I didn't run across fields with the men and boys chasing me, and being hit with sticks and made to live by myself in a small room and to wait for the bishop to come around to decide what would be done with me. So the running away was more like just going away.

I just left and walked down the road to the other road that went into town, and I stood there and a truck came along and I waved and he stopped and picked me up. It was fourteen miles into town and he asked me if I was a Hutterite and he knew, naturally, because of my clothes and the way my hair was done, like all Hutterite girls, and I said yes and he asked me what I was doing.

I told him. I said I was leaving the colony and this farmer, he said it was no use going into Taber, it would be best if I went to Lethbridge. He said it would be hard for me, and I said I knew two Hutterite girls who had gone away and they were still gone and that was about three years ago, and they must have got on okay.

I knew Lethbridge because I had been there, but I didn't know anybody and I told him this. And when we got there we drove around to this building and he got out and went in and came out with a woman and he said, 'Go with this lady. She is my cousin. Do what she tells you and you will be okay.' This woman, whose name I won't say, she was in charge of this home, and she took me in and told me I could work for her. So I did.

She asked me why I had run away, and I said I just had to. I wanted to read good books and learn things, and I listened in secret to the little radio my brother had, and I heard the news and the CBC and all these interesting people who were on the air. They talked of things I never knew about, these things I could not imagine. I could not imagine what a building was like that was eighty floors high. In Lethbridge I had seen these wonderful automobiles and I couldn't imagine riding in one. I thought, oh, what does Chinese food taste like? In an airplane, I wondered, oh, how could a person breathe air in them. I wanted to know about this wild dancing the girls my age did, not that I might want to do it, but why did they want to? I wanted to see waves crashing on rocks on the shore, and I wanted to wear a bathing-suit. You can see what kind of a person I was, and I can tell you, I was like most of the girls in the colony, but you could only tell these things to the one special friend you had in the colony. You knew she wouldn't tell and you wouldn't tell.

I had thought of going for a year, because I just knew there was this big and special world out there. Not just the houses and the kitchen and the barns and the yard and the men working on the machines and the same thing every day, the prayers, the church, the talk of farming and grain and the neighbours who were not like us, and all it was about, this life, was nothing. Just nothing, nothing, nothing.

I was very curious. You could be born in a colony and not be stupid, you know. There are some very smart people in the colonies, and they are very good at business. There are men in the colony who could build special machines for $1,500 that would cost $8,000 at the implement dealer, and they would be better machines. There were some smart wives in the colonies, too, you know, but they never got a chance to show what they could be. They could get the men to do things, and you know how? By showing them that doing it this way and not that way would mean saving money or making more money. Money is everything to a

Hutterite colony. They say God is, but he is not. It is money, so they can buy more land and get bigger.

Children are important too. Every woman has to have as many as she can. My mother had nine, and that was not unusual. But children, lots of them, so they could be taught to be farmers and farmers' wives and then they would buy more land somewhere else and split another colony. We called this splitting. People from other colonies from a long way were sent to this new colony. That is why money is so important, because they need more colonies. If too many people get into one colony, maybe more than a hundred, then trouble starts. Jealousy. Money problems. And stealing from the colony to go to town and sell something and get beer. Alcohol was a problem that could come up, too, although people outside the colony think Hutterites don't drink alcohol. I can tell you, some of them do.

When they found out where I was working, they didn't try and bring me back. A boy, I think they would have. They knew somehow that I was different.

I worked in the old folks' home as it was called, just doing kitchen work, and I knew all about that, because I'd been doing that all my life since I was seven, cooking and cleaning for the men and boys. So this job was easy. There was a girl there from Lethbridge and she said, 'Oh, they're not going to make me work such long hours,' and I asked her what was wrong with working long hours. I didn't know. I'd done it every day. It was the way you did it.

When I was the maid and clean-up girl, one old woman, who had been a schoolteacher, said to me, 'You're a Hutterite, aren't you?' Nobody was supposed to know at that time and I said yes, how did she know? I had my hair done nice and wore a white uniform and new shoes and I looked like everybody else. She said, 'It is the way you talk. You have a slow-moving kind of speech. You know English perfectly, but you really don't know how to speak it. There is no slang you use. You are not used to speaking it where it means something to other people. You use it for communication, but not for really talking to people.' That's just about the way she said it and I thought, she is right. And then I thought, when I went to a store to buy something I had noticed that the clerks looked at me strangely, as if they thought I might be from another planet.

Then one day the cook got sick and the lady in charge asked me if I could cook. Of course I could cook. One thing Hutterite women are very good at is cooking. Some of the things I had to use I wasn't sure of, but I cooked and cooked and nobody said anything. They said I was better than the other cook. The old people asked me where I had learned to cook and I said from the colony, and naturally they just couldn't believe that a Hutterite girl was not living in the colony. They were old men and women and all about the Hutterites they knew was from the old days when being a Hutterite was like living in a prison. I told them, yes, in some ways it was, but I told them things are going to change, and that was fifteen years ago and now I think you'll see some things have changed. The bosses know they have to be more liberal or else the young people will leave, and that will be the end of the Hutterites. That's true. You should believe me when I say that. The old ways are gone.

I never went back. If I had to meet my father for something about the family he met me in the Marquis Restaurant. I was changing every week, every month, and I was now the cook and I could have got lots of jobs – this was in the early seventies and everybody had a job. I had no desire to go back, although I would have liked to for my two sisters' weddings, but I said no. I met my brother Jake in town, and got him to smuggle gifts back to my sisters. Fancy underwear, with lace. My joke. No Hutterite girl or woman is ever supposed to wear that. Not ever. When we were little, we used to sneak out at night and run down the road to a neighbour's house and watch television. Oh, that was something. His wife was young and she'd show us her fancy underwear and we'd just oooh and aaah and gasp. How wicked, eh? That's the way it was. With my first pay I bought some beautiful lacy underwear. Maybe that's what kept me from going back to the colony. Anyway, that's what I bought for my sisters when they married.

I didn't go back, but some of the boys from the other colonies, they broke away. But most of them went back. Why? It is a very simple matter. Wives. They needed wives, and the only place they could get married was to a girl on another colony. The boys and girls about sixteen used to be driven around from colony to colony so they could look each other over, and if things seemed to mix okay, then it went on from there. Arranged by the bosses. Even though the boys dressed like city boys, they just couldn't get dates with city girls, or even farm girls. Oh, they'd get a date, but once they dated I think that was usually the last one. It was the girl's fault. She just wouldn't want to get mixed up with a Hutterite boy.

You see, there is still not the full freedom of the mind. They have been in the colony, born there as babies, and the colony is their life, and there is no other life. They go to school, and the teacher is not a Hutterite woman, and she has to be a woman teacher, but boom, once they reach their sixteenth birthday, in January or March or any time, they do not go to school any more. They work. They are part of the colony. They are given a job – hogs, cattle, the dairy, the machine shop, general work–and usually that is their job for life. In a box. A box with one hole in it. Through that hole they can see a bit of the outside world, but that's all.

Money, they don't need much of that, but there is sort of an allowance system now. Food, all they can eat. Clothes, all free for the rest of their lives. Black suits for going to town. Now they have houses for families in many colonies. They still all eat together. No cars, no motorcycles. No taxes to pay. No guns to go shooting deer in the fall. They are provided with a wife. They get everything but they have nothing. Do you understand me? They say, if you stay with us you will never have to worry about a single solitary thing about anything for the rest of your life. Just do your job and do what we tell you and everything will be fine.

I think that is why, when men break out, they nearly always come back. They don't get punished any more. But they go back because they just cannot function on the outside where real people live and work and laugh and have fun and do good things and bad things and hurt each other and love each other. They were not brought up and trained to do this.

For a girl it is easier. I don't know why, except most Hutterite girls when they come to town and fix themselves up, they are pretty girls. Pretty girls always get along, and besides, I think girls are tougher. When I was on the colony it was my friends and I who started getting sassy. Never the boys. It was the girls who wanted to run off to the Duecks down the road and watch television. It was the girls who would sneak away and pick up beer bottles along the road and take them over to Mr. Dueck and he'd sell them in town and give us the money. For lipstick. We'd put it on in secret. Oh, if we ever had been caught. The bishop would have come for sure.

I worked hard. It was just natural to me, and they thought I was very good. The old people started inviting their children for Sunday-night dinner. They paid, and it made a bit of money for the lodge. I made some wonderful dinners, and after each dinner they'd call me out to be introduced and the people would applaud. Can you imagine how absolutely wonderful that was to a little girl off a colony? People standing up and applauding my food and pies. And at Christmas, I was the one who got the most gifts. Every resident of the lodge gave me a present and every son or daughter gave me presents. Little things, sure, but it still made a pile this high.

I still haven't told you about the terrible thoughts that went through my mind in those first two years. Guilty thoughts, about leaving. I still can't talk about them, and every Hutterite who leaves has them. They terrified me, but then one day I said to myself, I'm not going to think about it all any more. No, never. And I didn't. I don't know if I was happier for it, but I wasn't unhappier. It was my final break-out.

I went to Calgary and got a good job in a restaurant and I married one of the cooks, really a chef. A German fellow. A very nice man. I didn't know him much but I thought it was time to get married, the old Hutterite business, and we've been happy. Two kids. Good jobs. Happy."

Six

The War, and After

❧
*We Made Money ... Arrowheads ... A Kulak Kid ... Leaving
Wetaskiwin ... War Bride from London ... The Canadian Way ...
Into the Early Twentieth Century ... After the War ... Harvesting*

During the First World War, 1914-18, the prairie regiments and battalions that
boarded the trains en route to Europe with bands playing soon ran slap into
the horrors of Flanders Fields. The toll of dead and wounded was appalling.
The Second World War involved less loss of life for Canadians but saw a great
deal more participation in the air force and the navy by prairie volunteers.
Western Canada was the site of most of the bases of the vitally important, but
still little known, Commonwealth air-training scheme, where thousands of air-
men from Britain, Australia, New Zealand, and other countries besides Canada
trained for war in the air, and transformed the local town's economy.

Factories converted to war production, and other plants were founded. Every
bushel of grain the farmers produced was eagerly bought. Equipment was hard
to get, and, worse, most of it was worn out from years of hard use. But they
carried on, short of help on the farms, often helped by German prisoners of
war.

But times were good. Money was plentiful, there was nothing to spend it on,
and the tight lid of the Wartime Prices and Trade Board kept prices at non-
inflationary levels.

After the war, tens of thousands of farm-born men and women put away
their uniforms, looked around, and asked themselves, what do we do now?
Often there was no place for them on the family farm, and no farms available
to rent or buy. Many used the skills acquired in the service or at trade schools
and began their own businesses. Thousands who would never have dreamed of
getting a degree attended university under Department of Veterans Affairs aus-
pices, and left the farms forever.

Almost unnoticed, the end of the war brought a new lifestyle throughout
the West. The cities boomed, as the expected recession did not occur. Towns
flourished. The hydro came through in the fifties, district by district. Minor
recessions came and went, but the even upward flow continued. Step by step
the farm and small-town population came to expect and then demand the advan-

tages of life enjoyed by those in the cities. And they got them. Good highways, thanks to the oil boom in Alberta, and hard bargaining in Manitoba and Saskatchewan. More and better consolidated schools, which meant better education for the kids who were part of the post-war baby boom.

In the few short years after the war, a quiet revolution had taken place.

🐦 We Made Money

"What did we do in the war? Okay. We made money. Crops just about everywhere were just about as good as you could hope for, and we were getting good money for wheat. We also had a good feeling about it all, because there we were, the farmers out here in the West who had had the hell kicked out of them by Eastern Canada during the Depression. And now what we were doing? You couldn't pick up a newspaper without reading that we were feeding the starving people of Britain and doing all this to help win the war.

We worked like the very dickens in the black market, too. My, my, that was hilarious when you think back on it. Help in winning the war, they said, and yet all these farmers were working just as hard on the black market taking meat into Winnipeg in their trucks. Whole sides of beef they'd butchered and wrapped in blankets and covered with stuff to hide it, and selling it to the hotels and restaurants there. Coming home with a sack of money, all bills.

They did it with gas, too. They had this purple gas, for farmers. People who weren't farmers didn't get it, and they had patrols out on the highway to stop you and test if you had it. But we lived in a crazy world then and my husband could get all the gas he wanted for the farm use–ploughing, cultivating, seeding, running the truck and tractor – and he didn't use one-third of it. He sold the rest. I can't remember what gas was, but if it was forty cents a gallon, then he could sell it for a dollar. People, you see, had to have gas-ration tickets and they couldn't drive much on them. So he'd just put a couple of 42-gallon drums into his truck and throw some things on top and go into Winnipeg or Brandon. You could sell it anywhere. He just would go into the St. James Hotel and sit, and before he'd have one beer somebody would come over, and, well, that's all there was to it. They'd drive to this guy's place and pump it out and my husband would come home. A three-hour trip and he'd have made maybe sixty dollars. I'd say it would be worth about six hundred dollars now, all things considered, and that's the way it was. You'd go away to sell it because it might have been bad if you sold it in town. The people there were such snitches, they'd snitch on anyone.

Another thing the farmers spent a lot of time on was getting their boys from going into the army. That caused a lot of snitching, too. Families with boys in the service didn't like people that had got their boys out or kept them out. A farmer was allowed one boy to stay on the farm and the others were eligible for call-up. Not too many of them joined up as volunteers. First, because there were so many Ukrainian, a lot of them didn't have enough education for the air force or navy. So it was the army. They just did not want to join up, these people. So, the boys would run away, work for a while on this farm, their dad's, and then go for two weeks to a cousin or a friend, and the Mounties would be looking for them, but they'd never find them. This went on all during the war. Everybody knew what was going on. But I must say this. It wasn't just the Ukrainian and Polanders over to the east there by the river, it was sons of English and American farmers, too.

I'm not one to hold with this idea that farm people are the salt of the earth, just nice and honest people. No, I've lived among farmers and the people in the towns around here and I know they can all lie and cheat and steal with the very best of them in the city. It has always been that way. So, lying and cheating with the conscription board was nothing new to them. They had just been practising for it.

I remember once, about 1944, we had this Dominion Day ball tournament and we had friends from Winnipeg visiting us and my husband was one of the organizers, so we all went to it. There were teams from Brandon and Minnedosa and over from Kamsack in Saskatchewan and Dauphin. Our friend, the man, he asked how come there were so many young and strong men playing. He thought they should all be in the war.

I told him, most of them are Zombies. Now, that was a hated name then. Men, born in Canada, who wouldn't sign up to go overseas and fight, so they stayed in the army in Canada. I said they were all farm boys and they'd been called up, and now there was the regulation that they could be released on leave to help with the harvest. 'But,' he said, 'this is July 1. This isn't harvest time.' I said, 'They were released for harvest last year. They just didn't go back to their camps, and nobody has come for them.'

Everybody made money in those days and there wasn't much to spend it on. You couldn't buy a new car or a truck, and if you got a combine or a new tractor, one of the new rubber-tired ones, people thought you had bribed someone. You couldn't do much long-distance travelling, and whiskey and beer was rationed, but that didn't stop anyone. There were lots of bootleggers with stills in the swamps and you could always buy it.

You could buy land, and cheap too. Like maybe you could pick up a section in 1943 for $12,000. I know, that sounds absolutely mad, but my very own husband did it. Off the widow Carter, who wanted to move to her daughter's place in St. Boniface. It hadn't been farmed that year and he seeded it next year, and I think there was about 580 acres of good land on it. The rains came right and the sun came right and what he got off that land in bushels, he paid for it that year. That's what you could do if you had the old thinking-cap on. To make it sound right, my husband bought that land, the 580 acres, for $20 an acre. It sold for $600 an acre last year, and it could have been sold for $750 four years ago but my son didn't want to sell it then. But most, they just sat tight. Saved their money and didn't buy land, because they thought there would be a big recession after the war. It didn't come, as you know. Things just got better and better for a long, long time and the farmers, they made a lot of money.

Now things are very tough and they're all howling their heads off and wanting billions from the government. Well, listen to me, I say they can go soak their head in a bucket. Don't they know what farming is? Up and down. Down and up.

Anyway, that's what I've got to say. We had the Depression and it was hell, not so much because we didn't get decent crops around this district, but because we couldn't get any money for our wheat. We were poor. Very poor. Then we had the war and everybody wanted what we had, and so that is why I think it was the best time of all. The shoe was on the other foot. We were kicking those big shots in Toronto and Ottawa. And we did a lot of kicking. Good, strong, hard kicking, and we all enjoyed it."

❧ *Arrowheads*

"My family came from Germany in 1935, when I was eleven, and my father got a job on a farm north of Edmonton owned by a

Scotchman named Irwin. My father would go to town with Mr. Irwin and people would say, 'Oh, Irwin's got a damn German working for him,' and this upset my father. When we started to get this kind of thing in school, it wasn't so good. The kids didn't know what they were talking about, but Hitler was big then and people said they could see a war coming, and they thought we were . . . you'd probably call it war-minded. We weren't. Anyway, the Schmidt kids got it at school. I had to fight sometimes.

Then, when I was fifteen, it was the war, and Canada was really into it. The Mounties came and got Dad and took him to Edmonton, and we thought they were going to put him in a concentration camp. He was away two days and then he came back. He'd told them about himself. How can a guy be a spy when he's working for a farmer out in the bush? They did dumb things then. I had more fights at school, though.

The next year our family rented a farm from a fellow who was a bachelor and had gone and joined the army. You know, that fellow didn't come back. He wasn't killed and he wasn't wounded, we knew he was alive and in Canada somewhere, but he just never came back to his farm after the war. By that time my father had got another farm, buying it, and we thought we were doing okay.

Anyway, when I was seventeen I decided I would join the army. My father didn't like it one bit. You know why. Over there in the fighting maybe I'd kill his brother's son, my cousin, or he'd kill me.

But you know how it is with a seventeen-year-old kid, a big and husky kid like myself. I was sick and tired of the farm and working and not getting any money for it, and all the other kids were spending a lot because their fathers had big farms.

I went to Edmonton to the army and there was a sergeant there and he asked me my name. 'George Schmidt,' I said. He didn't ask me how old I was. I was going to tell him I was eighteen. I was only seventeen, but I was big and looked older.

He said, 'Sonny, we don't have any Schmidts in this army. From now on you're George Smith. Take this paper and wait over there and a station wagon will be around to pick you guys up and take you to the barracks.' As easy as that. Like falling off a log.

So in the army I was George Smith and when I went back home to visit I was George Schmidt. I never got to the fighting. By the time training was over and they'd hemmed and hawed around I'd only got as far as England and the war was over. I was put in the Army of Occupation in Germany for a year and did okay because

I spoke the language. Lots of girls, lots of money, schnapps, and fun, my arm around a different girl every night. Then I came home and got my discharge. I went back to the farm for two weeks' discharge leave and then that was it for me. I never wanted to see a cow, or a root, or a stone, or a barn door again.

I took the machinist's trade and I've worked for all the big outfits, like Finning and Massey and them all. The Prairies are fine with me. I can't say I like the winters, five months of it, but that's the Prairies for you. That's where the arrowheads are.

About them, when I'd be picking roots and rocks for this Mr. Irwin I'd find arrowheads. Spearheads. Chipping stones. This had been kind of an Indian hunting-ground. I'd pick up a few and keep them. Hammers, heads, scrapers. I never knew what they were, but I'd put them all away.

That's kind of what kept me on the Prairies. I don't think there is a place where the Indians have been over the past five hundred years that I haven't been poking around in. I got thousands and thousands, bags and boxes and cases full, and I don't do anything with them. I am what you would call a collecting freak.

Now, in a couple of years I'm going to retire. No more of this travelling around with a box of tools. I never married, and I've got a little house outside of Edmonton, and one day I'm going to sit down and I'm going to start dumping this stuff on the floor and I'm going to find out what I've really got. Its sort of like my Loto Canada, the 6/49. I might have things in there which will make me a millionaire. But it might be a couple of years before I find out I'm a millionaire, once, twice, or three times–or just a damned fool with about a ton and a half of plain old rock.

Aw, it's been good fun. Kept me outdoors and busy."

🕊 *A Kulak Kid*

"It was a good time. I was twenty-two, I guess, and because I wasn't allowed to go into the army, but a lot of people were in it, I could get a lot of good jobs. Driving tractor and trucks for farmers and doing jobs in town. It was a lot of money.

In 1944 crops were still good, and I bought a quarter section. The down payment on my farm was one-third, $2,000. I can't tell you how hard I worked to get that much, but it gave me my farm.

I had no livestock, so in winter of 1944 I worked in Edmonton and made good money in a war plant as a driver. They'd let me work fourteen hours a day, and that was $1.10 an hour, good, and I saved a lot of money. I stayed with a Ukrainian lady who didn't have a husband. Dead. I had a room in the basement and I did the walks and cleaned out the ashes and did jobs around, and my rent was four dollars a week. I got a lunch she made for me in that, too. Five months of working all the time, at $1.10 an hour, that was an awful lot of money to put in the bank those days.

This lady had a daughter, Katrina, who lived with two other girls in a big apartment. She didn't want to be with her old mother, who only spoke Ukrainian, I guess, but she came over on Sundays to see her and bring her things. That's how we met. When I went back to my farm in April, I asked her if I could see her and she said sure. Like that, 'Sure, sure you can see me.' She thought I was just a dumb Hunyak. Well, what was she? A smart one? That's fine with me, I thought. Okay. These smart ones, they just think they're smart.

I saw her a couple of times that summer, and that winter I went back to Edmonton. The same place, the widow woman and the room in the basement. Smart old lady. Things were getting better with the war over and everybody coming home and so she put the rent up to six dollars a week. The first week I didn't do the furnace and she said, 'Why don't you do the furnace for me now?' I said, oh, for me to do the furnace and the walk and take out the ashes and fix your windows and take out your garbage, that would cost you about two dollars a week. She laughed. These old women are pretty tricky, you know. Nobody knows how to save a penny better than an old-country woman. She laughed and said, okay, two dollars, but your lunches, they'll cost you a dollar a week now. So that works out, see, to five dollars a week. But okay. I had a better job now at the factory, and I made $1.20 an hour and had five guys working for me. So.

That winter the factory only worked until Saturday at noon instead of all day like in the war, and I saw more of Katrina. She changed her name to Karen because she thought it sounded better. More modern. I didn't like so much all the lipstick she wore but I didn't say nothing. She seemed to come over more on Saturday afternoons now. She was working in a real estate office and she'd talk about being a real estate salesman. 'A woman,' I'd say, 'they won't have that.' She'd say, 'Then I'll make history by being the first in Edmonton.'

I had got a real big crop of wheat off that fall, averaging forty-four bushels to the acre, which was awfully good, and I got $10,000 for it. I was a rich man. I owned the quarter and I had bought another quarter on a real good deal and there I was. And I thought, how am I going to tell this girl I love her and I've got about $10,000 in the bank and I've got a half section – I'm not just the guy who shovels snow off her mother's walk.

One night when I come home tired and after I've washed up downstairs, the old lady calls down to me. I go up and she says, 'What are you going to do about Katrina?' I says why. She says because she's in love with me. I say, 'Well, I'm in love with her, too, but that doesn't mean there's gonna be any marriage. She doesn't know I love her.' The old lady says, 'Oh, yes, sure, sure, she knows. It's written all over your face.' I laugh and make a thing, you see, with my hand, to wash it off and I ask, what do I do?

She says, in Ukrainian, of course, that's what we're talking, she says, 'On Saturday afternoon she comes. I'm going shopping on White Avenue. You sit there, in that chair. She always sits here, this sofa, right here, and when I'm gone you get up, you big blockhead, and you walk over and sit beside her. The girl can't do everything. She's looked at you enough and you don't know anything about what she's saying with her eyes. You take her hand, you say to her, "I love you. Will you marry me?" That's if you want to. If you don't, you can get out of the house right now, get out in that snow and it's twenty below, and don't come back!'

Well, sure enough, when Mrs. Holinaty comes back from shopping on Saturday afternoon, there is Karen and me at the door to open up and we're holding hands and I've got this lipstick on my face and the old lady says, 'Good. I made some special cakes for you this morning and we've got a bottle of wine, too.' That's all she said.

So we got married. We didn't have one of these big weddings. Besides, we didn't know anybody. There were my people, the four of them, and a few friends and the Markowskis and Karen and her mother had moved down from north of Vilna after her father died, so it was just a small wedding. Honeymoon to Jasper, four days. You see enough mountains in one day.

We did some thinking next winter. I took off another real good crop, paid off the other quarter, and we thought, she didn't really like the farm and, okay, when you think about it, I didn't think it was so hot either. I'd spent two winters in town, and it was a lot better than the farm. I said, let's live in Edmonton. So we did. I paid the two oldest Markowski boys to get my seed in, and I took my two weeks' holidays to take off the crop. We did that for six years, and made good money every year.

But by then we had kids, and I had started this trucking company, putting all my money and twelve hours a day into that thing, and the oil business had come to Alberta, Leduc, Redwater, Golden Spike, all these, and I was getting real good contracts. I don't know what real good means to you, but to a kulak kid out of the Ukraine and no brains at all, the money I was making with a dozen trucks, twenty men, and a bookkeeper and a mechanic, we were on top of the world. Two kids, a good wife, the big house in the new subdivision, and me owning about thirty building lots around town, and the little farm for weekends at Spruce Grove, why I never thought I could have so much money! It was all pretty happy for me. For us. For our kids, too."

🐦 *Leaving Wetaskiwin*

"I wanted to get out of Wetaskiwin. My fiancé had been killed in Germany just twelve days before the war ended. I stood it as long as I could. I think my mother cried ten times as much as me. I think I somehow expected it. He had been wounded twice before, not bad, but I thought, unluckiness comes in threes. This would be his third time. It was, and that was the end of it for me. I just wished that people would stop looking at me as if my world had come to an end. It did there for a few days, but you have to get over these things. What good does it do, thinking about might be? It might have been me, getting hit on the main street of town while going to see him come in from the war on the bus from Edmonton.

So I made my mind up and I said Vancouver. That's because it was on the ocean and you know prairie people, there's something about the ocean. Look at the number of local boys who joined the navy. Anything to get off the land, maybe, because maybe they knew, way, way down inside them, that, well, that they'd be on the land again for the rest of their lives. I wanted to be by the ocean. For a while, at least.

Well, I was. I got a job at Woodwards department store. I was nineteen and had worked nearly two years in a general store in

Wetaskiwin, so I knew what store-clerking was like. I got a room for four dollars a week in a big old house in the West End. It was nice and quiet then, and tall trees and little shops. I'd buy a pork chop at Dennett's Meat Market and a few potatoes and vegetables at the Chinaman next door. I was making seventeen dollars a week, so I had quite a bit of money to spend. I don't think I spent more than five dollars a week on food. You could do it easily in those days. I had, oh, about six a week to spend and that was a lot. The beach was right there, and two blocks away there was Stanley Park. A good library you could drop in at after work. Swimming in the covered pool. Chinatown after work with girls at work, and, say, maybe six of you, and all you could eat. The bill would be five dollars, and about fifty cents each. So you could see, my money would go a long way, but there was one thing missing.

I might as well say it. I might have had a wonderful future in Vancouver but I missed old Wetaskiwin and its slow, slow ways and its quiet streets and nothing doing all the time. I was lonely in Vancouver. I admit it. I couldn't make real friends, and that's funny because it was after the war. There it was, full of people from other places and everybody wanting to know everybody, and here I was, belle of the ball at home, and I wasn't going any place except with the girls. Maybe I looked country girl but I tried not to. I tried to be big city. Sophisticated. Oh, sure, I read all the right magazines. I went to night classes. But I never had a date, and in those days I wasn't too bad-looking. I had had plenty of boyfriends at home before Ralph came along, so what was wrong with me?

That was October I went to Woodwards and by April I couldn't stand it any longer. I had to get away. They'd be seeding back home and everyone in the store would be talking crops again and I'd not be there laughing and helping customers and having a high old time and being with my own people. Somehow, and I can't put my finger on it, I felt that people who moved to Vancouver expected too much. They thought maybe that their social life would live up to those mountains, that sea, the boats, the flowers, and being green all year. It didn't work out for me.

One Saturday night I got a bunch of change and I walked down to a café on Davie and I phoned the man who ran the general store I worked for and I got him on the long-distance phone and I said, 'Hello, it's me. Millie. I'm in Vancouver.'

He was a big, jolly man, not a skinflint in a carload of him, and he roared out, 'Millie, when are you coming back to work for us?'

That solved my problem then and there. I didn't have to beg for a job, even ask for one. There was one, and he was asking me to take it. I loved that man then. You just can't understand the feeling I had. I held back crying, not saying I was so homesick I could die, and I said I'd like to come back. 'Great!' he roared. He was the kind of man who thought if you were long-distance he could reach you just by yelling loud. When could I come? I said it was Saturday and I couldn't leave until next Saturday. I could be home by Monday and I could start Tuesday or Wednesday. He thought that was great, and that was it.

What I'm saying is this. I just didn't fit in the city. I had to be in a small town. Like Wetaskiwin or Leduc or Olds or some place like that. I just wasn't a city girl. It was the people. The farmers would come in, and this was before the supermarkets, and they would talk. You'd ask how they were. There would be gossip. Talk. All this, you know, it is so simple.

Living on the Prairies, I am sure they are a different kind of people. They like you. They worry about you, like when Ralph was killed. They want to help, and when they say something, yes, and this is important, they mean it. There is no phoniness in people like that. The salt of the earth. All the time. Not just when they're talking to you, but after. You just don't find that outside the Prairies, I think. It is the prairie way. People, they are honest."

❧ War Bride from London

"Dundurn, Saskatchewan. I so remember that morning, with Jack so cheery and taking me to the farm to meet the folks, as he called them, and running into the store in this drab and dreary and perfectly awful little dump of a town sitting out there on the prairie.

He came out of that store with six ice-cream cones and two big bottles of a drink they called Kik. Orange Kik. He said this was a treat for us and the folks, for our coming-home party, bringing home his English war bride. Now, if you remember, Kik was the worst thing ever invented. It was coloured water, really. And the ice cream, vanilla. Nothing romantic like strawberry or cherry. No, plain, white, dumb, stupid old vanilla. Ye gods and little fishes! Can you imagine?

It was six miles to the farm, two miles this way, one mile that way, et cetera, and you know how those prairie roads are. Nothing in a straight line, although it looks that on a map. Turn here, turn right there. Even if I'd fled the place I'd never have found my way to anywhere. So I'm holding these two bottles of Kik and a bunch of ice-cream cones, and we finally roll into the farmyard and his parents and brother and sister come streaming out, all smiles and kisses, and hugs, and what am I doing?

I'm trying to get out of that bloody car with two bottles of Kik in one hand and six cones in the other, and feeling like a bloody fool.

Then I thought, oh, this is ridiculous, and I dropped the bottles in the snow and dropped the ice cream and did my share of the hugging, and we all went into the farmhouse. It was a big house, and the kitchen was big and it was warm and a friendly place, and I thought, 'Well, maybe this isn't going to be too bad, and we'll have our own place by spring anyway.' So there is lots of laughing and then one of the kids said, 'Oh, the treats,' and they both ran out.

The kids come running in, they're about twelve and fifteen, and they're yelling that the treat is gone. You know what happened? The two farm dogs had gobbled up those ice-cream cones. I mean it.

I started to laugh, and I guess that started it, because everybody got the laughs and Ma Patterson said, 'Oh, well, I've made jam tarts and we'll have them,' and we did. And that's how I came home, and Saskatchewan is my home now, it really is, and I never regret now that I came."

❧ *The Canadian Way*

"The first time I really met a grocer in Canada, I said to myself, what an incredible country this really is. My husband and I had arrived from England and a friend had rented a place for us and furnished it with a bed and a table and two chairs, just enough for us to get by, and with some pots and pans and dishes.

We took the streetcar downtown that night and ate. And next morning there I am walking down Osborne Street with my little net bag I'd brought, and the first store I found was the Red and White. I thought, what an odd name. There were quite a few around Winnipeg. They were tiny supermarkets, no bigger than an ordinary store, and they were painted red and white.

I was used to groceries in one shop, and greens in another, and then a visit to the fishmonger or the butcher and the stationery shop and so on, this here, that there, but here it was all on sale in this one store.

Fine, but it does seem a bit unusual, and I filled my bag with oodles of things, tea, sugar, bread, carrots, sausages, milk, so many things, and then I went to the counter and stood in line and a lady asked me if I was new. New? I wasn't sure what she meant and then I said, 'Oh yes, we just arrived from England yesterday afternoon.' My, that did cause a bit of an upset. Imagine, all the way from England last night and here she is shopping in this very store. My goodness. So many questions. It was all so friendly.

Then it was my turn and I laid out my things and when it was time to pay for all this, tea, sugar, and so on, I found I had left my change purse in the flat. I have never been so embarrassed in my life!

All these things that Mr. Beebe was tucking into the bags, a whole lot, and worth maybe six dollars, and here I was, not a penny to my name.

I said I was sorry but I'd have to put all the things back on the shelves as I'd come away without my purse and he laughed, a red-faced, jolly man, and he said, 'We'll just put it on your bill. Pay the end of the month. That's the Canadian way.'

I was astonished, as you would be too in my shoes, because after all at home it was all hard cash, pounds, shillings, and pence, and no nonsense.

And there he was, making out a bill in a new little book and telling me I could charge this because this was an acccount he was starting for me, and when I got over my surprise I said, what a very good idea. Maybe I'll just buy a few more things, and I did, and by this time it was too much to carry. I said, oh dear, and he said not to worry, m'am, the boy will deliver it in jig time. And he did.

I told my husband, what an incredible country. A person can walk in from nowhere and say she's from England and buy a lot of things and say she has no money and they let her take the things, deliver it to the door, and one doesn't pay a penny until the end of the month.

It seems all so silly now, but that is the impression that stays with me most when I think of coming to this country, and meeting such a nice and jolly grocer like Mr. Beebe the very first day.''

🕊 *Into the Early Twentieth Century*

"I came out of the war in July of '45, a wireless air gunner, thirty-two missions, no fighters up, the Germans didn't have any left, and our instructions were, 'Bomb on the edge of the fire zones.' Meaning? Why, we were just trying to destroy as much of every German city as we could. There wasn't much about war to it. Fly over, dump our bombs, and come home.

So, at the discharge centre in Calgary they said, 'Go home. We'll call you back for discharge when we get around to you,' and that was that, and I went home. Back to the farm. The old man and my kid brother had farmed it during the war, good crops and good money, although the Canadian farmers got royally screwed on the price. The Canadian government sold the wheat to Britain at a big discount, but that's a story that has never been told.

It's harvest time by now. I was twenty-one. Not married, of course. Not even looking around at that point, not me. And there I was, this one day, and I'm field pitching. Moving around to the hayricks helping each driver load up. Now, that is tough work. I remember it was a good year and those wheat sheaves were heavy.

And it struck me. Here it is, August of '45, and except for a few things, we must be harvesting and living just the way my grand-father did back in 1910 when he took up this homestead. Sure, a tractor now instead of the old steam engine, but the same principle was involved. The sheaves go in, the wheat comes out this spout, and the straw comes out another. We had horses, naturally. Plenty of them, I think we had about twenty. The horses ate the same, oats, same as back in 1910 or so. There I am in my GWG bib overalls. The same. A three-tined stooking-fork in my hand. They probably invented that a hundred years back. The same water-jug soaked down with a bunch of wet sack in the shade of the separator. The same sweat running off my face and chest, just as it was back when I was a kid of twelve and working on the place during the Depression. The same boots.

In the house, my mother, still at the big wood-stove all day, every day. Baking her own bread. Making butter. Selling cream to the creamery in Red Deer. Doing our shopping on Saturday night. Going to the same picture show on the main street. Picking up the grocery order. The guys going to the dance hall and the beer parlour, all the same.

So, look at me. I'm supposed to be a hero. I'd flown the battle skies of Germany, I'd seen cities along the Rhine river burning like a bunch of straw stacks in the fall, and there I am, leaning on my three-tined fork and I'm thinking this. We're doing things almost the same on this farm as when old Grandfather Martin came into this country with his wife and three kids and two wagons and some horses and a plough.

I'm thinking, we can fly over Germany, Lancasters, big bombers, and win the biggest war in the history of the world – and I come back and into the early twentieth century. Nothing changed. Not really. Horses. Milking cows at six-thirty in the morning. Separating. Mom frying pork chops from our own pigs in a big cast-iron pan on a forty-year-old wood stove that came in on that first wagon from the railway at Red Deer. Crockery, white with a blue ribbon around it, that came in with the old man, my grandfather. Drop it from 12,000 on a bombing run and it wouldn't break. They made things–harness, ploughs, forks, everything–they built them to last.

I thought, is this the place for me? My brother's life is this farm and he'll be on it until he dies, and I'm just excess baggage. I went away to war, they wrote me, I wrote them back, but life and things went on as usual. The same old ways. The same old tools. The same way of thinking, just like back in 1910 or so.

I thought, this is no place for me, and I told the old man so. Took him aside, just told him. He wasn't surprised. If anything, he was relieved, because there wouldn't be friction. I didn't fit in any more.

So I went off to Calgary that fall and studied and got my matriculation, two years in about four months. That's the way they did it with veterans in those days. You got what you needed to know and to pass the exams, and no frills and no fuss, and if you could stay out of the York beer parlour, you did okay. I started in at the U. of A. up in Edmonton in January, a half-year behind, but I worked fourteen hours a day and by God, I got through and in '49 I was away. Degree and all. Agriculture, the smart end of it. Working with farmers and not farming, getting a pay cheque twice a month, a government cheque, and not worrying about rust and too much rain, no rain, frost, caterpillars, wheat prices, and wondering what was happening to the farmers' world. I was with them but not a part of it."

🐦 *After the War*

"After the war everything changed around here and it was a good thing, in my opinion. What happened was that an awful lot of people decided that farming wasn't such a hot life after all and that they would be better off doing something else.

I mean, it was the army that did it. The air force, too, naturally, and the navy. Quite a few fellows from this district went into the navy. Mostly army, though.

But when they all came home they found a lot of things had changed. Farming had changed. They saw that not so many farmers, and maybe not even their fathers, had horses any more. We all love horses, don't we? Of course, but in the new way of doing things the tractor was the thing. The government realized that tractors were vital to bigger and better crops and so they didn't cut them out, the way they did cars and trucks for the duration of the war. They made tractors, and the rubber-tired ones were coming in.

Farms didn't need as many workers, because of the new machines. Combines were coming in, more and more of them, and farmers were getting out of cattle and cows and pigs. All of this. Besides, it was the older brothers who had gone to war, and the younger ones over the years had moved up, you know, and were taking over, and there wasn't all the need for so many men around.

Besides, they'd been away so long. I can think of boys who went off in '39 and didn't come back until '45. Six years. They were different. They'd seen a lot of the world. Done a lot of things they had never dreamed of. Dropped bombs. Been sailors and sailed those corvettes in the North Atlantic on those terrible convoy trips. Even killed men. All that sort of thing.

They saw big cities. London. In Holland, and Germany. They were seeing that there was other places in the world, not just the farm or the little village with its pool hall and the beer parlour. Even the towns they knew now looked pretty small and countryish, with the gravel main street all churned up with mud in the spring. They'd seen the big cities and they had lived and fought with boys from the big cities, Vancouver, Toronto, and Montreal. They'd got to know a whole new life, and not just the war life but the life of the big cities.

They had their gratuities and they had lots of money to spend and they could go to university if they wanted. Aggie school, or to be an engineer or a lawyer and maybe a doctor. There were all these trade schools, and if a young fellow just out of uniform wanted to be a welder or a mechanic or a shoemaker or a carpenter, or even a storekeeper, why, there was a course he could take and the government would pay for it, and pay him so much a month for board and room.

This was all there, then. They just had to ask for it. The government pleaded for them to take it. They'd say, okay, I'll take this course, or, I'll go to university. I'll try it. See how it all works out. And it did, you know. So many I know, they did it.

The Vogt family had five boys in the army and when they came back, my husband and I, we went to this big party near Christmas for them to meet all the people around again, and it was a big party. Believe me. And you know, by the middle of January four of those five boys had left for Winnipeg. There was no place on the family farm for them, and so they went to the city. These boys could have gone into the Veterans' Land Act, the VLA, and they could have got farms and money help, but they didn't do it. They went to school, courses, and one to the university, and that changed their lives. Only one of them came back and rented some land after, and he stayed for a few years but then he was off to Saskatoon and got a job, and so even he didn't stay on the farm.

They may have married girls from the district, but I suppose most of them married girls they met in the city or the bigger towns. That figures, you know, because at the same time a lot of the girls were going to the city too, taking typing and secretary courses, or working in stores.

The farms were losing their young people, but farmers being pretty smart people, they managed, because everything was becoming easier on the farm. Just as much work to do, of course, but the doing of it was so much easier. Bigger equipment. New ways. That's the way the Prairies changed after the war.

The farmers love their land. So do the ones who went away to the city or the towns, and they come back to see it again, at picnic time, field-day time, Christmas, the old home place, these times. But they know they can't live there any more, and so they are happy with their lives in the cities. I guess it all worked out for the best."

🦜 Harvesting

"The wife and I retired into a little house in Regina in '73 and my boy has the farm now and rents the rest, and he's an accountant with a second-hand-equipment dealer. His wife works as a home-economics consultant, so their times can be kind of flexible, moving vacations around and so on for the harvesting.

Early in August, I go out and batch for about ten days, just getting the combine and other equipment in shape. A bit of tinkering here and there. Sort of seeing it all came through the winter okay.

Not like the old days in the Depression when I was a young fellow, but more like the war years. Combines were coming into the country a lot then, but it was still the old ways for us. We just couldn't afford that stuff then, not coming off all those bad years.

We had the good old binder then. Four horses, and in that heavy wheat I'd use four of them in the morning until one in the afternoon, and then from two until it got too dark to cut, I'd use four more. Working real good and no breakdowns, you could cut about fifteen acres a day. That was good.

It was all stooking in those days and you'd have two men on that. They'd say a real good man could keep up to the binder. Well, I never saw him around this district. It was two men, and they could go a pretty good lick. The war was over and you could get plenty of help, husky young fellows, and they'd make three bucks a day and found.

Then you'd let the stooks ripen for ten days, sometimes two weeks if there had been rain. Remember, no combines. I'm talking about the good old threshing-machine run off the tractor. That meant you'd have eight racks out there working to haul the bundles to the machine. There was a man on each rack, and then we had two field pitchers, spikers we called them. They just moved around, helping each guy on the rack to load up. So you've got eight and two, that's ten, and me keeping an eye on things, and another man to handle the spout and keep things moving. You see, that's twelve, and then there's two others inside the bins moving the grain around when it came through the trapdoor in the top. Spreading it around. Getting the most in the bin.

Then moving the threshing-machine, if you were in a big field, or moving around, that took a bit of time. Just depended on how organized you were. This gave the teams and pitchers a break. They needed it.

I always wondered why the spike pitchers never got more money –those were the guys who deserved it. But nobody else did it, so I didn't. You couldn't move them around either, driving the rack, because on about four of those racks would be little farmers from around. They'd work for me, not taking wages, but then we'd move over and do their farms. They took a licking, those little guys. I said even if I went broke, I'd never get myself into the bind they were in, practically working for the other guy.

Working with a good crew, well, I'd say we'd take off fifty acres a day. If you were lucky. More if it was a light crop, but say fifty. In those days we only had the section and another eighty acres, so we'd clean up in ten days with no rain. That was good. That was when you felt good, too. It didn't matter what the grade was, or what the buyer would give you on grade, just seeing that steady stream of the golden stuff going in, that was good. That was money.

Now farming is all different. There's none of this five-o'clock stuff to look after the horses. Fed and watered and harnessed and then breakfast at six, and the first bundle thrown by seven in the morning.

Why, I never fail to get a kind of laugh out of it. It is a piece of cake, today. My son, he jumps into his car in Regina and he and his wife are at the place not much more than seven. I'm batching there and I've got breakfast all ready when they pull in, bacon and eggs, fried potatoes, lots of toast and jam, and a big pot of coffee. There we are, sitting and having a smoke and talking, and my boy Harvey, he looks at the clock and says it's time to get going. Out to that big combine and off he goes, and all day he's just moving it right along and doing a hundred acres a day, that's nothing.

Remember I said it took about fourteen men and sixteen horses and a few dogs to do fifty acres, in maybe twelve or thirteen hours, and they're all so tired at the end they just shovel down their grub and have a smoke and hit the hay. Well, Harvey and his wife, they do about a hundred acres, and he's sitting up in his cab all clean and fresh and listening to some Regina radio station. She's in the three-ton. She'll help me with the dishes and poke around, and about nine she takes out the truck. They've got this line of steel bins in the yard, and I open up the next one and soon, maybe half an hour, she's back, and we set up the augers and turn the thing on and there it goes in, and when it's empty back she goes for another. And she's just a slip of a girl.

They do that all the time, day after day. About eight, nine days, I reckon. That's it for the crop. For that year. So there's that $100,000 worth of machinery sitting there in the shed. Least it ain't eating hay and causing problems, and snow and blizzard and cold, it don't hurt that combine none. The only thing that's hurting, I guess, is the payments. There's always the bank. Not so much in my day, you can guess that, because banks were not places we went to much 'less we could help it. Then, mostly, it was ninety-day notes. Borrow for seed and pay back soon as you had the crop in. Times was tight as a bull's arse in fly time, them days, but we got along. Not so much with the help of that friendly banker. We just got along on our lonesomeness.

Now there's the quota, you know. Each farmer can deliver so much. When the new quotas come in, I just drive out there and unlock the bin and drive the truck up and unload four, five, six bushels times eight hundred, the amount they're going to let us sell. Then I spend a couple of days hustling that wheat off to the siding. The elevator man gives me a receipt on the number of bushels and grade and my son gets the money – and that's the way it is done hereabouts and everywhere now.

Let me put it this way. There ain't no sweat involved any more. Sure, there's a lot of worrying, because there's too much wheat in the world. Not good Canadian wheat, the best. But wheat. The wheat glut, they call it, though, you know, people seem to be starving as much as ever. But what I'm trying to say is, not much sweat any more. More thinking, more worrying. To me, sweat was a good thing. It kind of measured out how much honest work you were putting into the land."

Seven

Growing Up

Hiking Down the Road to School . . . The Happy Life . . . In the Deep Woods . . . Tonsils . . . The Wonders of Radio . . . The Good Old Summertime . . . Camping at Sans Souci . . . Just a Hired Man

Spring was the turning-point in a prairie child's life, the end of the imprisonment of winter and doing the chores morning and evening in darkness, with only the lights of Christmas to break the long siege. Spring meant work for everyone, and as the long summer rolled by, the boy of nine took his first step towards manhood by doing the harrowing with three horses on the summer fallow. Then harvest, the biblical gleaning-time of year, and endless chores for boy and girl. Autumn, and any mother worth her salt could think of a hundred extra jobs to do as the sun took longer and longer to rise, and the first venison-steak dinner was evidence of a successful deer hunt.

The West was a good place for children to grow up. Even if times were tough, they had few cares, no worries. In cities and towns and on the farms, the games they played were the same, kick-the-can, road hockey, hunting gophers for the tail bounty, hiking, building tree forts. Somehow, today's kids keep busy but they don't seem to an outsider to have as much fun. Maybe it is because all the old games have disappeared, or maybe we're all just getting old.

What child today would know you were speaking of a meadow lark when you said, "I was here a year ago, I was here a year ago"? Words to the birdsong. I hope there are kids on the Prairies today who know about the moccasin dance, learning on bob skates, making slingshots, smoking cat-tail fluff, going to the city for Eaton's Christmas Parade, and the pan of fudge made on the stove on Sunday night.

Hiking Down the Road to School

"These kids riding those big yellow school buses, they miss out on an awful lot. They get dumped off at the door and I'll bet they head right for the TV set. There's no more chores on the farm today. No cows, so no milking and no turning the separator and feeding the skim milk to the pigs and chickens. None of that. Gone with the wind. No forking hay down to the cows, no cleaning out the barn because there ain't one.

On these buses, they miss a lot of nature. You see, they don't walk. They ride miles and miles, sometimes as much as twenty miles, where we would only walk two and a half. All weather, and even in a blizzard you'd see us going, though mostly my dad would get out the horse and cutter and pile us four kids in. But the rest of the time we walked. Spring, winter, fall, you'd see us hiking down the road with our Rogers Syrup tin pails with our lunch. I always remember ours. It would be two sandwiches. My mother would smear the bread with butter or bacon drippings, and then there would be a nice slice of smoked moose meat or venison. Two of those sandwiches put a filling in you that would last until suppertime. There was always a couple of cookies and sometimes an apple. Apples usually came in the first few months after my dad bought a barrel of them, but then they'd run out. Oh, sure, and a pint of milk.

In the fall we'd pick rose-hips on the way home and my mother would make some kind of tea. She was Swedish from Minnesota and they knew about these things. I think, though, they got it from the Indians. The rose-hip tea was good for all sorts of illnesses.

In the winter when it was snowed in we'd get a frozen horse bun and we'd kick it all the way to school like it was a football, and then we'd kick it all the way back. A couple of miles sure pass fast when you're running and there are half a dozen of the neighbour's kids trying to kick that old turd around. There can't be any cheaper kind of entertainment than that, I'd say.

In the spring, for a few days anyway, you'd get a thaw and the drainage was poor and so there'd be all this water on the fields. Then in the night she'd freeze over, and that was what you called rubber ice. We had to go one mile up to a road and one and a half miles along it to the school, and with all these fields we could cut across the right angle, you see, and this was all flooded. You'd run and the ice would bend under you but not break and it was like swooping along. The only time you'd ever get that kind of experience was on rubber ice.

In winter, we'd take our gopher traps and set them in the ditches and through the bush on the side of the road, and we'd catch squirrels and weasels and sometimes birds, like the whiskey-jacks. Too bad about the birds. They'd freeze to death. The animals would, too, but that didn't matter. We'd take them to town and trade the skins at Scott's General Store, I think it was fifteen cents for a red squirrel and ten for a grey and twenty-five for a black one, and you'd get maybe a dollar and a half for a weasel. You had to do them right, on a willow frame and salt them down, but it was easy to do.

I remember these things, just walking to school and seeing the seasons change and the birds coming back. You know, the first crows, that was some excitement. Spring, that meant. And the meadow lark, dee-dee-dee-deedeedee-da, you know how it sang. 'Hello', it was saying, 'we're back. You can start seeding.' Yeah, the seasons changing. You don't see that much from a school bus full of yelling kids. You don't smell it anyways. That was something. Do you know you can smell spring coming in the air? I still can. You can't put a name to what you smell, it's just there. You can put your hand out and feel like you're stroking something new and warm, this air in the spring. Even the animals know it.

Some kids, of course, would come on horses. There was an orphan kid adopted by an old couple down our road and this Jamie kid, he rode this pony. Sometimes if I had a nickel I'd give it to him and he'd let me ride his pony home and I'd tie it to our gatepost and that was my fun. My nickel ride! When you got home you were feeling good."

❧ *The Happy Life*

"There we were, living in a dirt house with the cow and our pigs next door where we could hear them, and burning cow turds and straw to keep warm, all winter, and my father, he'd be away. You couldn't make a living on a farm in those days. You had 160 acres but only twenty of it was cultivated, you see, and with a big family the man had to work. My father worked for the railway. The CPR. He'd go in November and come back at Christmas and go away and sometimes they sent him far away. He lived in a bunkhouse and never spent a cent, and so this is the way we managed to keep going.

I wish people would stop writing these stories about the happy life on the farms in those days. It wasn't happy. How could you be all that happy when there you were, your father far away working for the CPR and your mother having another baby and the police saying you had to go to school when it was a long way away, and the cow gone dry, no milk to drink at all, lots of potatoes and turnips to eat, pig meat to eat, and snow and wind all the time and nobody but yourselves to talk to. Nothing to read.

I won't tell you what it was like when I went to school. You try going to school for the first time, you're eight years old and you speak Ukrainian and the teacher, she's talking to you in English. That's the way it was with me and my brothers and the other kids from the old country. After two years, when he was thirteen, my oldest brother quit and went cutting wood in winter in the Moose Mountains. He made a few dollars and came back and he could swear like anything in English. All the dirty words. He taught them to me and I took them to school and told the other kids. I guess they knew them, but I said them in class and got the strap. They didn't strap girls but they gave it to me. That was something.

When I was nearly twelve, my father sold his land and we moved to Winnipeg. No more dried cow plops. Now it was, 'Anna, you run to the store and get me a pound of butter, here is ten cents.' We went to a big school made of red brick. I went there another year until I was thirteen, and then I went to work. First, it was a tanning factory and then a bakery. What a difference. Oh boy. Then when I was eighteen I went to Eaton's, to the mail order, and got eight dollars a week. Rich, that was what I was."

🌿 *In the Deep Woods*

"I was just a little kid, nine or ten, I guess, when my big brother Alex and I would go out east to cut wood. He'd go about five times in the winter and my mother would let me go with him once, and because she always had a twinkle in her eye, that once a year was always a school-day. That made it so much better.

Alex was about eighteen or nineteen, I'd say, if I was nine or ten, but he'd quit school after about Grade 5 when he knew everything about spelling and writing and arithmetic that any farm kid needed, so he had been working like a man. That's the way farm kids in Manitoba were those days. School, you just got enough, and that was always enough.

This day I could go, after milking, and when it was still dark, of course, he'd hitch up a team to the long sled and we'd start out east. In those days the road petered out into a trail used by the wood-cutters and it wound along for miles, through poplar and scrub pine, and then we'd come to the tamarack forest. This is where the best wood was and there were no wood-lots. You just took a piece that looked good, as close to the trail as you could.

Then we'd tie Tony and Mac to a tree and throw a horse blanket over each one and my brother, he'd sharpened the axes and the saws the night before, so we'd just start to work. You never cut a real big one, over nine inches, because getting that on the load would have been too much. You took the smaller ones, and they were best for the wood-stoves in the house, too.

Alex would do the chopping, and when he'd cut them down, with my own axe I'd do the lopping off of the branches. Every twelve feet I'd chop out a deep V and this was where we'd start the saw cut. With a deep V you didn't have to fool around as much, and sometimes you only had to make about five sweeps with the big Swede saw. It was all done in what you'd call the time-honoured way.

I'd hear Alex chopping and the swishing, crackling noise of the trees coming down, and sometimes he'd stop and I'd know what he was doing because I'd be doing it too. He was listening to the silence. There is no other silence like that in the deep woods, nobody else around and just the white clouds above. Nobody for a million miles.

Then at ten o'clock Alex told me to get together a lot of the boughs and pile them and he lit them and they started to burn slowly, like they weren't going to start, and then in a few minutes we'd have a roaring fire. Alex would take an old pot and prop it with a stick, the pot full of snow, naturally, and we'd keep putting in snow until we had enough for tea. Throw a handful of tea leaves in and let it boil and then brew for a couple of minutes. With lots of sugar we'd have a couple of good big mugs of tea, and Alex would have a smoke. I don't remember that we talked much, although this would have been a good time to talk, two brothers.

Then we'd go at it, Alex taking another sharp axe. About an hour later he'd chopped down the poles and he went and untied Mac and threw a collar and towing harness on him and they spent about another hour or so hauling the trees out to the trail where we were.

You know, that one time, I'll bet it was twenty below, but I had to take off my heavy mackintosh, and so I was down to a sweater, and finally I took off that and was down to the last sweater, and I still wasn't cold. No wind got in there, and it was so quiet and still, it was warm when you were working.

About one o'clock we'd got all the logs off around the sled and we built up another fire and boiled some more tea and took out our sandwiches. Beef and bread, big thick sandwiches, two each. Each was just about a meal in itself and we put them on forked sticks and held them over the fire to thaw them and toast them. That's when the whiskey-jacks came around. They didn't come when we were drinking tea before, but they sure knew when we had food. They'd come right up to you. Wild, never seeing a human, but they'd come and take a big crumb out of your hand. Maybe two of them fighting for the same crumb. We'd warm up slabs of pie, too, and eat them, and what we hadn't eaten we'd throw to the jacks. When we'd done that, they flew away. They knew somehow that dinner was over.

It's time to get back to work and we worked fast, using a saw-horse to hoist up the logs and cut them where I'd V'd them. Then it was hoisting and shoving and pushing them onto the load. The first twenty-five or thirty were okay, you could handle them, but when the load got bigger, then you really worked, but with rope and using Mac for pull power on the last half-dozen or so, you got them all fitted in. You had yourself maybe one-fifth of your stove wood for the next winter.

Then we'd start home, slow, and you had to be careful, because the horses had a heavy load, even on sleighs, and it could be tippy and you could have the whole thing roll on you. But Alex, he was good with horses, and I held the reins and he walked with the horses. You see, it's getting dark by this time and there's a time between light and dark when it's harder to see than any time. It would be dark when we'd see the lights of the house.

We'd come in the lane and my mother and dad would be out to meet us, and Dad would help Alex unhitch and he'd take them to the barn to brush them down and feed them up, and we'd go inside and Mother would give us a cup of coffee. Real hot and good. Lots of sugar in it, that I liked. It was like drinking candy with a grown-up taste.

That would be a long day, hard work, but more than anything

except the baseball tournament on July 1, I think it was the day I remember most of all from my childhood."

☙ *Tonsils*

"Even today I'm not sure what tonsils do. You never hear of them any more. They're some kind of thing that you're born with, in the throat, and this was the time I remember in the Depression. Everybody had their tonsils out.

It was about my first week of school, at a little place called Rosser, north and west of Winnipeg. This day when school was over the teacher gave all of the new kids a note. She took a pin and pinned it to our dresses and told us to go right home and show the note to our mothers. When I got home my mother said that the next morning all the first-graders would be going to the General Hospital to have our tonsils out. We were supposed to wear our best dress and have our hair done so we'd look good. This was in 1933, because that's the year I started school.

Next morning I went to school and in the schoolyard there was a bus with some kids in it. They were from another school about five miles north of where we were, and we got in the bus and Annette Guerin started to cry. Little Annette was French and she had never been away from home, and she cried all the way to Winnipeg because she was scared. We stopped and picked up some more first-graders at another school and then into Winnipeg. I had never been there myself and I could see how big it was.

There were about fifteen of us first-graders, and the bus went to the hospital and my friend Annette is still bawling her head off and I remember the lady that met us, the nurse or matron, she was mad. Told her to shut up. You know how nurses can get.

We went in and there were two doctors there and two nurses and other kids from other schools, and they took us one by one into this room. There was a chair and you sat in it and it tilted back like a dentist's chair and the nurse put chloroform on you and pooh, you were unconscious. When I woke up, I was in another room and my throat was sore and kids were crying. There were four or five of us lying on the floor, and as soon as we came to, an orderly picked us up and carried us into another room and we lay on the floor again until we were feeling okay. I guess it was only a couple of minutes for each child and after a while the nurse came around and asked us how we were feeling.

My mouth was bleeding and they gave us swabs of cotton batting and on the way home we swabbed out our mouths. Annette was still crying and you'd have thought she was dying. None of us were hurt, it was just our throats that were sore, and the iodine, it gave us a funny taste. The boys, I remember, were yelling and saying it didn't hurt, it was okay, and we girls were just sissies. That was okay. I'd heard a couple of them crying, too.

Then the school superintendent, who was with us, he told the driver to stop at a store near Sturgeon Creek and we all went in and this man bought us all an ice-cream cone. That was five cents then, and you'd get vanilla, strawberry, or chocolate. We all thought it was wonderful. Having ice-cream cones free. We never got that at home, because all our fathers were very poor. There was never money for things like that, except on a picnic.

When we got back to the school, we were told to go home. This was only about one o'clock, as I remember, so we got half the day off and Annette and I walked home and that poor kid, maybe she got it worse than I did, because she was still bawling.

When I turned off at our farm and she lived up the road, I could still hear her bawling.

That was the way they did it in the good old days. You start school and yank, out comes your tonsils, and next year they took out your adenoids, and, honestly, I don't know what they are either. I know today they don't do it, and I don't know why they ever did. I asked my brother-in-law once, because he had a drugstore over on Corydon Avenue, and he said he thought it was something they did in England, so they did it too in Canada. You know, if the English did it, then it was right. That was the way an awful lot of people thought about it in those days long ago. England was always best.

Anyway, my mouth and throat was funny for a few days, but I still went to school. My friend Annette, she didn't come back for a week, and when I asked her why she didn't, she said she'd been helping her mother canning plums and killing and cleaning the big bunch of chickens they raised to eat in the winter. I knew she was wrong. You didn't kill chickens early in September. She just used it all as an excuse to get out of school. That was Annette. But she surprised us all, because when she was sixteen she ran away and joined the women's army corps by saying she was nineteen, and when the war ended she came back for a while and was quite a heroine. She was a pretty tough customer then."

ᕙ *The Wonders of Radio*

"We were living on a farm east of Strathmore there about 1936. I was eleven. My two brothers were older and my two sisters were younger. I remember my dad cutting up a length of alligator belting off the separator and cutting out soles and making tops out of the canvas from the binder, and we held them on our feet with elastic bands cut out of an inner tube. Darndest-looking things, but they were our shoes. Didn't cost a cent, because my dad didn't have a cent.

We walked four miles to school. A little white building and eight grades in it. Maybe forty-five kids, one teacher. The only reason it was warm in winter was because there were so many bodies in it. The heat from our bodies warmed the place up, and about noon it was livable. But we did our work, and we played outside at recesses and at noon. Imagine, if you can, about twenty-five boys and girls kicking an old soccer ball around the yard in the snow, and we didn't do it to keep up our circulation. We did it because we were having fun.

School was fun in those days. We were learning. Not many books, mind you, but Mrs. Johnston was a widow and she was a very wonderful woman and she cared about our young minds. And I'm told she did all this for $30 a month, and they took $12.50 off for room and board. Farmers were so broke in those days that she'd spend one month at the Gillanders', one at the Robinsons', one at the Campbells', and so on, so everybody got a crack at that $12.50, which was one awful lot of money in those days.

When I was twelve, that was the year that the wind just blew our family off the farm. That's why they called it the Dirty Thirties. Huge winds and dry land, and the soil just was sucked up and blown away in great storms. There are pictures of it galore, but that is one thing you have to see, be in, to know about first hand before you can understand what it is all about. That is nature at its very worst. When you see one of those, you know that your God has finally given up on you. No more, mister.

So that fall in 1937 we just moved away. I don't think the bank did it. I just think there was nothing to take, and they'd get around to us later. We put everything on the old truck my dad kept running on air and a prayer, as we used to say, and moved to Calgary, into a place that might have been owned by a friend of my dad or maybe the welfare people gave it to us. Anyway, we move into this house and somehow there is a radio as part of the deal, a big thing on four legs, kind of shaped like a, well, like the front-door opening of a cathedral. Wide here and it met at the top. This thing had two big batteries, the kind with handles at each end to lug them, and this first night my dad hooks them up.

Now listen. I was twelve, and I didn't even know there was such a thing as a radio. I hadn't heard anybody even talk about one. That's the God-given truth. And suddenly, whoof, out of this box comes this music, and then voices and more music, and, you know, I thought that was the greatest thing in the world, that some man could sit down and invent something like this. These stations on the Prairies and Great Falls and other American stations. Good God, man, you just can't understand what I felt. And we listened and listened. It didn't matter to me what kind of music they were playing. It didn't matter to me what the announcer was saying. Just that music and words were coming out of that thing.

Finally my dad shut it off. Maybe it was about midnight and that was three hours later than we went to bed. And I wouldn't go. I remember I went into my first and last tantrum. My mother years later said she thought I had lost my mind. Maybe I did. This is what the wonders of radio did for me, that first night.

I was smart enough that when I saw my old man going for his belt I scooted off to bed. But you know what I did? I stayed awake, and maybe about two in the morning when everybody was out cold I sneaked back into that living-room. I got down and I put my ear to the cloth covering where the sound came out and I turned it on, and I didn't hear a thing. Well, of course, every station was off the air. None of this 24-hour stuff. But I thought I didn't have it turned up loud enough, so I turned it up high. Then I gave the knob a little turn, and nothing, and a little more, and more, and more, and nothing happened. Then – and boy do I remember this! Middle of the night, you see, and reception perfect, and I banged right into that Mexican station at Tijuana, the one that you could hear halfway around the world it was so powerful. It sold phoney medicines and stuff like that in its commercials. Well, when I hit it, wham, out came the Mexican music, that mariachi music, trumpets and stuff, full blast. I knew I was a goner.

I heard my father's feet hit the floor and I headed for the door, even though it was almost winter, and I was stark naked except for pyjama bottoms. But he got me and he got that belt of his and he gave me the worst licking I have ever had in my life, before or since. The very worst. I remember it still."

✎ *The Good Old Summertime*

"On a warm and sunny afternoon in the summer we'd still be in our Sunday-go-to-meeting duds because we'd been to church in the morning and then the big family dinner at one o'clock and then about three, after a little snooze, my dad used to say, 'Let's go down to the park.'

We didn't live far, so off we'd go down to the Southside Park, and when we got closer we'd hear the band playing. It might be the Edmonton Fire Fighters Band, or a band from one of the regiments, or just a band made up of fellows who'd got together, and there they'd be, up on the bandstand playing away.

They'd start at three, and people would start arriving on foot and streetcar and plenty of cars, because even though it was 1934, '35, in through there, people just had to have that old family car for that Sunday drive. Now that's a thing you don't hear about any more. Going for a Sunday drive to work off the big noon dinner.

There would be families sitting around, plenty of children and young men and their girlfriends. The men in those years wore these white boater hats and some would be smoking cigarettes and these new lighters had come out. Flick, a flame. I was fascinated by these young men with their lighters. Everybody strolled around and there was an ice-cream stand with Popsicles and Revels and ice-cream cones and orange pop and everything was five cents. You couldn't get lower than that, but a nickel was a lot of money in those days. You got a dime a week for your allowance and that had to last. If you had a hot dog and Coke at the skating-rink Friday night, then that meant you couldn't go to the Saturday matinee at the movie house.

But anyway, the band played all the favourites. The old and the new. Like 'In the Good Old Summertime' and 'Moonlight Bay', and even 'St. Louis Blues', and they could play hundreds of others. They'd play three tunes and everyone would clap and they'd have a short rest and away they'd go again. Truly marvellous, all these young and old men playing so well, and they didn't make a cent, you know. If somebody paid them, well, sure, but I know there was never any admission or collection. Those were the fun times of being a girl growing up in the Depression, and I miss them.

They seem to have died out about the time of the last war. I don't know why, but I haven't heard of a band concert in the park for years."

🕊 Camping at Sans Souci

"This was back in Winnipeg in the mid-thirties, and my father was making twenty dollars a week as a book-keeper for a raw-fur auction house and darned glad to get it, and my mother, God bless her, was bringing up three kids, and I was about twelve then, and all of us were putting a brave face to the world.

Camping. Two weeks a year, and we talked about our last camping holiday up to January, and then we talked about the coming trip until July, when we went again.

My Uncle Jack had a car and he used to drive the family to a place called Sans Souci. This was a pasture up at the south end of Lake Winnipeg, and it had trees and the loveliest stretch of beach, sand, that you could imagine, and there were two rowboats that anybody could use. He'd unload us there, tents, pots and pans, food, little tin stove, water pails, and toys and clothes, and then he'd head off to Winnipeg and he'd be back in two weeks for us. This time we'd leave the tents and other stuff, the stove and such, because he'd be bringing somebody else, another part of the family.

It was really quite an arrangement. All summer, in two-week shifts, the Baileys and the Farmers and the Crossmans, all part of our big family, we'd each spend two weeks up at Sans Souci. The two tents were owned by all the family. One was a big bell tent, the kind the army used in the First World War. It was bought very cheaply. The pots and pans and dishes and cutlery, it was all give-away stuff, but it did the job.

So, all summer our family had this one spot over in one corner of this field right by the lake. There was a fire pit there which we'd built, a big picnic table and chairs which my dad and uncles had made, and a table to prepare food and wash the dishes, and a clothesline for wet bathing-suits and clothes was strung between two trees.

The owner charged twenty-five cents a day for our spot and there were about ten families who went regularly, every summer, so you could see that he took in quite a large amount of money in July and August. It was always full. Always. There were poor people and middle-class people like us, and people with more money than us, but it was all the same. Everybody, well, we were friends. The children played together and the adults sat around and talked. There was plenty for kids to do on the beach and exploring in the woods, and the older kids and adults played volleyball and baseball, and we all went fishing and in those days there were a lot of fish in the lake, mostly pickerel and perch swimming in schools in the patches of bulrushes near the mouth of the little creek. Our parents went visiting and played bridge and card games, and I remember it was a happy place. The sun always shone.

There was a Mr. Baker who owned a car and at the end of the first week he'd come around and take orders, and one of our fathers would go with him. They'd drive to Selkirk and buy vegetables and fruit and milk for everybody, and the back of the car and the trunk would be loaded high with food for the next week. Everybody ate steak that night. Steak and onions. With fried potatoes. Steak was very cheap those days, and hamburger was about seven cents a pound. We called them 'bats' then, the hamburgers, and we ate a lot of them.

So that's what we lived on. Porridge and toast in the morning. Milk as long as it lasted, because it was difficult to keep anything longer than two days.

For lunch we'd have sandwiches and raw carrots, and I guess the drink we had mostly was an awful concoction called Kik, which sold for eight cents a quart. It was really only coloured and sweetened water, but we loved it. Orange Kik. That was the favourite. For supper it would be hamburger or spaghetti or macaroni, or maybe a chicken, because a farmer from East Selkirk came around about once a week and would sell chickens and any other thing he had, like butter or buttermilk. Sour, you remember. He'd have a milk-can of it and it was probably five cents a quart, if that. But when it was cold it was the best thing I ever tasted.

Of course, Mother worked, cooking and washing the dishes, and my brothers would go and collect firewood in the bush and saw it and chop it, and I'd help with the dishes after, and cleaning up around our little campsite.

Mother and Dad slept in the big bell tent and the kids, we slept in the camping tent, your ordinary run-of-the-mill tent you saw everywhere those days. But I was often off sleeping with some other girls. That was part of the fun of camping out. You slept with your summer friends in their tents and giggled half the night, and my brothers, well, they did the same. It was like one big party for us, one that never stopped for two weeks.

At night, there was a big fire in the centre of the field, and every evening the families would gather around it. Maybe fifty people, and the flames soaring and the big logs being put on the fire, and the sparks trailing off into the night. We roasted hot dogs then, on a stick. I suppose they were only ten cents a dozen, and a bun was probably ten cents a dozen, so a kid could eat three hot dogs, slathered with mustard, and not break the family purse. Anyway, we'd sing, and I mean sing, for maybe an hour or more. All the old songs. You never hear them today. Songs our mothers sang before us, when they were our age. They seem to last forever.

Mr. Carter, there was a personality on two legs, he was always our master of ceremonies. He was a teacher at Earl Grey School, so this all came naturally. Everything was spontaneous, or so we thought, but I think now that he planned it. Mr. Heatherington had once worked for the Hudson's Bay Company in the Arctic, and he kept us enthralled every summer with his tales of the Eskimos and fur-trading. Another father who was a teacher told us how the world was formed, and I learned more from him about Earth and the planets than I ever learned in school. He was a wonder when he had the right audience. Singing, these little lectures, people telling stories, eating hot dogs and roasting marshmallows and not a drop of rain from the sky in those two weeks.

They were glorious days of summer then. Of course, we only had an inkling of what was really happening to the country because of the Depression. We just knew that times were harder and tougher than before, and we thought that everybody spent their summer holidays this way. You know, for a total expenditure of maybe twenty dollars.

But then it all ended. The last day, always a Saturday morning, we'd sweep out the tents and tighten them up and clean around our little area and pack up what we were going to take home. You know, our clothes and toys and fishing-lines and hats, and then we'd wait for my uncle's car to come down the road. In it, there would be an uncle and aunt and my cousins and they'd take our place at Sans Souci for the next two weeks. That's the way it went all summer. We were the ones who put up the tents because we were the first, and the last visitors would take them down at the end of August, and back they would go to the city.

It was sad to leave but it left us with so many memories for the next months until the Christmas excitement got into our little minds. Those summer days were wondrous times. Outdoors every waking hour – we got brown as berries. The macaroni casserole we hated at home, why, we just wolfed it down at the beach. It tasted great. Things like that. Seeing our friends again and taking hikes and sitting around the campfire at nights, hearing everybody singing the old songs. We all loved each other. Such happy times. Such happy days. I don't think one of us thought of what was to come, Hitler, the war, the friends we had who were killed, the sadness and the sorrow in our own lives through many ways, long after. Even now."

❧ *Just a Hired Man*

"I was an orphan kid and this farmer came up to Calgary and went to the orphanage and signed the papers and took me back to his farm. This was in 1930 when I was four years old.

I just wish he had taken my sister, too, but he just wanted a boy.

This man, my father now, he had this farm and three daughters and two boys, and he believed that everyone should work for a living. When I was five I would work, helping my mother in the garden and weeding and sorting and picking, and gathering chips for wood and snaring gophers and getting in the cows, and there are hundreds of little jobs to do when you live on a farm, you know, like gathering eggs. Another job was to take a lot of pieces of binder twine and I had to walk along every fence on that big farm and when I came to a fence post that was loose or if the wire had come off, I'd tie a little piece of binder twine to it and that meant that was a bad post. My father would come along and fix it. This was when I was five.

I went to school when I was six, in the old Rosea school three miles from our house. I could make out words and sentences even when I was four and in the orphanage in Calgary. They had a matron there who was a whiz at teaching. So I was fast in that school and the teacher put me in Grade 2 right away. So I went to Grade 3 and 4 and 5 and I studied at night, see. I worked at my chores and jobs and I studied like the very dickens and those teachers, why, I think they thought they had a university professor on their hands. Like I'd be in Grade 4 when I was eight and I wouldn't be doing my Grade 4 work because I knew it, and there would be kids in Grade 6 studying, oh, maybe geography, and if they didn't know the answer, then I'd give it.

When I was seven I was running the hay rake with two horses. People driving down the road past the field, they'd sometimes stop and look at this little kid on the sulky seat and when they'd pass by again coming back from town they'd toot their horns. When I was eight I was running the mower and doing half the morning milking and half in the evening. About ten Holsteins they had. Jake, the older boy, he and me would run the wood-cutting machine and sell the wood which we dragged up from the Oldman River, and we'd get the low-grade coal from the dump over near Coalhurst. Jake was about sixteen then, I think.

When I was about nine, and I still needed a box to stand on to harness the horses, my father put me on a five-horse team with 22-foot harrows in the big field, and I just picked that up easily and I was doing most of the work around the place, too, that a man would do. Not heavy work, like lifting, mechanical work. I could operate the crusher for the pigs and cows. I could run the tractor. I'd plough the garden and a lot of other things, and I could put a point on the cultivator shoes, and you'd think I was a real farmer and not just a kid who was nine years old. I was also going to school and by this time I was in Grade 7 and, well, looking back, I must have been some kind of a wonder to the teacher.

When I was coming up to ten, and it was time to go back to school, my father said there wasn't any need for me to go. He said I had learned all I needed. I could read and write and do arithmetic better than he could, and he'd only got Grade 6 or 7, and now he had this big farm and now he'd teach me to be a farmer. I think I should have said then and there that I didn't need to learn how to be a farmer because I already was a farmer.

The word got around that I was working on the farm and all the other kids in the district were going to school. Mr. Watmough, who was a neighbour, had something to do with the school, and he came over and talked to my father. 'No,' my father said, 'you can't make this boy go to school if he doesn't want to go.' 'He's got to go,' said Mr. Watmough. He asked me, 'How old are you, son?' I wanted to go to school but not Rosea, because it was too small for me then, and I said I was fourteen. 'Then you must be a midget,' said Mr. Watmough. 'Okay,' he said. 'Don't go to school. But read books. Read everything you can.'

That's how I got the rest of my education. Books from the Lethbridge library. Every Friday I'd cycle into town and exchange the books I'd borrowed for other ones. Two, three a week. I'd read until midnight, and I'd be up at five in the summer and six in the winter.

I had a mind of my own. You can understand that. When he took me from the home my father had told me that he couldn't leave me anything in his will when he died because I wasn't his family. It was later that I understood what he meant. About when I was ten. So I asked him, I wanted to get paid ten cents an hour. He said, 'Okay, that's fine. You keep a record.' He was kind of surprised after the first month when I gave him a bill for twenty-one dollars and some cents. But I had it all written down, in an official way. I couldn't believe how it would mount up, but it did. Twenty bucks was an awful lot of money in those days, but he was getting a lot of work out of me. Man's work. A lot of it. He said, 'Okay, I'll pay you fifteen dollars a month in summer and ten dollars in winter.' That seemed fair to me, but I said I'd do it only if he let me buy a calf from a neighbour and raise it and I'd get the money.

Oh, what's a calf? he was thinking. I thought, there is a lot of milk left over, because we were shipping cream, and I'll put up my own hay in the road allowance and buy oats. This is the way I was thinking when I was a kid. I bought that first calf for two bucks. I trucked that first one three miles, all trussed up and in a wheelbarrow, me pushing the thing. I sold him as a two-year-old for twelve dollars, as I remember, in the sale at Lethbridge. I was earning good money on the farm and studying all these correspondence courses in electricity and chemistry that I got from the school in Chicago. I worked hard, making this money and putting what I could into the bank.

I was doing a man's work, but I was still not too big. But I was tough and I was good at things mechanical, and when there wasn't enough work on the farm, okay, I'd tell my father I was going out to work. I might be gone two weeks and making two dollars a day somewhere and board and room and I'd come back and, lo and behold, there'd be a big pile of work for me to do. They hadn't done it. They thought they'd teach me a lesson. That was one time, I was fourteen. I said, 'Why didn't you do it, you bastard,' and he clipped me alongside the ear.

I think that clip on the ear did it. I stayed around for another year and I spent about half of it working around in town driving a team delivering coal, and a few weeks on the track gang, the CPR. When there was heavy work to be done, I always made sure I was back on the farm to do my share. That was okay. I grew up there and I still thought of it as home.

Then my father sold two calves I had been raising. Remember that agreement? Well, he up and sold them to a buyer who came around with his truck, and they were two-year-olds and he got about thirty-two dollars for them, and that did it for me. All those years of working for nothing and then for what was almost nothing. You'd have thought the biggest favour anybody had ever done to anybody in their life was for him to take me out of the orphanage. I thank him for that, but I can see now that it was just to put me to work my butt off. Look at the education thing. Taking me out of school when I was nine, while his own sons had kept right on going. That should tell you something.

Anyway, this was 1940 now and I was sixteen and there was the war going on, so I just cleared out one day. I said goodbye and I guess I was feeling kind of weepy, but my father didn't show it. He just wished me luck and didn't ask even where I was going.

I joined the army. There was no hassle about my age. They could see I could make good soldier material. I was in England, France, Belgium, Holland, and Germany. That's all the usual places. I was in transport, so I didn't get wounded, and I saw a lot of things, and when I was discharged at Mawata Barracks in 1945 I was just coming up to twenty.

There I was, back in '45 in September, and I had lived half my life. Really, I know a lot of guys in my position. Worked like the blazes when they were kids and joined up when they were kids, too. Maybe it didn't make us the greatest guys in the world when we got out, but there aren't many sergeants in the Canadian army at the age of nineteen, and that's what I was.

I had army grants coming for me and it was harvest time, and in

October I bought a truck. It just about took everything I had saved from before I joined up, and the credits I got from the army, about four thousand dollars, but it was a good buy. I went hauling grain and beets and spent the winter doing general work. I'd see the family around Lethbridge once in a while and we were polite to each other. Had coffee with my father once. We just talked about this and that.

I just put them out of my mind. Best that way. Why plough over old and dead ground. I just felt this way, that they'd taken me out of the orphanage to work, and all I ever was to that family was just a hired man. Nothing more.

But sometimes that was what life was like for an orphan kid on the Prairies in those days. The farmer, although he may not look like it, he's just a businessman, a factory owner, he don't care much for his workers. Same with a farmer. So I just put it down and away from me. No resentment. No bitterness. Not now. Everything worked out good for me and my wife. That's what it's all about, you know. Having somebody to love you, and you loving someone."

Eight

A Sense of Community

🕊 ===

It's Not There Any More . . . Great Big Old Folks' Homes . . . Bright
Lights . . . Farm Fashions . . . Death and Taxes . . . The Post Offices . . .
The Decline of the Towns . . . City Living . . . No Place to Go . . . Ever
Lived in a City? . . . The Cemetery

===

The Prairies are lonelier since the Dirty Thirties, mainly because the farms got bigger and there were a thousand more opportunities for the young to find a new life in the towns and cities. The blacktopped highways also drained away the vitality of the villages; the big city and its attractions and cheaper prices were beckoning only an hour or two down the road, and what's that distance in a new Chev sedan?

Today there are hundreds of villages in the three provinces that could be classified as ghost towns. Oh yes, people live there still, but they are old, retired, living in small white houses, watching TV, and wondering what happened to the way of life they once knew.

The closure of railway branch lines, the loss of elevators, hand in hand those two events helped kill the village, but the company economists could prove to the government that these branch lines were not earning money. Profit over people, the old, old story of the West.

But these villages – the hamlets blew away long ago – and the small towns have a stubbornness about them. They won't die. Or maybe they're dead and don't know it. They have a toughness, which, I guess, means a community spirit. Little events, parties, things that draw people together. They may be just names on a map now, population 75, but they are there, and they do symbolize the West, the spirit, the don't-give-up attitude.

"I'm staying," said an old man I met outside a small store, the only business in the village. "They'll have to take me out of here in a box. I was born three miles down that road, farmed west of here, and now I'm here. My wife's got her flower garden and vegetables. I'm the mayor. Don't have no council, no staff, no money, nothing. I elected myself. Somebody's got to keep this old place going."

✿ *It's Not There Any More*

"There's not much left of the little towns. Like they say, a lot of them just dried up and blew away. Names you never heard of, when old people talk about them. You might ask, 'Where was that?' They'll say, just down the Stettler line or south of Swift Current, something like that, and that was where a lot of people came from at one time, and then the place just died.

I think a lot of these places started dying the day they were born. Now, when you read the obituary column in the *Leader-Post* and it says someone was born in one of these places, you ask somebody where it is now and they say, 'Oh, yes, I remember that place. It's not there any more.'

If you went out looking for it, or came upon it just driving around, there would be a highway sign saying this was once it. There might be a few houses, three or four, maybe, and that would be the only way you'd know something had been there. An elevator or two, but they'd have been moved away, or burned down. A general store, a café, maybe, a blacksmith shop, maybe a filling station, but there was nothing to hold them together. An elevator that is closed or burned down, that takes the life out of a place. I've seen it happen.

They close down a branch line and boom, you've lost three or four little places, bang, just like that. The highway is rerouted, and that's the end. The Depression killed off a lot of them. People just moved north or to B.C. and never came back, and bigger farmers just took over the land. Or even before, a long time ago when the first immigrants came in, a lot of places were started and then they found out they'd put the place in the wrong spot. Sometimes it was because there was no good water supply. Or maybe the land was no good and the homesteaders figured they'd bought wrong or been suckered by the CPR or the land companies, and they'd try it for a few years, no dice, no crops, and they'd pull up stakes. The farmers would be off to somewheres else, and the people in the town, you'd find them looking for a new town.

After the war, highways did it too. Everywhere on the Prairies they were building new highways. None of this zigzagging all over the place. They straightened out these roads and made them into highways and a little place would find itself three miles from the highway. Now that's no good. The place is dead right there and then. They are still there, but it's only because the people who are left are too stubborn to move, or they are old and can't move.

After the war, when wheat prices were good, everybody was buying cars and trucks. Why deal at a little garage or bulk plant or a general store where prices were high when forty miles down the highway there was a big town. Four or five stores, a liquor store, a hotel, a couple of good restaurants, a bowling alley, so for a bit more gas and half an hour's more time you were where you could buy good things and pay less. Stands to reason.

Times change. The hydro came in. That sure changed people's thinking. The better roads. The trucks. People thought if they could live kind of nicely in a tiny place, they could live more nicely and all that in a bigger place where there was more things to do.

People's minds changed too, you know. They started to think that they just weren't a bunch of farmers stuck out in the sticks. With television they could see what other places were like. They would still be farmers but that didn't mean they had to act like people thought farmers were–like they didn't have to go into town once a week, on Saturday night, and do all their shopping and visiting. They could go in and shop any day they wanted. Just get out on the highway and go. The man, he wants a machinery part right away. So off he goes. The woman, she wants her hair done for a party on Friday night, off she goes to that big town, like Melville or Swift Current or North Battleford. See what I mean?

The tiny place with its general store, it wasn't needed any more except for emergencies, like you run out of flour or sugar or coffee. All the big buying was done where the big markets, and then supermarkets, were going.

A lot of things other than that. The schools. They started closing down the one-roomers. Hundreds of them. Busing the kids to the consolidated schools. Like they'd have sixteen or so school buses. No more village schools. Inefficient and too expensive.

If they had a doctor, he'd leave. The bulk-oil dealer, he'd find he couldn't make a living because of the stuff being delivered by tankers. The village council found they didn't have enough money to do anything. The main street would still be gravel and not maintained. Just no money, and the young people leaving as soon as they could and the old people getting older. It went on and on.

I remember, there was this place north and west of here and it was a Saturday afternoon and my wife and I were just driving around. It was in bird season and I had the shotgun in the trunk and I thought I might see a few prairie chicken. You know, they're not around much any more, too. Well, we're just out and we stop at this little dump. I need gas, but before that I stop at the general store and there's nobody around. I holler and yell but nobody comes out. So I drive to the gas station and fill up and I tell the guy, 'Hey, like, you know there's nobody in the store. You think something's wrong?' He says no, just try again. He's out in the back or off on an errand, he's around somewhere. Just help yourself, he says.

I drive back and the same thing. So I can't wait forever so I take two Cokes and two chocolate bars and my wife and I, we finish them off in the car. I take the empties back in and nobody around so I leave the money on the counter with the bottles and the wrappers, just to show him what the money was for, and away we go.

I'm not sure that says everything about these wide spots in the road that used to be places where people lived, a farming community, but it goes a long way."

🐦 *Great Big Old Folks' Homes*

"Fly over here in a jet liner at night at 30,000 feet, on a clear, cold night. What do you see? All these tiny little patches of light. That's the towns and villages, spaced out just like the railway put them there. And over there, if you look where you're heading, that big glow in the sky. That's Edmonton.

Nobody want to stay in a little place like this any more. There's nothing here, not for the young people and the parents, but especially the young people. No jobs. No money. No fun. No movie. No bowling. No bars. Like you could say there's just one hell of a lot of nothing here for them. I don't blame them. If I was young I wouldn't be here.

This town, and really it isn't a town, it's a village. Anyone can see that. But we've got a lot of retired farmers and their wives, they get a house cheaply here and they're near their kids on the farm. They go out on Sundays, visit, walk around the old place, and help in harvest. They talk to each other. The store's a kind of social centre and there's the pub in the hotel. They talk pretty well about the things they talk about anywhere, but they also talk about the past.

When you look at it, these little villages are really great big old folks' homes. And that's good. This town won't die. We'll be here for a while yet, I figure, and we do give the essential services. Bread, milk, sausages, gas, oil, magazines, and they've got their warm little houses and the television and . . . Yes, I never thought about it that way before, but these villages are saving the government a lot of money. These are big old folk's homes and the government doesn't pay a cent, and we look after each other. The way it works, everybody gets by and everybody's happy and that's just fine."

🐦 Bright Lights, Big City

"I know farmers. This store, I see them all in here. I'm seeing the sons and daughters of the people my uncle saw sixty years ago when he started this store. But it was sure different then. I'll tell you why. See that street out there? It loops about two blocks down and goes over the tracks and then you're on the highway, and in an hour or so you're in Edmonton, the big city. It is as simple as that. An hour and a half and you're there, and you know what they have there? Everything that we haven't got here.

We don't even carry clothes any more. Just a few things. Jeans. Boots. Underwear. Shirts and a few sweaters and windbreakers. Doesn't pay us to keep inventory. I can stock everything in here that a supermarket has, but the only thing is, they stock twenty times more. I have two kinds of toothpaste, Macleans, because it's cheaper, and Pepsodent, because I think it's good. They stock ten different times that many.

You want a part for your car? Sure, you'll get spark plugs or a fan belt over at the garage, but you won't find those cheap brands of motor oil, and you won't find a full range of radials, and you won't find parts you need. Nobody's saying this is wrong. The way things are, you have to go for the best bargain.

I keep enough things on the shelves here and in the back, why, nobody would really have to go into the big city at all if it was just the basics you wanted. But no, that's not good enough. I don't keep asparagus. I don't keep Money's Mushrooms. Avocados? Whoever heard of people around here buying avocados fifteen years ago, but now some woman will come in and ask if I have them. Of course I tell her I don't. If she asks where she can get them, I point over west and say Edmonton.

What I'm saying is, this store is just for people coming in for something they've forgotten, or run out of, and they need it in a hurry. Like a four-dollar order and they're just passing through going home from Edmonton, and they've got about three hundred dollars of stuff piled in boxes and bags in their pickup.

Don't ask me if I mind. I do mind, but I'm not saying so. This is business, and you've got to be realistic. These little towns and villages, they're just what I call Oh-I-forgot-something towns. They stop in and buy that kind of stuff. Same with the garage. We've only got one now. This town once had six hundred people in it and it used to support three of them, what with the farmers being extra and passing traffic.

I can see it. I'm the last person to blame them, because on some days I just leave Mary in the store and the wife and I go to town too. There you see things happening. You can do some shopping, like going right through town to the West Edmonton Mall. Now I don't particularly like the place, but it is some place, you got to admit that. If you had your office there, you'd never have to leave it. I don't know how many hundreds of stores, and shops, and restaurants, and submarines, and Ferris wheels, and skating rinks. Jesus! You never seen such a place.

What I'm telling you is, a farmer or somebody from this town, when they go to the big city now, they may go for shopping, but they go to get entertained. I don't know what comes first, the entertainment and the eating and the gawking at all the things and people, or hunting for bargains and buying up the stores."

Farm Fashions

"It kills me. It really does. A woman or two of them, mother and daughter or daughter-in-law, they walk in and they're dressed to the nines. I mean really good clothes. Good material and well cut and they know how to wear these clothes, and what's more, they know what they want. I can tell. I've been selling clothes for a good many years.

They spend quite a while in this shop, and I'm darn sure they've been in others. This mall has dozens of good shops for women. I'd say you've got as good a selection here as you have in any city in Canada, and that would include Montreal and Toronto too.

Then in walks a guy, and he's dressed in a windbreaker or a parka and he's got one of those tractor hats, a John Deere or a Versatile, something like that, and he says, 'I knew I'd find you here, honey. See anything you like?' Something like that.

Sure they have. Oh, sure. They'd buy out the store if you gave them enough credit. They don't ask for discounts and maybe that's the tip-off, because a lot of Edmonton people do. No, the real tip-off is the husband wearing the Versatile tractor hat. They're farm people and they're in town to spend money. She plunks down a MasterCard or Visa or American Express and we always ask them to put down their phone number on the sales slip. Just store practice. It's always an out-of-town number and we have to look it up later.

It's Tofield or Olds or Rocky Mountain House or up in the Peace River Country. Farm folk. Lots of money. Credit-card passers, I call them. They're really nice people to deal with, very, very nice, and in a way they don't want you to know they're farm people. But what I'm getting at is, the wife on the farm is not the wife on the farm I remember when I came here twenty years ago. That's a long time, I'd say, in the way it affects these women. They've learned a lot and they're not milking cows and slopping pigs like I used to when my husband and I sold the farm and moved to Edmonton.

But the point is, these women still live on farms, and big ones at that, but you couldn't tell them from city women. Not the ones we get in this store. This is a top store, as you can see, but this is where they head to, and they know fashions and they know what they want. The only thing that gives them away at all is the husband in the windbreaker and the tractor hat. Funny, but it's true."

🕊 *Death and Taxes*

"You know why there are no undertakers in these small towns? It must be something in the air or the water they drink, but these people live forever. They're here to eternity, I've always said. The only way to kill them off is with a baseball bat and I don't know, they saw you coming at them with a bat and they'd likely whip out one of their own and give it to you. They're amazing.

Everybody in the city, they spend most of their lives trying to ignore the fact of death, that we're going to die. Women of 70 trying to look 55 and women of 55 doing their darnedest to look 40. Below that, everyone looks 25, so you see what I mean. People don't talk about it. It is one of those big no-no's. It doesn't happen. You read the obituary columns in the *Journal* to see if you're still alive and my God, everybody has passed away. They haven't died. They've 'passed away'. 'Gone to a greater reward'. 'Are in the arms of their Lord'. All this stuff.

These people out in the towns around about, and on the farms, they live forever. I think it is because they don't think of death. Old Billy Jones, he's ninety-six, and there he is out on the goddamned combine swathing away to beat hell, and his wife Nellie, there's good old Nellie, she's ninety-four, and she's baked six pies and ten loaves of bread and it's only ten in the morning. I'm not kidding.

Last year I was out west of Olds looking at some land for evaluation and when I get back to the car it won't start. Okay, I know as much about a Honda as a hoot owl does, so I am having a smoke and thinking I'll have to hike to the next farm and along comes this old pickup. It has a hundred things wrong with it from the sound of it, a rattletrap, but its motor seems good and it stops and this old geezer gets out. This guy, without a word of a lie, he looks to be about a hundred and ten. Well, he walks up to this neat little '84 job I've got and I've already got the hood up and he says, 'Give it a roll-over.' Zzzzzzzzzrrrr zzzzzz. About twice. He takes a pair of pliers out of his overalls and he farts around and says try it again. Zoom. I got me a car again.

He's a local guy and I could have spent an hour with him. Talk about an interesting old geezer. And you know what he was mad about that day? He was eighty-nine, yep, eighty-nine, and the authorities whoever they were wouldn't fix up his flying licence. Not his car licence, his *flying* licence. I asked him, how did he manage to get a licence in the first place at his age?

He said, oh, no, he didn't have a licence. He'd been flying for years in his son's plane and never had a licence. Then somebody reported him and he had to go in and face the music. They said he was too old. They wouldn't give him a licence. I asked him what he was going to do. He said he was just going to keep flying. To hell with them. He'd just keep flying around.

You and I know that death is the big reality. You can evade taxes but you can't evade death. When your number is up, then you cash in. Not these people. They won't quit. I admire them.

In the old days they used to slap together a box out of wood they could find in the yard and put the coffin on the back of a wagon and the whole family would head out to the graveyard. If there was no minister, then somebody would say a few words and down he'd go. Not any more. It's all fancy. Embalming. Make-up. Why, I didn't recognize my own father when I saw him in the casket in the chapel. Without a word of a lie. It wasn't my dad. That body in there was a stranger in a suit and shirt and wearing a tie. My father, I never saw him in anything but a sweater and a bit of stubble on his face and he was a good man and he died a good man. And then they fancied him up.

I think that's what these old people are trying to avoid – what their kids will do to them when they're gone. That's why even farm people are going for cremation. You get a little urn of ashes, that's all. They may not even be real ashes. You can't tell, but you go out and scatter them somewhere and that's fine with everybody.

I travel around a lot and I'll say this, the best old people I've ever met are in the towns and villages and on the farms. They've got zip. Pep. Life. A couple of drinks of whiskey turns them right up into high gear, but usually they don't need it anyway. They've had a tough life for sixty, maybe seventy years and now they're settling down to enjoy their second life. Let them. They get up in the morning and there's none of this goddamned pollution. There's no bashing fenders trying to get into the city and do a job an eighteen-year-old can do. There's no fighting life. They're just sitting back, relaxing and enjoying it.

I don't know about sex with some of these old boys and their biddies, but sometimes, you know, I'm with them and the talk gets maybe a bit raunchy and sometimes I think I see one of those sly looks pass between them. That's when I wonder."

❧ The Post Offices

"What's all this damned talk about cutting out rural post offices? I mean it. Been on the television news and in the paper – Canada Post wants to cut out all these tiny post offices. And I'm telling you here and now, I don't think there can be one Western MP that's for it. They know the score. It's these bastards from the big cities, small cities, big towns, and all from back East. Not here, not in the Maritimes, not these places. Oh, they say, we got to cut out these little post offices in the villages to save money. Shit! The post offices may be little, but one thing these bastards don't know is how important they are. They aren't paying their way, these guys say. Of course they aren't paying their way, but in this country we're being taxed to death already and we're not getting one damn thing for our dollars. Except the post office mail and the CBC radio and television, and some pretty sloppy police work, most of the time.

It ain't the taxes though. It's these little villages. Hell, half of them are just retirement homes for farmers who've come in off the farms. A store. A garage. The hotel, sometimes, and a bulk-gas place, and that's about it. And in these villages, maybe the post office is in the store. Take away the post office, a few hundred bucks every month for the store owner, and he says to hell with it. The post office was the only thing that was really keeping him going, the bit he got out of it, and people coming in for their mail and buying this and that, little things. So they take it away and soon you got a real estate sign on it, For Sale. Can't you see this?

So the store goes. Nobody in their right mind is going to buy into that kind of a lousy proposition, so the village doesn't have a store any more. It doesn't have a meeting-place where these old people can meet when they pick up their mail. They talk, they gossip, they make plans there, and then they go home to their little bungalows and watch TV or just look out the window and watch a pickup truck going down the road and they call out to the wife, 'Jack Henry, that's his truck that just went by.' See what I'm getting at?

No store, what do the people do? Go to Davidson, which sure isn't any great flaming hell, anyway, or get into their fancy duds and off to Saskatoon. All that damn traffic. Trying to figure out that nutty street system. They do this, sure, maybe twice a month. Doctor or dentist, a show, dinner, visiting kids or friends, that kind of thing. So finally they say, this place is no good, and they move into the bigger town or even into the city, and there's another couple lost from the village. Then one day, all that's left is the filling station and bulk plant and that's for the farmers anyway, so there is nothing for the seniors any more. Nothing but a little village filled with old people waiting to die, and not doing a very good job of it.

Believe me, this is a very sad story. Villages used to be the life of the country. Some got bigger and became towns, and some just stayed villages, and some just dried up and blew away, but I'll tell you this. It wasn't because they lost their post offices – never, never the post offices.

This is the tragedy of this country. Down East in Ottawa and Toronto they don't give a fiddler's bitch any more about the West. Or about the old people. But damn it all, it was these old people and the other people in the village, they were the ones – and I don't care if you're Scots or Ukrainian or Polish or Norwegian, Finn, American, Frenchman, or ring-tailed bobcat – they were the ones who built the West. Grew the wheat, and it was shipped east, and bought the manufactured things which kept the Ontario manufacturers living like kings and employing tens of thousands of workers. And it's those people who are going to be hurt, those old people in the villages sitting in the living-room of those little houses, waiting to pass on to their great rewards. Damn sure, they're not getting much of a reward here on earth – and here's Canada Post saying they'll take away the little they got left.

And mind you, I'm only talking about the Prairies. What about those little widenings in the road in the Maritimes? Back in the bush in B.C. or up north of here, or north of Lake Superior? They're all getting whacked just because some slick con man who is head of Canada Post and pulling down $130,000 a year, he says the post office can save money by hitting the old people, the people living in the bush far from everything. And the whole goddamned worst of it is this – I'll bet you ten dollars right here and now that he's never been in a village like that. His advisers have never been in a village and know how important the P.O. is to them. No, sitting back there in Ottawa looking at a bunch of figures and saying, okay, 150 post offices have to go, they don't realize they're dealing with the lives of people. Good people."

✎ *The Decline of the Towns*

"A storekeeper, and yes, the post office, and the gas-station operator, and maybe the hardware store, lumber yard, if you've got one – we're the ones who see the decline of the towns. We know business gets less and less. Stands to reason. I think that if I went down to Brandon and I bought cases and cases of certain things when they're selling them cheap, soaps and canned goods mainly, I could probably get them cheaper than I get them from the wholesaler in Winnipeg. I know that doesn't make sense but it works out that way. Out here in the boonies, everything costs more.

But it's all too late. The school kids come in and buy. Some old customers are loyal, and they come in and do business with me. And people come in a rush, buy some smokes and rush out, and they're the ones who just forgot to buy smokes in the big city and use me. It's hard to live on that."

❧ *City Living*

"I should say that a large number of local kids, even though they were in the big city, somehow they wound up marrying boys and girls they went to high school with, did the same things with when they were kids. I mean, all those other people in the city, and one day there would be a wedding in the United Church in the old home town. I know. I went to enough of them.

How does that song go? City living ain't no kind of living. Willie Nelson or somebody like that. There must have come a time when they looked around that duplex or little house on that street and they'd just come back from a weekend on the folks' farm and maybe they're both thinking. I mean something clicks between them. City life isn't all that it is supposed to be."

❧ *No Place to Go*

"People say to us, when you folks retire, are you going to move to town? Like that, move to town.

I say, why would anybody move to town? If you move to town, then you've got no place to go. You're there, in town. On the farm, I can say to Bill, let's go to town this afternoon, and after lunch we jump in the truck and we're in Barrhead in about twenty minutes. Then we can walk around and talk to people and we're doing something.

If you're living in town, then you're there. So what does in town mean? You want to go somewhere else. You go to Edmonton. To the West Edmonton Mall, some place like that.

Where we are, we'll have three acres cut off from the farm, the part our house is on, and the garage and sheds. The new owner doesn't want those buildings anyway. So we've got our home and garage and Bill's tools and workshop, and remember that old garden every woman on a farm had? Well, I'm going to have that back again. When you were farming big like us, that was just something you couldn't do. I'm going to have a big garden and maybe a dozen hens and kind of get back to the way it was. Bill is handy with tools and he'll find enough to keep busy.

Farmers before, you know, they didn't retire. They just kept going until they kind of dropped of old age and tiredness. Not us. I'm looking forward to it, living still on our place. And when people say to me, are you going to move into town, well, I just say, whatever for? Living in town just takes the fun out of going some place."

✎ Ever Lived in a City?

"Oh, we knew what we were doing, Bert and me. We'd thought about it for five years, maybe more. It was always in our mind that when we both got to be sixty-five we'd sell everything, pack up, go through that dinner they always throw for people who are leaving, and we'd get in the car and we'd be in Victoria in five days.

That's what we did, and we knew what we were going to do. Bert isn't the kind of husband just to jump in, and me, I've always been the slow and cautious kind too. I get it from my father. Bert gets it 'cause he was born that way.

Two years before, we'd gone for a month and taken one of those motels along the Gorge there, the kind that a kitchen comes with it, you see, and we had about three weeks, just to look it all over. It wasn't bad. I'd say it was good.

That month we'd visit friends from all over who'd moved to Victoria, and they'd say, come out. The weather's great. Flowers in March. No snow. Lots of rain, but we knew that because here we were in it most every day. Everybody said, you don't have to shovel it. There was a lot of this kind of talk.

One thing I noticed, and Bert and me think this is pretty important. There were people who became British Columbians, just like there were people who stayed Saskatchewanian. There was a difference, and I'll tell you what it was. The people who became British Columbians, they didn't dress like they did back home. More snappy, and with all those stores to choose from and the money some of them must have got with farmland selling for seven hundred dollars an acre and being on the pension, they could afford it. Then there were the others who stayed Saskatchewanians, and dressed like back in Swift Current, which was kind of being careful.

Then next summer was the time to get ready. We'd both been born in the same month of the same year and when we both got sixty-five we said okay, let's go. Donny didn't want to buy the farm and Tom was in Ottawa with the government and the girls were married in Regina, so we told the agent to go ahead, and we sold the 480 acres we had and didn't renew the five quarters we leased, and then there was the sale. I told the auctioneers to go ahead, mark everything, and that took quite a while because they had to send people over, but they did it, and the auction was in early November. No snow on the ground, and the women's auxiliary had a snack counter going, and in about four or five hours, there went everything.

I'd see something going, and I'd think, I've got to get that back, I've had that for forty years, it's like selling a family friend. But then I'd say, oh, it's just Daddy's old chair and we never used it. It would go for eleven dollars or fourteen dollars or something like that and I'd feel sorry about it. But it was done. Somebody else owned it now, with all the pipe-tobacco smoke in the leather, and I'll bet they tried to get that smell out. I never tried. That smell reminded me of Daddy so much.

Next morning we went to the lawyer's office and signed the final papers on the old home, and one quarter of that was what my daddy filed in 1913 when he was just a young lad out from England. Here, with one stroke of the pen, two seconds, it was not ours any more. But we had all that money.

The big going-away party was that night in the hall, and next morning we started out, our car and Donny and Marlene bringing our stuff in the truck. We stayed with Bob and Lil in Calgary for two nights, and Bob and Bert had more than a few drinks and Bob was telling Bert how to be a city man. Scrape your boots before you come in the house. Don't spit tobacco juice. Why, Bert never used chewing-tobacco ever after I married him. But things like that. All in fun.

So there we were in Victoria and living in the same motel, and the first of December we moved into an apartment. The Fairfield district, ten minutes from the Empress. We had the furniture and stuff we'd brought, the bedding, linens, the dishes, pans and things, and paintings, of course, and clothes, and Bert's guns, and our curling-stones. We went to the Goodwill and got some of the nicest furniture you'd ever want to see, very cheap.

Have you ever lived in a city? I mean, can you imagine us, both born on a farm, me never off it and Bert only for his army years, always farmers. Always. Walking out the kitchen door in the morning and there isn't a thing to be seen but one neighbour a mile away. And then – and this is where the problem was – in an apartment. Why the whole thing was only about twice as big as my kitchen. I mean it. I really do. And there was a man and wife, say, only one inch from you through the walls next door, but you might never get to know them. I just could not get over that. Not at all. And when you walked down the street and smiled and said 'Good morning' to people, just Bert going out for a little stroll or me going to the store, oh, sure, they'd smile back and say 'Good morning' but I think they thought we were crazy.

Why, half the people in Victoria are retired people from the Prairies. What got into them? They did it when they were home. Why not now? That sort of surprised us. It just didn't seem to make sense to me. Why was it me or Bert who always said 'Hello' or 'Good morning'? Why didn't they say it? Had they lost their friendliness?

We were lonely. Very lonely. We just sat in that living-room and watched that 26-inch television and all the foolish shows. The game shows. Those soaps. Those people, Bert says must be right off the rocket ship from Mars.

One day in April we heard a neighbour had complained to the manager that our truck was always parked in front of the place, and it looked awful, she said. I thought, well, a person can't even park their pickup in front of their own place. It was only two years old and clean, a nice red, and half the people in Victoria seemed to have pickups or RVs or something like that.

Bert and me talked it over and he said he wasn't going to sell that truck for nobody, and one thing led to another and another, and it was spring and Bert had been reading the *Western Producer*. Finally he said, 'Jane, we don't belong here. They don't even curl the way we do back home.' I said, 'What are we going to do?' and

I knew what I wanted. I wanted to go back home, get a little house with a big garden and some flowers in town, a little place, but I didn't say that. Bert did the thinking in our family. I just pushed him a bit.

He said we were going home. Victoria was no good.

My heart just about jumped out of my skin. Oh, I was so happy, I jumped up and hugged him and I said, let's celebrate. Phone Donny. Phone Lil. Phone the real estate agent in Swift Current. Get him to send out a list of the places for sale, little house, a big garden. Phone the manager tomorrow and tell him we're leaving and tell him, oh, yes, tell him to tell that person she'll not see our pickup around much more.

That was about the middle of April, and the first of June, on the dot, we were back home in Swift Current, and everybody was saying why did you and Bert leave Victoria? All I said was that it was a nice city and yés, the weather was really nice, but it was not the city where we wanted to live.

You never saw two happier people. The first morning after we moved in and I was in the kitchen making breakfast, Bert came in from outside and he said, 'Do you know what time it is?' It was six-thirty, and I laughed. Then I knew we were back home. In Victoria sometimes we wouldn't get up until nine in the morning. Nothing to do. Why get up, eh? Why? Now we had lots to do, but it wasn't that. We were home, and when we were on the farm, in summer I'd be up at five-thirty, so we were kind of sleeping in, but we weren't. But we had something to do now. Boy, did we ever. Lots of things. Park your truck anywhere."

🐦 *The Cemetery*

"The reason I'm still in Shaunavon, I'm eighty-two, you know, is because the cemetery is here with all my kinfolk in it, including my husband and a boy and a girl. Everybody has gone that I know of, all my family, off to the Coast and Regina and, well, they just seem to be all over the place. I guess it would be best for me to move to Regina where my two girls are, but no.

I like this little town. I like the wind. I like the blue sky. It always seems to be a nice day here, and I walk downtown every day. There's still a few old faces and I do a little bit of shopping. If I need something for tomorrow, I don't buy it today. You know why? Then I wouldn't have anything to do tomorrow, although, of course, there's always the mail, but that doesn't count. Doing something, that means to me that you go into a store and you chat with the owner about things and then you buy something and she wraps it up and you take it home, and that way you've done your day's shopping.

But I guess the reason I stay is the cemetery. I walk out there twice a week when it's a good day. Sometimes I walk there when it's not a nice day. It doesn't matter to me. One day or another, they all seem the same to me.

This is a good little town. I like it here. I like the friends I have. And besides, the big thing, the cemetery is here."

Farmers

🐦

One farmer told me, "Why am I doing this? Because I like it. I could have left home at seventeen like some of them did, gone up to Calgary, worked around, but you know, a lot of them that did, you'd see them in town a year or two later and you'd ask and they'd say, 'Oh, thought I'd come back.'"

That doesn't tell the whole story, but no farmer is working from dawn to dusk, good years, dry years, if he doesn't like what he is doing. Nor do his sons, or his daughters who marry farmers, or work and live in town so they'll be close to "the folks". Farmers are special, in ways that I hope this chapter makes clear. Even the people who don't like them are worth a hearing. A farmer would tell you they're just jealous of his independence.

🐦 **The Boss**

"You're the boss. If you want to plant fifty acres of cotton when everybody else including the experts at the experimental farm are telling you to plant wheat, you can do it. If you want to go into pigs when everybody is making big money shipping canola, then you can do it. If you want to go down to Waterton for a week just when it's time to do your swathing, then you can do it. Everybody can tell you you're crazy, but if you want to do it, then you can. Your own boss. You've got independence, and I think that's what farming is all about. This dryland farming always has been a gamble in the South Country, so why shouldn't you be a gambler?

When Tom and I were farming and there was another spring and he'd be going out for the first day of seeding he'd say, 'Well, Janet, it's between me and God from now on.'"

❧ *A Tough Bird*

"The whole works is going down the tube, they say, these agricultural economists up in Edmonton and in the Department of Agriculture. Down the tube. Up the spout. No hope. All is lost. Goodbye. So long, Mr. Farmer.

That's what they say, and I don't believe it. The prairie farmer is a tough bird, tougher than you think. He could be lying on the ground and you're standing over him with a twelve-pound splitting-maul and you couldn't kill him. That's the way I think. He's been around too long and he's survived everything the weather and nature and God has ever thrown at him, and he's also survived about a hundred years of those absolute grade A brainless ninnies who get the top jobs in government. That is the scandal of the '80s. The mismanagement of this country's economy, the mismanagement of the farmer and how he works with his markets. The absolute devilishness of the banks, and that is the unknown scandal of the past five years.

Everybody blames the farmer. The farmer is the least to blame. Blame the government, their experts, their economists. Blame the banks. So leave the farmer alone. He's doing the best he can under times that would try a saint, and he'll survive in spite of the government boys and the bank managers. Mark my words. It won't be the same kind of country in another ten years, but the farmer will still be farming."

❧ *Worthy of His Hire*

"A buck for barley, and $2.60 for our export wheat, with quotas on it, I can't grow it for that, but I'm goddamned if I summerfallow this spring and watch the damned soil blow away. I'll plant, by God I'll seed just as much as I ever did, but this time I'm not selling her, not one bit.

You can't do business with anybody when the farmers down there in Nebraska and Iowa are getting $5.80, that's Canadian funds, right at the farm gate for their wheat. Not on your bloody life.

I'll try a few experiments, like putting on less fertilizer and a few other things, but I'm going to seed as much as last year and I've got enough bins on this place that I'll fill up. Then I'll wait. There will be money in those bins, that's a good thought. Just depends when I sell it, or if I can, and if I can get the right price. But I'm not giving it away. Not on your life, by God. I'm a farmer, and they say, every man is worthy of his hire. So is the farmer.

The wife and I will tough it out. I've been in this business thirty-five long years, more than enough to see good times and bad times. We've had drought before, and low prices and that wheat glut of '69, and we've always come out. We've still got the land, I own nine quarters of it free and clear. Better than a lot around here. And we haven't had to go to the bank yet. Next year that's a possibility. Not this year.

I'm not an economist. Thank God. I think they know less than we do about these things. But I'll be goddamned if I'll sell a bushel of barley for a buck and wheat for $2.60. It costs me more than that to produce it. There's no money in farming right now, but you'll see it turn around. It always does. Something will happen."

❧ *Hang in There and Hope*

"So you ask, why don't they get out of farming? Well, I guess some will. I can hang on, me and Margie and young Willy. Tighten the belt. Bite the bullet. Hang in there and hope. But I won't get out of farming, and why should I? It's my life. Always has been and always will be. What can a 59-year-old man do if he's been farming since he was a kid and it's his life? Nothing. That's what. I got all the skills of the farm and a lot of common sense and a sense of humour, but what good does that do me if I go into Lethbridge or Calgary and look for a job? First, my age. Number two, I don't know anything but farming this land. I got to stay. It's our life. As long as we're on this land I'm gonna farm it, and if I lose money every year, well, let me put it this way. This is our home. We'll always have a roof over our heads. I hope."

🐦 *Everything to Grass*

"You see, we've lost our markets. A lot of people just don't realize it yet, but they're gone, and when they come back, that's anybody's guess. The markets we've had for years, they just aren't there any more. The Americans and the Europeans have killed us off. There is no way Canada can match the subsidies those countries are paying their wheat farmers, and they never will.

So I decided, this spring I'm going to plant grass. Everything to grass. I'm going to go to the agricultural agent and find out the best and I'm just going to let it grow. All around us, there is going to be a sea of grass. Tall and waving in the wind. I'm not going to keep cattle or any of that. Putting fences in, too expensive. Nope, just waving grass all around, and when fall comes I'm going to burn it. Enrich the soil. Put nature's own nitrogen back into it.

That's what I'm going to do. For once, once in a long time, I'm not going to be worrying about a crop or prices or a darned thing. I'll just have that big sea of green grass, growing and looking good, and I'll just sit here and wait and see what the world is going to do."

🐦 *Poor to Worse*

"If the government is against you, you can hang in there long enough and beat them. You'll come out ahead somehow. The Toronto bankers, they'll try and wreck you, but keep slugging, get everybody else in the West to keep slugging away, and eventually things will even up. Maybe you won't come out ahead, but you'll come up even. That's all you can ask.

But the weather. Five good years, maybe, and then it hits you. It may not be hail. But it will be drought, that will come, and you can bet everything on that. Everything. There will come drought.

Or rain. Some years you go to church and pray for rain. Then there are years like last year. Take my brother. He's farming out there west of Edmonton, just north of Devon. A big place, good house, white-painted fence around the yard, a couple of palominos in the stable, and he's doing just fine.

Last August I'm out there visiting him and he's got the damnedest finest crop you ever did see. I mean, I don't think I've ever seen better in all my years, and for a week he and I are just jacking around getting his equipment in shape, and you know what? On August 30 he says, well, tomorrow we start. He's had some good pay-outs, but this is going to be a dandy, even if the price of delivery wheat isn't too great shakes. Next morning they're out there, and by noon it's raining. I mean raining. Why shit, this rain even made the papers in Toronto, because it just kept going, and I'm thinking, that poor bastard. A couple of times I phone him and yep, rain, a couple of days of drying, and then rain again.

So there you have it. Right through the duck-hunting season, into the moose and deer season, and he's still trying to clear that 3,000 acres of crop. He finally gets it in, October 16. It's not worth a thing then. The wheat dropped down two grades, down to pig feed, and the price, of course, the French and the Americans are making sure the price is dropping, and so what does a poor bastard do?

I phone him and he doesn't sound any different than he ever does. How was it, I ask? Poor to worse, is what he says. So I ask him what he's going to do about it. He laughs. I expect to get an answer that he's going to organize a protest against God and all his evil works, or maybe lead a march down to Washington and start banging heads. Not old Carl. Not that brother of mine.

You know what he says? Thinks that he and his wife will crank up the motor home and take off for Arizona or San Diego and get some sun for a couple of months. Now, when you look at it his way, that's the best thing to do. What in hell is the use of worrying? He can't do a darn thing about it. Nobody can. So go off to Arizona and sit around some trailer park and talk with a bunch of other farmers.

In my business here, if the same sort of thing happened, I'd be thinking of the least painful way to commit suicide. No, old Carl, he goes down to Arizona and sits around with a bunch of other prairie farmers and drinks beer and figures next year will be better."

❧ *Hooked on Fertilizers*

"These fertilizer companies make this product with the fancy names and numbers and then they send their field reps around and they can talk the hind leg off a mule, and then there is this big advertisement in the *Western Producer* or the *Leader-Post* and they got these big plants everywhere and they're just churning out the stuff. And you might say that these companies are standing to make more money in profits than the farmer on his grain. They don't take the risk. They just advertise it, and when they've got everybody brainwashed, they sell it and sell it, and when that batch of their fertilizer doesn't work no more, then they announce with a big hurray that they've got a bigger and better one. By golly, down the road their competitor has suddenly found a bigger and better one, and the poor darned farmer, he's in up to his neck.

Now, you read all the time about these heroin and cocaine people and how they're dying and how they are hooked on these drugs. I am going to tell you that I think the prairie farmer is hooked on fertilizers. And the way I understand it, when somebody gets hooked, then it is bad. I say the farmer is hooked on this fertilizer stuff."

❧ *The World's Toughest Critter*

"When we drive down from St. Albert to Pine Lake where my sister has a cottage, we pass the lovely farms. Houses better than half you see in the city. Not that they haven't got a right to them. I know they do. They work hard. And everything manicured and silver storage bins for grain, all in a row, and sheds for their machinery and equipment, and not a bossy cow in sight. Not for years.

When you visit these farms, and I do, loads of relatives everywhere, you see an aerial photograph of their farm. Some outfit goes around taking them and sells them to the farmer all framed. Let me tell you, those farms are something to see. You can see the farmer of today has changed completely. Not a pig sty in sight.

Quite frankly, after what we see going to the lake and visiting around, I honestly do not believe that these farmers are having such a bad time. Oh, I know, things are tougher, but don't you realize that the life has never been smooth. It always had its ups and downs. Either too much or too little. That is what agriculture is all about. The prairie farmer is always going bankrupt, after a few years of prosperity. That's the way the system works. Ask any farmer. Go ahead, and he'll tell you the same thing. Good times never last forever. And once you've hit the bottom, which we've done, things do get better. Five or six years from now, you know what? All this will be a memory.

The world's toughest critter is the farmer. That's the toughest job, and the next worst job is to be a coal miner. I know, I've done both. And you have some things on the credit side of your ledger that is not taken into account. The prairie farmer's experience. His skill. His courage, yes, and that other factor too. His optimism. The old bit, tomorrow will be better. He really believes that. And there's another factor in there which is as important as any. His wife, the woman who stands behind him, stands at his side, and often stands in front of him, protecting him when times get tough. Don't ever forget the farmer's wife. By God, no. She's the Plus X Factor."

✑ *Business in a Small Town*

"They come in here, guys I've known for a long time, ever since I set up my shop and they brought their welding to me and I always fixed them up and they paid me. And now they come in here with something to be done and they say, 'Johnny, could you put this on the book for six weeks. I've got a payment coming up and I'll get to you then.'

These poor guys, these guys who used to spend money like water, they can't even pay a sixty-seven-dollar repair bill on a piece of combine or rod-weeder. I know it's crazy. They're sitting out there on 2,500 acres of good land and a nice bungalow and a 28-inch TV in the living-room and $450,000 worth of machinery sitting in the yard and they are broke. I mean B-R-O-K-E. Yeah!

I say, 'Sure, Jim, Joe, Bill, sure, I understand, but please don't leave it until too late.' I tell them I got bills to pay, too. 'Sure,' they say, 'Johnny, you're the top of my list.' I think, Oh Jesus! He's got a list. How many on it?

This is the way you do business in a small town. You got to play along, hoping they'll remember you when the right time comes around. You shouldn't do it, but if you demand cash, they're gone down the road, and poor-mouth you, yeah, saying you're a skin-flint, a money-grabber.

I've watched them. They're driving these big pickups or the

wife's Bronco and they pull out of here, go down to the bakery, turn right, and I can look up the street and watch them come down the street and pull in at the hotel. They can be in there three hours, drinking whiskey sours or rye and water, no matter, and bullshitting a mile a minute, and then they pile into their vehicles and drive home. Hell, the money they spent in there in that time, that would pay one-third of the welding bill I just done for them. But no, booze and belly comes first. Poor but honest town mechanic comes second, and last. Huh!"

🐦 *Take the Farmer*

"Let's look at a farmer with, say, a thousand acres, just to keep it as simple as possible. Say $500 an acre, what the land's worth. You're looking at half a million worth of land that fellow would be farming. Take in his equipment and you have got to have another $200,000, the very least, and I'm being conservative, seeing as how a combine can set you back $120,000, and nobody has old ones in this district. Everything else he's got, truck and pickup, tools and buildings and house, and you're looking at another nice round figure. Say $100,000, being conservative.

Okay, add that up and it comes to $800,000, and we're not taking into account how much he owes the bank. Just that he can look around every morning and there's $800,000 staring him in the face, and mind you, I'm talking about the little guys. Section and a half.

Then go down the road to the city, or take Winnipeg or Edmonton if you want. It doesn't matter. You show me many people in the city who have $800,000 on the books. You'll have to look around. They all work at jobs there. House, maybe $125,000 and that would be a pretty fair one. What else does the city fellow have? Not much. A car. Three years old, $5,000 if it's in good shape. Maybe a cottage at some lake. Another $25,000, at most. Some RRSPs, but the farm guy could have them too. Darn little savings, I'll bet. Remember, all he's got is wages. Okay, let's be generous and the guy in Saskatoon, he's looking at $200,000, and the only hope he's got is his job and a pension at the end of it, and that's a long way away.

So, you're looking at two guys, a farmer at thirty-five with $800,000 and, if things turn upward, the chance to make an awful lot of money if he can hang on and retire with a couple of million dollars. That isn't unreasonable at all, if he can hang on for three or four years in this tough time. The city guy, he plugs along, two-per-cent raise this year, three-per-cent next year, and the same dull job. How many fellows working for a company like their jobs? I don't know, but I'll warrant not many do. In another ten years they'll maybe pay off that huge mortgage and that will give them breathing-space, but now, for that city guy, it is grind, grind, grind.

I think I'll take the farmer every time. It's a good life, and if he's smart he'll get through this mess. He can control his spending better than the Saskatoon or Winnipeg fellow, and if times get better, his land value goes way up. We hope it will. Your city worker, there he is in that machine shop, or factory, or office, working for the government, and he's got no control much over what's going to happen ten years down the road.

The young fellow farming, he has. From the day he buys his first half section, the young farmer is his own man. Lives or dies on his own decisions, and he's independent. He's a businessman, and that's something we often forget, but this man, the farmer, he has just one hell of a lot more going for him than most people think.

I wouldn't pity the young farmer, and most of the older ones are sitting mighty pretty. They own their land, and that's a mighty big bank account just waiting to be cashed in. No, farmers do a lot of moaning and groaning but I wouldn't count them out, not by a long shot, and I wouldn't worry too much about them. They'll do okay."

🕊 *Too Many Farmers*

"There are farmers I know who still think they are God's Chosen People, like in the Bible. Anybody who tills the soil is saintly. Sweat off the ploughman's brow is the only honest sweat in the world. The farm is the heavenly vineyard of the Bible.

That's a load of B.S. The farmer today, unless he thinks of himself as a businessman first and then a tiller of the soil in God's chosen vineyard, then he is a damn fool. And if he thinks of himself as a businessman, and he should, damn it all, let him ask himself what other businessmen would go on producing a product – wheat, barley–for which there is no market. For which there is no profitable return if he can sell it.

The problem, too many farmers. Too many small ones, too many old ones and too damn many inefficient ones. Get them off the land. If the town of Hannah had five big grocery stores and it could only support three, then two would go belly-up. That's the laws of business. But farmers don't seem to think the laws of business apply, and sometimes the government doesn't either.

The tear-jerkers say, 'Oh, but you would be destroying a way of life.' I say, B.S. What's the difference in the lifestyle of a farmer who sows wheat and harvests it, and a worker in a factory in Edmonton who builds washing-machines? Nothing, except the Edmonton guy puts in about two hundred days a year working eight to five. The farmer works about thirty-eight days a year, or so the government statistics say. There's no lifestyle involved any more. That began to go out after the last war, and by the time they brought the hydro in, it was gone.

I'll put it this way. If you pulled or yanked or led or bribed or dragged every lousy or inefficient or too old or too young farmer off the land, and their families, too, resettled them in the towns and cities, retrained them, and found them jobs, you wouldn't use up half the money the governments are spending right now on artificial prices, marketing boards, quotas, advertising, etcetera, etcetera, and on and bloody on. Just to keep the farm community afloat, with a lot of small and inefficient and over-bought farmers paying whopping big interest and slowly dying inside, day by day.

I wonder, has the government ever sat down and asked itself, why don't we ask the Western Canadian farmers if they want to pack it in? Give them a package deal which will let them get out with some bucks. Start all over again. They never thought of that. They never will. You know why? Votes. Bloody votes. How do you know but maybe the farmers just might jump at it."

🌸 *This Thing About the Farm*

"Now you take these farmers. They have none of these problems, the ones that give a businessman ulcers galore and make life miserable. First, they have no competition. Every farmer from Rocky

Mountain House over to east of Winnipeg, the whole darn Prairies and parkland, they sell to the same buyer, the wheat board, and they get the same price depending on grade. They don't have a union except their wives and kids, and their factory isn't going to burn down, and they don't have to advertise and never will.

There's no point worrying about prices, or what he can do about them, because he has no control over prices or the weather. He just goes along and keeps a smile plastered on his face. He's a businessman too, but he doesn't have all these worries.

I'm not too worried or concerned about these farmers, and their whining and moaning goes in one ear and out the other. I've heard it all before, I'll hear it all again. They always survive somewhere, somehow. The guy I'd be worrying about is the guys in the city and the bigger towns, but you never hear about them and the hard times they'd had to survive because the farmer has been having hard times. I'd say the small businessman is the forgotten warrior in all this, and that's too bad. He's just as important as the farm population. In fact, a lot more. The small businessman, manufacturer, dealer, he's the guy who does the hiring and selling and keeps a lot of these big towns and little cities going. They're the ones the government should be thinking about.

But you know what? It's this thing we've got about the farm. As though it was the most important thing in Canada. Wipe out every grain farm tomorrow and this country wouldn't starve. But we've got this thing about farms. Our parents, one of them, or our grandfather, almost for sure, came over to this country and hacked a farm out of the prairie or the bush. With his own little axe and plough, and two horses named Jack and Jill. The old story. A bit of the farm history is in all of us, so when we think of the Good Old Days it usually is about the farm. That's city people, I mean. So, whenever you get a situation like we've had the past few years, there always is a huge amount of sympathy. Oh, the poor farmer.

First, the farmer is not poor. Compared to the city man he is wealthy, in land. Second, I wonder if the farm is that important. Gosh, do you know that the state of Iowa grows more wheat than Canada? One U.S. state. The French grow more wheat. Wheat is only so important in this country because we've always been used to exporting so much. We've come to depend on wheat exports and the jobs at the Lakehead and Vancouver and on the railroads, the jobs that go with exporting wheat and barley.

It doesn't matter what anybody says or thinks. This financial business with the farmers will pass away and there will be good times. I've seen it before, the Depression and the late sixties and other times. Then it will come again. It always does. Don't worry, I say. Just sit back and puff your big cigar and relax. Nothing can be done about it. Everything takes care of itself. The world will go on."

🕊 *The Biggest Gamble in the World*

"A young fellow from our district, he went to the U. of A. and got his engineering degree and took a bunch of courses for two years at the Colorado School of Mines and then he worked in the office of a big company, Shell, I think it was, and was sitting pretty. A big salary and a wife and two little kiddies, and about ten years ago they sent him off to Saudi Arabia. Now, that was something, he told us. A huge salary, more than he ever thought he'd ever earn in Alberta, and a free house and a free car and free this and that and no income tax and he was just raking in the money.

Then, I guess it was five years or so ago, he got this hankering to get into farming, because, after all, he was a farm boy. He had all this money and he bought two sections, and remember, this was when land was high. His name was Allan, and I guess like everybody he just thought the good times would last forever. Well, he was able to put a good down payment on the land and the rest he got from the banks. I'd say it must have been half a million. Now just think about that. Half a million.

It was okay for a couple of years. He got good crops. Actually, you know, he was a good farmer. He had the farming brains he got from his dad, and he looked after things and paid off his payments every month on his land and his equipment and such, and they were doing pretty well.

Then, well, you know what happened. Two years in a row, down in this South Country, it hit us. No rain. The drought. The first year it was bad and the second time it was worse, and that was it for him and his family.

So, the same old story. The banks, boy were they glad to lend him the money when he bought the place. Now it was a different story. The bank sent their big shot down from Calgary to use the hammer on him. Oh, sure, they gave him every chance. You know how they do it. Figuring out ways to keep him afloat, and still it was only getting him deeper and deeper. There was nothing he could do. He couldn't borrow any more. Not a red cent. He couldn't pay on his mortgages and interest.

That's all there was to it. They took back the land. Gone. Everything gone. No point even fighting it. No one knew if we wouldn't have a third year of drought and his interest was just piling up and piling up and his equipment, it was four years old by then and it would go for a song. You know auctions. They are killers.

So there he was. A nice wife and two cute little kids. They're back in Calgary now and I don't know if he's even got a job. Probably not, the way things are. He works his heart out in the desert over there and then boom, everything he worked for for years and years is gone. Just like that. You read these statistics in the paper about the farmers who've been sold out. Well, that young fellow, he's one of them.

You can farm, and do everything right. The only thing you can't figure out is whether old Mother Nature is going to be on your side. You've got to figure she will be, but a lot of times, well, she just ain't.

He didn't take one thing into account, a thing that every farmer learns after a lot of years. He'd been lucky all his life. A good family, good student, good athlete, gone to university, and got this real good job way over there. None of that taught him the one big thing. He didn't understand that farming is the biggest gamble in the world. There is just no predicting Mother Nature. She's for you for about two or three years, and then she's against you. That's about the average. When she's against you, well, there's not a darned thing you can do about it."

🐦 *The Original 4-H Kid*

"When I was nine years old I was a gangly kid and so I could reach the pedals on the half-ton. And I was going all over the place for my dad, running errands to the neighbours and stuff like that, and I'd take the back road into Shoal Lake to get things and the Mounties never caught me once. I was twelve when Dad was driving the big tractor and I was driving the smaller one, and so I was doing a hired man's work, and that's not too out of line. I know lots of kids at school who did it.

There's a lot I don't know, the complicated things, but if Mom and Dad went off to Winnipeg to a funeral for two days, why, no problem, you'd see me running this place just fine. Just give me a list, here's what to do, and I'd do it.

When I graduate I think I'll go to Red River College for a year just to see what it's like, you know, and have some fun, stay with relatives we have in Winnipeg and just see how things are. But I'll be back. There'll be no problem with that, far as I'm concerned. I'm the original 4-H kid. I like the farm, and the girl I'm going to marry, she comes from a farm hear Newdale and she likes farm living, so in two years we're going to get married. Her father won't let her marry until she's eighteen. I'll be nineteen then, just right.

Maybe I'll have a farm some day. Not now. There's no way anybody can start farming today and hope to win. My dad's a winner, but he's been at it for forty-four years, since he was born. I'll just work along with him and we'll get a double-wide and park it in the yard and hook it up. That's the way I see it. Taking over the farm some day, getting married and having kids. It's the way she and I want to do it."

His Own Man

"Fifteen years ago when I was just a kid, fourteen, fifteen or so, I knew I was going to be a farmer, and my dad and mom would move to a little house in Gladstone or Minnedosa or even Winnipeg and I'd take over. Now I'm all grown up and been through Aggie at the University of Manitoba and I've worked with my dad for five years and been on my own for nine, and I know I'm never going to own my own place. It just is not possible. Dad is still a bit young to retire, but when he does he's got to sell to someone with cash, because they've got to buy that house in Gladstone, or build one, or, if they move to Winnipeg, pay $75,000 or so for a house. The rest will be interest they'll need to live on.

So unless Dad dies, the family farm will be gone, and that's a fact of life. You know it has to be this way. Your parents come first in their old age, they've worked hard and had tough times, but it is hard to believe.

So, all I can do is rent and farm, or lease and farm, and that way I'm actually working for somebody else. I'm prepared to do it because I just like farming. It's born and bred in me, but I know I'm really not farming.

A young fellow like me, twenty-nine, married and two little guys, there is no way he can get a farm. He can, if he wants to go into a huge debt and can find a banker stupid enough to bank him, but that's not the way. You're crippling yourself that way, even before you start. The little guy, the farm kid who grew up hoping to be his own man, that's gone now. All gone. The big buck has caught up to us, and it's all over."

The Best Crop

"Farming is a wonderful life if you forget the hundred and one things that are wrong with it, and what can go wrong, but it is an absolutely crazy way to make a living. I have farmers come into this office every week of the year and I explain a lot of this to them, and they know. Your average prairie farmer is not a stupid man. He'll look at me and maybe he'll grin and I know what he's going to say. He'll say, 'I know. Don't think I don't know that. But what else can I do?'

That's it in a nutshell. So, I guess the only answer is subsidies, billions of dollars of them, to keep them on the farm. You're preserving a pretty darn good way of life there. One, I believe, that's as important to the stability of Canada and its own good and welfare as any I can think of. Keep the family farm. Fight for it. Protect it all you can. I'm pretty bullish on the family farm for what it produces, and I don't mean grain. I mean people.

Good people. Important people."

One Flaw

"I've got a husband who is the finest man in captivity, the best that God ever made. He's kind and caring and loving and faithful and he's got a wonderful sense of humour. He has just one thing wrong with him. He's a farmer."

Ten

Oil!

🐦

*You Really Want Oil? ... American Over Canadian ... Oil Rich? ...
Thousands of Jobs ... Ambition ... The Seismo Guys ... One Hell of a
Fight ... Drill Mud ... No Future ... Easy Come, Easy Go ... One
Street ... Excuse Me, Sir ... This Malarkey About Oil*

*On a cold and grey February afternoon in 1947, Imperial Oil brought in the
Leduc Number One well southwest of Edmonton, marking the end of 133 dry
holes the company had drilled since it began operations in the province in 1914.*

*February 13, 1947, is a day every Canadian should know, for it changed the
ebb and flow of economics in Canada and made Alberta a true power in the
nation. And yet, amazingly, a former president of Imperial Oil told me Leduc
Number One was a fluke, a dart thrown at a board; if it had failed, come in
dry, the company would have suspended operations. The great Devonian Reef
had been found, and Alberta (and later Saskatchewan) became the happy hunting-ground for the world's major companies. New discoveries followed, year
by year. It seemed that almost anyone could find oil in those heady days.*

*The province's Social Credit government virtually turned the oil exploration
over to the world's major companies. In turn, they extracted the royalty benefits
that built a far-flung network of new highways, schools, community colleges,
universities, and hospitals, and made Alberta a rich province, a role it had not
expected.*

*It had its effect on all Albertans, plus the tens of thousands who poured in.
Hundreds of Albertans prospered with small businesses associated with oil.
Small independent Alberta firms sprang up and grew into robust companies.
Thousands of new jobs were created. It was Boom Town, but wisely managed.*

*And the people who participated have their stories to tell, about those days,
and about the ups and downs of the Oil Patch since.*

🐦 You Really Want Oil?

"The rest of Canada when they think of Alberta, the thing they
think of is oil. Filthy rich. The same way, when they think of

Edmonton, they think of Wayne Gretzky. It's not really that way
at all. Sure, there have been billions made out of oil, but Alberta
really is the same as it always was. Farming, the livestock industry,
towns and cities, and over there we've got the mountains and Banff
and Jasper. But when you really get down to the nuts and bolts of
it, the ordinary Joe hasn't done all that well out of oil.

Listen, when Leduc Number One blew in, and that was February
in 1947, most people said, well, they've finally found oil. We had
it in Turner Valley for years, boom times sometimes, but the Leduc
discovery well didn't change things all that much. I was a kid of
twenty working on this very farm, which was my dad's place, and
I never thought it would affect me. And it didn't.

Now look back. The Social Crediters were in power and Premier
Manning was running the show. Old Ernie, he was a smart cookie
and he had the good sense to get in some good advisers. Americans,
a lot of them were, but that was the only place he could find them.
We knew sweet nothing all about oil.

Manning found out pretty soon that this was going to be more
than just the Leduc field, and his advisers, the Americans, told him
that an awful lot of money was involved in the oil industry. Oil is
no damn good to you if you haven't got refineries, and the products
are no good to you if you can't get them to markets that sell it,
and we just didn't have the money to do all this.

Who had it? Guess? Well, that money was down south, just where
all the expertise was. So because Manning wanted steady upward
progress, the money poured in, from the south, naturally, and then
it went flowing out. That was his oil policy. It was right at the
time, I suppose, although you have a lot of criticism of it now. But
by about 1954, around there, he'd handed over the province to the
huge multinational oil companies. Gulf, Shell, Exxon, all those.
They wound up owning, leasing, controlling, you name it, about
seventy-five per cent of the oil and natural-gas resources of this
province. Just these six companies. I guess you could call it the
biggest give-away of natural resources in the history of the modern
world.

But as I say this, I also say that this was the way it had to be
done. Then, only these huge companies could handle the job. It
was a total denial of the principles of free enterprise – and that's
funny, because Albertans think they are Number One in the free-
enterprise business in Canada. But that's what it amounted to, in
the long run. Definitely.

There were no Alberta resource companies which could handle these huge projects, so the big fellows moved in, got the leases, buttered up the Socred politicians, did the survey work, drilled, brought in the wells, all of it. They built the refineries and helped finance the pipelines and built the petrochemical plants and everything.

I think it is safe to say that the Big Six, as they are called, that they pretty well owned the province. They called all the shots, and the government pulled the levers for them. I'd say it was the only way it could work. Remember these two things: Alberta or Canadian free enterprise just didn't have the know-how to do all this, and the government didn't either. Manning preferred to let the heavies do it, and he'd sit back and rake in those billions of royalties. That way, to a certain degree, he could control production and supply and price and royalties and the money would just roll in. And he'd spend it.

That's where we came into it. We, being us, the citizens of Alberta. We got new highways. A whole new school system, and the hydro into every cabin in the country. We got new universities and colleges. Little towns became small cities – and just look at Calgary! I remember when the Palliser was it, that was the be-all and end-all of Calgary. Now look, it's just an itty-bitty hotel down there by the CPR tracks. Same with Edmonton. It took longer, but there's a city that people don't take for granted any more. And all because of oil.

Oh yes, oil transformed Alberta. But look, when was the last time you flew from east to west coming into Edmonton or Calgary? On a clear night. Look down. What you see is what was there before. Farms. Every one of those little dots of light is a big yard light. Farms used to be a section, and now they average about three sections, usually, but there they are down there. Dozens you can see, way to the horizon. And the villages, the towns, the little cities, there they are all aglow, and you know there are people down there who have had nothing to do with oil. Some of their kids are involved in oil, but the farms, they still are there. Grain, cattle, hogs, year after year. It never ends.

There's only oil in places. We've had crews come into this part of the country and everybody gets all excited, but nothing. I say, you really want oil? What about the rights? You don't own them. After the Depression and the hard times of the twenties and before that, very few farmers wound up with pure oil rights. I mean, damn few farmers got rich. Personally, I can't think of more than four, and they're not around here.

I say, you want oil? You'll get money, but you'll have those nodding-horse wells all over your place. Trucks coming in, going out, upset, and there still won't be that much. Because, naturally, all of it goes to the oil companies, the refineries, the pipeline. Then there are the pot-hustling companies, they're the seismograph outfits, they test for oil. And the equipment companies, they've done well, so I hear. And the drill crews and those who own the rigs, and the towns, the motel owners, the cafés, the stores, the beer parlours. But this is just a small slice of the pie. Anybody connected with the industry seems to make good money, when oil is high in price, of course. For the rest of us, well, not much. A crumb here and there.

People will throw rocks at me for saying all this, but what the bedrock of this province is all about is still the land. Oil will run out. They can almost predict the year, because they're not finding any more. But those politicians and civil servants up in Edmonton, they threw all their eggs into one basket and that is oil. So, things go along like wildfire and everybody is proud of the Heritage Fund and we're lending money to poor old Quebec and Nova Scotia and building bridges and government buildings like they were going out of style. But what happens? I'll tell you. That bastard Trudeau and his gang back in Ottawa, they pull this National Energy Program on us. Whap! It hit like an atom bomb, and the government and the big companies, they were down for the count. Fifty thousand out of work in a few months. Jobs that never really came back. Thousands closing their houses, not making payment. Oh, my God, the sobbing. And then things start perking up, and then the price of oil drops lower and they take another big hit.

Not us. We're the farmers and stockmen and everybody connected with the land. We've had hard times lately and it's not likely to get better, no way, but if we hang in there, we've always got our land. That is the main thing. There is your ace, my friend. We have the land.

We can grow wheat and raise cattle and raise hogs. The people of Saudi Arabia and Mexico and Venezuela, they can't do that. So, even though times are tough, we'll have some kind of a market, and we'll have our land, and these nice homes of ours we've built

in the last twenty-five years. We'll have food and enough to buy
diesel and gas and we'll buy the second-hand clothes the city people
will have to sell to eat, and we'll survive.

You see, we're farmers, cattlemen, and look at your history
books. We are the survivors. We hang in. We eventually win out.
We invented the game. It's our set of rules. We eventually win."

ꙮ *American Over Canadian*

"My husband and I graduated from the university in Saskatoon in
1951 and we made a bee-line right for Calgary. This was where
the future was in Canada in those days for a young engineer.
The oil.

Oil is funny. Let me put it this way. People in the oil business
stick together closer than anybody I know of. There was the oil
community in Calgary, and then there was everybody else. We had
parties together. The wives met together for coffee, golfed together,
went to Banff, the families, and stuck together. You'd have a party
and it wasn't about what was happening in the rest of Canada or
in the world. If it related to the industry, then it was okay to talk
about it. Talk, talk, talk. It was just what this company was doing,
how it was going, and what this man was doing, or what he was
doing with his secretary and what the gossip was. Gossip. You
never saw the like of it.

And then there were the Americans. Boy, do we remember them!
They came up to Calgary in droves and it seemed every company
down there was building up a Canadian branch office. An engineer
would say he was working for such and such a company, but he
wouldn't say it was based in Houston or Tulsa or some place like
that. I think we were a bit ashamed to be dependent on the Americans, but that's where the money, and the experts, and the top
management came from. You couldn't escape it. And in their own
way, they wouldn't let you escape knowing that they were the top
dogs. Boy, and were they ever.

So you had the poor and simple Canadians at lower and middle
management and on top, always on top, the American bosses. Very
nice, oh, very nice people. A little crude, a little too mouthy, a
little too flashy, a little too this and that. Superior without the

right to be superior. But in the end, they were on top, and let's not forget that.

The whole thing, in a nutshell, is that I didn't like the wives, and I liked the husbands a lot less. I wasn't alone. They were just different. Or we were different from them. Same colour skin. Same colour eyes. Same two legs and arms. Same dresses. We used our knives and forks the same way. Same words, but boy, could they ever pronounce them differently.

But different attitude. We were, I guess, kind of Sleepy Hollow people. They were Indianapolis Speedway people. We went along quietly. They were rush, rush, do this, do that. I guess it was all a matter of upbringing and environment, when you really got down to it. Blackbirds fly with blackbirds. Crows with crows. Sparrows with sparrows. And never the twain shall mix.

And money. That was another thing. They had the money. Our husbands were striving for the jobs which would make them that money, but we didn't have it. If they lived on a scale of A, we lived on a scale of B, or even C. After about five years my husband had a pretty good job, shifting from his first company to another, but we had to watch our dollars. Our parties were low-key. You could afford about two big ones a year, and I'd say they would be classified as business parties more than anything.

In those days, it was who you knew, not what you knew. A wife worked as hard at promoting her husband as she could, and there was a right way and a wrong way to do it. I must say, if you studied these American wives closely, you could see they knew how to play that game. They were always older than us, so they'd been at it a long time. The American Wife's Game, support thy mate. You play it many ways. I won't go into them, but one of them was this. Your husbands' American bosses were the greatest guys in the world. Get it? None of them Good Old Boys could do any wrong. Comes to your house, gets tipsy, breaks a piece of your grandmother's china. Ah, now, I didn't want that piece anyway. It was getting old, you know.

The crazy thing was, they did not realize they were lording it over us. They actually didn't. I had a long chat once, a real let-your-hair-down kind of thing, with a woman I met frequently at the hairdresser's and we'd have a drink afterwards, and we had this talk. I let my hair down, all right. It must have been the sherry. I told her what we thought and felt. She was absolutely amazed. I think she was a little hurt, too. They just didn't realize it. I asked her didn't she feel the same way as I did when she was younger? Oh, yes, she said, but that's the way it was done, within the industry. Like a pecking order, see. Everybody did it.

Oh, yes, I could see that, but here it was American over Canadian. We resented it. And there were a lot of things we had to do together, like a Women's Auxiliary of a church. Within our company, within the industry. They were big on charity. Teas, raffles, things like that. It was rather stifling, but you had to go on with it. If they didn't like you, then their husband didn't like your husband. It was like that. Survival.

I think that's what we hated most, and in the oil community of Calgary, it was very close. The husbands lunched together and the wives were together, although, mind you, they had their own groups, American wives, and I'd have loved to sit in on one of those sessions and hear what went on.

Then they'd leave, transferred, and other men would come in to take the jobs and bring the same wives. It was a long time before Canadians in these American oil and gas and supply companies ever got anywhere. It still is the same, but to a much lesser degree, so thank heaven the younger people don't have to put up with so much of their good old American guff, if you'll excuse me. But that's the way we felt about it. They didn't know. They didn't understand. What was good for their good old country was good enough for good little Canada and the good little Canadian engineers and their good little wives. That was about it. Sorry, but I still feel resentment. Most of us do."

🕊 *Oil Rich?*

"You go somewhere, visiting relatives in Brandon or Winnipeg or out to the West Coast, and they see your Alberta plates and you get talking and they think you're rolling in money. That just isn't so. Not many farmers made it anyway in oil. Damn few. Not many had mineral rights. It all went down the tube in the Depression when they lost their farms, or they never had the rights in the first place.

So don't give me that business that Alberta is oil rich. Sure it's rich, but the people aren't oil rich. That's just something the rest of the country thinks. I can't take a hundred-dollar bill out of my pocket, if I got it, and say oil gave it to me. I could say keeping this little business going, that gave me the money. Same with the farmer. The farmer and people in the towns and villages, we really didn't benefit from oil, except the things like good highways and schools and museums. But actual money in my wallet, no sir, oil didn't do that for me. Hard work did it."

❧ *Thousands of Jobs*

"People drive by and they say, oh, look, an oil well, meaning they see us working on the drill rig. And say, the father is out of a job and the wife can't get one and the kids, they know that times are tough, and they all get talking and the father says that all the money from the oil is going down to those big American companies in New York and Houston and Tulsa, and the wife bitches that how come we never got any of that oil loot, and besides, what good has all this oil done for Alberta?

Well, if I was driving that car, I'd say, look at this fine four-lane highway we're driving on, you stupid bitch. Look at the hospitals every ten miles apart in the towns, it seems. Look at the schools you have, and remember what kind of a school you went to back in the fifties. Remember that, eh? And the computers the kids have; they can't read or write but they can sure make those expensive computers sing a tune. Look at the museums and the public buildings and the health service you got and take another look, lady. You've got no sales tax in Alberta, which means every damn thing you buy is six per cent less than in British Columbia. Blame oil, lady, oil did it.

And then I'd say, think of the goddamned jobs. Those office towers in Calgary and Edmonton, they just didn't go up by themselves. Some developer went around and talked to a lot of big oil companies, saying, you wanna beautiful new building to fit your company's image? So he signs up a bunch of companies and then he starts the building and gives jobs to hundreds of construction guys, and work for hundreds of suppliers, and then they move in. The companies say, oh, our old furniture is no good for our new quarters, so they go out and buy a million bucks' worth of desks and chairs and typewriters and computers, and guess who sells them and works in the places they sell them? Alberta people.

The company, it's in oil, so it has men going out around the country buying up leases, and somebody has to arrange the right-of-way with the farmers once they decide to drill after a whole lot of people have lugged the seismograph pots around looking for good vibrations, and a lot of well-paid people have studied them and said, we'll put a hole here. There's surveyors into the act, and then a local contractor gets the job to make the road and level the ground and dig the pit, because you can't set up unless the site is ready. More jobs. Then the drilling company, which is probably based right there in Alberta, it moves onto the site and then what happens?

The hotel owner in the little town down the road, why, he's just rubbing his hands in glee. He knows that drill crews work hard but they eat a lot and they drink a lot, and they got to sleep somewhere and he's got those eight rooms upstairs he hasn't rented in a dog's age and boy, is he ever happy. And so is everybody in town. The barber, if there is one, he'll give a lot more bean shaves, and the restaurant operator and the gas station, he's into the act and everybody is.

Then there's guys from companies that put in the valves, and you got to have tanks ready and a pipeline out, and then there's the truckers. These drilling outfits like to hire local people if they can, and truckers who may not have turned a wheel for a month are suddenly driving truck all day and half the night, up to Calgary, all over hell's half-acre. Then, if the well comes in and there's a set-up for them, there's the pumpers, and then that's it, they tear down the outfit and away they go. Maybe three hundred miles away or maybe only a mile away to another site if things look good, and the whole process starts all over again. More rigs. More guys working twelve and eight and twelve and then, whoopee, and people start looking for empty houses in the towns around, houses that their owners had pretty well given up on, and you could have more kids in school if it looks like a real big field.

But what do they do with all this damn black stuff? They had to build these refineries and the gathering systems, and the railway had to lay more track and order more diesels, quite a few million bucks at a crack, and that meant more jobs. And all the workers had to have work clothes, and Great West Garment in Edmonton was just a-churning them out, them Levi's, and the boot companies. Well, shit, why do I go on? You get the idea.

I'll tell you something. When the Liberals in Ottawa pulled the plug on Alberta with their National Energy Program, everything went down and I was out of a job. I got a job driving a cab in Edmonton, daytime, slow time, the worst time. So one day I pick up these two women from a big high-rise along the river. Young, about thirty-five, I'd say, and well-dressed, and they wanted to go way out east. So we're driving along and we're passing these refineries on Refinery Row and one says to the other, 'Aren't they ugly?' And this other one, she says, 'An eyesore. Somebody should do something about them.'

Well, if it had been my last day on the job and I didn't give a shit, I would have stopped the car and told them to get out and smell the air, and then I would have told those two proud beauties that those ugly-looking things are the only damn reason you're not pounding a typewriter in some office instead of driving around going to a party in a taxi.

'That's oil,' I would have said. 'When you're looking at them ugly things, you're looking at thousands of jobs. Not hundreds. Thousands of the suckers.'"

🐚 *Ambition*

"I guess a lot of us made our mistake when Leduc and then Redwater and then Woodbend came in, bang, bang, bang, like that, three oil-fields in a row. That should have told us something. If they can find three major fields in about five or six years, then there would be more.

That oil was a long time coming, but when it did, it was like somebody writing on a big blackboard, oil is going to be the future of Alberta. And so it was. But you know farmers. They're just like other people. Like Canadians. Somebody has to make that jump, then somebody else, then a lot, and when they see somebody doing good, then they might give it a try.

Now you take my brother Johnny and my nephew, Jerry, his kid. Back in '52. So when we weren't making out too good on the farm, they started work on the rigs and in the field in the winter – while we were waiting back in the house wondering when television was going to come along and give us something to do. They got out there, made money, and learned the ropes. At Christmas dinner, all family, he said, 'Ben, you gotta come with me after Christmas is over. I'll get you on and Sheila can look after the farm.' 'Oh, no,' I said, 'she can't.' Maybe she gave me a dirty look that time, but we still thought women couldn't do anything then, and just you look at what they're doing now. Running farms and businesses too. Doing it just as well as we can.

So my brother says, 'Okay, Ben, if you won't come, then can you lend me $3,000 and I'll pay you more than the bank rate? Keep it in the family, and you won't bust me if I go broke.' You see, his idea is to buy a GMC and go private trucking for these oil companies, custom rates. Cautious me, I say no, even to my brother. He takes no offence, 'cause I guess he figures I ain't got that much. I had, and just a little over, but it was too big a jump for me.

He went to the bank, put his section of land in as collateral, and away he went trucking. And in a year he had a second truck, Jerry driving, and he was away. I seeded for him next spring and we took the crop off together, and all the time he's working, and soon he's got another truck, and now all three of them have got 'Oil Patch Trucking' on the signs on the doors. He bought two more trucks, and he's up in Swan Hills that they're opening up, and those trucks are working sixteen hours a day. Then he takes in a partner and they change the name of the company. And today he's retired in Edmonton, he's got another house at Shuswap Lake, and he's going all over the world with his wife and they're having just one helluva time.

That's just one story. About a little guy, this farmer brother of mine on 640 acres and half of it slough and scrub, but from having no money, in ten years he's got more money that you can shake a stick at. No education. Grade 7, like me, but you didn't need education then. You needed savvy, and if you didn't want to work hard and long hours, you could forget it. You needed the right kind of wife, and maybe I didn't have that, but you had to have something that I guess I just wasn't born with. Know what that is? Ambition. To get ahead. Get in there and slug it out. And another thing. A long reach. The golden apple on the tree was just a little beyond your reach, but if you strained hard, worked real hard, you'd get a little closer and then closer, and then, gotcha!

I'm sorry I didn't have the guts to give him that $3,000. You know why? Because in those days working on your own for the big companies, if you had just a bit of luck you couldn't go wrong. Those were the good old days. There aren't too many good old days in farming. You're too busy thinking about the bad new days, that's why. If I'd given him the money, I know that him and me would have wound up being partners. I wouldn't still be on this farm. I would be retired and travelling around the country in high style. Fact is, I'd be at the Brier right now and staying in the Château Lacombe and living it up, instead of sitting in the house listening to the results on the radio.

The thing is, we had our chances on this oil-patch thing. It was sitting right here in our own backyards, just waiting for us. But no, what did we do? Sat on our duffs. Watched the parade roll on down the roads until you couldn't hear the damned music any more."

❧ *The Seismo Guys*

"Same old story. It happened everywhere. Those seismographic crews came through with their yellow trucks and their pots and all these guys, hitting a small town like this and putting up in the hotel, and they were here for a couple of months working over all the leases, and then they were gone.

These crews came in and they brought booze, but worse, a lot of them brought dope. Some of the girls went gaga over them and there was a lot of trouble. The crews were a pretty wild lot, and they knew about quiet little towns like ours and how to push it to the limit. Booze, marijuana, and those drugs, the chemical ones that send you up the wall. They did a lot of damage and the police had their hands full, and the worst were sent out and away by the company, but the replacements were not a whit better.

Some of the girls got pregnant, naturally. That's to be expected. But when they moved on, they left behind this dope thing, which is still around, and in the high school now. And those kids don't even remember when the seismo guys were here. Too young. But the dope thing hung on and hung on and left its mark on the next bunch of kids to come along.

And the thing is, they never found no oil. Not a drop."

◆ *One Hell of a Fight*

"You name it, I've worked in them all. Every field that came in the late sixties, early seventies, I worked on it. Swan Hills in the winter, fifty below, twenty-three straight shifts, no time off. Over by Drayton Valley, hotter than hell and all boggy country and every goddamned mosquito in the country was within ten yards of our drill site. Good hard work and sure, I made good hard wages. They had to pay to keep us. Some of those guys! The super looks at them sideways and they're off in their pickup, down the road and working again. I mean, if you knew your way around, then those were good days for jobs.

We'd come off a week of twelve-hour shifts. Too much trouble changing shift three times a day. Make it twelve hours, two shifts, and give the gang two days off and let 'em go home and see their kids or piss it up in town. We'd come off and a few of us would go into one of these little towns. You've seen 'em. Nothing to write home about. Main street. A few side streets. A few businesses, and if it was big enough, then a few stores and a couple of cafés, and the hotel. All the same. All bloody well the same. I musta been in fifteen, maybe twenty of these towns. All the same.

For three or four years these villages and towns in a field, around it, they just boomed. But nobody, nobody thought the rigs would be around long enough to put up a decent hotel. That's why you had these old wrecks, some of them brick, a lot of them wood. They'd been around since 1910 or 1920 and they were built to serve beer. Nobody ever stayed in them. A dining-room, though, and most of them, you could get good food. You know, pork chops and mashed potatoes, turnips, carrots, apple pie, pumpkin pie. That sort of thing. Big breakfasts too. I'll say this, cheap as they were in running the beer parlour, they could put up a good meal for you.

Funny, and I don't know how it was, but most of them hotels, they were run by Ukrainians. A lot of them. All called Nick or Steve. Nicholas, Stephen. Big fellows, and I didn't like them. They were the guys who made the real money.

Oh, yeah, a lot of them bootlegged. Nobody said a thing. Sunday, you'd see half a dozen company pickups around the back door if you stayed long enough. And I don't mean a couple of cases. Three or four was nothing, and a dozen, well, that just meant you were going to have a big party until the place opened next morning. A lot of money spent.

The Mountie? I just think he was told to turn his face. Stay home with the kids that day or get out on the highway and throw a few tickets around. But the Mounties were nice guys. Maybe they had to be. No use taking on a whole industry. A few speeding-tickets, any company will pay them. That's what I'd call public relations. Pay them and smile. But you lose a couple of guys off a site, like in the bucket for fighting and they miss a shift or two, well, Jesus Christ, one of these big company bosses could get awfully upset about that. Awfully. Like you'd say that was bad for the economy, and here's some punk little Regina Cowboy, he's the one who threw them in the bucket. No way. It just wasn't done that way. Not for fighting.

So we're working twelve-hour shifts, and when we get a couple of days off, we are rarin' to go. I've seen it. Nobody says anything about it, but we just know we're going to get in a hell of a fight that night. One hell of a fight. Maybe among the crew, like one guy has been riling up another and they can't have it out in camp. No way, both of them are down the road. But in town, let 'er fly. Or there'd be this good feeling in the crew, everybody happy with each other, no hassles, but you've got all this going inside you and if there is another crew or two in that pub, then something's going to happen. We didn't hate them. Shit, we didn't even know these other guys.

These Ukes who ran these hotels, maybe they just sensed it, just the way we talked or walked in or how we laughed. But they'd come over and say something like, 'No trouble, you boys, no trouble tonight. Okay? No trouble, be all happy.'

All happy, hell. Shit, we were raring to go and you could feel the rumble building up. Maybe six beers later, maybe ten, and then pow! It could start in the can or at the juke-box, like maybe somebody from one gang yelled at somebody from another, 'Ya playing that same old loud shit again?' Somebody from that crew would yell, 'Knock it off, ya pisscutters, we like it.' Then one of our guys would yell, 'Up your ass, ya creep,' and that would do it. Oh, God. I can see it yet. The farmers, they were off at their own tables in the corner, and they always minded their own business. So did everybody else. And there we were, going at it. Could Jack Demp-

sey have beaten Joe Louis? Who the hell knows, but we were going
to try and prove it. There you'd go, picking out one guy, and soon
there'd be a war going.

You gotta remember how it was then. We all worked for what
they called the independents. The smaller companies, not like
Imperial or Shell or Gulf. So, if an Imperial crew was beating up
on a Home bunch, we'd be staying out of it, and then our driller
would say, 'Let's all go in and help Home.' And in we'd go, and
we'd all beat the shit out of Imperial. That's the way it sometimes
worked. I mean, a bit of oil-company politics right down at the
ground level, one little crew against the fat-cat crew. It was dumb
and it was fun. Both ways.

They never lasted long. A few chairs broken and a lot of glass
and some blood here and there, and it was over. Hell, we might be
eating a steak with some of these guys a couple of hours later. But
it was the owner, the Nick or Steve or Joe, he'd be running around
and yelling he'd call the cop and he couldn't, you know. He'd get
black marks, for allowing ungentlemanly conduct in his premises
or something along that order, so he'd keep quiet. Maybe we'd
each throw in ten bucks, two hours' pay, for a hundred bucks of
good clean fun among a bunch of good clean kids. He'd always
come out okay. Yeh, maybe he liked those fights, made some
money on them. I notice he and his bartender never tried to stop
a good one. The whole bunch might have turned on them and
thrown them through the windows of their lousy joint. Those
money-makers!

Then we'd go to the cathouse. Sometimes it would be just
upstairs. Girls from all over. Maybe ten or so in one town. The
Ukrainian would rent them a $20-a-week room for $15 a night,
but they'd still do good at $10 a pop. Sure, or it might be over at
the motel or a house or two on the far side of town. Never right
in town. Everybody knew it. You can't change human nature, and
besides, we were finding the oil, weren't we? Can't deny that. When
we were gone, the oil would still go on. Service companies, new
business, new roads. They didn't care, we didn't care, so what the
hell was there to care about?

You moved around a lot. Six months on a job was pretty good.
If you were single, I mean. That got you a big pile of dough and a
couple of weeks at the Mac in town, or a motel and a car rental,
and a lot of good times and some girls. Or you could save it. I
never did. Nine years on the rigs, that was like a record, and

especially in winter, before I fell off a rig, a pure accident. Not even a skid or a trip and bang, there went my back. I got work in the city, no lifting, but there never was a life like on those rigs in them days. No, never. Lots of work, lots of money, lots of fun – and the only reason we did it was because we didn't have a single brain in our heads. Not a single one. Fun, though."

🕊 *Drill Mud*

"When I graduated in geology from the University of Toronto, this was in 1953 when things were beginning to roar along in Alberta, like a lot of guys in my class I was going to make a fortune in the oil business. After all, we were geologists, weren't we?

I went to Edmonton in June and it seemed my nice shiny degree didn't cut any ice with the drilling outfits. They seemed to be up to their necks in fresh and bright geologists and I sat in the office with a tough old guy, and I think he had an hour to spare or otherwise he wouldn't have been wasting his time with me. From Oklahoma or Texas, and one of the old-timers.

I remember him saying, 'Boy, can you smell out oil?' Well, I suppose that made no more sense to me than asking another geologist if he could smell out gold or copper. I was a smart ass, I suppose, and I answered that I wasn't sure if I knew what the smell of oil was like. This ruffled him up and I could see the interview wasn't going too well but I got through it, listened to a lot of his blarney, a lot of damned funny stories, and then he said he didn't have a geologist's spot open but he could get me on with a drill rig.

'Work a season with us,' he said, 'around the rig and with the crew and see how things are and you'll get more knowledge at that end of it and that will be a terrific experience.' Otherwise, he said, I could spend the rest of the summer trying to catch on where there just weren't any jobs. 'Take it now,' and he levelled his big horny finger at me, 'and you won't regret it.' So I did, signed on right there in that trailer he had for an office out in the equipment yard, and I knew he was doing me a favour. Hell, he could go out on Jasper Avenue and hire any roughneck he wanted.

They got me on a bus to Fort Assiniboine and I hitched a ride up through to the Swan Hills on a truck, and finally found the rig and reported in. Boy, I guess Joe College just stuck out all over me, and I paid for it.

You ever hear of drill mud? It is essential to the whole operation. Looks like cement and comes in one-hundred-pound bags, and when you're making hole a rig can use up a lot of the stuff. It's mixed with water and becomes mud, and it goes down the hole and lubricates the drill, because when it's down four or five thousand feet there is a terrific build-up of friction. Secondly, if there are fractures in the rock structure, the mud fills the cracks. That was my job, packing those hundred-pound bags. My God, I hadn't lifted anything heavier than a suitcase for a long time and I was out of shape. Packing those bags for twelve hours a day. The drill never shuts down except for a pipe change, and it was tough rock, so the going was slow. And that first day I packed and packed, and after four hours I was finished. After six hours I was dead. For the next six hours, with only a couple of breaks off, I performed a miracle. I worked while I was dead. But I got through the day, staggered to the trailer, fell on the bed, and slept right through.

Next morning I couldn't get up, but two of the crew just hauled me out, shoved me into the shower, and guided me into the cook-shack and just about fed me. That day was worse. In fact, I'm not sure I remember much of it. The next day was bad, and here are these guys getting me into the shower and into bed and into the cookhouse, because they wanted me to stay. Otherwise, *they'd* have to lug the drill mud. To make it short, I survived the first week, and from then on it was easier, and in a month when one guy quit and a new guy came in, I moved up and he went through that living hell I had.

My introduction to the oil industry, and I never forgot it. I stayed on, through that winter, next spring and fall, and I was a pretty seasoned guy when I got my final cheque and headed off to Calgary.

This is important. I went into Imperial there and made out an application and the next day I saw the personnel officer. We talked a bit and then he made an appointment for the exploration chief, nice guy, big rough hands like the old guy up in Edmonton that time. He asked me why I'd worked on a rig for nearly a year and a half, and I didn't tell him it was the only job I could get. I said I knew a degree really wasn't worth much, and I wanted to learn the business from the ground up, so I did.

Big smile on his face. He just stood up, stuck out his hand and said, 'Welcome to Imperial.' "

🕊 *No Future*

"Four of my five boys worked on the rigs and in the fields for a time, like five or six months at a time, but their heart wasn't in it. There's nothing glamorous about oil, let me tell you. If you think so, you've been looking at movies. The real stuff, it is just hard work and long hours and sometimes it is downright dangerous.

I'd always tell my boys to ask for the hard work, where the rig was hell and gone from anywhere. Camp living. They got board and room if they were near town, too, but towns have beer parlours, and drill workers, there is something about them, but they just can't keep their noses out of a mug of beer. It's ruined a lot of them. One of my boys turned into an alcoholic, and he's still fighting the booze. The second, he fell off the platform when he was working as derrickman and down he went and smashed his shoulder. Some small-town doctor put it back together and didn't do much of a job. He walks like this, his shoulder kind of hanging over this way.

They learned, what I'd been telling them, the four of them. There's no future working on the rigs. Sure, the money is good, but there's two things they gotta learn. Be careful to not have an accident, and stay out of the beer parlour. Two of them didn't.

But there's no future. You want to be something in that business, you go to university. It's a caste system. The companies want workers, tough guys who can stand that noise and heat and cold and the long hours. That means a lot of money, but it's no damn good. All they'll ever be, maybe toolpush. Not superintendent or anything up there in the big money and responsibility. I mean, no future. Give a guy maybe eight years at that life and he's burned out. He's finished. And then he's not good for anything."

🕊 *Easy Come, Easy Go*

"There was a joke going around a couple of years ago which went like this: Oh, Lord, please send us another oil boom and I promise this time I won't piss it away. That's close enough.

I remember one December I made more than $5,000 working on a big rig north and west of Breton there. Kind of hillbilly country, and it was winter and cold as a billy goat's ass, and it was one of these deadline jobs. Anyway, we were doing twelve-hour shifts, and there was double time and triple time and bonus money, and Christmas and Boxing Day were in there, too, and somehow that month's pay came out to about five grand. I thought at the time, that's $60,000 a year, and that would be more than the personnel guy was making in Calgary, the guy who hired me.

I was twenty, no education, no experience, strong and tough as an old range bull, and I had no brains at all. After the income tax came out of it, I should have put half or more of it in bonds or the bank or these mutual funds or done something with it. But I was single and didn't give a shit. This would go on forever. It would never stop. Alberta would still keep pumping out the oil and we'd keep putting down hole and those cheques would just keep coming in and I'd be off to Mexico or Hawaii and living it up just something fierce.

Twenty-eight days on the rig, twelve-hour shifts, eat, work, sleep, work, on and on, working our butts off. We really earned our dough. That country was tough, and the toolpush was tough, and the company was tough. Tough but fair. They wanted hole and we gave it to them. Supply truck would come in at 3 a.m. and we'd hop out of bed, unload for an hour, back to bed, and there was four more hours' pay. Like that. They wanted the job done.

Easy come, easy go, and fly down to Calgary and see my folks for a week with a wad this thick and visit them the first night and have dinner and then back downtown, and I wouldn't see them the rest of the time. Downtown, the best hotel in town, U-Drive, the biggest and best vee-hickle, booze, night clubs, girls, the works. New clothes. New clothes for whatever girl I'd picked up for the week. In and out. Easy come, easy go. Shit. You couldn't believe it. Here I am, twenty-one, twenty-two, and living like a sultan.

I sure learned that money has a language all by itself. First morning, I always stayed at the International Inn, and I'd lay a ten-buck tip there for breakfast and that waitress sure didn't forget you. She'd just be there before you even sat down, big smile, hey hey, but it was great. Kid of twenty-two.

Then the NEP hit us. I'm still not sure what the NEP really was all about, but I know how it hit us. Not at first. No, we still went along, but in a few months this rig, that rig, was heading for the States. No money in drilling any more, and if you don't have that, then that's the start of the slide. And by God, one day we finished off a job and thought we'd be moving with the rig. It was moving, all right, but into a yard at Edmonton. Still there, I'll bet.

No jobs, no money, no girls, no Cadillac U-Drives, no nothing. Just lots and lots of nothing and some good clothes and a Rolex watch I had to pawn along with my $800 golf clubs.

Now, that was me. That was like a lot of guys who worked on all those rigs. Guys from B.C., Saskatchewan, and all those Newfies and their nutty accents, we're all in the coal-bin. But there were family men, too. Guys with a wife and kids, you know. They got it worse. Like they had mortgages and wives and kids and a front lawn and a back lawn and a lawn-mower, and worst of all, they had that big mortgage. I don't know how many hit the coal-bin that year. Twenty thousand, maybe? About that. Jesus, it was rough on those guys. And these weren't guys who screwed around with their money. Not like us. But the way it is on a rig, when the job shuts down, everybody goes. There's no sentiment, if you know what I mean. Sorry, fellows, if we need you again we'll phone you.

Remember, I'm not talking about the thousand other guys who work for a big outfit. I don't know bugger all about them. They all had their problems, too. I'm just talking about guys like me, working on the site and hourly wages and no union and so it's Goodbye Charlie, and that was what it was all about."

🕊 *One Street*

"We live on a cul-de-sac. Maybe twelve or thirteen homes, all nice big ones. You never get to know your neighbours well in this city, but you got to know enough about most of them. Let's say that every family there was connected to the oil business in some way. This one was in oil, and so was that one, and that one was a big lawyer for Husky, and across the street, that one had his own rig-servicing company, and, well, let's say it was a very affluent street.

We'd have a block party every summer for the kids and parents. We'd rope off the end of the street and have barbecues going right in the street and a table for beer, and hot dogs and fizzy drinks for the kids, and we'd all get together. The last one, I can still remember the talk. Oil was booming. Calgary was booming. We all were booming and prosperous, and it would never end. The gist of it was, this little street and Calgary and Alberta was the best place in the world to live and we lived in it.

Then came weasel-face Marc Lalonde and his energy program. The big companies began cutting middle-management staff, and the rigs started heading south of the border, and everything started to slow down, and then it stalled. I don't think I'm being dramatic about this but a feeling of real fear spread through this province, and when that happens, it just multiplies. More and more, those high, those low, out they went. No jobs. And most people in those days lived pretty close to the line, because they thought the good times would roll on forever, would never stop.

And then it happened. The first 'For Sale' sign went up on the street. It had been years since I'd seen one of those. Do you know what? Within two weeks there were four more. That's five. Five out of twelve or thirteen, and every one connected with the energy program and the Liberals. That's right, the Liberal government, and if you think people in Calgary are ever going to vote for them, you've got another think coming."

❧ Excuse Me, Sir

"The story I'm about to tell you is true. Okay, I'm going to lunch the other day and in front of the old Herald building a chap stops me. I'm alone and he asks if he could speak to me for a moment. He's about my age, fifty-five or so, and he's well dressed. I noticed that. But in Calgary somebody just doesn't stop you at noon and ask if he can talk to you for a minute, everybody's so damned busy trying to get something done, but here he is. So I stopped. I don't know what he is but I've got a moment, and he tells me he's an unemployed executive from Edmonton and he has no money and if I could help him out, a dollar or two maybe, it would mean a lot. He has no place to stay. No money at all, the way he tells it. Just his manner and his style, I guess, the way he talks and looks me in the eye, I've got to believe it.

I don't know what made me, but I said I couldn't stand out here in the cold but that I was going to lunch. Maybe he'd like to join

me. I'm darn sure that wasn't quite what he'd expected, but he said yes, and we crossed the street and went in and got a table and I said, 'Okay, tell me about it. You mean in this whole city there's not a job for you? Anything?'
Understand this. I was only curious. Eating alone, what the hell? He was just like anybody you'd do business with. Hair trimmed, business suit. Clean shirt and tie, and even a briefcase. Executive type.
He gave me his name, and let's just call him Tom Brown. He said he'd been let go from a middle-range executive job with a medium-sized firm, and when he told me what he'd done he had enough of the jargon that I knew he did have some connections with the trade and with companies. He named a few, clients of his firm. Big ones I recognized. He was frank. Played it honestly, I thought.
He had a wife and two children and they'd apparently lived quite close to the line and when he got his dismissal – lack of business, he said, and others went out the door, too – they had nothing. He had no Unemployment Insurance, naturally. So he and his wife split. She got welfare for herself and the kids in Edmonton and he was drawing it in Calgary. That's why I'm calling him Tom Brown. You just can't do that, and with the computer set-up they'd nail him if he tried to pull anything fast. But splitting, and each drawing welfare, that apparently is okay.
He was sending his full amount of welfare to her and he was, get this, in his words, 'living off the streets'. That's a hippie term, I thought. But with this guy, he used it perfectly naturally.
We ordered. He had a mushroom omelette, dry toast, a small salad, and coffee. What any businessman would order. I waited for him to order a drink, and he didn't. He either wasn't going to try and push his luck, or he just didn't have a drink at noon.
I asked him how he lived, and he said, 'Well, in some circles they call it panhandling.' He smiled. I was getting to admire the guy. Here he was telling me something, and I believe honestly, that he was doing something that I couldn't do in a million years. He said he did it every day at noon, 11:30 to 1:30, but because it was late and about 1:30, he'd finished for the day, or until late afternoon when he tried it again. He said he'd pick out a man of his own age, dressed well, and always alone, and he'd stop him. He had his little pitch, of course, and it was so natural you just had to believe it.
Here's the smart part. If he didn't get a positive reaction in fifteen

seconds, and he told me that was a long time, he'd say, 'I'm sorry, but I've taken up your time. You're busy, so I'll let you go,' and he'd start to move away. Don't laugh at this. That was the thing that triggered it off. When he appeared to be rejecting his, well, call him client if you will, that's exactly when the client was most likely to pull out his wallet and say, 'How much do you need?' or 'What will help you?'

Do you know how much he was making a day? Give a guess. He said a good day was forty or fifty dollars a day. Now, I don't know if that is good or bad. I suspect it is good. I was doing some mental arithmetic and thinking, two dollars a person. That's twenty. He couldn't possibly make twenty positive contacts a day. It just wasn't possible, but he said it was. I thought, Christ, this guy is working five times harder than any of our salesmen, and they've got their customers lined up.

He told me a lot more. Not too much about himself, but he did give me his card, his old one, with his wife's Edmonton phone number on the back. So far, in that category, he was legitimate. When I got back to the office I called Information and yes, they did have a listing for that name.

But he had a good car. He said he just could not do without it. What he would do when he had to renew the insurance I don't know. But he lived in a fifty-dollar-a-week room with hot and cold running water, toilet down the hall, one of those cheap hotels over by Centre Street. He at least had a home base. Apparently there are places downtown where you can buy a good breakfast for about two bucks and he filled up there, and he said it was usually two Big Macs and fries at night, so his food bill was absolutely minimal. He pointed out he rarely ate lunch, but maybe a hot dog and coffee at an Orange Julius. That was all.

There's a twist to this. Isn't it always? Every night he'd go back to his hotel and he had six of these little bottles the airlines give you and he'd fill them up with vodka. Put them in pockets so they wouldn't show. Then he'd take his briefcase and go to a good bar and sit at a table, buy a vodka tonic and nurse it and pop in a shot from the airline bottle or go to the can and drink one. In about an hour and a half he'd order another vodka, and so that's how he spent his evenings. Maybe ten ounces, but he said it didn't affect him. Never had, he said, and never would. Maybe. But he said the bars were warm and there was activity, people, and often he'd strike up a conversation with somebody, and that was something he absolutely craved. He was a good talker. Graduated from the University of British Columbia, he said. Took night-school courses there, and then headed out for this part of the world and did well, until . . . Well, you know, it has happened to a lot of fellows.

You know, I liked this guy. I asked him if he told this story to people he met in bars and he said no. Never. He just told me because I had asked the right question. I guess I did. He told it well. Well educated, no doubt of that, and he knew a lot of the business world, politics. He'd travelled a lot.

I wanted to help the guy. That had been nagging me right along. I thought, here is a guy who would be a credit to some organization or company and I told him so. He thought it over and he said, yes, he could see my point, but he'd been doing this for a couple of months now and he kind of liked it. I asked him, for Christ's sakes, why?

Every day was different, he said, and when he'd been in oil service production, every day was the same, the same work, the same faces, the same troubles. Always the problems were the same, he said. Oh, you know, I could believe him on that one.

So here he was, broke to all intents and purposes. Quite broke, but never flat broke. Living in a bums' hotel, but wearing a $450 Dunn suit, fresh shirt, and tie. By the way, he said he did his own laundry in the room and used a traveller's iron. Did his own underwear, his own hankies. Walked into a different bar every night, made busy looking at the papers in his briefcase until he could talk to someone, and then back to bed. Yes, the guy said he liked the life. He was sending about fifty or sixty dollars extra to his wife every week and he asked how many businessmen with a wife and kids and a big house, how many of them can give an extra two hundred dollars or so to their wives every month, right out of their pockets? Boy, he had me on that one. I sure as hell can't.

We had a very pleasant hour. Very entertaining and very instructive. When he left, I put him on my expense account and I thought, should I or shouldn't I? He'd just cost the company about seven bucks, but what the hell, and when I put back my credit card I took out a ten-spot and when we were on the street I gave it to him.

You know what he said? He said, 'I was wondering how much you'd give me. You're in my Gold Card bracket. You've now paid your dues.'

I liked that. I should have said he had a real sense of humour.

Now next time he sees me he won't go after me. I've paid my dues. But I think I'll go after him. Take him to lunch. Slip him a ten-spot. That was just about the most enjoyable lunch hour I've spent in a long time."

❧ *This Malarkey About Oil*

"You can talk all you want, until your hide is blue, but you can't get over the fact that agriculture is still Number One in the West. Don't let anybody give me this malarkey about oil. That's a money-maker for the big companies and for the government and for a hundred thousand people, maybe, but it is still not a people thing. See what I mean? Only a few people are involved. All the decisions are made in Dallas or Tulsa or Calgary. You drill a hole, you get oil, and that's it. The oil goes off to a refinery and the crew moves on to another site. There isn't much involvement with the people.

Now, you take farming. Fly over this country at 35,000 feet. As far as you can see, farms. Wheat. Summer fallow. Houses. Towns. Villages. That's where people live. That's where the farmers live. The towns and those villages, and those sidings with two elevators and a couple of houses. The farmer goes to the town or the village and that's where he buys some of his groceries, his parts, his bulk fuel. Everybody depends on each other, town and farm. You see? And the whole shebang, all rolled together, they have all these connections with Lethbridge and Red Deer and The Hat, and these cities have their connections with Calgary. Don't you go about telling me that Calgary is all oil and nothing but.

I'll put it this way. If the agriculture community of Western Canada went over on its tail, dead, and the same thing happened to the oil industry, which would make this country the worse off? Don't answer. You don't have to. The agriculture end of it would kill us."

Eleven

A Feeling of Home

I Grew Up in a Cave . . . Deer Among the Graves . . . The Land Is Still Out There . . . Home at the Cabin . . . The New House . . . A Frog-Swallower of a Sale . . . Tearing Memories Out of Your Own Heart

One fine day in May I was travelling around with a friend in his pickup and he pulled into a yard, overgrown with broken trees, sprawling bushes, and old buildings, grey and falling down, and he pointed to the largest and said, "Doesn't look like a house, does it? But my grandparents brought up six kids in that thing there, and I was born there, too. It's the old home place. I could pour some gas on the whole thing, I guess, and just let her burn, but it's part of this country down here. I'm keeping it for my memories."

An old but sprightly woman from Edmonton travels around to talk to elementary students about her times, and when she tells them immigrant farm people lived in houses made of sod and dirt and tar-paper, they gasp. She asks, "Well, what's wrong with that? They were warm in winter and cool in summer. They cost nothing to build. Maybe your own grandmother lived in one of these soddies. Ask her."

But most of the pioneers who first came to the Prairies made an attempt at building a wooden dwelling. The bachelors erected shacks, but families built the two-storey houses which have been called the only distinct style of architecture the Prairies has ever had; you can see a typical example on the cover of this book. Trees were rare on the Prairies and of poor quality, and good lumber was expensive to import, while in the bush country up north many homesteaders built log homes.

We cannot imagine the crowded conditions today; I have talked to people who came from families of twelve, fourteen, even sixteen children. Every child, even the toddler, had jobs to do, and the large kitchen, with its big stove and the warm glow of its kerosene lantern, was the heart of the home.

Today, the small farms are gone. Only big farmers can survive. The homes are modern, mainly bungalow style, with lawns and flowers, and almost all of the old pioneers, the homesteaders, are in the cared-for cemeteries.

The old ways of the farm are gone, as they should be, and the relics of that life are in museums, as they should be. But sometimes in the lee of a small rise, you can still see the old homesteads, built there to catch the sun and protected from the chilling north winds, and that is as it should be too. They stand there as silent reminders of a hard life in a tough land.

🐦 *I Grew Up in a Cave*

"Oh yes, I grew up in a cave. From the age of seven until I was fourteen, when my father decided to build a house. We thought nothing of it.

My father had come out from Bukowina, which is part of Russia now, and it was three years until he could bring my mother and me and my younger brother out to Canada. We went by wagon for two days from Wetaskiwin, going east to where the Round Hill community was and then to his homestead, and there was our home. Yes, it was a cave. He'd dug it into the south side of a hill at the bottom and it got lots of sun. That's the way it was done. Three sides of the house was dirt and the side with the door, it was wood. The floor was hard clay and you could sweep it and the rain never came in because, you know, it was a cave. He must have spent hundreds of hours just digging it out.

It had two bedrooms, one for Nick and me, and one for my parents, and the rest of the cave was everything. I mean it was the kitchen and the dining-room and the living-room and the storage room and, well, you can just imagine.

But it wasn't bad. We never thought all that much about it. We knew that one day we'd have a house, but there was so much to do. My mother and my brother and me, we lived alone there most of the winter because my father was working in the lumber camp up north of Edmonton to make money. You couldn't make a living off a farm in those days. The money from him working in the bush kept us going while we built up the farm. In the winter we looked after the cattle and the pigs and chickens and our four horses. He came home twice. Once at Christmas, and then about the middle of February, and then he'd come in the spring with the money and some presents he'd bought in Edmonton and things for the farm. When it was all counted out on the table, there wasn't all that much left. Just enough, I guess, to put us through the summer until we could sell things.

You know, I liked that cave. It was dry and it was always warm and it had two windows, and the light came through them. There was a big stove and the big pipe went across the top and out the front and the heat from the pipe helped to warm the house. When you shut the fire down at night, it would burn for a long time.

Our place was near the Battleford Trail, so that meant we had lots of visitors. Men with teams and hayricks would stop the night and they knew my mother wouldn't have much food so they brought their own. You know, a piece of meat, a loaf of bread, meat pies, and this was in the winter, so it was frozen, but my mother would thaw it out and feed us all. These men, maybe families, they'd have breakfast and then go on to Wetaskiwin. On the way home they'd stop again, very tired, but they'd have some more food to cook and then they'd lie down on the floor in their big coats and sleep. Sleep and snore. Snore, snore. Oh gosh, some of those people really snored.

About twice a year a Swedish preacher would come, Preacher Larsen. He'd hold service in our cave and people would come. He'd say, I am coming again on December 15 and six months later, on December 15, there he would be. The neighbours for a few miles around, there they would be with food, and there was a lot of talk and good fun. There were Canadians and English and Dutchmen and Germans, Ukrainians, Norwegians, Galicians, everybody, and a few Americans, and this preacher thought, well, I can't preach to everybody in their own language, and a lot of people don't speak English yet. So he'd preach in Swedish and throw in some English words. That way, everybody understood him a little. My mother asked him why he just didn't preach in English, and he said he preached better in Swedish. That was his way.

The policeman would stay too. Once, he had a few drinks out of his bottle because he had been riding for many hours in the cold, and he got a bit tipsy and he wasn't the stern policeman then. He told jokes and he said that this was a funny place he liked to stay at, because the family lived in a cave and the stock and horses lived in wooden sheds. He thought it should be the other way around. When he'd leave, he'd give my mother or father a piece of paper saying they had given him two meals and a place to sleep, and they were to cash it at the police post in Wetaskiwin. My father never did. He said it was worth it just to have a man around who knew what was going on in the world. You see, Wetaskiwin was a town and they had the telegraph on the line from Calgary to Edmonton and the news came over the line. It would be weeks old, but it was still news.

Well, that was my home. A cave with a hard clay floor, and we never thought anything about it. It was not until I was fourteen and a new baby was coming that my father decided it was time for a house to be built. It took him two years to get the lumber and everything for the house and then one day in July of 1915, here came the neighbours. From all over, with saws and axes and hammers and everything, and they went to work on the house. In two days they had enough of it up that we could live in it. I think maybe twenty men worked on that house, hammering and building walls, putting on the roof, making the two chimneys and putting on the shingles and making the rooms. People went home at night to feed and milk, but they came back next day, and Mother and I had to feed them. It was like threshing-time but more so because there was more.

That was the end of the home in the cave. It was just used for storage from then on, and a place to put young calves at night and young pigs if coyotes were around. In 1917 the farmers had been getting good crops, big ones, and good prices at the elevator at Round Hill, and my dad bought a Model T car. He tore out part of the wood front and then the cave became a garage."

🐦 *Deer Among the Graves*

"When I was a kid on the farm and we'd come back from town on a Saturday night, there was a bend just at the cemetery and our lights would always pick out two, three deer eating among the graves. That always gave me kind of a funny feeling. You never saw them anywhere else. To this day I'm not sure why they preferred graveyards, but I have an idea – and I'm not sure I was so wrong when I was a kid, about that funny feeling it gave me.

One time I asked Dad when we went by, and he didn't say anything. But then next week we went into town in the truck to get some stuff from the co-op and on the way back he stopped by the cemetery and he took me inside. I remember it to this day. There were the old graves, and because this had been an Anglo-Saxon district, there were granite tombstones. Mostly a Scottish district, for that matter, all these Scotch names, McGregors and McLeods and Macleods and Duncans and the James family and a lot of others, and he'd point to one and he'd tell me a little about him. How they came out and saw the Souris River Valley and how good it looked, and I guess we're back in the 1890s. And how they wrote and told others to come, and how they hacked out their farms. What they used. How little money they had. How hard they worked and how they froze to death, and how they built their churches and before that they worshipped in somebody's kitchen every Sunday. How they survived.

He told me how the wives worked with them in the fields. Jobs like picking rocks and hauling brush into piles and burning it. Cutting ice. Stooking, and today you can't imagine women stooking. Where would you find a farm with a thresher these days? But I remember women in the fields, and they weren't just taking the afternoon lunch to the men, either. They were stooking in the hot sun. He knew most of these families in that cemetery. This was about 1930, and I'd be about ten years old at that time.

He talked about them as though they were still alive. I can remember the last place he took me was in the near corner where our people were–Grandpa and my father's oldest sister, Margaret, who died of pneumonia when she was fourteen, and his brother who died in the war, and his was just a marker, not a grave. A few cousins and a couple who died in the flu epidemic after the war. Maybe eight graves in all.

That was a funny time for me. And I remember my father saying, 'John, I'm glad the grass is green here, and I'm glad the deer come here and eat. It makes me feel good that they would think this is kind of their home. Somebody's watching over them here.'

Maybe a year after that we buried my grandmother there. I remember not minding her being laid to rest after a lifetime of hard work in a place where the grass was green a lot and the deer came at night to watch over them. It made me feel good.''

❧ *The Land Is Still Out There*

"It's so many things. The wind, always there in your face, making the chimes on the porch go clinka-clink-clink in a musical way. The sunrise in the spring when I'm making breakfast for my husband when he's going out to seed. I look out the window and there it is, so big and red. Another good day. Watching that big yellow school bus going down the road. All those nice kids in it. Walking down the lane in early June and there is our wheat, all green, and blowing in the wind, moving all the time. Getting it into my mind that I should make a few loaves of bread and some buns and scones, and the smell. My husband coming in after work and saying, 'Hey, give me one right now,' and me saying, 'Wash your hands, they're all covered with dirt,' and him saying, 'No matter, it's good clean dirt.' Well, it is. It's our dirt, isn't it? The way we make our living, growing wheat.

Driving into Calgary and seeing a play in the new centre and my husband's fidgeting at first, and then when we're going home he says, 'That's a darn good play. They were pretty good.' Listening to the sound of the shotguns over by the slough when the boys come home for a Sunday dinner and they go out and try for a few ducks. The big dinner we have, about fourteen of us, everybody laughing and talking and Deirdre, John's wife, has brought a couple of fancy bottles of wine and we're sipping at it, like we do it all the time.

Going into Olds on a Saturday and all the people on the street, all of us shopping and saying, 'Gosh, this is more fun than shopping in that mall in Red Deer.' Taking people home with us for dinner. Potluck supper. Just sitting around talking, crops and prices and who's doing this and that and laughing at some pretty mean gossip of people in the district or yacking away about what is going on in Edmonton or Ottawa. Somebody is sure to say, 'Those politicians, they're all alike.'

And in July, just locking the door and driving away in the camper and if we see a road going somewhere we take it, looking at other people's places. You can spend two weeks just driving around Alberta and not doing a thing. Like the little towns, sitting in the beer parlour at night, and in fifteen minutes you're playing shuffleboard and in half an hour you're at a table and meeting some new people. Like, do you know so-and-so, and yes, they knew his cousin or daughter and away it goes. And all the time you know the wheat is growing, getting ripe, filling out, and soon you'll be harvesting again. Wonderful. But you can't sell it, maybe, not for your price. You don't think of that. Tomorrow is another day. Things will get better, because they can't get worse. A bit of a laugh out of that one.

And harvesting, the coming and going, the boys back from the city helping out, driving truck, all the things to be done and the wives, Deirdre and Beth, helping around. City girls, both of them, and to them it's fun. Like Beth saying, 'How could they ever invent those machines?' My husband Gerry saying that, 'Well, they just improved a bit on what the Egyptians used to do with a flail and a blanket woven of reeds. Not much difference. Today it just costs a lot more.' And fall, and we still have the church dinner, chicken and dumplings, apple pie, pumpkin pie, ice cream, coffee, and the Ladies' Auxiliary makes two hundred dollars and we all have fun.

And then winter, and everything gets so quiet and we think, why not go to Victoria and get one of those motel rooms with a kitchen in one of those motels along the Gorge? Can we afford it? Yes, he says, and then Christmas comes and a couple of birthday parties, and there seems to be so much to do, curling in Olds, a few parties, a trip to see the West Edmonton Mall just to say we've been there, and Gerry working on the machinery and, why, it seems like there is no time for anything and no time to go to Victoria. The blizzards, and he says, 'Here's another coming down the road,' and we're shut in for a few days, though not really, because we've got the skidoos and when it stops we get them going and go racing across the fields and down the sideroads and stop in at neighbours' and have a cup of coffee. Then home, and Gerry says, 'No cows to feed and water, Mom,' and I say, 'My goodness, what has farming come to these days?' and we both laugh and I think, it's not such a bad life, you know. I guess we'll have to leave it some time, but we don't think about that. The boys won't ever come back and I don't blame them. No worries for them, always a pay cheque every two weeks, but that's not for us. The little brown cheque every month, the pension, that's the only cheques we'll get, and my husband says, 'Free from the government, what a way to run the country,' and I always say, 'Free, my foot, we earned them. It's people like us who kept this country going, wouldn't you say?' and he laughs. A kind of Wayne and Shuster routine with us.

And then it's spring again, and that big red sun coming up and Gerry's coming in for breakfast, after just walking around a bit. It's something he's always done, something that stays over from the days when we did have a big barn and cattle and a couple of horses and some cows and chickens and pigs, and he just can't break the habit of going out and seeing that everything in the morning is the same as he left it the night before.

Farming is always the same, you know. No cows and chickens now, but the land is still out there, black with some snow still in the hollows, but almost ready to be seeded again, starting another year. Just like it always was."

🕊 *Home at the Cabin*

"Talk all you want about Winnipeg and what a lousy place it is to live in a lot of the time, the winter's cold for weeks at a time and the spring messy and dirty and all that wind blowing guck into your face and hair, and the mosquitoes and tent caterpillars and the heat in summer, or maybe it's raining every weekend and twice as hard on long weekends, but the old place still has a lot going for it.

On Friday in winter we're both home by four and everything is laid out in the hall and into the car in fifteen minutes and we're off. It's getting dark before we're thirty miles out of the city heading for our lake in the Whiteshell. As you may know, that's a provincial park by the Ontario border. There's no place like it, and it is better in winter than in summer. Like, there's nobody there and that's the way we like it.

Oh, sure, it's okay in summer too, being isolated, but you'll always have somebody from the city popping up. You know, the old cheery 'Hi, there! We were just driving around and we thought we'd pop in and see you guys.' Oh, yeah! Tell me another. So, there's another day of reading and relaxing and swimming and just being ourselves, another day shot.

We get to our cabin, and that's all it is, a cabin, about six, and we usually have to slog the two hundred yards from the road, right through new snow. Fresh tracks. Deer. The odd moose. But fun.

John lights a lamp and I'm filling up a boiler with snow and we've got this all down to a science, you see. John throws the kindling into the stove and puts on dry wood, and in a few minutes the fire is roaring, I mean it is really roaring, and in ten minutes you can see the red creeping up the pipe. That's how primitive the place is, in a way, but I'll tell you this. Heat that comes from a wood-stove always feels better than heat from radiators or electric heaters.

By this time John has lit the big Coleman lamp and we look

around, or I do, as John has gone out to the car and is hauling back all the stuff on the toboggan. Isn't it crazy how much stuff you have to take to the cabin, and I mean every weekend?

The cabin is fairly roomy, twenty by twenty-four, with a bedroom at one end, and next to it the washroom and Porta-potti, so that gives us about twenty by fourteen as the main room, where we do everything, cooking, eating, reading, and, of course, entertaining. There is a huge window which looks out over the lake and there is a dozen and one things I've got to do, but it becomes routine, opening up the place every weekend, blizzard or no. We've actually gone down when there wasn't another car on the road. Anything to get away from the city.

By this time the pail of snow has melted and I pour it into the reservoir and pack up the pail again for more water, and I'm laying out the stuff for our meal, because by now we're hungry as bears. I've made a salad the night before and sliced the chunky potatoes, and there is this huge thick steak and raw onions, and we prepare a meal, and oh boy, what a meal! What a meal! We take a few minutes out for a good and big Scotch before I whip the stuff on the table and then we dig in. That is one of the real good times. The wind may be howling. We don't care. It might have started snowing. Who gives a damn. Steak, rare. Salad. Red wine. Thick bread. I don't think you can ask for another thing in life but to have a warm cabin, the stove crackling, a good meal inside you, and the world of people and teaching and hassle a million miles away as the mind flies.

Then it's about ten or so and John stokes up the fire and puts the damper on and we get into our skidoo clothes. The best time is coming, what we've been looking forward to for a whole week. The thermos of Scotch and hot water goes into a small haversack and we leave and go down to the shed where the machines are and John pours in the hot oil while I hold the big flashlight and pull, pull, yank, and in about five tries he's got one going, and then mine, and we're just raring to go. We go down the ramp from the shed and on to the lake and away we go, just soaring, swooping, gliding, circling and making figure 8s, and just having the time of our lives. I'm telling you, there is nothing like it. Nothing at all.

There we are, just two people on this lake. It's about five miles long and two wide, and in the winter, in the night and with the stars and sometimes a big moon and all that whiteness of the snow, it is like another world. Not in this world. We can yell and scream all we want, and open them up and race for a mile and just stop and take off our balaclavas and listen to that overwhelming stillness. John, he can hear the stars crackling and sometimes I think I can too. There's no feeling like it. Besides, it makes you sexy.

There, off down the lake at the end, our light. Whenever we want to go home, and we think of our cabin as home, not the apartment. This is our home, this wilderness, from Thanksgiving Day until the May 24 weekend, this is our home and there's nobody around.

We'll stop and just sit for a few minutes taking it all in, the cabin and the pines and the quiet, and that big black sky, and we'll have a few drinks out of the thermos and then we're away again. Up and down the lake. A mile up the river, just ramming and banging along, and I always wonder what the beavers in their lodges are thinking. Those Crazy Canucks. Hah!

Then we head for home and the wind whipping in our faces and both of us yelling our fool heads off. The light getting closer and, wow! Nothing like it. Nothing in all of God's white earth, I say.

We run our skidoos up on the ramp and leave them there and you get into the cabin and it's nice and warm and cozy and John, he tosses a match into the fireplace. In two minutes it is blazing away. That's when you look at your watch and say, my God, is it really midnight? Were we there, out on the lake, for two hours? Well, we were, and that's the beauty of it all. There is no time out there. It is timeless. I mean it.

We'll sit in front of the fire and have a good stiff one and munch on what's left of the potatoes. We'll talk over the things that happened to each of us last week. Talk about money. Talk about this and that. Us, mainly.

Then we go to bed, this huge double sleeping-bag I made, made by sewing two Woods Arctics together, and we sleep like lambs. Just unbelievable! You're asleep before you know it. You're talking, and then, snore.

In the morning I can hear John lighting the fire and then I hear him down at the lake chopping the hole in the ice where he's put a stick. Then he comes in again and putters around and I can hear him taking a spit bath with the heated water and then, the fool, he runs outside and takes his snow bath. I'm not kidding. He rolls around in the snow, wearing only a pair of moccasins. He's back in, yelling, and that's when I get up. By the time I'm washed and dressed the place is getting warm again and cozy and he's gone out to the hole and brought in one or two good pickerel. The place teems with them. In winter, that is. In summer, with all those fools in the big boats towing a raft of kids around, they go and hide.

Okay, I'm going to ask you this. Is there anything better than having breakfast on a beautiful Saturday morning, the sun shining down, the snow everywhere, and a whiskey-jack pecking at the window wanting a handout and you're eating pickerel just twenty minutes out of the lake, with fried potatoes and sliced tomatoes and toast with jam and coffee. You can just lean back and think, a whole day ahead. Anything you want to do. Reading. Loving. Hiking. Just sitting and watching yourself unwind and become a human being again. You just let peace and quiet take over. John and I, we actually live for those winter weekends. Our life in the city is just putting in time. Our life begins when we open that cabin door. Maybe we can't go on forever like this. But again, maybe we can. We're going to try."

🕊 *The New House*

"Just about one of the happiest days of my life was when we moved into our new house. The last thing I did in the old one was slam in the dampers of the old wooden stove I'd slaved over for umpteen years, and there was nothing left in the house but the coffee-pot and some cups and saucers and the cream jug and the sugar. The men had moved in everything else into the new house that morning. I picked up the coffee-pot and the cups and the sugar and cream and I walked out of the old house and along the fence about a hundred feet and into the new bungalow and I put the coffee-pot on the new electric stove and I sat down. I said to Bill, 'Now we're going to have morning coffee in a decent place.' And we did. We sat and drank the coffee at the table and I looked around and thought, I can't believe this. After twenty-five years, a real new house of my own.

You'll find a lot of farm women who think this way. The new house, like a bungalow like ours, that was the last thing you got. First there was the Depression, all those sad years, those awful years, and then the war. The rains came and wheat was two dollars and more a bushel and they'd take all you could grow. Now, wasn't that nice of them? Then after the war there was supposed to be a big recession. It didn't come. Things got better and well, first there was the new tractor, the big Number 8 with the rubber tires, and then there was the combine, and well, I couldn't complain about that. Then there was the new truck, the three-ton, and the new car, the '49 Chev. All in this time, Bill was picking up eighty acres here and a quarter there until we were up to two sections. Pretty good, seeing as how we'd started with nothing in '28, just taking over his father's half section place. This is it, where we're on, and of course the house was there too. The old house.

Then it was my turn. In '49, and a real good crop and good prices, and I put my foot down. No more living in that old house. I raised three children in that house, and I don't know how many young pigs I had in boxes around the stove keeping warm because it was too cold out in the barn for them. And baby chicks, why, I couldn't count them. Hundreds over the years. The kitchen was like one big incubator.

So I said, this is it. I'm having my new house even if I got to go to town and truck the wood out here and bring a couple of men with me to build it. He says, 'Oh no, no, of course not, this new house I've been saving till the last because its gotta be done right.' Something like that, you know. Bullfeathers, I'm thinking, but no, he's right for once. We spend a few afternoons that winter drawing up the plans. We figure, we'll still keep a big kitchen and a small dining-room for when company comes and a living-room for parties and cards, and then a bathroom. A big one. Water pressure and a bathtub and I thought, good, I'll have a bath every single day. You never do, you know. You just say these things.

Oh, you go on like this. And three bedrooms. 'Why three?' he asks. 'Why not?' I say. 'Because I want them! Don't you think the kids are going to come home visiting?' He says, 'They're gone forever,' and I says, 'Don't you bet on that one, mister.' And guess who was right? Me. It goes without saying that at least one of those two extra bedrooms has been busy half the time we've been in there. Kids and grandchildren, you know yourself how it goes. They may be grown up and far away but you're never shut of them. We can't complain. We're blessed with good kids, even when I can think of times I could have wrung their necks.

Now it is June and I'm in my new house and the men have moved in the furniture and I'm sitting at the same big table as in the old house and there I am, and I'm drinking the first cup of coffee in my new house and I'm thinking, well, this is really nice, all clean and shiny. But then again it isn't. You know what I missed? First, the memories. There was twenty-five years of memories in that old kitchen. Of kids. Of neighbours coming to me with their troubles and their sadnesses and saying, Beryl, what shall I do? Or Beryl, do you think you could help us? Things like that, and meetings of the executive of the local CCF and WA meetings and Christmases and birthday parties and back in the old days the threshing. Fifteen men would be in that kitchen twice a day, dinner and supper, and eating like they were going to the Arctic and would never eat again for a month. And the kids. The two kerosene lamps I used to light up for them, and that was before we got the power plant. Coming home from Dunedin school, all cold in the winter, that three-mile hike in the snow, and me giving them hot cocoa and cookies and listening to them and their crazy gabble about what went on, and them doing their homework at night. After homework we'd all get together and play cards for half an hour, snap, hearts, old maid, all the simple games, and then it was off upstairs to bed for them. Bill and I, he'd have his pipe going, and maybe it was during the Depression and, oh, my, we'd wonder. Can we keep going? Or maybe, because I was the practical one, I'd be saying, is it even worth while trying to keep going? Then he'd give me that look of his and I'd know we'd be farming until we'd drop, and on that very land too.

I guess I haven't thought of it much, but there's no better place in all of Canada to learn about farm life on the Prairies than right in the kitchens of the farmhouses. That's where it all happened, all the things, the good and the bad, the loving and the fights. The counting out of money to see if there would be enough for Christmas gifts in the Depression. And during the war. Young Bill was in the SSRs and we'd get these letters from him overseas. Bill would pick up those blue envelopes from town and we'd wait until the milking and supper was over and everything cleaned up and then Bill would open the letters, maybe five of them. They were numbered, you see, so you knew which one to read first, like 108, then 109, and so on. He'd read them and we'd know. Even when he was in the hard fighting, terrible fighting as we found out when he got back, those letters told us he was okay then. We didn't dare let ourselves think that those letters were maybe five weeks old and a lot could have happened then. Course, they'd have told us quickly, so we would have known.

But that's beside the point. And the parties we'd have. The kids bringing their friends. Oh, I'll tell you, keeping those kids in line when they were teenagers, that was a job for ten people.

You know, I was sitting there with that first cup of coffee in my new home and I thought, well, here I am. I've got what I wanted. Running water, hot and cold. A really souped-up hydro plant so I could use the electric stove–this was before Sask Power came along, a couple of years. Clean walls and big windows and cupboards galore, and a shiny floor that would take a mop just as easy as whistling. All this, and well, I still missed the old house. So many memories. Good and bad. Soft ones, which kind of make you weep, and hard ones, the kind you would sob over if you remembered them too much. All of these things.

I remember, it was about 10:30 and Bill always came in from the yard or work if he was around, looking for morning coffee, and he came in and I told him right there and then. Like, now is the time to do it and there never is going to be another time. I said, 'Bill, you go right into town and see if there's anybody wants the old house, and if they do, they got a week to get it down and away. I want it gone.'

He sure knows me well enough that there is a time when I don't fool around, and he says, 'Well, Carrothers was in the post office the other day and he says he's got a family of these DPs from Europe coming in next month, and he didn't know where to put them up. Maybe he could take the house out on skids. Been done before.' I said, 'Never mind going to town, you get on the phone to Carrothers.' And so he walks over to the old house, because that's where the phone still was working, and he comes back and says , 'Yep, Carrothers just got himself a house for five hundred dollars. Be over to look at it this afternoon.'

That was the way it was done, without a word of a lie. In two weeks it was gone and the half-basement filled in and no more house. I just had to get rid of that house. I don't think I could have lived happily in my new and shiny bungalow with that old place over there with all its memories. I was going to have to start building up memories for my new home, and, of course, I did. New memories which are old memories now."

🐌 *A Frog-Swallower of a Sale*

"I'll tell you about Mickel, the neighbour I had down the road until last year, and I'll tell you about Mary. He had about 750 acres and you'd say he's pretty small potatoes, but Mickel and his wife Mary, they worked awful hard and he looked after his machinery, and all his kids were gone to the city to be schoolteachers and accountants and housewives, but being a good Polish bunch, they'd come back in harvest and lend him a hand.

He could handle it okay and I'd go over there and help out if I saw he was getting into a bind, but when he got up to seventy and that was the winter before last, he fell off a ladder and broke the old right hip. At that age that is bad. Old bones, brittle, and it could end farming for you.

So we're sitting around home one night and Mickel phones and he says, 'Peter, Mary and I are going to town and we're selling out. You come here, and I give you the first choice before the auction man comes. Okay?'

I say okay. But I go over there and asked why they were selling out.

Too old, he said. His hip was giving him trouble. He couldn't work like he used to, and I know that was sixteen hours a day a lot of the time. But he said he couldn't figure out the government forms and the income-tax vultures were always after him, because he insisted on trying to make out his own returns. They just weren't making enough money any more and besides, they both had the pension and besides, Mary wasn't feeling too well. For a guy who had decided in ten minutes that he was going to pack it in he had a lot of reasons.

You gonna sell out everything cheap? That's my next question. That pickup out there would be worth at least a hundred. What about the windmill? Going to give it away? What about the buggies and all that antique machinery? Five dollars? Ten dollars? Twelve? I said he'd be giving it away if he put prices on it like that, and the auctioneer would take his twenty per cent and where would they be? With a handful of ten-dollar bills and not much else.

Besides, I told him, you do it right and you'll get a lot more for your machinery than you think. Times are tough, and people are looking for equipment that has been taken good care of, a full line and all in good shape.

We had another drink and I said not to call the auctioneer in town until I came over tomorrow and we'd go over it all. I had a sneaking suspicion that he could sell most of it at a good price in one great big garage sale in the spring, and that would give him about three months to get ready.

Dot and I went over next morning and we had them kind of excited by this time and we all went around the yard and the house, and it took nearly all day but we listed everything that wasn't absolute junk. We decided to have a monster sale, a dandy, a stem-winder, a frog-swallower of a thing. And it was Mickel and not us who suggested that I run it. We'd get ten per cent of the proceeds and we'd do all the work and it would be fun, because apart from curling and a bit of visiting and cribbage, TV, there isn't too much to do on a farm in the winter.

Dot wrote to about ten papers around, and they printed her little stories, and in the six weeks before the sale she wrote up advertisements and put them in these papers every week. Sort of teasing them along. For farmers who wanted a bargain. For antique-hunters. Junk-hunters. Everything you want. Old-time stuff. I must say, they were pretty good.

She then put one big ad in a week before in the *Star-Phoenix*, saying free lunch and refreshments, sandwiches, coffee and cake, and you didn't get that at other sales, and besides, it was from eleven in the morning until four in the afternoon on a Saturday, so it was like a holiday. All we had to do was pray for sunshine.

We labelled everything and I put what I thought were fair prices, and all the equipment was spread out in the next field, all ready to be started up if somebody wanted to, and the antique stuff, loads of it, lamps, rugs, glassware, furniture. Oh, you just name it, everything.

It was a beautiful day. One of those early spring days when everything is just perfect. We had Mickel's kids in from the city to help, and people started to come in at about nine, even before we opened. It was cash only. Bring cash, the ads said. And they did.

A sale. A picnic, that's what it was. It could go into the *Guinness Book of Records*. They bought everything. They even tried to buy stuff that was just lying around and not for sale. Junk. There were about ten or twelve offers on the Chev pickup. I could have sold it ten times. They even bought the windmill. I asked the guy what he was doing with it and he said he didn't know, but he'd always wanted a windmill of his own. They grabbed at the antiques, and one woman bought six sets of harness, collars and all, and she said it was for her rec room. I sold an old hen-house to another guy from Saskatoon for forty dollars and he was going to use the old boards for lining a room in his cottage. All sorts of these things, and all these farmers and people from the town and Saskatoon and as far away as Regina, and all of them there having the time of their lives. Eating Mary's cake, drinking coffee, eating bits of garlic sausage and her sandwiches and then charging off in another direction to look for something else.

In about five hours they cleaned everything out, and we took Mickel and Mary and all their kids and *their* kids back to our house and we had a party. A big meal. I'm not going to tell you how much Mickel made, but I can tell you this. It was a hell of a lot more than if he had had an auction and everybody knew he was selling out and everything had to go.

The land and buildings were sold in a week. So, in a few days we watched them drive off to Saskatoon with the stuff they kept in this van and I thought, goodbye Mickel, goodbye Mary, old thing, and I hope you enjoy life in the big city in your little apartment. It would be a rude shock, and I wondered if they would survive it. I really did. Mickel was looking pretty down in the mouth those few days after his big sale, despite all the money he had pulled in.

About June they came out to see us and the wheat was showing good, real good, and I thought, oh-oh, I'm happy again. And when they drove into the yard I thought, oh-oh, I'm going to hear a long, long tale of woe and there will be tears and wondering why they had left the old place.

I've got news for you. They absolutely loved it in the city. They absolutely adored it. And there's Mickel in a New York Yankees baseball cap and a flowered shirt and, Jesus Christ, would you believe it, this old Polack is wearing shorts and sandals. Mary was good old Mary, of course, nothing changed her. But that old bastard, the only thing missing was a tennis racket in his hand.

Fifty years on that place, and they'd left it without looking back. At first I thought he was putting on an act, this wasn't for real. But it was. For him, and for Mary. When Mary said it was for real, how good it was, I knew it was. Mickel might try and fool you, but Mary was straight down the gun barrel with you. When she said they loved it, I knew they did. Living like a king and queen and acting like twenty-year-olds."

❧ *Tearing Memories Out of Your Own Heart*

"My husband used to say, 'Emily, we've just got to get rid of a lot of this junk. It's forcing us out of house and home,' and I'd say, 'Oh, George, these are my memories.'

Now he's gone and I've lived alone in the house for six years and it's just too much for me, and I'm going to move into the Pioneers' Home over on Third Avenue. And it's just too much for me to think about. I've got to be out of my home by the end of June and it's already the middle of May, and I just don't know what to do. All those rooms and the attic and the basement, and I'm not even going to think of the shed and the garage. I honestly don't know what is in there. Stuff nobody wants, I guess, but you know how it is.

I tried already. My daughter came over from Calgary when I decided to sell the house, and she wanted to help me. We took the back room, the one Benjy and Harold used to sleep in, and we went in there, and finally she just got so frustrated. She'd say, 'Mum, you know you're going to have only one room in the home, so you don't need this,' and she'd show me something, and I'd say, I don't know. That was back in December and the house sold in February, so I've had a long time to try and decide what to give away and what to sell and what to throw away, and nothing seems to work. My brain just can't cope with it.

Mary is in Calgary and Harold is in Toronto and Benjy, he's in Los Angeles, and they've all got homes of their own and they wouldn't want anything. Why should they? I know, I know, most of the stuff I have is junk. It was good when we bought it, when my husband had the store, when we were starting out and the children coming along, but it's like everything else, I suppose – all the things we thought were so important a long time ago, they aren't important any more.

You know, that house is more than eighty years old. My father built it, and he planted those huge poplars out front. I was born in that house and married in it and when my father died, my husband and I took it over. I got it in the estate because I was the child that stayed and looked after him. So there are a lot of memories there. You've got to think, my whole life is in that old white house. It wasn't worth much, being wood and not too modern and all that, but I have all of my life invested in my home.

Now I've got to leave it. I'll still be around, but I've got to be practical. Oh, yes, I know, thousands of women like myself have had to go through this, and I guess some of us were more practical than I am. Then again, a lot weren't, being like me.

But I think I'll take what I want, and sell the rest, and then give away what's left and say, 'Emily, it's done and gone with. You've got the rest of your life to live and you've got to get on with it, now.' I guess there is no sense in fooling around with things like this. Do it now. Say now, and do it. But it is going to be hard. Like tearing memories out of your own heart."

Twelve

Progress?

🐦

Progress. A slash through the tall timber, cut by the first homesteaders with an axe, became trails which widened into roads of a sort, enough to handle one wagon. Then came the twenties, and grading was done and gravel spread and culverts laid. Then came the Dirty Thirties, and desperate farmers paid off their meagre taxes by improving those roads, good enough for a car but not good enough for comfort. After the war, a frenzied road-building program went on everywhere and the Old South Line road or the Jacob's Hill Cut-off underwent some fine-tuning–widened and ditched properly–and then the asphalt gang came and laid out the long strips of hardtop.

You could now get from here to there in two hours, a far cry from here to there in two days in a horse and buggy.

With fast transportation, the cities grew larger with farm trade, the towns with a purpose for existing hung in and prospered, and the villages shrank–the store, the post office, the service station, and the beer parlour. Of course, the crossroads hamlets just dried up and blew away. A whole way of life gone, or changed, or improved, or made worse.

The progress in the West mentioned in this chapter is a mixture of good and bad. But it shows that one thing is certain: take that first step, and you can't go back.

🐦 *Your Friendly Banker*

"Eddie and I are walking around the yard, kicking tires, you might say, and I know something is not right. Finally I ask him. I say, okay, son what's on your mind. Fine, that opened him up and he starts telling me about his latest go-round with his friendly banker.

It seems he had a mortgage coming due on a half section. I said, so what? Mortgages come due all the time. Okay, what's the land worth, I ask him. Well, he bought it for $105,000 about six years ago and then everything went crazy and now he thought it was worth $225,000, if land figures in the farm paper meant anything. But the problem was, his mortgage on the $90,000 that was left on it, it had been ten and a half. Now he goes in to the banker, and it was twenty-one per cent. I told him, look, things are rough, and we've got no control of it at all. It's done in New York and London and even Tokyo these days, and you and me and every one of us, we just pay up but cut our losses when we can.

I told him the only thing to do was sign on the twenty-one-per-center on a one-year deal. Seeing as interest rates have got to go down, on a one-year deal he can ride down with the rates year by year, or six months by six months if they'll let him. Sure, I said, the things are sky-high and make no sense now, but ride them down and you'll come out okay.

That's when he said to me, 'But Uncle Les, we signed a five-year mortgage just last Thursday.'

I looked at him as if he were daft, and I asked him how that came about. As if I didn't know. Oh, he said, the banker said that was the best route for him to go. Tie him to twenty-one per cent for five years when in two years people would be paying fifteen per cent and like now, paying eleven per cent.

I sat down on that machinery box and I explained the facts of life about refinancing to him. You know, Eddie is maybe forty-five, and nobody had ever told him about this. Certainly his friendly banker hadn't. Hadn't he read any books? Well, his wife had. Oh, sure. What about his tax accountant, the smartest of them all? No, not a peep. I thought, Jesus H. Christ! No wonder farmers are in trouble. They're like little kids.

When I explained it to him, he agreed. It made perfect sense. But that's the way it goes in the high country. Stick it to 'em.

I've often wondered. I know banking people. Golfed with a few of them in my time. What gets me is this. How can they live with themselves after they pull off a deal like that? The customers, their advertising says, we look after you. Come to your friendly banker. Isn't that how one goes? And yet, these guys in the branch offices, they must be brainwashed, that the customer is a stone to be kicked around. I couldn't possibly sleep at night if I was that banker dealing with my nephew and I didn't give him all the options open

to him and then let him make up his own mind. But for him to
go into that office and have the mortgage renewal already prepared
for him to sign, that is criminal. No, not criminal. But it is immoral.
Well, end of story. Eddie lost that half section. Just couldn't
handle that twenty-one per cent. Game over."

❧ *The Banks*

"I got absolutely no sympathy for the banks. None at all. They
were all around here when prices were high, offering these young
fellows all the money in the world to buy land. At their high
interest rates. Money for land. For brand-new equipment, com-
puter-driven kind of stuff. For to build new houses on that land
they bought at those crazy high prices.

Now, there they are, grabbing it back, and you've got farmers
around here who just as well should just walk away from their
places. They're never going to pay off their debts."

❧ *None of These Banks Any More*

"By 1929 we had about fifty acres of our quarter, SW-23-37-26, we
got that fifty acres broken and disced and harrowed, and we broadcast the wheat by hand, my wife and my daughter and my two
boys. We didn't have a seed drill. Then we harrowed over it and
waited for rain.

Everything came right for us, that year. Soon there were the little
shoots of green and then the wheat came up. Up and up. I'd watch
it every morning. Then it was high and there was going to be a
good crop. Then it was hail. In five minutes there was nothing left.
It was just a big muddy field and nothing more. No wheat.

We got by that year. Me and my boy Steve, he was twelve, the
oldest, we went stooking and harvesting for farmers around Tar-
nopol who had been lucky. No hail for those guys. That way we
got through the winter, and it was a bad one, down below fifty
below lots of times.

Next year was when they say the Depression hit us, and I know.
We got a neighbour to seed our land that spring and we had a good
crop until July. Then no rain and hot winds all the time, like a
furnace. There was no crop that year. My neighbour came over

and he looked at it and said it was not worth cutting. Okay, I said, and this time my boy and me, we went all the way over to around Birtle there to find work. He got one dollar a day and I got two and when it was over we had about $120 to get us through the winter and spring. That was for food. We made it because we didn't spend anything but what we had to. That was a bad year too.

Next spring I got to have seed wheat, which I don't have. I gotta have seed, and the seed we need comes to forty-one dollars. That's when I go to the bank. They won't lend me forty-one dollars. It is too small, the manager says, and we got these rules, see. They will loan me fifty dollars, but they won't give it to me unless I get two other people to sign it. That means, if I get burned out again by drought and not pay, then my two neighbours, they got to pay. I think this is very bad, but I don't know what to do, so I have to borrow from the bank and get two signers.

Next crop, that year, it is not so bad and I can haul enough wheat into town and sell it. Prices are very low, but I pay off the bank and I say, I'll never go to a bank again. But I have to, see, other times later on – but this is a thing I hate doing now.

Then, a long time later, a bunch of men in town and some big farmers, they get this idea of a credit union, where people can be like a bank. There is a lot of writing to Regina and things like that, and about a year later we get our credit union. I am one of the first to put my five hundred dollars in and then I'm a member, and when it gets going I take my money out of the bank and put it in the credit union. I'm over and finished with banks. Our credit union has maybe nine million in it now, all the people's money. It's ours and we do with it what we like.

You go into town and you see a guy getting out of his truck and you can go over and say, hi George, how is everything doing with you? He says fine, and how are things doing with you? I say fine. You are talking to the president of the credit union, which is your bank. He is your neighbour. He is not some guy sitting in a big office down there in Toronto and making a million dollars a year.

None of these banks any more. They had their chance with us and they made it very bad for all. All of the time."

🐦 *The CPR Was God*

"Everybody talks about how terribly hard the banks are today on the farmer, but I don't think they can stand up to what the CPR did in those early days.

My dad had filed on a homestead near Fairlight and he and mother worked so hard they got about seventy acres broken and seeded in the first three years and built our house and a sod barn and some sheds and they were doing fine. They could see that in a few years they would be doing just fine. They could see a good life ahead of them.

Then the CPR decided to build a line between Reston and Wolseley. I guess their charter with the government said they could do it, but they didn't ask. They just grabbed off a right-of-way right through our farm, right through the crop that Dad had. It was ninety feet wide, that right-of-way, right across the whole quarter section, and that meant they took about twenty-seven acres, and they didn't even ask. Mom told me the surveyors just came through and then the work crews and before they knew it, there it was. A railroad. It cut Dad's crop land in half so he had about twenty acres on one side of the railway line and about twenty acres on the other, with the line and its fences and everything in between.

They never got a cent for it, even though my dad and other homesteaders hired a lawyer and did everything, but it was no good. In those days, the CPR was God, king, the law, and everything, and that was that.

Some neighbours were worse off. The rail line even went through a couple of their yards, cutting right through, and if a house or a barn was in the way, then that was just too bad.

The homesteader couldn't fight the railway. They say the railway opened up the Prairies. I'll say this too. It sure opened up a lot of wounds that were never healed. My dad never forgot that, because it meant he really had to start all over again."

🐦 *The Travelling Radio Show*

"In 1935 the Bank of Montreal foreclosed on my brother Benjamin's farm. They could have done the same to fifty others in the area twenty miles each way from Morse but they only chose a few, to show the other farmers that they could do it. 'You're next if you don't behave,' that's what they were saying. They couldn't do much else but behave, no crops, cattle being taken by the government at one and two cents a pound because they couldn't feed them, no feed, no money. The dust storms, some eight or ten days in a row–the Black Blizzards, the newspapers called them, but that was a phrase that never caught on. To us it was just the dust storms, and it wasn't black. It was greyish-brown, the colour of the good land that was blowing away into the Atlantic Ocean three thousand miles away.

This was about 1935 and radio was coming into the country. There were stations around, in Regina, the CBC transmitter at Watrous, and you could pick up Cincinnati and Cleveland, Chicago, Minneapolis, Winnipeg. These were the days of Fred Allen and his funny wife, and Jack Benny and the feud he had with Fred Allen, and Fibber McGee and Molly and their crazy cupboard. And they were broadcasting the Maple Leaf games out of Toronto and the World Series in October, and the Joe Louis fights from New York. 'A right, a left, two more rights, a left, a right and he's down, and Joe Louis, the Brown Bomber, wins again!' There was everything on that radio. I can say this, it was bigger than television is now. Not big in that people listened to it seven hours a day like they watch television, but big because it brought something into their hopeless lives.

In walks my brother Benjamin. No money, but he had sold his equipment, such as it was, and his furniture, and I think he told me he got something like $165 for everything. But he had sense enough to get on a bus to Regina, and he went to the people who had this radio dealership and he got the selling rights for that part of Saskatchewan. Oh, there were dealers in the small towns, like the garage man would handle them, but they were just there. Benjamin wanted to be free to go anywhere and sell, and he'd handle everything. He'd sell to the farmers, the people in the towns. Anybody.

It was the RCA Victor one he started to sell. He put some money down and signed some contract and they gave him two models. I can remember the big one. It stood yea high on four legs and was pretty fancy. There was a smaller one without legs but just as good, but not as fancy.

This was in the spring and he went around for two weeks and rented a hall in every town, spacing them out so he would do five a week, Tuesday to Saturday. Then he put advertisements in the local weekly newspapers saying he would be there with his big radio show and saying how cheap these radios were. That they could pay for them, say ten dollars down and two dollars a week for about fifty-two weeks. This kind of thing.

I went with him on his first night. We rattled down to Mayronne in that old Dodge truck he had and sure enough, when we pulled in, the garage man knew we were coming. Two newspaper advertisements had done the trick, but we put up some posters on the main street and looked at the hall. Then he strung his aerial from the flag-pole and about fifty feet to a telephone pole and hooked up his two radios, with all the big batteries, and we were ready.

Now, Tuesday is not a town night for the farmers. Saturday is. So we were a little worried. We shouldn't have. First, it was free. There were all-day suckers for the kids and free cigars for the men and little Japanese fans for the wives. You could buy everything for less than two dollars, but it was the right thing to do. It put everybody in a good mood.

Then Benjamin got up there on the stage, and you'd have thought he had done it all his life. He told them about the radio, how it was going to sweep the world and children could learn their schooling from it and you would hear kings being crowned and world-championship fights and, of course, so important, the World Series and the Stanley Cup. Baseball and hockey were very, very, oh, very big on the Prairies in those years. And he told about the National Hockey League games on Saturday night, the Metropolitan Opera on Saturday afternoons, and the soap operas, *Pepper Young's Family* and *Ma Perkins*. These were things they only had read about. Then he went over to one set, the big one, and he turned it on and there was that ten-second hum and then, here it came! Music or a play and he said that on Monday night that was *Lux Radio Theatre*. Everybody knew that one.

He let the people listen for half an hour or so, and there Benjamin was, twisting the dial and looking up and shouting 'Chicago!' or 'Salt Lake City!' He was quite a showman.

Then he told them about the cost. He told them he had two ways for them. They could pay cash, and then he laughed and said that only the politicians had cash. These farmers and townsfolk didn't have a hundred dollars. Most of them didn't have twenty. So they could go on the instalment plan, and he explained it and how they'd sign a contract and they only had to send their eight dollars in at the end of the month, and in a year the radio would be their own, free and clear. He told them about trade-ins and how they could be sent in and be repaired, and the manual which showed them how to hook up a good aerial and ground wire for almost nothing. If they bought, they'd have their sets in three weeks.

Eight dollars was a lot of money in the Depression and sometimes a man wouldn't make much more than that after his groceries were bought, but this was something different than that. He told them it was a chance to break out of their misery. Yes, he used that word. Misery. They understood that. People could live lives better than they had been for three years, and don't think the Prairies didn't have real hard times even before the Depression. Oh, it did. You just never hear about them.

There might have been 150 people there. That would mean maybe forty or fifty families. And that night we sold nine contracts. Everybody wanted the big one. We sold nine, signed, sealed, and delivered, and nine cheques or dollar bills for ninety dollars, the down payment. Delivery in three weeks, or less.

That was for one night. In '34 Benjamin's total crop brought him no more than three hundred dollars. Here he'd made a third of his year's work in one night. You see, he got the ten-per-cent commission, so he kept the deposits and the company in Regina handled the contracts and all the paperwork and the worry and fretting and people not paying.

We did about the same the next night in Cadillac, and even better the next night in Val Marie, and that was a part of the country hit harder by the drought than the others. I think we then went up to Shaunavon and then to Maple Creek, and that was Friday and we did even better. I think we sold fifteen radios, because there were a lot of ranchers who were still holding on, and they had money.

I know that Benjamin had more than four hundred dollars in commissions, and there was still an awful lot of towns and villages to go. But another crazy thing. When we got back to Morse after the first three weeks out on the road, guess what was waiting for us? At least twenty letters from people who had been at the meetings we'd held, and they all wanted to buy our radios, and they all had cheques or money in it.

I asked Benjamin, if they're doing this, why don't they buy them from Eaton's, where they're cheaper? The answer, simple, of course. Eaton's didn't send out a radio to everyone to see what it was like, and Eaton's didn't have salesmen going around and asking people to buy, and they didn't have the instalment plan, and that was it. The instalment plan was it. Ah, that did it. One hundred dollars at once is just too much to think about. Ten dollars, why anybody can find ten dollars somewhere. That was it.

That summer we went to every part of southern and central Saskatchewan, just working out of the little old village of Morse. We sold more radios than anyone ever had in the province, and the money just rolled in. By September, when I had to take over my first school, I had driven Benjamin thousands of miles and we'd met thousands of people. We'd sold hundreds of radios.

Benjamin made many hundreds of dollars, up in the thousands, and when it was over in September for me, he gave me a cheque for three hundred dollars. That was more than I was to get teaching at the school for the whole year in the Onion Lake district, believe me. He also had paid me five dollars a week for driving him, and I got my room and board, and a chance to see all those towns, too. It was quite an education for a girl of nineteen.

He couldn't do this in winter, of course, and when he tried to do the same next year, in the spring, the radio firm in Regina said nothing doing. They weren't going to let him make so many thousands of dollars while they did all the collecting and had all the headaches. They sent out their own men, three, I think. But they didn't have the knack of it and they didn't do any good at all."

🕊 *The Coming of the Hydro*

"When you read these historical books on Saskatchewan, they write about the Riel Rebellion, and the Indians, and when the CPR came through in the 1880s, and what it meant for the West and Canada. They go on and on right up to the present day, but there's one thing that never seems to get mentioned. It was the most important thing of all, I think, and that was when the farms and villages and little towns got the hydro.

Now it may not seem like a big thing today because everyone takes it for granted, like you flick a switch and it turns on the yard light on a cold winter morning, or you hear the thermostat kick in the oil furnace, or if you've got four dual milking-machines, you just stand back and watch them working away. That's electricity.

Before that, farming was a real chore. I mean, it was hard work. It is still hard work, but think what it was like with no electricity.

The hydro, just to give you one example, made the farmer's wife's job at least twice as easy.

She could turn on the electric stove in the morning and in a few minutes you'd hear the bacon frying, the eggs sizzling, and the coffee percolator going. Before that, you'd have to put the twisted paper in the box and then a bit of kindling and sprinkle coal on the top and light it and you'd wait and wait and wait. Then the cooking could start, and when the fire was roaring in that old Majestic stove, it would start heating up the water in the reservoir and, well, I won't get into it all, but even making breakfast on a cold morning, that was a long and hard bit of business.

And think of the heat. I mean, in the kitchen. The thermostat would keep it warm all night, and you'd dress in a warm bedroom and go downstairs to the kitchen and shave in real hot water and when you went to the table, you felt good, and all that hot food ready to eat, it would be a pretty nice way to start a long day.

They did it on a grid system. They didn't light up the whole province just like that, bang! A section maybe forty miles by forty miles would be wired, the poles put in, the substation set up and the houses wired, and the government came along and inspected the wiring and then you were ready to go. In our area, and this was in May of 1952, they had a ceremony in Yorkton and they got an old boy, the oldest man in the district, and after the speeches were done, he pressed a button and everybody went home and flipped the switch and there were the lights. You'd plug in the toaster and felt it heat up.

Course, all this cost a lot, but farmers were in pretty fair shape by then, all the good crops during the war and good prices and after, and I'll bet you the business that increased the most in those years when Tommy Douglas brought us the hydro, I bet it was the little electrical shops which sprung up in every village and town. They must have done a landslide business. Everybody buying. Think of it. Thousands of farms, and every one of them getting the hydro, and that means tens of thousands of appliances and all the other things.

Some people were a mite stubborn, though. Like my wife's sister, they're farming over west of here, and she said she couldn't cook right on the electric stove. Couldn't do bread right. Couldn't do a roast worth a hoot. Shoot, she'd do a roast the way you tan leather, lean and roasted right through several times until a ten-pound roast came out weighing six pounds. Anyway, she had the old wood-stove set up again in the kitchen, right next to the new General Electric. If that made her happy, fine and dandy. Still couldn't cook meat worth a hoot anyway.

Just one thing. Wood. Ever see those woodpiles in the yards in the fall? Yea tall and this wide, like an old straw stack. And that was just one winter's wood. You'd have to buy it, and that was expensive, or go over to the river forty miles away with a farmer's wood permit and cut it, haul it, buck it into foot-long size and stack it, and let it cure for a year before that scrub poplar and fir, tamarack, would burn. Now, all gone. Flip, and you'd see those coils heat up red. Put your hand over it. Hot. That's what it meant.

Not like in the old days when my folks came out from the East, Peterborough, in 1890. Why, I remember my grandfather telling me he and some neighbours would take hayricks and go south and west of here for about sixty miles where it was all unbroken, and they'd pick buffalo chips that had been around hardening into stone for twenty years, maybe, and they'd take home a load of these things which would last most of the winter. Burned like coal, he said, lots of heat. But it was a five- or six-day trip, and they'd camp out. Their vacation, take their guns and live off the land. Took along a few jugs of moonshine, too, I'll bet. Shot deer on the way home for the winter. Now he'd go crazy if he saw us just flip a switch and boy, there's heat.

No, I don't think it was Louis Riel or the CPR or any of the wars or the Saskatchewan Wheat Pool or the Wheat Board that was a really historic thing. To my mind it was those couple of years when the whole of Saskatchewan lit up like a Christmas tree. That's another thing. Great for the kids. They had lit-up Christmas trees."

◆ Coming in with a Bang

"They said the hydro would be ready in August, and this was 1955, but there were some hitches, as there always are, and it wasn't until the middle of October that they finally sent us letters saying it would be turned on at eight o'clock on the night they were going to be ready.

Naturally, everybody in our district had been getting his houses and barns wired and inspected, and electricians were making a killing, working day and night and Sundays, too.

A city person cannot really imagine what a big event this was in our lives. There is just no way. I mean, it took the farmer out of the secondary class. He was the same now as the people in Regina and in the towns and villages. Now the poor sod-buster, us, out there in the dark, we would have the hydro.

Then came the big night, and everybody had had their place wired for weeks, so at ten minutes to eight everybody for miles around turned off any light they had on, and put the electric light switches to 'On' and sat in the dark and waited. Four minutes. Three. Two. One. Eight o'clock! And wow! In our house everybody started hugging and laughing, just like at a wedding, and out came the beer and the wine and the whiskey, and there was going to be a party.

My brother Jim had climbed our windmill down by the barn and he came back and said it was something, just seeing those lights popping on in houses for miles around, all over the prairie, and hearing the yells. People going out into the yard and whooping and yelling.

And suddenly there was this hell of a boom. An explosion. A terrific blast of a roar and I thought, 'Oh, my God!' It was like the crack of doom. The windows shook. You never heard anything like it.

A few days later we found out. The police don't know to this day. But it was brother Alex. He always was a scamp, even when he was little. He had worked on construction during the summer, bridge-building up on some river north of here, and every time he'd come home on the weekend he'd snitch some dynamite. All summer, and he had about forty sticks, he figured. He was planning this. He'd dug a hole in some pasture on the next quarter to our home place, a kind of no-good farm of mostly pasture and scrub that nobody used much except for cattle. He'd dug this hole about two feet deep and he'd bundled up this dynamite with a long fuse, and when we were all waiting for eight o'clock and the hydro, he'd snuck out. Then when the lights went on he waited a few minutes, and then he lit the fuse and high-tailed it for home.

Then it went off, and boy, did it ever go off. Heard for miles, because it was a cold night and the air was still. Just this tremendous boom. People talked about it for weeks. The police went around looking, talking to people, but, of course, nobody knew where the sound came from. Nobody knew nothing until that smarty-pants told us he'd done it and he took us to the spot. You could see the hole.

Even today people around talk about the day when the hydro

came, and they always mention Alex's bomb, just as though it was as important as the hydro coming."

♔ *Trains Were Friendly Places*

"When I was a young girl and then got married and my husband and I had our four children, we lived in Biggar. That's on a straight line west of Saskatoon, the place where they've got that sign on the highway saying, 'New York is big, but this is Biggar.' People sure remember Biggar from that sign.

Biggar used to be a railroad town. A lot of railroaders and their families lived there and everybody knew everybody else, and we'd always use the CN to get into Saskatoon. It meant going a long way back if you were going west to Edmonton and the Coast on holidays, but we'd get a pass. The railroaders had passes and they'd slip it to the husband and he'd ride free. Nobody would know. Everybody did it.

Then you'd get on the transcontinental train, to Winnipeg or Edmonton, the Coast, and it was such a good trip. Those big velvet seats and the butcher boy coming through with his magazines and candies and sandwiches and then he'd come through with coffee. There'd be people eating their lunches they had brought, big baskets of chicken and ham sandwiches and pie and cake and cookies and fruit, and they'd try to share it with you. You talked to everybody and you made friends, even for a short way, everybody was so friendly. It was nice, and the kids could play in the aisles and the men would go into the room at the back of the car and smoke and maybe do a little drinking and talk about everything. You felt like a family on a long trip, saying goodbye to new friends and meeting other people getting on. Then you'd go clanking along and stop here and there all along the way and see new sights.

Let me tell you, going by passenger train was a real adventure, and there was always that whistle blowing. Blowing for a village or a road crossing. At night you'd wonder what the people were doing inside the houses where those little yellow lights were. The yellow was coal-oil light, this was before the hydro came in about 1952, I guess. You were warm and cozy in the passenger car and you hoped they were warm and cozy in the houses you passed.

But the best of all was going to the dining-car. The head waiter would go through all the cars calling breakfast or dinner or lunch, two servings, and you went in and all you saw at first was the whiteness of it all. The white tablecloths. Whiter than white. And the car was elegant too, all soft brown colours, and the waiters, dressed in black and so neat. Some were Negro and some were white, but it didn't matter. I think dinner was about $1.50, which was a lot in those days after the war when prices went up all over the country, but it was worth it. You tipped the waiter a quarter. 'Leave a quarter,' I always told my husband. 'George,' I'd say, 'he's a Negro fellow and I don't think he makes much money. Give him fifty cents.' And it would be pulling teeth for my husband to leave fifty cents for a three-dollar meal, but it was worth it. You see, they travelled from Vancouver to Winnipeg and you usually got the same waiter, so if you tipped him good the first time you ate, he would be attentive to you. Remember those little dishes of celery and radishes they'd bring you? Well, if you ate those up he'd probably bring you another. If you were a friendly person, you'd have him as a friend by the time you reached the Coast.

And the food, the food was so good. I can see it now. The white tablecloths, and the napkins, and the plates of roast beef, and they had a special way of roasting the potatoes and doing the peas. The bread came in a silver dish with a white napkin over it. The cutlery. Oh, yes, I remember. It was sterling silver and heavy. You could tell it was the very best. Nothing but the best in those days.

Going to the Coast like we did every summer, you'd get into your berth and the train would be swaying and the whistle going oooahhhooo and you'd see the lights of the little towns and with the clickety-click of the rails you'd soon go to sleep. I was never afraid on trains. They were friendly places and I guess you could call them the most democratic thing anywhere in the country. What I mean is, if my husband and I were going alone and two other people sat with us, they could be aristocrats from England or orchard people from Vernon or a big shot from Vancouver, and I've met all three of those kind of people. I remember them still. Really friendly, wanting to know about the life you had, where you lived, and you'd get into some lively conversations. People talked a lot more, I suppose, because they knew they would never see you again. Some of the stories I heard in all those years of travelling by train – then you'd say goodbye at the end, or they'd get off, and that would be that.

Yes, I've taken VIA Rail. Yes, it's a train – but that's about the only thing you can say about it."

✎ *School Buses*

"When they set up the big school districts, you know, maybe they were helping the farmers more than the kids. What I'm getting at is the school buses. When they went to the consolidated-school-district plan, of course, they had to bus the students in and out, five times a week, September to the middle of June, and that meant decent and efficient transportation. School buses. You understand?

Who drove those school buses? It wasn't a full-time job. Two hours in the morning, two when school was out, and in the early days it was pretty damn low pay.

I remember my brother. In 1947 he had come out of the air force and got married and they bought a quarter section, down there near Granum. They literally didn't have a bean. He had the DVA, and Margaret had saved up some as a nurse, but by the time they settled in and got some equipment, they were broke. I mean broke.

The thing that kept them going that first year was Jack got a contract to drive school bus. He had to buy the bus, and because it was just after the war the government had to put some sort of priority on this kind of equipment, so he got a priority on a school bus. Then he had to pay his own gas, and the first two months he got that on credit from Old Man Tilley at the Imperial station, and, of course, he didn't have any other income. They'd just bought the land, and made the down payment on the bus, so things were real tough. And when all was said and done, that total contract for that school year was worth seven hundred dollars. Not seven hundred dollars to him. When all was paid off, payments and gas, he probably netted two hundred dollars, but that was a godsend. It really was. It got them through that winter and spring, and it was a bad winter for snow and cold. So it was $200 for a year's work, you could say.

But what am I talking about him for? This is about today. All over Western Canada there is thousands of these buses. Our kids got to have the very best education so they can leave the farm and go to college so they can go east to Toronto where the big money is. So, buses. Thousands of them.

Damn it all, I've never seen times when they were tougher than right now. The last three years, you could put it. Now think of the thousands of farmers who are keeping their heads above water with their school buses. Those school-bus contracts, that's the only real money that's coming in. Year in and year out, that's sure money. The cheque every third of the next month. Sure as death and taxes. I wonder, yep, I wonder, how many farms are kept in groceries with the school-bus contract, or the school-bus wages."

🐦 *Not About Women's Liberation*

"We stayed out of it too long, thinking the men could run things and get things done. Now we know a bit different. The women have to get in there and fight with the men too, and in some ways take over some of the things the men were doing but not doing very well.

I'm not talking about Women's Liberation. Far from it. I'm far too old for that. A woman of sixty, she should leave that nonsense to the women of twenty-five who have nothing better to do. As far as I'm concerned, I'm liberated, even in town here, and that goes for farm women I know, too.

I'm talking in the field of common sense and doing things that can be done. I'm talking about using your common sense and hard work and figuring the best way to do things. We've got a lot of experience in these things, you know, and we can put them to work.

There should be women on the boards of the wheat pools and marketing boards. We should be more into government, getting our ideas across. Some of us are pretty good writers and we could be writing pamphlets and, for that matter, making speeches. This isn't Women's Liberation. This is liberating the West from Ontario and Quebec, showing them we mean business.

You just take the Women's Auxiliaries and the like about three steps further and you've got a pretty strong force. We've stood behind our men all our lives, most of the men are what we made them, so now it's time to step out in front. Grab the reins and get the wagon moving down the road. These days, it would be a new Cat, a big bulldozer but with a woman's touch at the controls. We've put it off far too long, I figure. We just need a few strong women to grab hold, and it wouldn't be too long before things would happen. Don't be silent any more. Be strong and holler more. A lot more. Yell real loud."

🕊 *Political Clout*

"I look around, and twenty miles each way, so that's forty by forty, that's 1,600 square miles and that's a pretty fair chunk of acreage. Well, in travelling around and talking to people and looking, I figure that in five years half the farmers on that land today could be out of business. In five years. That is, if things stay the way they are. It could be worse in other areas. Could be better. But I'd say this part of the country is about average. Average farmers. Average crops. Same rainfall. Same drought. Same hoppers. Same land prices. Same interest rates. Same price we pay on our machinery. Same taxes. Mostly the same of everything. And same prices too.

And what is happening? Jesus Christ, I'm not even sure. All I know is it's pretty damned hard to make a living on the farm today. You gotta have a lot going for you and you never get it all together at the same time.

What the farmers of this country need is political clout. Back in Ottawa they just ignore us. We're pretty far down on their list. That's Ontario and Quebec talking to Ottawa, and Ottawa saying, 'Okay, fellows, we'll look after you first.'

Farmers used to have some political clout in this country. We could go down there to Ottawa and tell those politicians they were doing us wrong. We'd say we want this and give them the reasons for it, and they'd think it over and say, you know, they're right.

Farmers need a union. Oh, I know, don't tell me. We've got half a dozen of them, all fighting among themselves, and all they do is pay high salaries to the top guys. They do surveys and they get stuck away on the top shelf. I know all this. They send delegations to Ottawa. Please, sir, they say to the minister, can we have an appointment? They sit around for fifty minutes with the minister of agriculture, pleased as punch, and then he says, 'Well, thanks, boys, it's been good to talk to you, and I'll have my boys look over this brief of yours.' End of story.

They're all the same. Liberal, Tory, whatever. What does it matter.

Forty or fifty years ago the farmer had clout. Maybe thirty-five per cent of people lived on farms. That's across Canada, not just the Prairies. The farm vote, that was big, and politicians couldn't ignore it. That's when the minister of agriculture was a big man. Like Jimmy Gardiner, for one, he practically ran Western Canada. When old Jimmy stamped that little foot of his on the platform, the whole country practically shook. The farmers and the people in the towns and villages could elect governments then.

Now, how many people on the farms? Maybe four or five per cent. That is political clout? No way. That is nothing. We are outnumbered. We are surrounded. Even the people in the small cities, the towns, they are not too much a part of us in a political way. We get along because we have to. But the distance between the farmers in the West and the rest of Canada, it gets wider every year. Nobody listens to us. Nobody, and this is worse, nobody talks to us. They don't say, okay, you've got a problem. How can we help? They don't even know we've got a problem down there in Ottawa. The trouble is, we're trapped. Nobody listens, yeah. Nobody listens. And we don't know how to talk.

It is hopeless, I tell you. It is just going to get worse. You can blame the French government for manipulating the European Common Market and forcing down the price of commodities, and all the subsidizing that goes on. You can blame the Americans for falling for it all like suckers, as they always are. Blame Ottawa, just as she stands. The capital city. Blame the Tories. Blame the Liberals before them. They've sure as hell got nothing to be proud of.

But I guess in the long run, the way the cat's tail hangs, you gotta blame us . . . ourselves, I mean, for letting all this happen, because, damn it all, we saw it coming. Saw it pass by, and then it was just too damned late. It's too late now. We are in real trouble."

Thirteen

Ranchers and Others

❧

*The Finest Ranch Country in the World ... Lost to the World ... Good
Grass Makes Good Beef ... The Herder's Dream ... Range Fire ... Free
Range ... Ranchers Are a Different Breed ... Sweet Revenge ... Deer
Cows ... Nodding Horses ... A Gun for Texas ... Pet Deer ... Coyotes
... Home Brew ... Pasteurized ... Mr. Sheep ... The Hog Business ...
And Pigs Get Slaughtered ... Getting Your Goat*

Ranching provided the glamour of the West; there was nothing romantic about
being a homesteader. The foothills country of south and central Alberta proved
ideal for the grazing of herds, and by 1900 there were scores of brands registered.
Cynics say the Calgary Stampede was begun by the big ranchers, who, knowing
only a few of them could hang on against the push of the homesteaders and
their barbed wire, started the world-famous rodeo to remind future generations
of the ranching heritage. If so, they succeeded.

The problems are different today, but the rancher is still the man in the pickup
truck – rarely on a horse any more – checking his herds, looking for rustlers,
breeding up, watching the market closely, his wife by his side as his top hand,
both hoping tomorrow will be better. Sharing that philosophy are all the other
types of people on the land trying anything – sheep, goats, pigs, even (in the
old days) home brew – just to get by.

❧ The Finest Ranch Country in the World

"You never saw country like the prairie for growing cattle. You
just can't imagine it today. Rich, oh! Nobody has ever seen country
like the Prairies were in those days. It was the finest ranch country
in the world. There was the finest of grass growing high, and pea
vine, vetch, lots of good water. I used to raise monsters and not
one of them so much as got a handful of oats. Not like today.

There was this butcher in town, Johnston, and he said, 'Bring
me some beef,' and I said I'd bring him two quarters and he said,
'How much will they weigh?' and I said I'd bring him two quarters

and each would weigh two hundred pounds. Off a cow, mind you, not a steer.

He said, 'You can't,' and I said I'd bet him. Two hundred pounds a quarter. Oh, those were enormous animals in those days. Johnston said, 'I'll bet you any amount of money you want,' and I told him he didn't have enough money, so I didn't bet him.

Well, I went out with one of my Indian cowboys and I pointed to a big cow and he slaughtered it right there, turned it on its back sliced it down its belly, wrapped two quarters in canvas, put it in the buckboard, and into town we go. I'll tell you. Those quarters dressed out at 210 pounds a quarter. Johnston was new to that country and he couldn't believe it, that we could grow range cattle that size. Don't think the man ever got over it."

🕊 *Lost to the World*

"School? I practically had none. Just a few grades. Not enough to get by these days, but in them days it didn't seem to make no differences. Most boys were just like me. My education didn't amount to a row of pins. I learned to read and write and I can get by on that. A farm kid in our district, well, not too many got more than just getting by. It was the same with all of us, but in them days we didn't care none.

Most fellows didn't go on. They was needed on the farm or they went out to work for somebody. Some went cowboying for the big outfits south and west of here and we never saw them again. Once a fellow became a cowboy he was pretty well lost to the world. But anyway, about schooling, I didn't want it and it didn't need me."

🕊 *Good Grass Makes Good Beef*

"I can see my old grandfather sitting right there in his chair, that pipe of his going out again and again. That man smoked more matches than anybody I ever knew, and he'd talk about the good old days. They weren't good old days, really, because those old-timers had a tough life. Ranching sure as hell wasn't like you read about, none of this happy cowboys singing around a fire and long herds being trailed up to the Pat Burns slaughterhouse in Calgary. It was just plain hard work and I remember him saying, 'Good grass makes good beef.' He was saying, of course, that the good old days back in the early 1900s was when the ranchers had big spreads and there wasn't much interference. You had your herd and a couple of the best bulls you could afford, and you did the best you could. If you made money one year you probably lost it the next year–the blizzards, the big ones, the five-day ones–and you started all over again with what you had left.

But you had to have that grass. You had your deeded land, a couple of quarter sections, and then all the rest, for miles and miles around, that was free range, open range, and that was why you had your two round-ups, one in the spring for the branding and the one in the fall when you cut out your big steers and the old cows and you moved them to the rail point and shipped them. That was ranching then. What was left over, you got through the winter with, and you hoped for chinooks to clear off the snow so the cattle could get at the grass, and no disease, no wolves.

'Good grass means good beef,' he'd say, and what he was talking about was homesteaders – and barbed wire. Barbed wire meant homesteaders. I don't think he had anything against these people who came up from the States and from Manitoba and Ontario and Europe, who grabbed off their ten-buck homestead. But they put up barbed wire and that meant the end of the open range. A guy with three or four of his neighbours and their little 160-acre patches, they could louse up a whole ranch operation. In four years they'd proved up and sold out to some other nut who thought they could farm in this south country and moved to the town or gone back to where they came from. But the damage was done. They'd screwed up the range, pure and simple. Ploughed under that good grass, and registered homesteads along the river and creeks and taken it up, and they had the law on their side. Once the sod-buster from the East had registered his claim with the land agent, then there wasn't much that the rancher could do.

It all went to hell pretty fast, it seems. Only a few years, maybe five, after the railway hit Calgary and they started shipping east and not trailing down to Fort Benton, the homesteaders started coming in. They knew their rights, and the ranchers didn't stand much of a chance. A house here, another there, a few, and then a school and then a store and you've got a settlement.

By this time, says my grandfather, the homesteaders were getting pretty well settled in. Schools and towns and churches and stores and post offices, and in a big bit of country there are three ranchers and fifty or sixty homesteaders—and the politician, who is he going to toady to? The farmers, naturally, and the rancher would be left sucking the hind tit.

Let me put it this way. The Old West as we know it in Canada, the way it was won was with the Homestead Act and the CPR. Ten bucks for a quarter section and the rangeland all surveyed and staked, and there wasn't much left for the guy who ran a couple of hundred cattle, even a thousand, on land that he knew wasn't his.

Being a cowboy was no big thing. Like being a rancher was becoming not such a big thing. After 1900 there wasn't much of the yodelling cowboy any more. Just a lot of hard work, a lot of working with cows, which aren't your smartest animal, and calving in a blizzard, and hell, we're not even speaking about wolves and there were quite a few of them. Sometimes bears down from the mountains. But mostly blizzards and drought, and when you had less and less land and everybody building their herds, you had overgrazing, and that was another bad thing. No rain, no grass. No good grass, no good beef. Poor beef, and you're not making even your own wages. That was the size of it.

So there are all these poor bastards all through this part of the country, hoping, looking at the mountains for the next big winter storm and not seeing it coming. A blizzard, she'll come up in an hour and you've got your fortune out in the hills, in the coulees, the bottomlands, and you can't get them out, and they'll drift with their asses to the wind and you can't find them, and three days later you find them and they're all dead. That's the way it sometimes happened. Is that any way to make a living? Not in my way of thinking.

Of course, the whole thing is changed now. Today's ranching, I mean, you get up in the morning and go ranching in an All-Terrain Vehicle and come in for lunch and mess around the house trying to figure out your income tax. Then you say to hell with it and take the wife and kids into Calgary for a big meal of Chinese food. Not a chicken or milking cow on the whole damn place. Comes in these cartons.

No, the way the old man told it long ago when I was a kid, it was Churchill's blood, sweat, and tears, and God got his two bits

into it, too, because of the weather. Now it's how good a bull you
got, and how many of these cattle with the fancy French names,
and when you've got your calves up to a certain size, you truck
them off to a feed lot and sell 'em and let somebody else do the
worrying. You worry that you'll get a good price, and the company
who owns the feed lot, he's hoping the price of barley will be so
low he can feed them critters up and make a profit. All the time,
the city housewife is screaming about the price of beef. It's always
too damned high for her. It's always too damned low for the guy
raising them.

Funny, ain't it? Me running off this way, talking about my grandfather who was an old-timer, a real rancher, and I don't think I
know any more about ranching than any other trucker. Yeah, I'm
a trucker. So much a mile, a $35,000 rig, second-hand, long hauling,
and I still probably make more in a year than my old grandfather
did. But I remember what he'd say, and what ruined the old way
of life was homesteaders. Barbed wire, politicians, votes, and where
the deer and the antelope play, that is all farming now, six-section
farms, and no grass. Remember what he said. No good grass, no
good beef. That says it all."

❧ The Herder's Dream

"I was working for Dumont, the rancher, doing odd jobs around
the place and they had this new herder, a man named Robinson. I
said one day, did he want to take a magazine with him while he
herded, and he said no, not that day. Every day I'd ask him the
same thing and finally he said, 'Helmer, I can't read.' It turned out
he had been raised on some lonely ranch down there and he'd
never had a chance to go to school.

Then one day the boss sent me out to his range to give him
something and as I rode up I saw him lying on the ground, looking
at something down there, and I thought that was sure funny. I
swung down from the saddle and knelt there beside him and you
know what he had done? He'd taken his very sharp knife and he
had cut dry weeds, and with the pieces he had built a tiny but very
complete section of square corrals with an eight-cornered roping-
corral, gate bars and all, and he even had a big squeeze-gate built,

and a snubbing-post in the centre of that corral. His corral was five bars high and each square corral was connected with the other.

Well, I just looked at it and at him. I thought that here was a man who didn't have no education and wasn't going to get anywhere in life except being a herder, but he so wanted to be a rancher that he'd spend his time with his knife and a bunch of dried weeds and sticks building up a little spread, corrals and gates and even a snubbing-post. I thought, one man and his impossible dream."

❧ *Range Fire*

"When I came in to this High River district about 1900 there was no houses. You could go for miles and see maybe not more than four houses and no fences, just the prairie and the grass this high, up to my waist, and you could look as far as the horizon, and it was just like a big waving carpet. The finest ranchland in the world. And believe me, when you got a fire started, believe me, it was a fire too.

I mind one that started just east of our place and it went right down to Brooks, and anything that was in front of it, well, it just went. Houses. Barns. Everything. There was nothing could stop it, rivers, nothing, coulees, nothing, it just kept going, and with a wind behind it, well, I never saw it, but they said it could run down a man on a horse. You see, the horse would tire, but the fire would just keep coming. Of course, the horse would be terrified, scared as the very devil, and that made him panic. Forty miles, sssssssswooooosh, just took the whole thing out. Crossed the Blackfoot reserve and took out everything on that, and the whole country was black as coal. But when the rain came, the grass came up just as green as anything you ever saw in your life. Just beautiful, most beautiful thing I have ever seen.

Some fires were set so the new grass would come up, but the Brooks fire was accidental. A fellow was herding some cows and he stopped to light a cigarette. You know how you flick the head of a match with your thumb? He did it too hard, I guess, and the head of the match flew off and fell into this dry grass, and instead of smacking it out he decided to get his cattle out of the way, because they were in front and a north wind was blowing, and by the time this cowboy got to the fire it was away on him and going to the south. In five minutes all the men in the country at that time couldn't have stopped it. The flames were twenty feet high and just going like Billy-be-damned."

🐦 *Free Range*

"In them days you just grazed your stock wherever you goldarned wanted them. You could be the biggest rancher in the district and you wouldn't look like it because all you'd have was a funny little house and a corral and a few sheds and a bunkhouse and that would be on your 160 acres, your homestead, and then you grazed your cattle and let them run all over the country.

You could say about a fellow, 'Oh, he's just got a little outfit out west of here,' but somebody else would say, 'Yeah, but he's got more than six hundred cattle,' and that would make him a real big man. Looks counted for nothing in this country in the old days."

🐦 *Ranchers Are a Different Breed*

"There's nothing romantic about being a rancher. Forget that. I know of more things that go wrong with a ranch that can louse you up than if you're just a farmer. Grain or mixed farming, doesn't matter. Ranching is a tough way to go.

If they get a drought year, then they've got the problem of hay, feed. You can't run cattle all year round when we've got a bad winter with snow, as cattle, as you probably know, aren't like horses. Horses can get down to the grass by pawing away the snow. A cow can't do that. Too dumb, or she's never learned and she's carrying a calf and they need a good diet, and so you've got to bring them in and feed them. That means hay. If hay was poor that year, then there's nothing that jumps higher in price so fast in price than hay. You see, they have to truck it in from up north. There are guys up north of Edmonton who just pray that the south part of this country will have drought.

In the old days beef was lean. Grass-fed, no marbling, just a good chunk of red meat, no fat. And then people didn't like that. That's one of the reasons we had that big rise in feed lots. They'd buy 'em small and fatten them up and that produced the veins of fat. Okay, then with this cholesterol thing the food writers in the papers said meat had to be lean again, with not much fat. Everybody was going to die of a heart attack if they ate this fat meat. So now we're back to lean meat. You see, all this gets complicated, and it's just one of a hundred things the rancher has to think about. Just one of a hundred things.

But he puts up with it, because ranching is a way of life. His old man was a rancher and he inherited the home place and the leases. Leases are what you get from the government, so much a quarter or an acre and it's yours to graze on. Most ranchers, if they say they've got 10,000 acres, they mean they've got 320, really, and that's the home place. The rest is leased, and the government controls the leases. This way they're sort of weeding out the poor ranchers – you know, the guy who's on a three-day drunk when it's calving-time and all hell is breaking loose.

It's a hard life, a hard-working life. When you got cattle, you just don't lock the door and go off to Arizona and tell the neighbour to look in every couple of days to see if the heat is still on and the place hasn't been wrecked by these kids from town who seem to make a living just going around raising hell. No way. You got a ranch, it's a thirteen-month-a-year job. You're always checking and fixing fence. Checking water-holes and pasture. Moving bunches from upper to lower pasture, to better water, and worrying about water and looking for sick cows. When you've got four hundred or five hundred, that's a lot to look after.

You worry about rustling. Yep, there's some of that around. In the night or, hell, even during the day, a rancher hears a shot from a long way off. He says, 'Oh-oh,' and he's on the phone to the police, but not much good it does him. He gets there after an hour or two of looking, say, because where the cattle are then, that's not where the dead one is. The cattle have spooked. If there's anything that'll drive a cow nuts, it's the smell of blood. They get the hell out of that place. So, maybe he finds where the steer went down, shot, and the guys from town are long gone. Throw it in the back, put a canvas over it, and they're gone. Some fellows I know lose two or three a year that way. A lot of money, when you figure in one year three big 800-pound fellows just shot and taken away. That buys a lot of groceries. Hazard of ranching. No fire or lightning, but a city slicker with a .22 semi-automatic loaded with long rifle shells. Does it every time.

They're a different breed, these ranchers. Different from farmers. They have a feeling for it all. Not that the farmer doesn't either, but mostly the guy who ranches, he's out in the open air a lot. Not sitting on a $125,000 tractor pulling $60,000 worth of equipment and then sitting around mostly and watching his grain grow. Naw, that's not fair. But a rancher has got those big, high skies, all so blue, little clouds passing over and they're out riding, although a pickup truck or one of these three-wheeled All-Terrain Vehicles is more like it these days, and they look and the mountains are out there, looking pretty. They look down into a valley and a herd of white faces are down there around the dugout and, you know, that's a pretty good feeling.

They're different people. They're happy with their life, what they're doing. They got insecurities too, but they kind of put that aside. They want and they get the good things in life, and they got these bonuses on the side. The rancher, he's a friendly guy. He'll talk to you, tell you everything. Everything about it all, except the size of his herd. That's a no-no. Ask him how many and he's mighty shy about that. You don't ask a city guy how much he makes. Then don't ask a rancher how big his herd is. But, sure, troubles he's got, but he knows he's high man on the totem-pole of the good life. Good food. Good friends. All the fresh air he can breathe. The feeling that, even in bad times, life can be pretty good.

They don't make a lot of money. I don't know any rich ranchers. Big companies that ranch, yeah, sure, but the little guy, the guy on the horse, looking at his own brand and thinking, that's my daddy's brand, or my granddaddy's brand, and it is the only one in the world like it. That kind of makes it unique. I know, if I was ranching, that would make me feel pretty good. I'd call it freedom in a way, shaped into the bottom end of a branding-iron.

You go to a wedding, say, some cousin in Calgary gets married and there's a reception. You know how guys stand around and kind of size each other up, not knowing each other. One guy says he's an oil engineer. Another runs a trucking business, say. Another is an accountant, a doctor, a lawyer, whatever. Then this quiet guy with the face all burned by the wind and maybe a suit that don't quite fit, you know, like off the rack at Sears, and he says, 'I run a few head down south and east a ways from High River. Foothills kind of place.'

I've seen it. One, maybe the accountant, he says, 'You're a

rancher?' The guy says, 'Yeah. Don't get up here much. Kind of keep close to the place mostly . . .'

You can see the look in the eyes of the other guys. It's like a kid getting a new bike and they say, 'Gee whiz!' They've got respect for him. He isn't just this guy, any guy. He's part of what they call the Old West. He's history, heritage, I guess, is the word. There they are, stuck behind desks, being just city men like ten thousand others, and he's a free man, going it alone, his wife and kids making it go. This rancher is what they would like to be. No matter how important or wealthy these other guys are, this man is really the man they want to be.

If I was a rancher, I'd feel pretty good about that."

✒ Sweet Revenge

"I remember the exact day I blew my stack. It was about eight in the morning and I was going to town and I took one of the back roads to look and see if one of my bunches of cows and calves were doing okay and along this road I see vehicle tracks. Know where they were going? Right through my neighbour's fence. They'd driven the vehicle straight through the fence, busted it, pulled up about four posts before the wires snapped. I thought, Jesus Christ. This is it.

This kind of stuff had been going on for years now, and this being the country it is, there ain't a house within miles and they just were getting away with it. There was this gully about two hundred yards away and I thought, that's where the bastards are. Hiding the truck in the gully and gone hunting. There were no tracks coming out and I thought, okay, let's look into this situation.

I had a big box of that cubed sugar I carried in the cab to feed some of the horses I had running up in the hills when I'd go up to look at them. Stuff I'd buy and let them feed up, and then ship to the slaughterhouse in Fort Macleod. To me, horses are just another cash crop, and there's a big market for the meat in Japan.

So I hike over there and sure enough, there's the truck, not even locked, and the registration is a Calgary guy. Screw this, I said, these guys drive all the way down here, 185 miles, hunting, and they go around busting up fences. Know what I did? I unscrewed the gas cap and I dropped in about a dozen of them sugar cubes I'd stuffed in my pocket. That's what I did. Then I just walked back to the truck and away I went. Never thought another thing about it. Tit for tat, by God. Those guys would come back and drive home and somewhere around Nanton or up around Vulcan that Bronco they had would go cough, cough, sigh, and they are dead. That big motor, she's so gummed up with gasoline laced with sugar that she ain't going to go nowhere.

You know, that's a $400 job if it's a nickel. Stuck down there at Vulcan with no goddamned motor any more. And I didn't think anything about it. Didn't even tell my neighbour. What he don't know, well, that won't hurt him.

And that was only the first time. Not a month later I'm out this Saturday morning and this is part of my own place now, two sections I lease for spring grazing, and there's this wire gate busted. Tracks in. None out. I think, this is funny. There's two vehicles in there, two sets of different tracks, and I walk down and sure enough, in a kind of bluff there's a three-quarter-ton and a two-horse trailer. Name on the side of the trailer, from one of those cute little five-acre hobby farms just south of Calgary. You know, white fences, cute little six-horse barn, huge, big, big house. Gentlemen farmers, they call themselves farmers, but these guys work behind a big desk on the twenty-third floor of one of them skyscrapers telling a lot of other people what to do.

Okay, out comes the sugar. Maybe fifteen or twenty I put in. I figure a guy who's got a two-horse trailer and can go riding out in my hills all day after busting my gate and shooting my antelope to boot, my deer maybe, he can afford a more gummed-up motor than the guy in the $15,000 Bronco. The only thing I felt sorry for was the horses. When they break down near Nanton or Stavely there ain't no livery barns around any more where they can be stabled. But to hell with that noise. I don't care. A man's property, you got to respect it, else what's the use of it all.

And it's always these city guys from Calgary. I mean, just who in hell do they think they are? My neighbour, this Herbie south and west of here, he did it differently once. He surprised two guys in a pickup coming off his land after busting a fence. He just stopped them and said he wanted $500, and no fooling, and he wanted it then. Jesus, he said they put up a fuss. Then they got real nasty when he didn't back down. They said to hell with you and other choice language and he just said, you write me a cheque for $500 now or else I pick up this mike and I'll radio in to the wife and she'll phone the Mounties and then we'll talk it over like sensible gentlemen. One guy reached in his pocket and pulled out his wallet and handed him five $100s. Just like that. The guy was actually carrying a roll of $100s. Calgary sportsmen, but they weren't in their office on the twenty-third floor of some skyscraper telling people what to do. They were facing one mighty angry rancher."

🐦 *Deer Cows*

"My son decides to retire early from working in the oil business in Calgary and he's always wanted to be a rancher, so he buys this ranch, the cattle and everything, way over by Millerville. The real estate man, he knows that part of the country, and he tells my boy to go to a shop in Calgary and have a bunch of 'No Hunting' signs made of steel. That means he'll save money when the hunters from Calgary come out and start to fill them with bullet holes. The bullets will just bounce off.

Then, he says, when hunting season starts, round up your stuff and put them in a corral by the house and don't let them break out. Get a few big sheets of plywood, he says, and get somebody to saw them out so they like they look like cows, and paint them up some and put them over by the bluffs, just kind of nearly in among the trees. The hunters, he says, will fill them full of bullet holes, but they won't be your cows, so you'll save money that way too. And when they find out the cows are decoys, they'll get so mad they'll head off to some other part of the country.

It worked, too. They fired at the signs to make sure their guns were working, and they fired at the plywood cows. A cow and a deer look an awful lot alike to some of these city fellows."

🐦 *Nodding Horses*

"Now that we're telling ranchers' jokes, did you hear about the fellow who had the big spread west of High River, and the oil boys come along with their seismic gear and take these tests, and six months later they come back and they say to him, we want to put our rig right over there, about a hundred yards from his house.

He says okay, go ahead, and for a few weeks there's the damnedest mess and commotion and noise you ever did hear, but sure enough, they get themselves an oil well. Then they say they want to put in another, because just one well ain't no good, so he says, carry right on, gentlemen. Another hundred yards from his house, on the other side, and a few months later they got these two nodding horses going day and night pumping up that oil, and life, well, it kind of looks better. And one day he goes into the post office in High River and gets his mail, and there's a cheque from the oil company for the first royalties and the thing is for $14,000.

He looks at it and says, 'Boy oh boy, this is the most money I ever made out of ranching in any year!' "

🐌 *A Gun for Texas*

"I was in this sporting-goods store buying a new golfing glove and the salesman was helping me, but you have to try on quite a few before you get the right one, so he said for me to keep looking and he'd serve a man who had come in.

I could hear their conversation. They were maybe ten feet from me and this man was a rancher and I guess he was west of Nanton out in the foothills and he wanted a gun. The clerk asked him what he was going to use it for, and this rancher said he was going to Oklahoma and Texas on some trip and there would be some trap-shooting at these ranches he'd be visiting, and he wanted a good gun. The clerk said, oh, in that case, you'll be best with one of these, and he took one down.

The clerk showed him a gun, and I could see it wasn't a bad gun. He said the price was nine hundred and something. Say, nine hundred and fifty dollars. The big guy picked it up and sort of fooled around with it, and I could see he didn't know much about guns. A rancher, and he couldn't even get the heft of it.

No, he said, wasn't there something better, and the clerk said no, that was the best one in stock right then. Well, this rancher got kind of angry and he said, 'I can't go down there with those Texas fellows with a nine-hundred-buck gun. They'd laugh me off the place. Those fellows have guns that cost ten thousand dollars.' And he asked if there was a place in town where he could get a gun like that. 'No', the clerk said, 'no, this is all we've got.' The guy said, 'Okay, if you don't want my business I'll try Woodwards.' And out he went.

The clerk came over to me and I was kind of laughing and he asked if I knew who he was. I said no, but his face looked kind of familiar. He said he was so-and-so, from such-and-such a place, and he was a big rancher and was always in the paper yelling for more subsidies and grants and this kind of thing for the poor rancher who was being beaten into the ground. That kind of thing. On committees all the time and going to Ottawa and raising a lot of dust about how a rancher couldn't make a living selling cattle any more because of the government and those bureaucrats in Ottawa.

But there he was, complaining that he couldn't buy a five-thousand-dollar or ten-thousand-dollar shotgun in a little shopping-centre sporting-goods store which maybe sold one of those nine-hundred-dollar guns once a year."

❧ Pet Deer

"About the end of September, the farmer I worked for started putting out a bucket of barley chop every morning and every night at a little bunch of trees at the foot of the garden, and the deer started to come. There were about five or six deer that came all the time. Free breakfast, free dinner. In about a month they would be standing there when I'd take the bucket and I gave them names, from the story, Donner and Blitzen, you see. I thought, what a kind thing to do.

Then one morning when I came into the kitchen he told me to take a knife that was on the table and we went out. It was frosty, cold, I remember that, and the deer were out there and we walked towards them.

Then bang, bang! He just put that rifle to his shoulder and shot, bang, bang, and one buck just fell right there and another made two big jumps and then fell down dead.

I couldn't believe it. This farmer had shot the deer, the pets. Like bang! One. Bang! The second. Then he took the knife and cut both throats and the blood poured out, and we went back to the kitchen and his wife asked him how many. He put out two fingers and said, 'The two bucks.' Just like that.

When we finished breakfast he got the tractor and we took the deer to the shed and hoisted them up and he cleaned them. He was good at it.

I asked him why he had done that, feeding them, making pets of them, and then shooting them, and he said, 'Winter meat. All that grain they've been getting makes the meat good. Not too gamey now.'

He said they did it every fall that way and I thought, okay, I've learned something more about Canadians and how to farm. You make pets of deer and then you kill them for dinner. Then I started thinking about it, or I started thinking his way and it made sense, just like slaughtering a steer for meat. But I'll say this, it sure was a shock to me. In Germany they didn't do it that way."

🕊 *Coyotes*

"Our family has been in Canada since, well, for 280 years or more now, and my grandfather came out west from Quebec in about 1864 or so and it was all wild then, no English or Ukrainian then. Just the little town of Winnipeg and a village at Portage, and then there was Brandon further up the river, just a small place, too, so you can see the Thibodeaux go back quite a ways.

When the farms filled up all along the Assiniboine River, the coyotes came in. They like to live where people are and they lived on roots and mice and things they could catch, and if somebody's horse died and they hauled it down by the river, the coyotes, you'd hear them yapping down there. People say coyotes howl but they don't. They sort of ki-yi-yi-yip a lot, and then sometimes what might be like a howl. You'd hear one, and then over there by the bluff, another would answer and then another back there, and they'd have this conversation. It was nice to lie in bed at night and hear them.

Sometimes at night they'd try and get into the farmyard and steal a chicken or a duck. We had dogs and they'd come rushing to the door, and my father would grab his gun and go out and fire a shell. That would scare them away, but they'd come back. Sometimes they'd be around in the daytime, too, and sometimes they did get a chicken. My father didn't mind all that much. He said he just figured it was a bonus, that chicken, for the coyotes killing so many mice and rats and other animals we didn't like.

Then in the Depression, I remember, they started to get more and more. You could go anywhere and see them, and then you'd see them more in fours and fives, like wolf packs. And one day a man from Wawanesa, that's the insurance company for farmers, was trying to sell insurance to my father, who was so poor he couldn't hardly make a living on our lot, and he looked out and he said, 'What's that?' And my father said, 'Oh, just a coyote. They're thick as thieves around here.' This man was from Winnipeg and it was his first trip along that south part of the river where the coyotes were and he was excited to see them.

A couple of weeks later this man wrote my father a letter. He said he had friends in Winnipeg, big shots, and he'd told them of the coyotes and they wondered if they could come out and shoot them. Would my dad help them? These men were from the Manitoba Motor League, which was a fancy club of rich men and they owned the old Hudson's Bay fort at Lower Fort Garry and this was, they figured, better than playing golf.

My father wrote back and said sure, come on out, and he would charge them four dollars each a day and my mother would feed them and they could bring their own horses if they wanted, or they could just hunt the coyotes on foot. My father would take them to where they were, and my brothers and me, we'd sort of herd them up from the river to where the men with their guns were.

The man wrote back and he said they'd be out two Saturdays from then in the morning. My father thought, he's bringing a couple of friends, and told my mother that three or four men were coming for dinner and instead of having it at noon like we always did, we'd have it at supper-time instead, around four so the Winnipeg guys could eat and go home by daylight. This was late September, getting dark early.

You know what? Without a word of a lie, five cars came into our yard. There were twenty men, and each had a shotgun, and there was a truck with three horses, and another truck with a bunch of dogs. My dad counted, oh boy, twenty times four dollars each. Eighty dollars. That was more than he made off the farm in a month.

My dad sent my brother running off to the Cadieux place to get three of their kids, and he and I sort of worked it out with the men from the Manitoba Motor League. The kids would go along the willow flats by the river and beat pots with big spoons and yell and drive any coyotes that were down there looking for muskrat and beaver.

My mother made a dive for the root cellar and began to bring up vegetables and quarts of peas and bottled pumpkin for pies, because she knew there was going to be a lot of hungry men coming to eat. One of my sisters, the middle one, she went and borrowed all the plates and cups and forks and knives she could from the Cadieux and the Hammer family, just saying, 'Give it to us and we'll pay you a dollar when we bring it back.'

That day was crazy. We all went out about ten o'clock and we ran like wild savages, back and forth, and there were a lot of coyotes down there and you could hear the shotguns going bang, bang. Rifles, too. They were getting something, for sure. When we got up to them in the field they were gone, and they had shot, oh, I guess, about eight coyotes. The dogs were going crazy and you could hear the men on horses off in the distance firing away still.

Then the men on horses and the others came back and they had three or four more, and I could see my father scratching his head. Here they'd shot more of the coyotes around, maybe half, and he was thinking, maybe this isn't so good. But he didn't say anything. This was about two in the afternoon when all this was finished and it was too late to go anywhere else, so we all went home.

These were big jolly men and they were having a wonderful time and my mother had a big feed ready for them. When the food was being set out in bowls and dishes, they sat around and had a few drinks from their flasks of whiskey and talked about what a big and wonderful day it had been. It sure was, but maybe not for us. I wondered about all this, too. What would we do next time, if they wanted to come back. I wouldn't hear the coyotes at night. I felt sad about that.

Okay, so the men all had a good meal. We'd even brought in milking-stools from the barn and made a bench out of a board and two old nail kegs, and so we got them all managed. They ate and ate, and this was just French-Canadian food but you'd think they had never, never in their lives eaten anything so good. I got to thinking, this is fun.

When they finished, a big man who seemed to be the boss, and

I guess he was because I heard he owned a mine up north, he said to my mother, 'Fine meal, ma'am, and what do we owe you?' Like that. My mother didn't speak English hardly at all, so I said, 'It's a dollar.' The men laughed and said it was worth the best money could buy. So the men gave my father a five-dollar bill. Each of them. That was four for the shooting and one for the meal, and my father had meant that the four dollars would include the meal in it.

Then the men got in their cars and trucks and drove away, and my father had about $130 because some of the men were so happy they had given big tips. We also had about twelve coyotes we could skin out and we did, those that weren't too badly torn up by the dogs, so we had about eight skins we could sell easily. And we boiled up the meat with barley and fed it to our pigs.

Next year the men wanted to come out and do it again. By that time, my father had thought it over, and he figured that was enough. You need coyotes around. They may be skinny creatures but they ate a lot of mice and rats. And besides, he said, he liked to hear them yelling at night like I did, too, and so that was the end of the big coyote hunt. I think it was good that one time, but not a lot of times."

🕊 *Home Brew*

"Down around Elie and, you know, over to Headingley and down to Starbuck and in and around there, we got crops in the Depression. Thing was, see, that we didn't get any price at all. I mean, we were better off than the poor fellows and their women in Saskatchewan, but we didn't get any price for my wheat. In '29 it was good, up there over a dollar a bushel, and then by '32 I remember I got a fair crop and I had to sell it for thirty-seven cents a bushel. You didn't need to be a book-keeper to see you were broke.

There were no jobs, either. In the twenties, a fellow could hop the railroad and go into Winnipeg or down to Brandon and he'd get a job. That is, if he needed one. And then there were no jobs. Not one for love and money. Just nothing.

So, things were awfully tough, and especially on a lot of the French-Canadian families around there with big families. You know, eight or nine or twelve kids wasn't too much out of the ordinary. Feeding them, putting clothes on them and shoes so they could go off to school, that took a lot, and then because they was good Catholics they had to give so much to the church. That church of theirs, they didn't let up on them any. They had to pay up.

So what I'm going to tell you about is home brew. A lot of people drank around the district. But then along come this Depression and nobody has any money for the hard stuff. We didn't drink beer then, beer was kind of considered a city kind of drink. Farmers and in the towns, they drank the hard stuff, and when it got so a bottle was as much as you could feed your family on for four or five days, then you thought twice.

Then there was the low feeling that so many people had. It looked as though the roof had fallen in on us. I felt it. I'd get real depressed. Everybody did. When you feel that way, you want something to cheer the spirit, and booze did it. There was always a couple of families that made home brew, and you'd buy from them. So you'd go to one of these places and buy a small bottle, which is about what a mickey is today. You had to bring your own bottle and exchange it for a full one. A ketchup bottle, that's what I used. Or if you wanted a quart, a milk bottle was the best.

It was real hard stuff. I mean, when I'd get home or some place where I could take a few belts, I always made sure I had some cranberry juice or saskatoon juice, something like that, just to mix it with. This home brew, it had a punch, it could hit you hard. Tasted awful, too. But it was something, well, it would make you feel better for a time. A lot of the times, a few of us would go hunting, and each of us would have a bottle, and by the time we got going, those deer or rabbits or ducks, they were as safe as any animals in the world. Couldn't hit a thing.

Then it got so that we said we should make our own, and from what I've read, they were making it in half the farms in the West. I had my own little still. It was easy to make. Just a big pot and you threw everything in – potatoes, raisins, prunes, anything that would ferment – and you boiled it up and then you strained it and you let it ferment some more and you strained that, and then you had this thingamajig and this distilled the alcohol out of it, it coming out in drips from this steam system you had rigged up. All you'd want would be a gallon, and then you'd take the thing apart and hide it in a hole and cover it up and you'd let the brew sit for a few days and then strain it and she was ready. You put some syrup colouring in it for colour and to make it taste better, and there you had it. Cost nothing. That was the way to do it.

Then when things were getting very hard and you felt hard done by, you could haul out a bottle and sit around with somebody who was in the same boat and you could do some drinking together. You'd say, 'I'm gonna quit this farming business, get a job in Winnipeg.' He'd say, 'Don't be a fool. You've got a nice little place here, and things will get better.' Then after a few drinks more, he'd say he was gonna quit, sell out, and get a job in Brandon. You'd say, 'You can't. You got a better place over there on the Lido Plage Road than I've got here, so why quit? Next year will be better.'

I guess some guys became alcoholics like they do now, except I don't remember that word. I guess they just called us drunks.

Then I took four cows to the Canada Packers in Winnipeg. My oldest boy and me, we took these cows in and I had a bottle with me. The boy was driving, and we had a crack-up. Bust a wheel. By the time we got there, the buying for the morning was done, but a fellow came along, an independent, and said he'd buy them. When we'd unloaded them at his corral, I pulled out this bottle and said, you know, have a drink.

This fellow thought it was pretty good stuff. It had cranberry juice mixed in, and he said, well, where could he get more of this. My son pipes up and he says, 'Oh, Dad makes it. How much do you want? It's eight dollars a gallon, and we'll deliver it. Much as you want.' I was going to stop him right there and then, and then I see this buyer is thinking. He says, 'If you can deliver me four or five gallons a week, I'll take it.' No ifs, ands, or buts. Now I'm thinking, five gallons times $8 is $40, and four times $40, that's $160, and I just could not believe it. That was more than a banker made. A lot more.

I said, you're on. First delivery, two weeks from now. Right here, at three in the afternoon, rain, shine, snow, or hail, and we shook on that. I couldn't believe it, and on the way home I started thinking out loud, how was I going to make five gallons a week? And we decided right there and then to have one big one, and put it in a small shed. It wasn't tough to build, and I won't go into it all, but we didn't have it at the house, or close. It was over in the willows and swamp by the Assiniboine River and that was because, if the Mounties found it by the house, I'd be in jail in no time.

Over by the river, if they found it, well, you know, we'd have lost it, but we wouldn't be caught. That would have meant a year in Headingley, and it would have been the end of me. Of my family, my wife and kids. Going to jail then, well, people wouldn't think that what you'd done was to keep your family alive. They just thought of going to jail.

For two years we delivered that home brew, faithfully, you might say. Nobody knew. Just my wife and my two oldest boys, and we'd buy our coal in Winnipeg, anthracite, so nobody would see the smoke. No smoke. We bought our spuds and sugar on Selkirk Avenue in Winnipeg. An old man who didn't mind how much you bought. The nice things we ate, we bought in the city. I bought my cousin's truck and said I could only pay him ten dollars a month. Playing poor. That's how we got away with it, doing all this at night, and taking this five-gallon keg into town under a load of wheat. I had a big tarpaulin and I guess the neighbours never noticed I always brought the load back with me.

Well, that went on for two years and we did real good. Saved a lot of money, and remember, I think a dollar then was worth twenty dollars today.

So we quit when we had two thousand bucks ahead. It was hidden. We sold the place, and it was only 240 acres, hardly enough to live on anyway, and we lived in Vernon for a while, and I didn't do any more of the home-brew thing. I never got caught, but I think it was about time I did.

I think it was hurting me a lot, and it was hurting my family. They didn't understand what was going on. There was a lot of fighting, arguing, in among us, and finally I thought, it's this business. So that's why I really quit. I was small potatoes, but it was getting too much for me to handle.

Once I sold the last batch and we got rid of the farm and got in that truck with our stuff and the wife beside me and the kids in the back, you know, heading that spring to the valley where the apple trees were, it all suddenly went away. I guess you could say I was free again."

❧ *Pasteurized*

"Three years after my wife died I married this new teacher who came to town and she and the kids took to each other and I knew it was going to be all right. I'd had a bunch of housekeepers but none of them lasted, and I don't really blame them. Two little boys to look after and everything else, and after a month or two they just left.

I think the cow was part of the problem, too. I'm the only guy for twenty miles who still has a cow on the farm. I like it, and I don't mind the business of milking twice a day and scouring out the separator parts and bowl and all that. I like having our own milk and cream. But there are always times when you've got to get away early and you can't scour out the separator, and a couple of these women just wouldn't do it. I might come home late, too, after dark, and have to milk, and that would put them in an upset, holding dinner, that sort of thing.

My new wife, she knew I had the cow, and knew about cleaning the separator. She had another reason for not liking it. This milk was not pasteurized. That was her big problem. She'd come from the city and all milk was pasteurized. Okay, that's fine. But I'd been brought up on milk and cream straight from the cows, and my two sons had, too, and it hadn't killed us yet. No matter. That milk was not pasteurized.

Then I found out that when she went to town, she was buying these cartons of pasteurized milk and cream, and throwing our good milk out, and pouring in this store stuff. I thought the milk tasted funny, but I never said anything. Then I found out. This was costing us a lot of money. She wasn't wasting the cream, though. Richest stuff you ever saw. She was taking it into town by the quart and swapping it off with the grocer for other cream, so that didn't count.

Anyway, this evening we talk about it and I tell her, look, if you feel so strong about all this, I'll do this for you. Tomorrow I'll take that cow in to town and have her pasteurized. I should have done it a long time ago, I said. That was just perfect with her. All smiles and so on.

Next morning I put the sides into the pickup and I coax Bossy up some planks into the truck and tie her and get off to town to do my good works. I park behind the café and go in and spend an hour shooting the breeze with the coffee club, mostly retired farmers, and then I drive home and let the old girl out into her little pasture. That's done.

My wife said, 'How did it go?' I said 'Fine. They took some tests and gave her two needles and she let out a couple of bellers and now she's all fixed up. No problems any more.' 'Oh,' she says, 'that's wonderful!' Happy as all get out.

I sure hope she never reads this book."

❧ *Mr. Sheep*

"Sometimes people come to me and they're looking for something to get into to make some money, what with the farm-gate price of wheat and barley down at the bottom, and they think it might be a good idea to get some sheep. I'm Mr. Sheep in this part of the country.

I say, go ahead, spend the winter reading the books and visiting some sheep farmers and look at the figures and watch the market and talk to your banker and talk to some more sheep farmers. Then if you decide you want this kind of life, remember just two things.

One is, sheep are not stupid. You're not dealing with a cow.

The second thing is, sheep-farming is kind of a one-on-one situation – it's you against the sheep, or them against you. If you want some co-operation, and you're going to need a lot, just make sure that when you want them to go this way or that way or do something, make sure you do just the opposite. You want them to go into this left-hand chute? Okay, then try and make them go down the right-hand chute. That way, they'll go down the left-hand chute.

This way, I tell them, you are going to have a fine relationship with your sheep, and I wish them luck."

❧ *The Hog Business*

"With the money I got from selling off an eighteen-acre piece, I figured I'd go into some hogs. I'd met this guy who had a big hog operation at this agricultural meeting at the Olds College and we got to be good friends in the two days of this seminar, and he was making out real good. I phoned him up and he said to come over.

So, the wife and I drove over this nice day and sure, I could see right away, this fellow was in the Big Time. His barns all new, farrowing-barn, a bigger one for weaners, and one for feeding and finishing, and those pigs never saw a bit of real sunlight until they were moved from the finishing-barn to the truck, and in a few hours it would be lights out for him. It was a real nice operation and clean, clean as a housewife's kitchen. You could eat off them floors, and they used high-pressure hoses to clean them out and everything was done automatically, mostly. There wasn't much bend-over work, not much lifting work. Automatic feeding, lights went on and off when they were supposed to, and when we went through, he gave us a couple of white coats to wear. Like we were visiting in a hospital.

Then we went back in the house and I remember it was Early Times bourbon he poured us, at eleven in the morning. First, he talks about the economics of the business. You know, barley low and hog prices high and going higher, and so he was doing real good, this guy was. He figured it was going higher, but once the American farmers moved back into hogs in a big way, once they got smart, it would be a fight to the finish with them. He looked for the price of barley to rise in a couple of years and so that was a bit of poor-mouthing on his part. No, he wasn't saying I should not go into the business because it would be competition against him and others, just saying like it was. Prices so high couldn't last. You know that. Everything in farming goes in cycles.

Then he talked about hogs, the right kind to buy, and he thought for someone starting out the Large White and the Landrace would be best bets for a couple of beginners. Landrace, he said, you could have a splayed-legs problem and I didn't know what that was but I got the idea.

Then he got into the breeding boars, and that's where I got an inkling about what this was all about. He said he had eighteen boars. Eighteen for three hundred sows, I thought. What's wrong with these fellows anyway? He was talking like a scientist, this boar would give his offspring this quality and they figured another would give them this, and so on. It was like he was trying to breed a super hog.

But he got off that and said he could sell me a couple of boars because he bred them for sale too. I didn't want to ask how much right then, but he went on about back-fat placement and teat placement. I thought, tits on a boar? What goes? And they have to have the right feet and toes because they'd be on slippery concrete a lot, and the testicles shouldn't be too big or too small. Now what kind of advice is that to a wheat farmer? And the penis should slide in and out of the sheath just right. Well, I thought, how do you know? Isn't that the pig's job, the sow and the boar, to know that?

He went on and on like this, him sipping his bourbon and me and my wife just nodding and things flashing through my mind. He'd already told us a hundred and fifty things we shouldn't do and not one thing we should do, like should we go into pigs. I mean hogs. Pigs seem to be a dirty word when you're dealing with pigs. Hogs. The boar, he said, is the most important part of the whole thing. That figures, I guess. Whoever I bought from, he said, I should see them in operation. Meaning, of course, well, like in action. And he almost cracked a smile when he said that when it was over, it was important to check if the big fellow was out of breath. Well, I will be doggoned.

At this point my wife spoke up and she said, 'Now, this is all very well and fine and you've got a wonderful place here and you've told us a lot, but Will and I only have $28,000.'

His wife was at the stove and she turned around and I still remember her saying, just like this, she said, 'Don't. Just plain don't. Dick is going to give you $28,000 worth of advice in the next five minutes, and two years from now you'll thank us. Just don't. Stick to what you know.'

And he said his wife was dead right. It was no place for amateurs trying to run a grain operation too. He said he had a half-million investment out there, what we'd looked at, and he still owed the bank a big pile. If he couldn't see too much daylight ahead after twenty years in the business, then we'd lose ours in a year, and besides, with only that much money we had no business even thinking about the hog business. He said leave it to him and other big ones and the Hutterites, and take the money and go down to Reno and have a big blast. Said we'd do better down there than in the hog business in such an itty-bitty way. He said it all so definite, and with what he'd told us there was nothing to do but finish my drink and shake hands with him and his wife and thank them for saving us $28,000.

Then you know what I did? Me and the wife, we took his advice and we went down to Reno. One of them package deals. She played Keno and I played automatic poker and we ate like kings and saw a lot of stars at the casino shows – and we came home with more money than we took down."

🐦 *And Pigs Get Slaughtered*

"We're laughing now, I guess, those of us that are in hogs. I can't remember when it's been better. Just can't remember when the price for barley has been so low, and I can go to any neighbour and load up. We get dinged by the feed companies who make our supplements but they've educated us enough through their advertising that we got to have them. I suppose we do. But it's the same with the wheat farmer. They get dinged every year, higher and higher, by the fertilizer companies, and there's a scandal that somebody should look into.

I've got two hundred gilts. If you've got under fifty, you can't say you're really a hog farmer. That many sows just won't support you, not with the equipment and business and capital you have to put in. I'd say with one hundred, you'd still be on the borderline. But two hundred sows is nice and comfortable. That can be handled easily with hardly any outside help.

We're laughing now, and we're the ones who are buying the new trucks and such, but our turn will come. Barley won't stay as low as she is, but while it is down there, more and more people will be coming into the business. They'll push up the price of barley, and more and more pork products will come on the market. Then that old pendulum of supply and demand comes swinging back at us. Too much pork, down go the prices. The little guy hoping to make a quick buck, he's the first to go, and then the middle guy, and then the bigger operations, we'll be finding it so tough we'll be wondering why we ever thought hog production was the right way to go.

It's the law of supply and demand. But the guy who always gets hit hardest is the guy who does the supplying. That's me, and it will always be me. The guy who does the work takes all the chances."

🐦 *Getting Your Goat*

"When things got really tough and the bank took one section away from me, I held a conference, a pow-wow, and I said we'd have to cut way back or we'd wind up busted. The first thing we're gonna do is buy a cow. No more milk at a buck a litre, stuff you can't drink anyway, so weak you could spear fish in it. No, a cow's the answer. Great uproar. Who's going to milk the cow? You, I tell the kids, you guys. And collect the eggs. What eggs? Big uproar. The eggs from the chickens. We're going to save money like nobody has before.

First, to get milk you have to find a cow, and do you think we could find a Jersey? I mean one under five hundred dollars. You'd have thought every one was a special pet the way they were priced. We heard that a guy over near Breton had a few for sale, but when we got there they were gone, but he persuaded us we didn't need a cow. What we needed was a goat, and he had just the one. One hundred and seventy-five bucks, and she'd milk like a son of a bitch and we'd have enough and more to sell to people with bad stomachs. Goat milk is so rich and it digests in twenty minutes or so, and if you don't pasteurize it, you can sell it at two bucks a quart. She was a Sannen goat, a pretty thing, and I could see we wouldn't need to build any cow-shed. So we wound up with two goats, three hundred dollars for the two of them.

I got them home and on the way we stopped off in Leduc and picked up a book on goats. It turned out to be no good, because it was written by one of these hippie types, you know, back to the land. What this writer was talking about was having fifty of the damned things so he could become a capitalist and have other hippies working for him looking after his goat empire. So, I thought, we had cows when I was a kid. What's the difference. Hay, some bran and molasses, vitamin supplement, a couple of pounds of grain a day. You couldn't go wrong.

Then the chickens. We wound up with thirty layers, Rhode Island Reds, and three roosters, and that meant another house. A chicken-house. Half for the goats, a partition, and half for the chickens. That was eight hundred dollars, and would you believe it, the county made me submit plans and take out a permit. Jesus, what's the damned world coming to? A guy can't throw his money away without a permit.

So, in about a month's time, there we were. How are you going to eat about twenty eggs a day, what with this cholesterol thing still hanging around. And milk, the best in the world, you bet, but three quarts a day? We'll make butter, I says. Then I find out that you can't separate cream from goat milk without a big process, so no butter. Cheese, yeah, but it looked like a big investment for two pounds of cheese a week and I wasn't about to be like that hippie capitalist up in the hills who was looking to corner the cheese market of New England and Boston. So, to hell with cheese, and drink some more milk, kids, it's bloody good for you.

Do you know how long this damned nonsense went on? A year. Winter comes, and egg production drops off to four or five a day and we can handle that, and then they stop laying. Winter, the goats have still got to be fed and watered and exercised, but for two long months they are dry, just like the chickens don't cackle no more when they drop an egg. The farm is barren.

One day I says to the wife, 'What is all this costing us? We got chickens and goats to save money from Safeway, but I notice we've been buying Number One Large and 2-per-cent milk regularly this last little while.' My wife says, 'I've been waiting for just the right moment, and this is it. You're starting to get your senses back.'

There it is. On a sheet of paper, all nicely laid out. One column, how much the goats and the chickens and the feed and the shed costs, plus three dollars an hour for labour. The thing is astronomical, like $2,000 so far. On the other, how much we'd have paid for eggs and milk for the same time, something like $450. The bottom line is, while we're providing de luxe hotel facilities for our guests, they are costing us an arm and a leg.

I looked at her and she looked at me and I said I was going to declare bankruptcy, and I went to the phone and got the farmer from Breton on the line. I said I was going to give him a bargain. Two goats for $150. He said he'd be in tomorrow, and I kind of expected to have him say, 'What took you so long?' "

Fourteen

Indians

❧

Garbage Dumps . . . Damnation in the North . . . The Lousiest Land . . .
The White Man's Big Mistake . . . A Hell of a Way to Live . . . A Modest
Proposal . . . That Indian Bunch . . . Total Frustration . . . Another
Indian . . . Leaving the Reserve . . . This Indian Thing . . . Hitching a
Ride Home . . . Like Lepers . . . Back in the Bush . . . The Bright Lights

I'm sorry this chapter has to appear. It does not make pleasant reading. But there is nothing pleasant about the plight of our native people on the Prairies – or the rest of Canada – today. Any book that ignores the Indian situation – "The Problem", as whites call it, and everyone knows what they are talking about – is taking the easy, or cowardly, way out.

There is little comfort to be gained from what these voices – native, Métis, and white – have to say. But if this book has a purpose, it is to show how people see things, and how they talk about them. We learn something not pleasant, but important.

There are a thousand "experts" in this field today, and in hindsight they agree that all former government policies were wrong. Still, they cannot agree which policies would have been right. Round and round they go, unable to agree on what should be done, although about three billion dollars annually is poured into this "hole", and the problems continue to grow.

Once they were proud, these tribes, and strong, civilized, and successful by their own standards. They warred against each other, but that was part of their life. Their final defeat came not at the hands of the whites in any battle but by treaties. When the buffalo was exterminated, their livelihood was gone, and everything began to crumble.

Today, their culture is very fragile, although stronger than, say, twenty years ago when they discovered there were legal and political ways to fight back. It has been a tough and highly controversial struggle, and there is no end in sight.

Who is right? Or, who is wrong? What is to be done?

I am no expert, and I have little faith in experts who seem still to be applying the white man's thinking to a problem they cannot understand either.

What follows are "voices" on both sides of "The Problem".

❧ Garbage Dumps

"An old wartime buddy of mine, John Kerr, he and a friend flew up from Minneapolis and they picked me up and we flew up north, fishing and just looking over the country. A hell of a trip, just eight days. Lots of fish. Lots of fun. Just three old guys out on kind of a spree.

But we flew into a lot of these Indian communities, Indian and Métis. We'd need gas and there was always the chief or somebody or a fishing lodge on the lake where we could buy gas. Naturally we did a bit of walking around.

I came away being ashamed I was a Canadian. More like it, I was ashamed that those two Americans saw what they did in those villages. More to the point, I was ashamed that I was a Canadian and those people up there, that they were Canadians, too.

Johnny and his friend were just too polite to say anything, this not being their own country, but I was shocked. The squalor. The housing. You wouldn't keep your hogs in some of those buildings, and I mean that. Nothing to be the least bit proud of, nothing at all. Those poor devils up there, they lived in a kind of poverty that I hadn't realized. They had nothing. Their houses were falling down, and God knows what they ate. There was one store we bought some stuff at, and most of it was junk food, nothing that seemed to have any good nutrition in it. They lived on fish from the lake, of course, and what they could shoot, but the kids were living on cheap chocolate bars and cans of Pepsi. That was about the size of it.

And I know as well as you do that most of the money they had was welfare, welfare, and more welfare. There was no work up there. They couldn't even have the little bit of dignity of being on Unemployment Insurance and saying, well, at least I worked and earned the money I'm getting now.

Everything came in by the plane. The booze came in by plane, and from what I saw, plenty of that came in. God knows what freight rates they were paying. I mean, if it had been a white community, a mine or something, their rates would be a lot lower. Everything seemed geared to screwing these poor Indians.

What hope has a kid starting life in one of those places? The school in one, it was the worst I ever saw, and there was a new teacher every year. They just couldn't stick it. When an Indian couple has a baby there, I'd say they are signing that kid's death

warrant the moment he is born. There is no future. If they go
south, there is less future. You know how it is in Regina where
they all seem to wind up? Not that they aren't smart kids. Just no
opportunity, and who do we blame?

We blame the Indians themselves, but I guess the real blame
winds up on our shoulders, and especially the bureaucrats in
Ottawa and Regina. In the long run they're the guilty ones, but
this business has been going on so long that it now appears
perfectly normal.

Those people who kick about the natives in Regina, let them go
up there and see for themselves. I've seen three or four of those
native villages now and I can say this. The government in Ottawa
has no right, absolutely no right, to bitch and scream and so on
about South Africa. I've got a feeling that South Africa is doing
pretty well in that department, judging from what I've seen on the
TV and comparing it to what I saw up there. We have no right to
call them down. None at all.

Those places up there are garbage dumps. No more or no less.
They are just garbage dumps of people."

❧ *Damnation in the North*

"I saw an advertisement in *The Times Educational Supplement* and
it said that Alberta was seeking teachers for northern areas. It said,
in effect, they were looking for teachers willing to teach in the land
of the wild moose, in isolation, in temperatures that could reach
− 40 Celsius. As I had experienced absolutely none of this, how
could I resist? I was hired.

The government would pay my way, but as I was penniless,
nobody would lend me the rest of the money I needed, and the
day before I was to leave London, I went in desperation to the
London branch of the Bank of Commerce. No, they told me, there
was no way. Sorry, and all that. But I asked to see the manager as
a last resort, and he was an elderly Scot who had been to Canada
as a young man with the Hudson's Bay Company and you know
what? He said it was against the regulations and rules to make such
a loan to an emigrant, but he would, and I'm glad to say I repaid
him within a few months.

All I saw of Canada was the inside of the Toronto airport and the inside of the Edmonton airport, and then I was dumped out on an airstrip of a little Cree and Métis village about seventy miles east of Peace River, and then that was when I had my first impressions of Canada.

Four days later I was living in a Roman Catholic mission. It was a four-room building, and it was quite an experience. I shared the place with a priest from Belgium and his assistant from rural Quebec. The priest was young, and all he cared about was getting the sporting papers from Belgium and tape recordings of the parties his friends had at home and he'd go to bed early, and his assistant and I would sit around and drink the church wine and read the soccer news in these sporting papers. But this brother was a Québécois and he was passionately convinced that his purpose was to save the local natives from damnation. He used his power crudely, like a crusader swinging an axe against the infidels.

The government, in all its wisdom, had recently resettled the Indians and Métis from their traditional village and put it down beside a new oil-company road, because they thought it would make communication better to Peace River. Of course, the natives bitterly resented this, and those few families who did try and buck the government, well, they just couldn't make it work. They just could not maintain their traditional lifestyle.

The Indians rarely, if ever, displayed their real feelings to the Roman Catholic clerics, since the church had the power to strip the Indians of all their rights and to literally deny their existence. You can imagine a young and idealistic and urbanized Englishman, myself, not a Catholic and not French-speaking, suddenly finding himself in this situation. Can you even believe this was possible in 1967? The year of Expo 67? Canada's one-hundredth birthday? But it was all too true.

The rest of Canada filtered in through weak radio signals and occasionally a newspaper from the outside arrived, but we were in complete isolation and in the time I was there, I learned a great deal about the people, and about the inherent hypocrisy, the fallacies, and the blatant racism of the white man's attitudes and policies to the natives.

I could see I was doing no good there, and that nobody could under the conditions that existed, and I got out. There was nothing else to do."

ꙭ The Lousiest Land

"When you go south of the Battlefords, across the river and down
south, there's good farmland all the way. Good grade-two land,
and well looked after. Some good farmers down there.

Okay. About twelve miles south, I guess, you'll come to a sign.
Says it is an Indian reservation. Okay, look carefully. It is scrub
land. Sloughs. Hilly. A big gravel-bed in places. Anyway, you don't
see any farms, and I don't think there is a farm more than five
acres in that whole reserve. I don't know what they do for a living
except collect welfare and fill up their yards with old Fords and
Chevys. Maybe they trap a few rats in spring, shoot deer in autumn,
or maybe some of them have got jobs in North Battleford or with
farmers. I've never known anybody to know a native off that
reserve. You see these little houses tucked in off the road, shacks,
but you don't think about the people living in them.

So, you're driving along maybe another ten miles and on the
other side of the road there's another sign, like the one you saw a
ways back. Okay? End of reserve land. Right then, start looking
hard. Know what you'll see? Farmland starts again, good land, well
looked after, grade-two land again. Just like that. Good land starts
again right at the reserve boundary.

And that, my friend, is how we treat our native brothers. We
find the lousiest and most messed-up piece of land in the whole
country over there and we call it an Indian reserve and we dump
the whole bunch on there a long time ago, and there they've been
ever since. Living, somehow surviving, as if they weren't a part of
Canada, and as if they weren't Canadians. That's us. The white
man."

ꙭ The White Man's Big Mistake

"Start up north as far as you want to go, work down, Hay River,
all those little reserves scattered the hell all over the place, these
Lubicons, down to Edmonton and way west of there, Red Deer,
Calgary, Gleichen, Macleod, Lethbridge, all over the damn place,
and they've all got the same problem. Indians. Half-bloods, Métis,
status or non-status, it doesn't matter. Problems.

Whose problems? Ours, because we pay the taxes that keep these fellows and their wives and their kids going. And their problems, well, their problem is that they had the wrong parents and grandparents. Go back far enough, I guess, and the big problem is that they were here first, and the white man came along and right there – sure as shooting – that's when the Indian problem began.

Look, just listen to me. You think I haven't thought about this for a long time? I'm right in the middle of it half the time. I know what the problem is, or I mean I know how it all started.

Listen, it's this. Our ancestors came into this country and we said to ourselves, 'These people are goddamned savages.' Well, they were, by our lights, but from all I hear they were doing okay. They ate, they had the buffalo and the deer and moose and the fish, and they even did a bit of farming in their own way. They had their own God, the same as the whites and the Arabs had their Gods. They didn't have it all written down in a Bible, but they had a religion and their own laws, and because they had been around since the Ice Age it all must have worked for them.

But then something happened. The white man came along. At first they got along pretty well. The trappers and traders had iron and steel hatchets and guns and knives, and that was pretty hot stuff for a guy who had been chipping stone axes. And then, now listen, and then came the whiskey. The rot-gut. Then it was no going back. I still don't know why, but there is something about an Indian or breed and that is, he can't handle booze. I could tell you some stories.

Another thing was the missionaries. The Catholics, they came and said there is this thing called heaven and if you join up with us guys, you'll go there and never have to worry about a thing for the rest of your life. Then came the Anglicans and they said that those Catholics were a bunch of shits. Join us. Then the Baptists, I guess, and others, and they had the poor Indian so damn confused they didn't know what to think, and the whole bunch of missionaries, they treated these people like slaves. They would have been better out on the bunch grass with their horses and bows and arrows and leather tents than working with those damned missionaries. Take it from me, I've listened to the old people. The things that went on with those missionaries, you wouldn't believe it. All in the name of saving souls for God, you understand. They were right. Everybody else was wrong.

I'm an old-timer, but I've seen all this and I got a lot from my daddy and his uncles too, going a long way back, and all the time, just like now, in Ottawa and other places, they've been pouring money into this whole Indian business. You see, they made one big mistake. They are still making it, only bigger, and it's costing them ten times more money, and ten years from now it will cost them twice as much more. Long ago, back after the Riel Rebellion, they said, 'We'll have to change the Indians into white men.' Did you ever hear of anything so damned stupid in your life? Let's change Russians into Englishmen. Let's yank a few guys out of one of those black African countries and make them into New Yorkers. Dumb! Dumb! And, naturally, the way they went around it was to say, 'We'll make them farmers.' Just about everybody in the West in those days was homesteading and making a damn poor and almost-starving living off of 160 acres with only 30 broke to wheat, and they say, 'We'll solve this Indian problem by turning them into white farmers.'

You know, you sit around the pub with a beer and you think about this and you ask yourself, 'Was there ever any common sense ever used when the white man from Ontario came out to this country and decided to make it work?'

Say you and I are in the beer parlour in Fort Macleod and there's a couple of Indians over at another table and I say we go over and join them and okay, they are good guys. I know them. They sit where they sit. We sit where we sit. If we want to get together we do, but we don't talk about things like this.

Now, there's one fellow named Joseph who comes down from Calgary every Friday night. Believe it or not, he has a good job in a big oil company. A superintendent or something. Drives a three-quarter-ton pickup, brand new with everything, loaded. I couldn't afford it. And I say, 'Joseph, my friend and I have been talking, about your people. . . . '

See, but a funny look will come over his face. He'll talk machinery and drilling and what kid in town is pregnant and who did the dirty deed, or he'll talk cattle or baseball or these Olympics coming up. But mention that stuff and, well, you're going back into something not very nice. He knows. Jesus H. Christ, but he knows. Picking sugar-beets at the age of eight, that's just for starters. I think he did a couple of stretches in the can at Lethbridge for drinking, fighting, things like that. Hell, that's normal. Alberta's jails are full of Indians. But forget that.

But I say, 'Friend here,' and that's you, 'friend here wants to know what happened. I'm telling him about the white man, the traders, the missionaries. All of that. How did it start, eh?' You don't ask a direct question like, 'How come so many of your people are so fucked up, Joseph?' No way. Never.

I can see him now. He's a good-looking fellow and smart, and he'll think a minute and then he'll tip that Stetson of his up about a quarter of an inch and rub his thumb down the side of his face and you know he's ready to say something. He'd do the same thing if you asked him to guess the weight of a two-year-old steer, but something is coming. Remember, being the guy he is and working with maybe fifty or sixty white guys, as I call them, although they might be Polacks or Chinese or Pakis thrown in, he just might lift up that glass of beer of his and kind of push it at you a little and he's saying, 'Here. This is what happened. This stuff.' Alcohol. That would be your answer. You'd have it right there. Bang!

Alcohol, rot-gut, then disease, starvation, tricky government lawyers, crooked government land agents, rotten government Indian agents, missionaries who would screw a snake if they couldn't find an Indian girl. Ranchers who burned them out, which is funny, because the tribes did a lot of burning out of grassland of ranchers, but who was there first? The bands, of course. Lousy schools, these residential schools where the kids got a Grade 8 education which made them damn good farmhands at a buck a day, when a dumb immigrant without any English was making two bucks a day. See what I mean? The whole system was rotten.

What I'm saying is this. We made our big mistake when we said to the Indian, 'Look, chief, this way you're living is no good. Look at those clothes you're wearing. Why, a white man wouldn't be caught dead in them.' No matter that they'd been wearing those kind of clothes for centuries. And then they said, 'Now, chief, you got to send your kids to school. Do you want them to grow up to be an Indian like yourself? No house, no stable, no cattle, and just a few of those scrub ponies you got out there, do you want that for your kids, chief?' And then he's sure to say, 'You better learn to farm, chief. You just can't go chasing around the mountains shooting elk and grizzly and catching a few beavers in the spring. You've got to come up in the world. Plant wheat, grow it and sell it, and then you'll be like us, nice clothes, nice house, and you can put fences around and string them with barbed wire and nobody can come on your property.' Jesus H. Christ! Didn't they know the way the tribe lives, sharing everything when they weren't killing each other? Barbed wire! The white man's final answer. Fence every goddamn thing in and then put up big signs saying 'Keep Out, You Bastards'.

And then he sees the chief has got a fine sorrel stallion and he says, 'Chief, that's a sorry-looking horse you got over there, but I need another and how's about we swap? I got a fine bottle of Hudson's Bay rye here and we'll swap, even across. Okay? Make you feel good?' By this time the chief is feeling good all right, good enough to murder this bastard, but he's got a thirst and he knows whiskey, that trader's rot-gut poured into an H.B. bottle, and he swaps. And he drinks it. And then, my friend, that's the beginning of the end, for sure, and that's why my friend Joseph, sitting in the hotel at Macleod, would have said everything if he'd just lifted that glass of beer and pushed it at you one inch and what he was saying was, 'This is how it all started, and this is how it will all end.'

What's he going to do? Nothing. What about me? Nothing. You? Nothing. Everybody? Not a damn thing. It is just going to go on, and I hate like hell to say it, but it all began when we tried to turn the Indian into a white man. What did we get? Look around you.

Sure, I like them. Joseph, I say, he's one of us. He's got a good job in Calgary, that oil company, and he does his job and so he's now a white man. That just ain't right, but it is in this country and right across the country. It's like this. Some are good guys, they got good women, they got good kids, everything. They got their own fears and sorrows, but they don't have much happinesses. They're only good to us if we see one and say to ourselves, 'There's a good Indian because he acts like us, has that nice house and he keeps it painted, and the yard isn't full of old wrecks of Ford sedans, and his little girl has a part in the school play.' Jesus! Did you ever hear of anything like that in your life?

Joseph's just one. There are hundreds like him, doing okay. Some have farms. They got little ranches, drive truck, work on the rigs, pull their weight, haul their freight, and, you know, they are good Catholics too. But we go back a long time in our memories. It's like a long time ago somebody planted a seed in our brain and it said, like a radio message, 'Watch these guys.' We've been doing it ever since.

No, I've got no answer. We look at it a million times, fiddle and fool around, and nothing is solved. Maybe there just isn't any solving to do, and that is just too damn bad, because a lot of good people are going down the drain because of it, them and us."

A Hell of a Way to Live

"Last fall I'm driving down from Yorkton to Regina and it's getting dark and there's this man walking ahead with this pack on this back and, well, I thought, he's obviously going somewhere. You've only got a couple of seconds to make decisions in that light, and I thought, Indian. A white man would be hitch-hiking. This guy is making it alone, probably figuring nobody would give him a lift. But he's got a pack, probably going home. Finished harvesting for some guy, I think, and heading home to the wife and kids. Little Black Bear Reserve, maybe Pasqua.

I slam on the brakes and he comes up and slings this pack in the back of the half-ton and gets in. You know how they mush-mouth, 'Thanksh, mishter, she's good to have zhiss ride.' I ask him where he's going and I'm right. He's off the Pasqua Reserve. Going home, and that's all he says – and this guy is no mush-mouther at all.

I stop in Melville for a bite and coffee and we go into this café and, you know, when you're with an Indian, long black hair, work clothes, I guess that is the only way you're going to feel it – the hostility. In that café, when we walked in, the conversation stopped. There's another of those guys. What's he want? What's he doing with that white guy? Or, more like it, what's the white guy doing with him? I actually felt it. Then we sat down, had our bite to eat, talked of this and that, and left. It had started snowing by that time and so I was keeping my eyes on the road with not much time for talk, and when I dropped him off at his road, he said, 'Thanks for the ride and the coffee. I appreciated it. Thanks again,' and he got his pack and that's the last I saw of him.

But I thought of it a lot. What a hell of a way to live when you go into a café, an Indian, and you get the shit-look from the kind of scruffy bastards who hang around those highway cafés in this part of the country. At least he was working, and he offered to pay for the food. Those other guys, I know their type. Work fourteen weeks, quit, collect Unemployment Insurance for forty-eight weeks, and just raise mischief and trouble the rest of the time. Or they're on welfare and their wife or girlfriend works. And here they're giving this guy dirty looks.

No, I didn't find out why he was hiking down the highway as dark was coming. He had money. He said he'd worked for a combine for six weeks further north so he had money. I wondered why, after he left, and I can't come up with an answer. Maybe he had his bellyful of them sleazy looks in Yorkton and just decided to get the hell out."

❧ *A Modest Proposal*

"It's known as the Indian Problem, in capital letters, but if the average citizen sat down and read the statistics, the reports, they would see a problem that is enormous. Downright horrifying.

Let me put it this way. Once an Indian, man or woman, leaves the reserve and comes in to Regina or Saskatoon, for many then it is game over. They've left a world almost totally subsidized by the Canadian taxpayer, right, but it was a world where they had some measure of security. They were among relatives, the extended family, grandparents and parents and children and uncles and nephews and cousins all living together. I mean, they had protection and they understood how the system worked for them. There may be ninety-per-cent unemployment on a reserve, but with government money flowing in and a support system for medical and social problems in place, at least they could handle it. They were fed and housed and clothed.

But when they come to town, goodbye. There aren't many Indians with more than Grade 9 education. Without a matriculation diploma, Grade 12, you can just forget any kind of meaningful work. Part-time jobs, and these days they are very hard to find. No decent places to stay either, and landlords are very discriminatory and won't rent, unless they've got a dump so run-down that no other person would pay a dime to live in it.

In no way, shape, or form are they admitted into white society. All doors barred, all windows locked. So naturally, they turn towards where their people are, and that's the Skid Road. This is where they are accepted, where the bars will let them in, and the cafés will let them eat. Oh, sure, they could go to any bar or restaurant in any city, but let them try it. They'd find out very quickly what quiet harassment is.

They might have an alcohol problem when they left the reserve. Now they're sure to–their friends drink, so they drink. They want to be accepted, and they find that a few good belts makes them feel that their problems aren't that bad. Their friends shop-lift to get money for booze and chemical drugs, so they do it, and they get caught. The second time they're off to jail, or fined and can't pay their fine, so they're off to jail, or they get sentenced to one hundred hours of community work and they don't show up, and they're off to jail. Another statistic.

Would it shock you if I told you that about ninety per cent of the women in the women's jail up at Prince Albert are native women? At any one time? Or that seventy per cent of Indian men will have served a jail sentence by the time they are twenty-five years old? Or that in an average year, about sixty-five per cent of all the males in Saskatchewan sentenced to prison will be native, but the natives make up only twenty per cent of the population?

I mean, this gets real scary. Then I ask you to think this over. Go back as far as you want. Find out the number of commissions and reports that have been done by earnest and decent people, including politicians, and the billions of dollars that has been poured into native programs and buildings and projects and businesses. Count the tens of millions of man and woman hours poured in, too, by social workers, teachers, prison guards, politicians, civil servants, and ask yourself this question: What has been accomplished? C'mon, try it some time when you've got a week to spare. I can predict your answer.

You've got to take a whole race of people, from Nova Scotia to Vancouver Island, and what are you going to say to them? Get some pride? Get some education? Stop the booze? Stop the drugs? Stop the wife-beating? Stop every goddamned thing and smarten up? It's gone too far. It started too far back. Good men have retired from the Department of Indian Affairs crying in frustration over a career finished and nothing accomplished, because they know that nothing they did meant any difference.

I'm not one of those DIA men, but I've come to the conclusion that there is only one solution. That's why I won't even give my name. Every do-gooder around the world would come down on me. But if every Indian child below the age of ten was taken away now, right now – away from their parents, away from the reserve, and out of the cities – and brought up in the white way, with the other population of Canada, then maybe you'd have a chance for them. As it stands, a native child born in this year, 1987, doesn't have a chance in white society and never will.

I know, I know, there are unbelievably huge problems involved, and besides, it wouldn't ever happen, the Charter of Rights, the Constitution, and all that. But if it could be allowed to happen, building a whole new race of natives, a whole new native culture, you'd save some. Every child under ten today, and every child born into a native family from now on, whisk them away to safety. Kids are resilient and they seem to forget easily, and in a new culture they'd survive and flourish. I'd be willing to bet they'd even out-perform the white kids, most of them. But the way they are now, hopeless. They are being brought up to meet failure early and totally.

All this will never happen, of course. An article on this would never see the light of day. It is unthinkable. People don't do things like this. My rebuttal is, we're not talking about things that are unthinkable. We are talking about the survival of a race, and the qualities of survival are in those children under ten, right now, today, who have not yet realized how degrading, how hopeless, it is in today's world to be an Indian.

You will never change white society and its rejection of the native people. It is fixed, firm, and fast. That deep-seated racism will always be there. It's an inherited thing now. But you could change the native society by creating a new one, from the children. That could work, but it will never be given the chance."

✐ *That Indian Bunch*

"I been waiting a long time to tell somebody this. I don't know what the solution is. Maybe there isn't one. But something has got to be done about our people.

I mean, I don't know who is at fault. Us? All those guys back in Ottawa in Indian Affairs? Maybe. Maybe they should put a few educated Indian guys in that department so they could say, hey, you guys are doing this all wrong. What you're doing is worse than before. Because that's the way it always seems to work out.

Our leaders, they ain't Indians no more. They talk about our nations and our confederacies and our this and that, as though all the Indians in Canada are the same. We're not like each other. But these leaders and some of our kids who get to be lawyers, they think they've found the gold treasure chest. They say they represent us. Sure, we elected them or we put these lawyers in charge of what we got, but to them it's just money in their pockets. To the white guys at Indian Affairs and in the government, they talk one way, and to us they talk another way. And these lawyers, they go off to university and the government pays every cent of their way and they're with white people for about five years, and then they're lawyers, and they're not Indian people any more.

In between these chiefs and lawyers and the bureaucrats down in Ottawa, you're gonna find us. Just the poor Indians. We can't do anything. We got no say, and we look on the TV and there's a bunch of them raising hell. Drumming. Dancing. Singing our songs. Hell, man, we don't do that when we're by ourselves having a good time. We sit around and eat and have a few drinks and talk about kids and money and where the good fishing is. What we're gonna do, maybe try and get a new house, or trade in on a better truck. Does that sound familiar to you? Well, it should. That's the way you white people talk when you've got a family party going. Talking about kids and grandchildren and who dies, and sorry, that's too bad, isn't it?

But these leaders always after land claims, and this drumming and those phoney Indian costumes and that drumming and ki-yi-yiing. That's a laugh. That's not us. But these chiefs and lawyers tell the people, they say, the only way you can get attention is to have a media event. They phone up the television stations and they come out with the cameras. Some young girl reporter who doesn't know what she's talking about, she's up there with the chief and he's spouting off this Indian talk. He's laughing at her, but she don't know it. And there's the people, the white people, they're sitting in their homes watching this on the Six O'Clock News. I know what they're saying. They're saying, oh, it's those goddamned Indians again. What do they want? And the wife will say, they want half of British Columbia or all of downtown Winnipeg or all of Quebec or some such foolishness, but that's the way it comes across on the TV screen.

All I want is to be treated equal. I don't want aboriginal rights. All that stuff went out the window a long time ago, we're not

Indians any more in that way. The Riel Rebellion in this part of
the country knocked that thing on the head a long time ago. We
want to be treated like we are people. Damn it all, we are Canadians,
aren't we? We got feelings too. We can do more than work for
some farmer or get on doing dirty ground jobs in some factory, or
working on a garbage truck, or things like this. The Joe jobs, the
nothing kind of things.

Like me, I'm a welder. I walked around Regina for two months
looking for a job, and I'd say I had eight months' training in the
industrial school in Edmonton and look, here's my certificate.
Look, right there, it says top honours. This man can weld anything,
that certificate says. Did I get a chance? No, they just look at me
and see this dark skin and say sorry, chief, nothing open around
here yet. They never give you a straight no. They can't. This here
legislation, because they advertise for a job and I show up, I got to
have the same chance as a white guy. Of course, if it was a white
guy and me, both applying for that job, the white guy would get
it every time. Ten times out of ten. Don't kid yourself. That is a
true thing I'm telling you.

Okay, I get on with an outfit. A good one, and there's lots of
work. But I can see what the guy is thinking, I'll hire this fellow,
but he better watch out. No drinking. No Indian time. No goofing
off to go fishing or hunting. That kind of baloney. The guys in the
shop, they are okay. But you know what? They are watching me
too. The boss, the super, the guys with me, they inspect my welds,
cleanness, evenness, strength, and they're always wondering, will
he make it? I was a good welder and I am better now, but they're
thinking, he's Injun Joe and he's going to screw up.

There were times I wanted to. Get drunk, see my friends downtown, buy them beers because I know they got no money. Maybe
go back home and buy everybody a lot of hooch and we'd all sit
around and get drunk. But I don't do it.

One time I nearly did. Nobody would rent us an apartment.
They don't take no kids. Jesus, we went to apartments where we
saw kid's toys, bikes and stuff, in the hall and the janitor would
look at us and smile and say, 'Sorry, we don't take children.' Maybe,
'Sorry, that ad's been filled.' They don't say they don't want an
Indian family in their nice apartment block.

Finally, we get a house. It's not in Indian town, but it is a working
district. Guys like me. I got the tip from a guy at the shop and he
comes with me and Johnny's one tough guy and he sees the real

estate agent and he gets the key and then we drive over to see the house and it's okay. Needs a lot of cleaning up but it's got a fridge and stove and all the stuff. Okay, I'll take it. We go back, and the real estate agent sees me and says the house has been rented. That's after he looks at me. He thinks the house was for Johnny. Well, you should have seen it. Johnny leans across on that guy and he says that if he don't produce a lease contract in one minute, he's going to the phone and he's going to phone Shumiatcher and he's the best lawyer in town. He's going to phone the *Leader-Post* and this company's name is going to be all over the front page. He's going to phone and get me on Johnny Sandison's TV program. He's gonna phone Civil Rights, Human Rights, the provincial premier, and it was kind of funny, Johnny got kind of wound up and didn't notice that this poor little squirt of a real estate guy was already shoving the lease deal at us before he got past the TV program.

So, you see, I didn't even get a house on my own doing because I'm an Indian. I fix that house up better than any house on the street. The owner, a nice lady, pays me to buy the paint and brushes, and I'm at it after work and on two weekends. I do the yard, the lawn, put in flowers, and I give my wife money to buy the best curtains she can, and she's a smart girl and comes back with three big pots of red geraniums for the front window.

School. Our kids are seven and nine then, so it's elementary. I think there may have been a couple of other Indian kids there. I ask the kids how they're doing. They say fine. Do the other kids play with you? Sometimes. Hell, I know what sometimes means. It means only when they have these group games. Ring-around-a-rosy stuff. I tell my wife to dress our kids better than any kids in school. I can do it, I'm making more than fourteen dollars an hour. I know that little girls have birthday parties at that age, but my kids, they don't seem to get invited. That doesn't bother me. I seem to have figured that would be the way it was. Nothing you can do about prejudice by the parents. Too bad. Best you forget these things.

But, you know, life goes on. We get to meet our neighbours on either side, across the street. Talking together, that sort of thing. The first time the guy across the street comes over and wants to borrow my Black and Decker drill I know it's going to be okay. I'm not an Indian any more. We're not 'that Indian bunch over there' any more. We're neighbours.

That Thanksgiving I take two neighbours goose-hunting where I know there are geese and nobody else does. I take them to the reserve, up north of here, and they bang away, get their limits. Happy as a pig. That really broke the ice all the way clear to the bottom. The women started asking my wife over and they saw she wasn't just any Indian woman. She's educated, was a teacher up North Battleford way on a reserve school. My Marlene is a lady.

Well, you could go on and on. That's us. We're doing fine, but let me tell you this. We're the lucky ones. I just can't put my finger on it. The whole problem is too big, so big you can't imagine it. You can't say, okay, we'll take all these Indians over here and we'll do this and that for them. We'll make them into good Canadian citizens, with jobs, with kids that don't muck up, with all this stuff. It won't work. It has to be done on an individual basis, man for man, woman for woman, family for family, each one trying to do the best for what's right for each of them. Then you might get somewhere.

But right now, honestly, I don't see any hope. It is just going to get worse, and worse, and worse."

☙ *Total Frustration*

"An Indian kills somebody, his wife, his girlfriend, or just some guy at a party, the cops never have to look far. Hell, the guy is probably sitting in a chair in the house with the knife or the broken bottle lying on the floor. 'That's him. He did it.' They don't try and run away. Usually they're too drunk to do it. Or two big cops come into the bedroom and wake him up and haul him off and he asks, 'What have I done?' They say he killed his wife or his best friend. He doesn't even remember.

No, I'm not being harsh. That's the way it is so often. Solving an Indian murder is no big deal. They'll admit it. 'Sure, I killed him. He drank all my bottle of wine.' That's a reason for murder. 'She was playing the radio rock-and-roll too loud and wouldn't stop.' Another reason. You'll find that booze is mixed up in all these killings.

They're a gentle people out there. They look after each other as best they can. Leave them alone and make sure there is no booze around and they're a different people. I know. But once that booze gets in . . . that is the killer. Not the knife. Not the deer rifle hanging on the wall. Not the lamp with the heavy base that they club somebody with. None of that. Any cop will tell you. Any social worker. Anybody involved with them.

But remember this. Go into any liquor store and you might see a buck buying four cases of beer and a gallon of cheap wine. Then another buys three cases and a bottle of vodka, and another guy comes in and he does the same. They sell it to them. They can't refuse to do it. There is no such thing as the old Indian List any more. That's when there was a list of bad offenders in the booze department and they couldn't buy the beer and wine and vodka. But not now. And that liquor-store clerk knows they're probably all heading for the same party and there's going to be enough booze there for a hundred people, not just the ten or fifteen who will be there.

I never know why they do this. Desperation. Insecurity, I guess. Total frustration. Imagine that society was a jail to you. But the bars were invisible and only you saw them and you knew you couldn't get through them. That's what your average Indian on the Prairies, that's exactly how the poor bastard feels. We don't see the social and employment bars, but he sees them. Christ man, he can reach out and feel them. They're damned real to him. He can even shake them, and they don't give an eighth of an inch. He's in prison. We put him there, and that's for sure.

I don't know the solution, but I don't think there is one. This has been going on for a long time. I'll tell you a story. I know a government welfare inspector, and he was told to fly around up north there and visit all the reserves and see what was going on. Well, he soon found out. And when he came back after six weeks he'd be telling everybody he met, his friends, 'It's going to blow. It's going to blow up north.' Boy, he meant it. He'd hold out his finger and thumb real close together, and he'd say, 'It's just this far from blowing. There's going to be a bloody revolution. You can smell the hatred and the fear up there. The frustration.' You get the hang of what he was saying.

But here's the point. While he was going around telling everybody that the situation was going to blow, he was writing his report. Then he handed it in, and one day I asked him if he'd put all this about it all going to blow in his report.

He said no, he hadn't.

Now, think that one over. Isn't that what is wrong with the

whole damned awful situation? The liquor clerk knows all these braves are going to go to a party and everybody, even the kids, they're all going to get drunk and there's going to be trouble. The government inspector, he goes up north and comes back shocked and frightened and he doesn't put a bloody word of it in his report.

We've got problems. I think we've got problems we haven't even figured out yet."

🕊 *Another Indian*

"Here I am, I'm fifty-six, and when I go in the liquor store in this town I always feel kind of funny, like people looking at me and saying, oh, there's another Indian, in here to buy some cheap wine and go over to the railway bridge to get drunk and pass out.

That is one hell of an awful way to think, but I do. This is where the Indian is today in this country. We got more right to be in this country than anybody, and they did to us what they're doing to people over there in Africa now. Why the hell should I feel guilty about going into the liquor store and buying a two-litre bottle of wine?

These people, the ones looking at me, they're buying Scotch and rye and vodka and they'll go home and get drunk, and they're the ones giving me these looks. Me, I'm taking this bottle and going home in my Bronco, and it cost me $19,000 five years ago, so I'm not poor, and my wife and me will have a little supper and watch TV and have a few glasses of wine. Not to get drunk. No, no, not at all. Just enjoying ourselves.

I got a good job and we got a nice house and our kids, they seem to be doing okay. Better than the white kids, anyway. I know that. They're good kids, all got jobs. But this is the way white people teach their kids to think about Indians. It's from the old days. Oh, just a bunch of drunken Indians out there on the reserve, fighting and killing each other.

What the hell can anybody do about something like that? I mean, I don't know, it's been going on for so long. Seems like forever."

🕊 *Leaving the Reserve*

"She's easy to leave the reserve, oh boy. One morning you say I'm not going to put up with this no more, all this drinking and fooling around and the fighting, the kids breaking into people's homes around and in town, and you say, okay, I'm going.

My mother didn't want me to go. She said things in Winnipeg would be worse. There's no place to work there, nothing to do but be on Main Street and all that wasting your time and seeing a friend go into a beer parlour, you follow him and maybe this guy will buy you a beer. That's what she said. Look at your brother, she says, he's in jail and then he's out and then he's caught doing something with another guy and now, she says, look at him. He's in the pen.

Look at your sister, she says, and that's when she starts to cry, and that is a sorry kind of story, too. She's on the streets, just a kid. When I'm working around Shoal Lake for a farmer and doing some jobs, a little time driving truck, anything I can get to help my mother, this sister of ours, she's only sixteen and doing no good in school and she's drinking too much, and one day she gets on a bus and down to Winnipeg there and soon somebody comes back to the reserve and says she is a whore. I don't like to use that word but this fellow says I seen this nice-looking woman outside the Marlborough Hotel and when I get up to her, you know what? It's your sister and she's peddling her ass. Wants me to buy some. She don't recognize him, he says, and he's from the reserve by Birtle there and he visits our place lots of times. That was too bad.

She's gonna die, my sister. Somebody is going to take her out of that hotel where we find she is a lot, and they're going to beat her all up. She's just a little Indian kid. There's something wrong all around this business and I'm not ready to say it's because she's native. She being the fastest berry-picker in the family, even trapping up north and she was good there, too, and all these things we do that the white man says we stopped doing a long time ago, we still do. There is I'm damn sure a lot of living off the land still left in our blood.

I'm not going to use no names because of that sister of mine and my big brother, but I can tell you this, mister, not so much for them as for my mother. She is a . . . a perfect lady. She's not old, but she had six kids of us and she, well, I'll tell you a story. A few years ago I asked her how she was such a perfect lady. You know, even though we had a shack and not much money and my old man gone to Thompson and working out of there going north into the bush every month, my mother keeps this shack clean. We all get clean clothing to go to school, and she tells us about when she was a kid and then about her mother and grandfather and father and how they lived in those days and I say, 'Mom, how come you are so perfect?' She said that she learned all the good things from her mother, but all the useless and dumb things from the nuns at the Catholic school. Okay, got that? And then she said when she unlearned all the things the Catholics had taught her, then that's when she came perfect.

Oh, yes, leaving the reserve. It's easy. Somebody's going to town and you get in his car and give him five dollars for gas and you go. I said I was going and make some money and come back and help people. That was when I was twenty and Mom meant a lot to me and had her church and friends, and I didn't hang around with them others. You got into a lot of trouble that way. The Mounties, you're driving along the road with a couple of guys in an old car and z000000m, there they are, and they think you've done a crime and search the car. You haven't done nothing, you're just going to town. 'It's ten o'clock,' one of these cops says. 'What are you going to town for?' 'Chinese food,' we say. Something like that. 'Show me your money,' he says. 'You ain't got enough,' he says. 'Turn around and get the hell back on that reserve.' My friend Billy says, 'It's a free country,' and he says to the cop, 'What's your number?' The cop says, 'Here's my number,' and slams Billy in the face. 'Now, get the hell out of here.' He's one of these new Mounties that are always showing up. Somebody some day is going to do something bad to a fellow like that. We're just going to town for Chinese food and it was me, not my friend, that had the money. I think about a hundred dollars that time. I'd been working.

Sure, okay, enough of that business. My friend, he's going to Winnipeg in this old Chev, but the sumgun she breaks down at Portage and we walk into town and it's lunch-time and there's this Indian hotel on the main street and we go in. We are having two beers and then we'll eat and this guy stops and asks if we want jobs, picking raspberries. The farmer said if I worked hard I would do good. Okay, I can tell you this right now. I worked hard, but I didn't do very good, but I didn't mind.

It was a farm that had Mexican people up from Mexico to work and they lived in little shacks. You know what? These shacks were worse than anything on our reserve, but they were the happiest people you ever saw. The government or the farmer flew them in from Mexico and they worked for Canadian money and then they went home by this plane again, and they had more money than any of the people in their villages. But you know what? They were working for wages that no Canadian would work at. Too low. But those guys sure loved Canada, and I guess Canada loved them because nobody else was going to do that picking. That's how I became a Mexican, I tell people.

I stayed there for three weeks and not for the money. I couldn't pick like those people could. Laurie could, I'd say, and she's the sister I told you about in Winnipeg. I picked because I needed the money and I got to like these Mexican people an awful lot and they liked me. But the real reason, I think, was to know what it was like not being a native. I don't mean that. I'm still blood, Cree, I'm proud of that. We haven't got much of our history written down, but the old people, when I was a kid, they used to tell me stories about some really, really good people who were us. A lot of things have happened to us guys and women since, but anyway. I stayed because I wanted to know what it was like not to be where these people I'd seen all my life were, and seeing how their lives sort of changed a lot.

Maybe a month, I tell the owner I'm going and he said stay. No, I said, so he drove me to town and I caught a bus to Winnipeg, and the last thing he says is, 'Stay the hell off Main Street.' Sure, I know what Main Street is. That's Indian Town. Teepee Village. Skid Road. They got all these names. I don't go there but once, to walk up and down it and see, well, that was a pretty ashaming thing. I go into one hotel beer parlour and I look around and it's about noon and what I see, I wish I hadn't seen. There are the whole bunch, all the brave Indians in the country. Drunk, half drunk, starting to get drunk, and it's only twelve o'clock. I have one beer and go.

I'm walking out and a fellow stands up and says, 'Give me five dollars,' and I told him to fuck off and he throws a chair after me, crash, it hits another table and I just get out of there.

Next day after walking around and finding a hotel that looks not too bad where I sleep that night, I walk around again just seeing things, and then I see this picture gallery downtown. It's got some Indian stuff in the window, so I go in. The lady comes up and asks if I want something and I say no, I'm just looking at this picture and that one. She knows I'm native, but I think she sees me different. I've got on a good jacket and good pants and I've got a haircut and I talk nice to her. Just looking around. She asks me what I think of the pictures, and I guess I get up a little nerve and I says it's just that same old stuff the guys out on the West Coast do. A long time ago somebody gets an idea for this kind of painting and then everybody else does it and I tell her I think a lot of the things she's got hanging on the walls have been done by white people anyway. She's a nice lady and she laughs and she says I'm right, the paintings are all the same but there is nothing else. There's nobody else in the store and we get talking more and she says, would I like a cup of coffee. That surprises me. Then I don't know all that much about white people, but I know enough, and this is not the way they're supposed to treat me.

Okay, here's what happened. She's got a little office at the back and we go there and she's asking me who I am and what I do and, I know now, she's trying to find out a lot about me. I'm having a good time and I tell her and when a customer comes in the store she tells her assistant to look after them. She wants to talk to me. I tell her all these things, all the things I never told anybody before, and I get kind of brave and I tell her that me talking to her is like me talking to my mum. This gives her a laugh, and then she says, 'Johnny, would you like a job?'

Boy, that sure surprised me. I said yes, right away. That was what I had to find soon, so she says, 'You come back here tomorrow and we'll see what we can do for you.'

I go to a movie that night and have a big meal after and then I sleep and next morning I go and see her and she said a friend of hers had this farm with horses out near Selkirk and I could work there. What she's saying is that Winnipeg is not a good place for a new guy like me. I know this, and I take the job. So that night she drives me out there and I meet her friends and we talk and the next day I'm working. This thing is a farm job, but I've got a little trailer and there's a little TV in it and a kitchen, a stove and fridge and a table and a bed you pull down, and it sure is pretty good. There's a toilet and a shower in the barn and I use that and I eat dinner in the house and then I start having breakfast there and I like it.

I had a darn good life and a good time, and I saved all my money and I bought the '78 pickup off the farmer. This man, he was a good man. He had a business in the city and his wife worked at a college there, teaching, so they were away all day and I was the boss. I did everything. You could say I owned that farm, but I didn't. On Saturday they would go around with me and I'd show them what I'd done, and I'd say I needed money to buy paint or a new tool or take something into Winnipeg and get fixed and he'd say, 'Johnny, you do what you think is best. My wife and I were just about going to sell this farm until you came along.' One day he said, 'I'm going to give you a raise of a hundred a month.' His wife would hand me a parcel after dinner a few times and there would be a nice shirt or a nice sweater and I'd say she shouldn't do that and she'd say, 'Now you just go back to your teepee and try it on, and not another word out of you.'

We did a lot like that. They would joke with me about teepees and eating moose nose, which I'd never done, and things about Indians, and if they gave me a drink before dinner on Saturday I'd say, 'You put any tobacco juice and lye water in this to make me drunk?' The kind of things the traders used to do in the old times, like my mother told me. Lots of joking.

The thing I liked was when they had a party on Sunday afternoon and they'd ask me over. I'd help serve and pour drinks and have a couple myself and talk to their friends and their kids and we'd have some good talks around that big fireplace. The thing I liked best was when some friend would say, 'I'd like to hear what Johnny has to say about this?' So I'd tell them. A lot of things they would never know about. How our people thought. Why so many of them were just poor drunks down on Main Street. I didn't say, 'It's your fault.' It is and it isn't. But they'd all listen to me. We had some good arguments, but not really. Just talk. People telling what they think.

I remember one day, the visitors were leaving and I heard one woman say to Maureen, my boss, I guess, and this woman said, 'I wouldn't do too much of this, Maureen. It might go to his head. You never know.' I always remember those words. Then she looked around and saw me there and put out her hand and smiled and said, 'Johnny, it was delightful to meet you.'

That's when I thought, it never . . . damn it all, does anything ever change?

But I didn't let it bother me, and my bosses, they never invited those people back to their Sunday parties on the lawn or to dinner. Others, they came, and new ones too, but never that woman and her husband who was a big doctor in Winnipeg. I know why. My boss, Maureen, she felt ashamed and we never talked about it. It just wasn't what you talked about, but I know. These people were awfully good people.

Then they had to sell their good farm because, well, I don't know.

Maybe they just wanted to live in the city. We'd had a bad winter and living on a farm twenty miles out, it wasn't so good. The new owner didn't want me, although my boss told him he was a fool for not, but no, he wanted someone else.

I'd been with them for four years and I wondered what I was going to do. I'd take the truck into Winnipeg at least once a week to get things, like supplies and feed and things, and I knew it very well, and I could go into a good restaurant and eat and have a beer and, oh hell. What I'm saying was that I didn't know how I'd do. I was sure still an Indian, and you know people in the city, they look at you and think, 'What's he doing away from Main Street?' There's just something in the way they look at you. Anyway, I hadn't seen my mum for two years, since she'd been in hospital there for an operation, so I thought I'd go back home for a while.

So I went home to the reserve, driving my nice pickup and in my good clothes. And you turn off the pavement on the highway and you hit gravel and when you get to the reserve, you know you're there. The road gets worse. Those shacks, you think, don't they ever paint them, and then you think, oh, if DIA [Department of Indian Affairs] don't do it for them, they'll live in them till they rot. My mum was fine. My sister, she didn't know where she was. Not in Winnipeg, we knew that. I'd tried to find her. My brother was in jail in Vancouver, I knew that. Nothing was different.

I'm not with my mum and my little sister an hour when there's a knock on the door and then it opens and a guy I went to school with, he comes in. Doesn't even say hello. Just says, 'Johnny, let's get over to Russell and buy some boxes of beer. They got a new liquor store there that'll knock your eyes out. Then we can go to the hotel and drink with some guys. Most of them will be there.'

I thought, 'Oh shit. Is this what it is again, over and over?' I said, 'No, I don't drink that way,' and he said, 'Okay, white guy, give me the keys and forty bucks and I'll go and bring some back.' Just like that. I said, and this is a kid I grew up with, I said, 'Get out of here, you . . . ' well, I'm not going to say what I said. He slammed the door, and a few seconds later there's this crash and I run out and he's thrown the axe for splitting wood right through the windshield. There goes my hundred dollars deductible.

My mum and I drive around even with a bashed windshield and we see people, and some say it's nice to see me and others, well, they aren't so nice. I'm not an Indian any more. I still belong to the reserve, I can vote on it, I could even start a business on it and not pay income tax. I can do anything on it, including getting drunk and beating up wives and kids if I want. But I'm not an Indian any more. I been around white people, nice white people, too long. I don't know what I am. That's my trouble. In two hours I don't know what I am again, just like when I was a kid four years before and knew I had to get away and find out what I was. Do you see what I mean? I can't explain it. I'm a guy with an Indian face and a nice white man's sports jacket. That says it all, I guess.

I stayed with my mum and sister two more days and I did a lot of fixing up of little things wrong that they couldn't do. Then I drove to Portage and got a new windshield and after that I thought, what will I do? I went to the man with the berry farm at Portage but he couldn't use me, but he did remember me. I'll give him that. He remembered my name, but it was hard times for him and his family and they didn't need help.

I did what I should have done first. I went to Winnipeg and got a room in a motel and then I phoned the man I'd worked for at Selkirk, and he said to come over. He's got this big business out near the airport and I walked into his office and you'd think I'd been away a year instead of just a week or so. He's happy to see me. I told him. Just the way it happened. Home. Mum. That shit of a guy I went to school with. The whole thing, and then I said I wanted a job. He thought, and he said, 'Johnny, I can pick up this phone and get one of my men and then send you over to the warehouse and you can go to work as soon as you get the right clothes. But I don't think it would be good for you. I think you'd be happier on a farm. I've got a lot of friends who've got places, out along the Assiniboine or south of here, and why don't you let me try?'

I know he was trying to protect me from myself and others downtown, treating me like a kid in a way, and I was twenty-four or so then, but I'll tell you this. That was what I was hoping he would say. When he said it, I knew it was what I wanted.

No more story. He got me a good job on a big stock farm, a little trailer same as before and good people. I never let them down once. I got good pay and my board, my meals, all the things and they gave me free gas, and this was a big farm. Some day I'm going to run that farm all by myself and I've got a woman I want to marry. She's got two kids, but that will be fine with me, and when it works out, I know how to build a house. I got it all worked out. She and me, we've done our figuring and this is the best way. I don't think a native should marry a white woman, and that's why I like this woman. She's from the Philippine Islands and works in town in a dress factory, and when we get it all sorted out, money fixed up, get a bit of land, maybe ten acres, I'm going to get a house on it and keep working on the farm. I've got to do what's right for me and for this lady and her kids and then our kids, and going to Winnipeg or Brandon or Regina or somewhere else, that's just not the place for our people. It's best the way I do it, like we been planning to. That way it'll work out. I just don't want anything bad happening to us. We ain't married yet but I feel that we are already a family, this thing we have, and there is no way I'm going to spoil it. This thing is for us and nobody else. Don't we deserve it?"

This Indian Thing

"You know, I hate to be going into a liquor store. If there's a lot of people there, I kind of hang around, sit in my truck and wait until I figure the place is almost empty. And when I go in I see the people, and the clerks looking at me, and they say, 'Oh, there's a drunken Indian,' or 'There's an Indian going to buy a couple of bottles of wine and go somewhere and get drunk.' They don't say, 'Oh, there's a man buying two bottles of wine to take to his daughter's birthday party,' or something like that. No, these people think we're just going over there and sitting beside some garbage cans in a back alley and guzzling down the whole damn works.

It's in your mind, in your heart, this Indian thing. You walk around, and okay, so my clothes aren't good right now, but they're workingman's clothes. I work on a crew, five men, electrical work, and I've got as good an education as the guys on my crew and I got the same trade-school training and I got four years' experience with this company and you know what? Right now, even working today, I think they still think of me as just another Indian. And one of those guys is from Yugoslavia and another is from Denmark. Hell, we were here long before those guys, but that's the way they think. Even the immigrant guys think that. Now, that's a hell of a thing.

I feel it when I walk down the street and when I get out of my truck, which is an '86 three-quarter-ton, and they're thinking, how can an Indian own a new truck like that? I know that.

You should come with me to one of these fancy men's shops in the mall. I walk in and I'm looking, say, for some socks. You think anyone will serve me? Finally I pick up three or four pairs and I got to walk to the cashier and then there's some young fellow and then they're nice to me. I bought something, you see. I made money for them.

Look, I've got a good education and a good wife and three kids. I've got a good job, pays eleven dollars an hour. I pay my bills and my rent and the wife, that woman is the cleanest person you'll ever see, I bet you. Everything scrubbed, and the oldest girl going off to school clean as clean. We don't drink, except a bit of wine. I make things with my wood-working tools in my basement and we go to church too. I'm no different from my neighbour next door who, when he sees me cutting the lawn, I don't think he believes his eyes. What does he expect me to do? Cut it with my tomahawk?

But you're looking at a guy with one big inferiority complex. It's this wide and that long, and I've had it ever since I was a kid up in the Meadow Lake district. I don't know how I got out of there. It took a lot of guts, I tell you, because that was my home, the reserve. Then it was Saskatoon and it doesn't take long before you're down on 20th Street where your friends are, and you can feel safe among your own people there. But let me tell you, that's the most dangerous place in the world for an Indian or a Métis. That place is the end place. I was there for six months and I don't know how I survived. Drinking. Fighting. All that. You see a new face and you wonder where he comes from and he's just been let out of jail. Time after time.

Anyway, here's what happened. I got to get off 20th, so I take a bus to Regina and it's worse. More of us and no place to go, but I find out you can take courses and I take one in welding, which doesn't do me any good, no jobs. Then I take one in electrical and the school gets me on with this company. The foreman the first day he takes me aside and he said, 'Look, kid, it's not me and it's not the rules, but every day you're with us you're on probation.'

He meant that somebody in the front office would be looking at me all the time. I tell him I don't mind that. I won't be drinking any more and I don't and I'll be in on time. It turns out it's the other guys who get in trouble. Big hangovers. Not showing up. One guy was getting ready for a big wedding that night and he drank a mickey of vodka at lunch. In this café, two trips to the washroom and the mickey was gone. He was no good that afternoon and nothing happened to him. The boss knew. Me, I'd have been gone.

I think the main reason I came to Regina was this girl, Josephine, Josie, off a reserve at Meadow Lake. She had come to Regina and was working as a clean-up girl in the hospital. I liked her and thought maybe something would come of it. Well, as you can see, it did. I got a wife, that's Josie, and three little kids and a job.

This is not something we talk about with others, but we do among ourselves. A clerk at the check-out at the supermarket the other day asked her if she was from Fiji. Josie said no, she was born up north. Well, that clerk was surprised. See, she thought no Indians dressed like that and had money. This is ridiculous, isn't it? Me talking like this and we're Canadians.

Nothing's going to change. The whites are going to go their own way and not give us any credit at all, and we just got to live our own lives, with the few friends like us. There are quite a lot, you know. They say there's 25,000 natives in Regina. Why not say half live good lives and don't cause trouble? I know lots of them, and some of them are good friends. We don't go over to Alabama North on the west side of town. We just stay in our own little place and mind our own business and live and let live."

🐦 *Hitching a Ride Home*

"I was driving through to Winnipeg and I'm coming up from Lethbridge through Taber to get on Number One at Medicine Hat and just outside Taber I see this person hitching a ride. He's small, just a kid, and I think he's a local kid just going down the road and so I stop. It's about eight in the morning, dark and cloudy and looking like rain, so I'll give this kid a lift for a few miles.

When I stop, he gets in and puts his sack in the back and away we go and I got a look and I think, 'Oh-oh, it's an Indian.' That's a natural reaction in those days, but I say hello and off we go. I can't turn him out now. I'm not that kind of guy. So I ask the usual question, how far are you going, and I hear, 'I'm going home to Regina.' Boy, did I turn my head quickly. It wasn't a boy, and I remember saying, 'You're a girl.' She said yes. So I have an Indian kid with me and she's a girl. Oh boy! Just a little bit of a thing. I asked her a few questions, like the first being how long she had been hitch-hiking. Her answer got to me. She said she'd been standing by that road since three o'clock the day before. About eighteen hours and not one person had stopped. Not even some guy in a pickup who would let her ride in the back. No, I guess, because they saw she was an Indian. Nice country around there, I thought. I asked her where she had slept and she said in the culvert, and believe me it had been a chilly night even though it was summer. God, I thought, could one of my kids have done that? She told me she worked in the beet-fields and had to get back to Regina because she had to see her baby. Getting better and better, isn't it?

Well, I'm barrelling along and she's too shy to talk anyway, so we just listened to the cowboy music on the radio, and we get through Medicine Hat and suddenly I thought, she probably hasn't eaten. I was planning to barrel right through to Regina but I asked her. No, she hadn't eaten since breakfast the day before. Some breakfast, I'd bet, in a beet-picker's shack. Was she hungry? Yes, she was hungry. You bet she was hungry.

So, we're coming up to Maple Creek and there's this new motel out on the highway and I think, shall we go there? Would they serve her, this Indian kid with straggly hair and old black clothes, among all those tourists? I knew they had to, but I knew she and I would get a lot of stares, and you never know about these outfits. Maybe a Mountie would be casually waiting outside when we finished. What was I doing with a minor, an Indian, out on the highway? So, to hell with it, I swung right and went into the Creek and we went to the Commercial Hotel there. They've seen enough Indians in their one hundred years, or whatever it is.

I got us a table and got her seated and I told her to stay there and when the waitress came she was to order a cheeseburger for me and whatever she wanted. Oh, I told her I was paying, sure. Then I went to the washroom and then into the beer parlour and had two fast beers, about ten minutes, and then I went back and she was sitting there looking scared. It appeared the owner, not a waitress, had come over and questioned her. What was she doing here? That kind of thing. She said she was with a man. Well, the owner said that when the man came back she would take the order. Nice, eh?

Then the owner came over, and believe it or not, she was a nice and kind-looking woman, like your mother would be, and she had a chip on her shoulder. Picking on me, of course. She saw my cigarettes on the table and she said they didn't serve people who smoked. Holy mackerel, this was long before this anti-smoking B.S. came about. I think she didn't want to serve this Indian girl.

Anyway, we order, me a cheeseburger and pie and coffee, and she says the same, she'll have the same, but with milk, so I told the woman to bring three hamburgers. She gobbled the first one down, and when she reached for her pie I pushed the other burger at her and told her to get on with it. She did, and down went the pie and the milk, and when I went up to pay, the woman asked me if she was a prisoner and was I taking her to court? That really got me. That's what she thought. Why else would a middle-aged man like myself be with an Indian? I told her it was none of her damned business. No Mountie followed me, so I guess she didn't phone the cops.

Away again she began to open up. They'd been thinning beets for a farmer. She called him a Hungarian, probably second-generation. The whole family, her mother and aunt and uncle and six or seven kids, had gone in a truck to work in the beet-fields. Christ, she said, she'd only had the baby two months before, and here she was doing this beet-thinning, which is no easy job. Apparently they worked by the acre, not by the hour, so how much they made depended how thick the thinning had to be and the weeds. She said she had made only thirty-two dollars in nine days of work, under that boiling sun, and she became very weak. Besides, she was going crazy wanting to see her baby back in Regina. So she'd decided to hitch-hike home to save money, or so I thought, and when I asked her how much money she had, she said, 'Two dollars and a little bit.' Apparently the farmer paid the mother the money she had earned. So no wonder she was standing out on the highway with her thumb out. That got to me.

The family came from a reserve north of Lac La Ronge, way up in the bush. Right to Regina, she said, because they couldn't live there any more, all the drinking and fighting and no work, and, as she said, nobody would do anything to help them. That was a couple of years ago, and they'd joined the Indian community in

Regina. Two families had a small house, she said, and that's where her baby was, being taken care of by someone. She was just sixteen. The usual story, I guess. Or at least the one you always hear. Indian kid comes down out of the bush and is pretty and somebody gets her to go downtown and it happens. She didn't know who the baby's father was and she said she never would. I remember her saying, 'He was just a guy and he bought some chips and cookies and we went to his room and drank wine. They're all like that,' and I guessed that there had been others. Hell, of course there had been. Bloody sad.

She really was a nice kid. It came out, you know. She liked good music and she did want an education and she wanted to be a nurse. Wanted to go back up north and help her people. Wanted to meet a nice boy she could marry, have kids and watch them grow up. She really had a lot of depth and savvy for one so young, and in such a tough life. I got so I was admiring her.

When we got to Regina, she said, go this way, go that way, and we were into a place that might be considered Regina's slum area, if they have one. Pretty drab little houses, old unpainted houses, and this was Indian Town as I saw it. The place was dismal, and she said to let her off there, at this spot, and what do you do? You feel lousy about the whole situation, but what? I reached in and pulled out a ten-spot and gave it to her and told her it was for her. Not to give it to anybody else. Just for her. Have a good meal with it tonight, and she said she would and got out and took her pitiful little sack of clothes, and ran up the steps of one of the houses. Turned around, waved, and then she was gone. Inside. People watching this, a big new Montego sedan letting her out, a white guy driving, fiftyish like me, and I thought, she'll have a lot of talking to do about this one tonight. I just hope they didn't get the money off her.

I've often wondered about her, what happened to her."

🪶 *Like Lepers*

"People in Regina don't talk about it, but I think everybody has a story or two. They say they won't go downtown, after seven o'clock the only people downtown are natives. That may be true in a couple of places, but they won't go downtown. Fear of getting mugged, stabbed, that sort of thing, but I don't think it happens. It's not in the paper, but then again, it might have to be a serious crime by a native to get in the paper. Maybe that's being kept under the rug too.

It has been my experience that all the real harm they do is to each other. They don't bother white people. They just beat up on their own people, because when you get right down to it, they are ghettoized and who else do they know? The Indians in this town are like lepers. We don't see what's going on and we ignore them, even though we are fully conscious that they are there. Like the blacks in Alabama, I'd say, maybe twenty-five years ago. That's the way it is.

Good people, I know, are trying to do something about it, but what do you tell them? Go back to your reserve? Go back to some shack on a pine-tree reserve with polluted drinking-water and no decent school for the kids and a lot of booze coming in on welfare day, and two or three families living in those shacks the government puts up for them, the ones they tear down for firewood in winter? Ah, it's all a crazy system. Both the welfare and government people playing a game and the Indians and Métis playing their game, and neither realizes it is a deadly game.

But here in Regina, you know, life goes on. We've got our Rough-riders, such as they are, and our civic pride, and our Canada geese on the lake, and the Tory government and the civil servants to protect us, and people go downtown and see these poor people and they say, like I wish they'd just go away. Well, they aren't going away."

🐦 *Back in the Bush*

"Métis, sure, include them too. They're part of us. They go through what we go through, too. We don't have anything. We live in poor houses, old shacks, the white man would not live in. The food we eat, it is not as good food as you people eat. We have no money and you people, that's what you have a lot of. We don't have nice cars and pickups. All our stuff is cars and trucks the white man doesn't want. The white man. I don't see him living on reserves and his kids taken from him and put in foster homes. The white man, well, look at him. Everything is for him. The cities are for him, the schools, the colleges, they are for him and they don't want the reserve Indian in the schools and even in the cities. They got to let us in, but they won't give the Indian a chance when he is in the city.

The white men and women make the laws and they elect the politicians, and the politicians, those guys they don't even want us in their ridings. That means they got to think of us sometimes, like when we raise some hell with them, and then most of their thinking is, how can I get these guys off my back? We got nothing for our kids and nothing for ourselves, and the happiest thing the white politicians could do for the white man is to push the Indians as far back in the bush as they can, then forget about us. Just pay us enough money to live on in poverty and not think of us. Get us out of sight so the tourists in North Battleford and Saskatoon won't see us. So the whites in the cities won't see us. Bad for business. The Indian is bad for business. That's about it."

✤ *The Bright Lights*

"It's inevitable. The natives will be urbanized in just a few years. The move to the cities is under way now and has been for years, but it is increasing. Every day. Go down to the bus station. The number of natives getting off the buses from up north are many more than the numbers getting on and going home.

They may say it is a better place to find jobs, the cities, but that's not so. There are no jobs for them in the cities on the Prairies and they know it, but they know the cities are a much better place to spend their welfare dough. The bright lights and all that.

All right, can you blame them? What is there for them on the reserves? I'll tell you. There is nothing. There are no stores. No laundromat. No beer parlour. No good school, and no garage for their cars and trucks, and, well, in a nutshell, no nothing.

You see, the white man has got them hemmed in. The reserves, no matter how big they are, they don't have villages on them that you can call villages, like with some commercial activity. But there are towns on the outside of the reserves, and that's where the natives have to go to do business. So, look at it. All these tens of thousands of dollars of welfare money pour into the reserve but, whoosh, out it goes again, out to the white man's towns and villages, his stores, his beer parlours, his garages, his laundromats, and so on. It's a no-win situation for the Indians, and when they're not wanted in the towns, or the businessmen think they are a nuisance, well, the Mounties kick them back onto the reserve again until next welfare day. Nice, eh?

So, they say, why should we have to put up with all this crap? Well, they don't. They can go to the cities, and what do you find there? Regina, they say there that twenty per cent of the population is now native and Métis. You're looking at maybe 25,000 of them. The same with Saskatoon, maybe fifteen per cent. Edmonton. Calgary. Winnipeg has always had a big problem as long as I can remember. Everybody in these cities just refers to it as 'The Indian Problem' and they don't have to go into specifics. Everybody knows exactly what they mean.

The natives find they can cash their welfare cheques just as easily in the Main Street beer parlours in Winnipeg as on the reserve at God's Lake, Oak Lake, or any lake. They find they've got their own areas, like hotels where the clientele is native, and stores and cafés where they can hang out, and there are even cops on the beat who are sympathetic to a lot of the Indian problems. They find more of the government services they need, within walking distance. There are centres run by agencies to help them, feed them, get them over rough times, look after the kids if the old man and woman are both thrown in jail. Schools, some of them are almost all native, especially in the core area of these cities, the old part of town.

In other words, if you view it from a strictly native point of view, there is no longer any reason for most of them to stay on the reserve. Lousy housing, for one thing. Isolation in many cases. Neglect by government, almost always, just giving them enough to get by. The old ones stay. That is their home, and they will die there and they know the city offers them nothing. The younger ones, the family ones, there is no life for them. Lo, the poor Indian. He can't trap any more. He can't hunt. There are no more fish. There are no jobs, none at all. Unemployment is above eighty per cent on most reserves and the only employment is part-time, when somebody wants a ranch hand for two months or a farm labourer for the harvest. Not much more.

They know this. And they know that a lot of their relatives and friends are in Winnipeg or Regina, and they seem to be making out okay. Of course, in the long run it is a no-win situation for them, but hasn't it always been that way? I can't think of any time in the past fifty years that I've known them that they got a fair shake. They didn't ask to be born native, remember that. So consider our attitude towards them, even from the time we first started to read. Cowboys and Indians, and the cowboys always winning. It goes on from there. Right down the line.

Fine, so about this urbanization. It is coming fast, and in a few years, maybe twenty, there won't be many natives on the reserves, and maybe not even that many reserves, for that matter. The natives will all be in the cities. Not the towns, they're not tolerated there. But they can lose themselves easily in the cities, even though they have a high profile. The whole gang, tens of thousands of them, they'll be in Regina and Winnipeg, Calgary, Saskatoon, and Edmonton. You better believe it, because it is coming."

Fifteen

Jobs

✍

The Work-Hard Part ... A Tall Crop ... Addicted to Railroading ... In Praise of Education ... On the Tractor ... The Way to Make Money ... And That's the Way You Do It ... Then the Union ... Sugar-Beet Slaves ... You Really Want a Job? ... Praying for a Job

To anyone who remembers the Great Depression, a job is something special–any job. You'll hear about some of those jobs in this chapter. In the tough times that hit the West in 1981, that same desperate attitude towards jobs came back as you'll see.

People talking about their jobs tend to be interesting once they get wound up. There's a fair variety here, all the way from secretaries to "slaves", and, as you'll see, some of the people I talked to got really wound up.

✍ The Work-Hard Part

"You asked how a guy without education could do on the Prairies? Okay, so around Edmonton isn't what you'd call the bald prairie, that's south. We've got some hair on the top, trees and sloughs and that. But how can a guy do? This is how. First you get an education so you can write and read, and the arithmetic stuff is important, but it's not that important. Geography? Read the *National Geographic*. Watch the public broadcasting on the TV.

Then, have a good wife. Teach your kids manners. Work hard. Say it three times. Work hard. Work hard. Work hard. Always think the other guy's gonna try and do you in. Don't try and do him in. You lose friends that way. But protect yourself. Work hard. Think all the time: can I do this better? That sort of thing. Love your wife and don't fool around. She's always your best partner. Think this is the most wonderful country in the world and treat it that way. Get your moose in the fall. Work hard, and pray for as much luck as the next guy gets. Then you'll be even. Then the work-hard part comes in, you're ahead and you win. That's how it's done. That's how I did it."

✒ *A Tall Crop*

"When they finished the railroad into Flin Flon in 1931, my dad went back to Nipawin and he looked around and then he filed on a homestead. He said he spent a week looking for the ones with the biggest trees. The land agent didn't know what each quarter section was like. They were all just little parts on his map. So my father filed on the one that had, he said, the biggest trees anywhere. Good ones, tall, very tall, straight grain, and he knew what he was going to do. So he got 160 acres of timber for ten dollars.

Then he looked around for a portable mill. He didn't have to look far. This was the Depression and the woods were silent. Nobody was cutting. He said, well, life must go on, some people have money and people always need lumber. So he bought this mill, and this was November by now, time was getting on. But he knew what he was doing, because he'd been a foreman in the bush.

The farmers were off the land and just sitting around and he said he could go out on the main street and whistle and he'd have fifteen men in ten minutes. He got them and I know this, he treated them well. The camp, or I mean this homestead, was about eighteen miles away and he said he'd put them up, feed and board them, or they could live at home, and if they were there on the dot at eight in the morning they'd have work. Most of them chose to live at home.

He set up the mill and all that goes with it, stables for the horses, and a truck and what we'd now call a pickup, a car with its rear sawed off and a box there. There was an office and a small kitchen, and just he and half a dozen guys worked out there. That's how it worked. A man could bring his saws and file and work alone, but they needed men with teams too, so they got paid by the horses and the man. And my dad said he put in a bonus system, and it worked. The men worked harder, and they got their bonus, and my dad said they were very happy with it.

All this time, he was doing everything in his head. He had a few children's scribblers, and a pen, and that was the way he did his business. But when the job was cleaned up in April and the men went back to the farms for another try, my dad sat down and worked it out. First, you remember, he was just rough-milling. The lumber, or most of it, had to be sent to a planer mill in Nipawin. So, my father figured, I'm really just working for that planer-mill guy. He looked around and he found a planer mill at Onion Lake, one that the government had set up for the Indians and it hadn't worked out. He got it dirt cheap. But back to the scribblers. He found out that with his expenses and wages being high, he still made a lot of money. Maybe $5,000. I know that is hard to believe, one man making that in the Depression, but I'm sure that's what he told me he made.

There was a lawyer in Nipawin, and my father went to him. Here is this guy in bib overalls and some scribblers in his hand, and he's telling the lawyer what is going on. He said the lawyer, who probably made $1,000 that year and figured he was darned lucky, was amazed. Here was this immigrant and he had this problem. He was making so much money.

The lawyer said Dad would have to become a company. So he did. Then he'd need another officer. So Dad said, okay, Mr. Lawyer, what about you? I can imagine just how fast that lawyer snapped him up on that. Very fast. The lawyer probably thought, here is this dumb Bohunk, and in the end I'll wind up owning this company. It didn't work out that way, but you know how lawyers are.

Dad's men had cleared off that quarter and okay, you could say he was cheating by moving next winter on to another quarter that had just as many wonderful trees. He didn't see it that way. First, he'd given the people for miles around the cheap lumber they needed. Secondly, he'd cleared off a whole quarter, which would have cost another settler hundreds of dollars to do, so he was handing some poor guy what could be a very good farm. Third, as Dad used to say, it was up to the government to change the law if they thought he was doing wrong. You see, in that way he was thinking like a lawyer.

But anyway, that's what he did, and every year he got bigger, until he had four outfits working at one time, and everybody wanted to work for Wasyl. He was fair and he was honest. He'd never cheat you. If you cheated him, though, look out. An eye for an eye. No doubt about that. He had the look of an eagle, seeing everything. One mistake and you were out, and no matter how good friends you might have been and how good the contract, once and you're out. Money wasn't his God but loyalty, that was important.

He had faithful and hard-working crews every winter. He kept his machinery in good condition and he bought the best hay for the teams, and oats too. He fed his men well and if they were sick, they got paid anyway. He was a good man. He looked after things for everybody, and there was no trouble about anything.

And he was only about thirty-four or thirty-five when he was a big man, because he'd stuck to the woods, and by now he was selling the lumber all over the Prairies. A town would figure they could afford a skating-rink, even though times were tough, and somebody would see this little ad in the *Free Press Prairie Farmer* and they'd write. Wow, they couldn't believe his price. So, another carload sold. He did that all the time. He paid his men cheaply, but they worked like the dickens. They knew he was honest and they'd get the bonus. Then they were sitting on top of the world. They'd have had no money, maybe, if they'd spent their pay month by month, but in April, there they were with this big wad of dough, and it was the Depression and nobody had any. But they had, and they could go back to the farm and start again with some money. My dad figured all this out, you know. He was quite a guy."

❧ Addicted to Railroading

"If you came from a big family, like maybe twelve kids, ten, not unusual in those days, you would know that a couple of the boys, at least, would go for the railroad. The CPR was the one us three brothers worked for. Then there was the CNR. I don't know why, but it was always considered the poor relation, the worst of the two roads.

You really had to go to the city if you wanted a job on the railroad. I'm not even sure they hired for the section gangs in the little towns, but I don't know much about that because most of the gangs were made up of what we called Gillies. These were immigrants who came from the province of Galicia, but whether Ukrainian or Polish or Russian, you got the name Gillie. No harm meant by it, really. Just like somebody born in Scotland, he was called a Scottie. Or a Limey, although I don't think Englishmen worked on the section. It was too tough. They were usually fellows who didn't know how to work or were lazy, or thought working with their arms and backs was just too good for them. A lot of resentment against Englishmen in those days. People tended not to like these guys.

But my brother, the oldest, Ronnie, he went into Moose Jaw and they said nothing doing here, but try down the line, meaning Winnipeg, and they let him ride the caboose of a freight going east. They did things like that in those days. This was in the early twenties, when he went. Sixteen, I think he was. Oh sure, he got on. No trouble in Winnipeg. That was where everything was on the Prairies in those days. All the trains passed right through, and the CNR, too, and up from the States. The place was full of railroaders, what with the two big stations, the big railyards, huge, and the shops and the immigrant sheds for the new people coming in.

Well, there was my brother Ronald, his first job, proud as punch, and he came home to get his stuff and Dad said, what was he doing? He was going to be a call-boy, the lowest on the scale. They gave you a bike and you pedalled all over Winnipeg, night or day, and you told the crews when they were to report. You see, not many people had phones in those days. Businessmen, firms, government, people with money, yes, but an ordinary person did not have a phone. Who would you phone? None of your friends had them either. It was thought of as kind of a luxury.

I started out as a call-boy, too, but about seven years later and this was '28 and I got seven bucks a week. That was good, but only because I chose the overnight shift, twelve hours. Six at night to six in the morning and you'd be pedalling the old bike in twenty below going out to East Kildonan to tell some fireman he had to report for a five-o'clock call. Train going west. Mixed freight. They did it the hard way in those days, nothing easy like making up the crews two days ahead of time.

Billy was in between, and he went to Moose Jaw and got on as a wiper in the shops. That was dirty work, being in among grease half the time, grease up to your eyeballs, but you were better than a call-boy because you were closer to the locomotives, those big steamers, with the noise and the heat and the yelling. I always thought there was a kind of excitement working in the shops, getting those big brutes ready for the road, fussing around them, slicking them up good, then seeing them move out slowly to the table and being swung around. Then huff, whump, huff, whump, as they moved out into the yards.

So, we were a railroading family, the Jennings. Out of eight boys, three working on the road, and Jack, he died of rheumatic fever when he was a kid, and the other boys drifted off, working for other farmers, but three out of seven was pretty good. A farming and railroading family. The split was about right. For a farm kid with some ambition it was best to go railroading. Like Buck Crump, president of the CPR and living in Calgary now, he started off in the shops like we did, right there in Revelstoke in the mountains. Made it right to the top. A lot of others did too, but not as high as him. He hit the jackpot. He was the one who converted from coal to diesel, turned the whole thing around.

Then, about '31 the Depression hit us. Trains still kept running, but some guys were laid off, and then faster and more of them, but somehow me and my brother Ronnie hung on. We took pay cuts, like ten per cent one year and ten per cent another, but by then I was braking. This would be about '36 then, and there was the unions, and they did what they could for you but times were tough. Boy, were they ever tough. So there wasn't much talking back to the company. You were all in the same boat, them and us in the union. I remember I was making about forty cents an hour and you couldn't kick about that. It was good money for them days, but with a wife and little boy, it was tough.

Then, of course, there wasn't much hope of making it up front in the cab. Engineer, fireman. Them jobs worked on a certain amount of pull. If you knew somebody higher up, say a superintendent, then you'd make it up the ladder. If your father was an engineer, then you stood a good chance of being an engineer one day. If your old man was a conductor, then he'd be around head office, Western, a lot and he'd know the higher-ups, and that would give you a start. Who you knew, who your old man was.

One thing, though. You were like a big family, the CPR family. All their lives, men on the Prairies, they worked for the one company. You see, it was such a hell of a big company. The train traveller, he just sees the conductor and the train men, the black guys in the sleeper cars and the diner, the waiters. But it was like an army, with fifty people working behind each person on a passenger train, making it all work. Like cooks and flunkeys and the immigrants on the track gangs, and the bridge and building gangs, and the station agents, hundreds of them. The telegraphers and the clerks and then the roundhouses where the engines were repaired and the shops, like the big ones in Montreal and Transcona and Vancouver and in Moose Jaw, the towns that depended on the railroads. Then there was the hotels, like Banff and Lake Louise and the Royal Alexandra in Winnipeg. In every city they were the biggest, so they were like the centre of the city. The Palliser in Calgary. Everything happened there for Calgary. On and on. The CPR was the big thing in the West.

You felt you were part of something so very important. Trains in the night. Trains in the day. Always going. Always full, taking wheat to Vancouver and Montreal, bringing stuff back either way. All steam locomotives then, huge ones for the mountain grades, yard engines, and everything in between. All made in Canada. The Dorval shops. And you thought, or I did, maybe the CPR is the greatest thing that Canada has ever produced.

There was a lot of complaining, too, like the company never had a decent pension scheme, and when it was time for quitting, a lot of pensioners were in a pitiful financial state. That was too bad. But there was this terrific loyalty to the company–and even if they were living on beans and bread and not much else and no money because of the poor pension, they would still be loyal to the company. The company was their life all their life, and when they retired, you'd see them sitting around hotel lobbies or in cafés or the curling club, anywhere, and they'd be talking about the company and how wonderful it had been to work for it.

I didn't suffer, because in '42 I joined up. Didn't have to, as most railway jobs were frozen, vital to the war economy. When I got out, I took myself off to university and that was the end of any thoughts of railroading for me. Teaching, that was the safest job of all. Stick in there and wait for your pension. No problems. Just do your job and stay forever. But no fun out of it either. No family. No loyalty.

Both my brothers, Ronnie and Billy, they're dead now, but they were CP men till their dying breaths. You never could say a bad word about the company to them. Pay not too good, lousy bosses, and things changed so badly for the workers after the war, just terrible, but they stayed on and loved it. It was love for that company. No, it was more like a terrible loyalty. Like they were addicted to railroading and couldn't leave it, and they never did. In fact, all they could talk about was railroading. Nothing else, just their days on the road. Ronnie an engineer, Billy a conductor. Railroading was their whole life."

🕊 *In Praise of Education*

"I had the mail route between Lethbridge and Medicine Hat, the pickup and delivery end of it to the post offices, and then when I moved up to Saskatoon I hooked on to a route like the one before, and I knew that I was never going to get anywhere driving a mail truck but there was Darleen and the baby, so I had to stick to it.

There was night school at the university, though, so that's the route I took. Three times a week, the extension courses, where you could enrol in dozens of courses either at the city schools or the university. I went the business route, and nobody said, oh, don't take this business course or this computer course because it will be no benefit to you because you're just a mailman. Canada Post. You know what the public thinks of us. Boy, I do. Well, I wasn't taking those courses just for the fun and games of it. Not on your life. In about four years I had as good a background in some of these business courses as any kid graduating from the U. of Lethbridge or the U. of Saskatchewan. I know that. I work with some of them now and nothing they can do here impresses me one little bit.

One thing about education I've found, it's a lot of fun to learn. You're among younger people and there also are a lot of older people, so it's a nice mix and learning is fun. You help each other, and from what I learned in my four years of extension classes, it was enough to get me a good job. I had to work for it, to show the company what I could do, but I could do it. I got this accounting job because of those courses. Without them I'd still be driving Her Majesty's Mail."

🕊 *On the Tractor*

"Can you imagine a twelve-year-old girl today driving a tractor? All day? That was me back in the Depression. I had a job and my father didn't.

He was a farmer and we lived north of Barrhead and this one

summer he told me I'd have to start to learn how to drive the tractor, and I spent a couple of hours doing it, just driving it around the yard and up the lane and down the road a bit, and then he said I'd learned enough. I'd go and work on the summer fallow because the Russian thistle were coming up. He had road work to do for the municipality to pay off his taxes. This was 1933 and farmers had no money to pay the taxes, so they worked.

So I did the summer fallow. The word got around and people would say, 'Oh, there's Hermina Levy out there on her dad's John Deere. I saw her there. Working the summer fallow,' and one day my father heard this and he said, 'Yes, and she's better than any of you guys. A woman is better at sewing a seam in a dress than a man. Well, you look at what she does and she's better at driving my tractor than any of you guys. She does that field like her mother was sewing a dress.'

In those days a woman always got a lot less money than a man even if they were doing the same job. So these guys thought a girl would be paid less than a man, and a man got maybe three dollars a day, eh? So one day a neighbour asked what he would charge for me to work on his tractor and my father said two dollars. That's how I started.

I went to work for old man Hesterman that year, and because he had two tractors I did part of his fall ploughing, too, and the word, you know, it got around. He was five miles from us and I'd get on our horse and ride there and I was always on time, and being a Dutchman, he liked that, and I didn't stop for a smoke or do any loafing. In town that winter I guess he talked about it, and other farmers got the idea.

The next year was 1934 and things were worse, so I worked for one-fifty a day. Long days, too, those farmers knew how to get the most out of a person. But it was money. I was thirteen then, and I guess I weighed about eighty-five pounds, but I could do the job. Farmers had different tractors and I could even give that big flywheel the right pull and kick and get it going. No electrical starts then, you see. It was priming it right and then giving it a little kick and then up, and bang, bang, bang, and away it went. One farmer said he could sell tickets just to watch me starting a big tractor.

Some days it was only ten cents an hour. It was one-fifty a day and maybe that was fifteen hours. You'd work hardly until you couldn't see. I was so tired, I'd get on my horse and sometimes I'd be asleep on it, and how I didn't fall off I don't know. But it would take me home and my mother would hear the horse coming, I guess, and take me off and give me some soup and her bread and put me to bed. I'd sleep maybe five hours, and then I'd be away again.

Every penny, it all went to my father. We needed the money. When you've only got a small farm and nobody is paying anything for anything . . ."

✎ *The Way to Make Money*

"I was in the artillery for five years, four of them overseas, one where the fighting was, France, Holland, Germany, and then I got home and I had nothing. I mean not that much money, and a wife and two kids I hadn't seen all that time, and no job. The artillery, it don't teach you no trade, and I'd been sort of a handyman and farm worker when I joined up in early '41.

I couldn't go to university after the war because I didn't have the education, but they had the Veterans' benefits thing and it would send you to courses and pay you. First I took a carpentering course, about four months. Then I took a welding course, and that meant going to Winnipeg, but that worked out. I took that about four months and then I flamdoodled them into giving me a mechanics course. Five months, I think, and then an advanced automotive course. They sure pushed us hard through these courses. Those were ten-hour days and I learned and worked hard every one of them hours. Don't get me wrong. I wasn't cheating anybody. It was like the government paying us back for all that time in England and in the fighting.

This was the start of '47 about this time and I thought, well, better start making a living. So I took the bus to Edmonton where we'd lived before the time I enlisted and I got my truck. I'd bought the truck in 1940 just before I suddenly decided to enlist, and put it up on blocks in my mother's garage. Now, you have to know what it was like then. There were no new trucks, the war and all that, and none being turned out yet, and I had this brand-new truck. A '40 Chev half-ton. She was a beauty. I got her licensed up and drove home and every time I'd stop for gas or a meal, people would ask me if I wanted to sell that thing. I'd say no, but they'd say how much do you want? I'd say how much will you give? Why, they were willing to pay double, and I said no, no thanks.

And then one guy in Davidson, he says he'd pay me double, about $1,300, and he'd throw in a '36 Ford pickup for free, and I thought, well, maybe I'll think about this. In our advanced mechanics course the truck we'd worked on was that kind of Ford. We drove out to his farm and I looked it over. It wouldn't run, but I had a pretty good idea why it wouldn't. This guy was a big farmer but he didn't know much about machinery. I said no to $1,300 and I said I'd be able to sell my new truck for $1,750 in Regina. Now, this farmer, he'd made a big pile of money in the war with wheat and cattle and he didn't even blink. He said $1,800, and I said, throw in that truck? He said yes, and I said, okay, lend me your kid to steer the old truck, and I got a tow-line on the old truck and away we went to Regina and we pushed the old truck into the garage at our house and I got the Chev and the kid back late that afternoon and got my $1,800 in bills. I caught the night bus back to Regina and there I was, looking pretty good. I figure $1,800 is about $10,000 in today's money, and I had a truck I could work on.

Gosh, it didn't take much. The worst thing wrong was it needed a fuel pump and some new brake linings and springs and a rad, and I scrounged those up around town in one morning. I think I might have paid $125 for the lot, and the best thing was, the rubber was still pretty good. I scrubbed out some of the rust on the body and painted her up and put an advertisement in the *Leader-Post* saying I had a good '36 farm truck for sale and I'd guarantee it for a year.

That's where I found I had some business sense. That guarantee bit. It wasn't worth the paper the thing was written on, of course, because I wasn't a company, but I got six phone calls the first day. I thought, oh boy, I'll ask $800. You know what? Three guys came the next night just about the same time and they're running it around the block, and they can't see anything wrong with it and one guy, like we're all standing out on the street, and one guy says he'll give me $900. Right now, and he's reaching for his wallet. That guy was a war worker, I'll bet, making big money and saving it while I'm off in Holland getting pneumonia that last winter and nearly dying. I say I gotta have a trade-in. That's when another guy, he says he'll give me $800 and his car, and it's at the curb, a nice little '34 Dodge sedan. I knew that car had to be worth $300 at least, and maybe more. I ran it around the block twice, good brakes, good rubber, everything seemed to be okay, and I said fine, you have a deal.

So that was another $800 and I took that Dodge and put about a week's work on it, tuning it, replacing the fan belt, a twenty-cent deal for that, and cleaning and scrubbing it up and putting on some paint. And in one hour I sold it for $500. One ad, maybe fifty cents or something, just one ad. This was the way to make money.

And then my wife heard that a Mrs. Cranston down the street was selling her house and going to Winnipeg to live with her daughter because her husband had died a few weeks before. She said this lady was going to sell her furniture and I thought, why not? Cars, trucks, furniture, what does it matter? I went down there with my wife and she introduced me and she said two second-hand dealers had been in that day and I said how much did they offer? She said $300 for one and $275 for the other, and I said to her, I will give you $400 right now, and I hadn't even seen the stuff except what was in the parlour. Boy, did that please her. She said yes, and I wrote her a cheque right then and there, Bank of Montreal, and when she took me through the house I thought, boy, oh boy, this is something. This wasn't the days when everybody was going after antiques, because it was all new and shiny stuff they wanted, but I knew there were enough people in Regina who still cared about good old furniture.

I told her, Mrs. Cranston, I will hold a sale next Saturday, and she said she'd be in Winnipeg by that time. Everything left would be mine. I thought, boy, and I asked her how much she had got for the house. She said nothing yet, but she'd been thinking of $2,000. I mean, this was a good house. Big and roomy and family-like, and I hadn't even been in the basement yet or the attic.

I get excited when I tell this story. I said I'll give you $1,900 cash right now and you'll be still a lot of money ahead because you won't have to pay the real estate commission, which would be $200, and then your lawyer and everything. You use your lawyer, I said. I'll pay the lawyer.

My wife is standing there flapping her arms and jaws and I said, don't you like this house? I mistook her, what she was doing. She was practically jumping around for joy.

Next morning we're down at her lawyer's office and the papers are signed and the cheque is okayed at the bank, and I own the house, and she is out by Thursday. I drive her to the station and I ship about twenty boxes of her stuff on the CP and she's gone.

I don't know nothing about this kind of furniture but Gert has an idea and the first thing she does is put a tag with $100 on the big sideboard in the dining-room. Twenty here, $15 there, $6 there, you know, and $40 on good stuff, and I say she's crazy. She said she wasn't, and she got on the phone to her mother in Moose Jaw and she came over next day, and yes, she said, this is wonderful furniture and she said, put ads in the paper, and this was okay. Then she said something I'd never heard of before. She said put ads on the radio station, lots of them, and she sat right down and wrote up an ad for the radio. I thought, this will never do, all this money, but a radio ad was something like two bucks, and we put twenty-five on the air on Friday and Saturday. Every time you turned on the two stations it seemed I was hearing one. And two ads in the *Leader-Post*. Big ones, on Friday, they cost twenty dollars each. I thought I'd go broke this way.

Well, I didn't. No sirree. I just wasn't prepared, me with my Grade 10 and farm work before I joined up. But my wife and her mother, why, they took to it like a duck to water. All the stuff we found in the attic, in the basement, we had it out on the lawn, all scrubbed up by nine in the morning, and the people came. It was like a holiday. If you knew what Regina was like in those days, no more Regina Pat games, no curling, no going to the cottages yet, this was early in May, why it was like the circus was in town. And one of the first to come was the lawyer who'd done the papers on the house.

We sold everything for cash or cheque that day. Everything, and there was my wife running around, and me sort of standing there with a dumb look on my face, and her mother at a little table writing receipts and taking in the money hand over fist. Know how much it all sold for? I know to the penny. One thousand, seven hundred and forty-four dollars and fifty cents. Remember it still. Take away the four hundred dollars I paid for it all and that left about thirteen hundred bucks. Maybe six days' work.

And the two second-hand guys, they came up to me after and just shook their heads. One wanted me to go in with him, and I said no, I don't know anything about this business. The one little guy just shook his head and walked away, and the other, he said he was over on Albert Street and he asked me to come and see him if I changed my mind.

We moved in and I spent a lot of time in bits and drabs doing work, fixing up things that were wrong, and so the carpenter thing came in good for me there. A year later she was a pretty fine-looking house, and we sold it for $5,000, $2,000 down and an agreement for sale.

That's the way I got started. In trucks and cars and furniture and then houses, and I always worked out of the new house we had built over on the northwest side. Brand new. And I'll bet I made more than the biggest banker in town those years, and I only worked when I wanted. Trucks, cars, houses, farm machinery, and then farms, and all out of the room I had in the basement. I always said you can win if you try and work hard."

And That's the Way You Do It

"From the time I was a little girl, maybe nine, I always felt I wanted to be a writer. I'd write poems, about the animals on the farm, things I'd do at school, going hunting for birds' eggs in the spring, harvest time, things like that. They were child's poems, not very good even for a child, I suppose, but I'd send them off to *The Western Producer* under the pen name of Red Winged Blackbird and three of them were printed.

When I graduated in 1968 my counsellor was very disappointed when I told her I was not going to college. She asked me what I was going to do and I guess I said I would go to Calgary and take a business course and get a job. She said I just couldn't go and work in an office. But I did. I saved enough for the tuition in the commercial college in Calgary and I stayed with a cousin who had an apartment and I did fine. I took the shorter course, the one without shorthand, and I graduated from that in five months and they sent me to Shell. That was fine. I was hired right away and it was a fine building with a cafeteria and all the people were very nice, but I found out that for what I was doing I didn't need to take a commercial course. An older filing clerk can show a new kid like me how to file everything in an hour and a half.

I was happy there and I got a room, a large one with a tiny, tiny kitchen, and I shared the bathroom with two other people and I was happy. I didn't know anybody, just the girls at work. I guess my mind is curious enough to be a writer because I'd spend Saturdays and Sundays exploring. Taking buses all over the city, getting off and having a cup of coffee and going back on the next one. Or I'd take long walks. Or at nights, if I saw where there was a free lecture or film, I'd go to see that. I wasn't trying to save money, really, but I was trying to find out what a city like Calgary was like. I thought this was important.

I also enrolled at a night-school course in creative writing at Mount Royal. I thought it would help me. What a collection! I mean, there were perhaps fifteen of us and they were nuts there. I mean nuts. Maybe three or four. And housewives, a couple of schoolteachers, and a doctor who wanted to write when he was probably making ten times what the instructor made.

And the instructor! I mean, here he was instructing in creative writing and he'd never written a thing. Oh, I mean he had written a lot but he didn't seem to have had anything published. No books, no poems, not an article of any kind. But he'd spend the last half-hour of each class reading something he had written, going on and on and waving his arms, taking all the speaking parts, and then he'd slam the thing down on his desk and say, 'And that's the way you do it.' I thought to myself, fine, if I ever do any writing, that is not the way I would do it. Even I could see just how bad it was.

One night he asked me to stay late as he wanted to talk to me. Of course, he didn't want to talk to me. He had had his eye on me. Oh, I could tell. He drove me home in this old car of his and we stopped for coffee and here it was all spouting out. How he was a great writer and he was in this hick town and nobody appreciated him and he was meant to be more than a schoolteacher teaching writing at a hick college in this hick town, and on and on. I kept thinking, he's lucky to have a job.

He had a wife and I suppose he had children, but he started taking me out. I was only eighteen and I didn't care. It was a chance to get out, and besides, I really think I would have had to be the aggressor if anything happened. I think that's what he wanted me to be.

Looking back, I think he thought he was being Bohemian. Whatever that means now. We went to the opening of art shows that year, to cocktail parties where some oil company was unveiling some murals for their lobby. Little parties where everyone sat around and drank red wine, and they talked about their work. I mean, in capitals, Their Work. What they were working on, the novel or the play, and then they would be famous. I've never heard of one of them in the past twenty years. Even at that age I knew what kind of company I was in.

No, these were just people who worked at Mount Royal and the University of Calgary or worked for the big companies and were just stopping off in Calgary for a while until the world discovered them. They talked and talked and talked, about Their Work, and mostly about themselves. Talk, talk, talk, all about their little own selves, and these women reading poetry. But awful poetry, awful stuff. When she'd finish, there was one professor who always smoked a pipe, and he was the one they all looked to for judgement. He'd take a couple of puffs and sort of cock his head and say, 'Excellent, my dear. I do believe you are truly finding yourself.'

Oh, another thing. About this time the Calgary writer James Gray had written a book called *The Winter Years*. Everybody was buying it, and a girl at the office loaned it to me. Wonderful. I hadn't known the Depression, you see, but I'd heard my parents talk about it a lot. So it was pretty close to home to me. One evening at one of these parties this professor with the pipe asked me in front of everybody, 'And what are you reading, my dear?' Everybody was 'my dear' to him. I said I was reading James Gray's book, and there was this silence. I had committed a sin. A common, ordinary writer like Mr. Gray. Writing about common, ordinary things. Horrors! Shame! This prof puffed that pipe of his and said, and I remember, 'Rather commercial, don't you think, my dear?'

My time for running with the smart literary set of Calgary ended just about then, because I said, if you mean commercial means making money out of his book, yes, I'd say it was commercial. I'll bet he's not always over in a corner writing out applications for Canada Council grants. And I said Mr. Gray was writing history, real history, Western Canadian history, about what happened not too long ago.

It couldn't have been the wine, as I usually only had one or two glasses of their dreadful plonk. No, it was frustration at all the phoniness of these poets and poetesses and writers and playwrights who had never seen a line published for which they had been paid anything. Just standing around at their cocktail parties trying to act like Lister Sinclair, suave and intellectual. And all that rot.

I'll make it short. That was the last soirée I was asked to. It seemed the way that society worked, my friend would have suffered because he was escorting this philistine around. Little old nineteen-year-old me. It must have hurt him because I was good for his ego, but his literary friends mattered more. That suited me fine. I met a lot of funny people and was a guest in a lot of truly smashing homes and ate a lot of very good food and I learned one thing. If you're going to be a writer, then stay away from people who play at being writers. Write yourself."

🕊 *Then the Union*

"When I came out to Calgary from Yugoslavia, 1962, Dalmatian Coast, I was twenty-eight. A big guy, that was me. You see. Look at this arm. I just spoke a little bit of English, not too much. As long as you can count the numbers, that's all you need to know.

I got a job in construction. In three weeks the foreman said to me, I am going to make you a sub-foreman. I said okay, that is fine. He saw that I knew how to build houses, the old-country way. The immigrants, they know how to make money, how to do business. That was me.

In six months I had my own business. That was when Calgary was booming. All that oil, everybody had money. In a year I had ten guys working for me. The foreman who had made me his sub-foreman, that guy, he was working for me now. When I wasn't out in my truck looking at more lots to build houses on, or inspecting another house, or maybe talking to a man and his wife who wanted a house built, then I was working with my guys, and the foreman I hired from the other job, he was my foreman. That's the way I worked.

Then it was 1965 and I had about thirty men. All working for me. I said, I will get bigger and bigger. Drive a big Cadillac, you know, have lots of money, be a big shot. Then the union comes in, they want to sign up my crew. No way, I say. I pay my guys good. I chose them, they're my kind of fellow. Work hard, and that's me working right along beside them. Saturdays. Sundays if we have to. Everybody makes good money.

The union, Carpenters, Building Trades, they get a guy working with me. Sure I hire him. He looks okay. But he's a spy, and in a few days he's talking to my guys and saying how good the union would be. I wait. Then another of my guys comes to me, this time an Italian, and he asks me do I know what this guy is doing? I say yes, but I don't do anything. I'm paying all these guys good money and I look after them and it's me paying the government. I mean, I'm a real businessman. Everything is on top of the table. Then it gets too much. The government comes in and says I got to have a union election. I say, how many men can I have and not have this election? He's this real snotty guy and he says it doesn't matter, there's gotta be an election. I say okay, and I go to my guys and this is what I tell them. I'm not having no union here, and those who want to vote for a union, just put your names down on this paper and I'll send you your pay. This was my way of doing it.

After that, I'm real surprised. Out of about twenty-five guys I only got seven left. But these other guys? They quit, and I think, something is gone crazy in this country. Why do they quit? Making good money. They get everything a union guy is going to get. Why quit? They like me. I like them. We get along. Sometimes on Friday when we quit and go to the beer parlour, sometimes I'll buy fifty dollars' worth of beer.

So, after four years building houses, I say to hell with it. That's the way it is, then that's the way she's gonna be. I had my seven or eight guys left, all hard workers like me, and I'm back to being what I was four years ago, but it is okay with me. I am a little little little guy again and I can build houses good. I got all these little headaches now, but no big ones. No union headache to come. I'm too small. He's just a little bit of spit, the union boss tells a friend of mine, we don't want him. When he gets bigger, we'll nail him. He don't play it our way, this union guy says, we will kill him off. That's nice, isn't it? A union guy, Building Trades Council guy, talking that way. He's not talking about me. This guy is talking about jobs for human beings. Canadians. You ever heard such a thing? No. No.

Just building good houses for nice people, that's good for me. I make money, they get a good house. Everything is fair. We're all happy. No government coming around snooping. Too small. No union. Too little, too small. Just a little bit of spit like this guy says."

❧ *Sugar-Beet Slaves*

"We didn't like the way the Canadian government did things. What they did to us caused us very much hard work and sorrow, and we lost a lot of time.

In 1964 we went to the Canadian immigration in Germany and applied and our papers were all right. But then we got a letter to go see them and then they told us no, we did not have the proper qualifications. I don't know what they were expecting but my husband was a master mechanic in German terms and I was a good woman, a hausfrau, and we had four fine children and quite a bit of money saved. No, they said. Sorry, but we are not taking anybody any more. We thought, why did they call us in then. Why?

We went back home and said, well, that is that. They don't want us.

In two weeks we got another letter. It said, if you would sign a two-year contract to work in the sugar-beet fields in Canada, you can go. We talked it over and we thought, well, sugar-beets grow only three months in summer, and we could work in a city near there the rest of the time, so two years would not be a long time.

So we signed, and they sent our family to Lethbridge and then to Taber to a family of Hungarians. They treated us badly. The house they gave us was two garages, and they were just one board thick and there was no water and just one light bulb in the big room and nothing to cook with, just a couple of pots and a frying-pan and some dishes. And we had to work from dawn to dark for this farmer hoeing the beets, and the pay was worse, far worse than we'd got in Germany. All of us were working.

We were slaves to that farmer, because he had the contract, and he said if we didn't work for him and do what he wanted we would be sent back to Germany. This is the truth.

We found out there were others like us, around Raymond and Picture Butte, all these places. People like us from Germany and Poland and Holland. This was a scandal, but nothing was ever done about it.

I don't know how we got through that winter, but we did. God, it was cold. The children were crying from the cold. There was no sympathy from the farmer, and his wife was worse, and she was a Canadian. I don't know how we lasted. Anything would have been better, but there was that piece of paper we had signed. It didn't say it would send us to a life of pure misery.

Then in the spring we heard that a family at Raymond had just left and gone to Calgary. They were making good money and had an apartment. And the immigration people knew where they were, but they had done nothing to them. Then my husband said, okay, we go. And that Saturday when we got paid the little bit we had coming for the month we waited until the farmer and his wife had driven into Lethbridge, and we got a farmer to drive us to the bus depot. We waited and waited, thinking the police might come. But when the bus came we got aboard with our suitcases, and that was the end of it. Nothing happened. Nobody said anything. They knew what things were like. They knew we were slaves.

It was a very bad way to start life in this country, but we worked very hard. And maybe my husband and I didn't make a lot of money, but we brought up five children, and we educated them, and they went to university and they are all in business right now, or teaching, and they are doing very well. And so it all worked out okay in the end."

You Really Want a Job?

"I came from Camrose, but we built houses all over the country. My dad and me. I've been a carpenter since I was just a little kid. He had me pounding nails when I was ten and he showed me the right way to drive a nail home and I don't think in fifteen years I've ever bent one. We built houses and barns and three and four houses at a time, community halls, business blocks of four stores and three suites above, all the way from Fort Assiniboine down to Red Deer.

Then in 1981 the work quit. Nothing. It just dried up. Only little jobs. This was when Alberta got the hell kicked out of them by Trudeau on the National Energy Program. In three months we saw it happen. We finished the jobs our crew was doing and then, wham! I mean wham! There was no more work.

My dad was fifty-five and he was pretty well fixed, owned the company and had no debts, and there was a little work around, like renovations, and he could keep a couple of men busy, but it was all itty-bitty stuff. He told me it would be best if I went out on my own and came back when things perked up.

Sally and I headed for Calgary. That seemed the best place. This was in November and I figured there would still be a lot of work. No new stuff, but finishing-up work. A lot of those skyscrapers.

I was non-union, so I headed for the non-union contractors, and

I'd go in and ask. Sorry, not today. When? Oh, maybe never. That's the attitude they had. I asked one guy, a clerk in the office, what the rate was. He said they had been paying eleven dollars but now they were going to pay nine dollars. My God, my dad had been paying me thirteen dollars. My God, my dad had been paying me thirteen dollars and benefits.

This was about the fifth place I'd hit that day and I was kind of bushed, so there is a beer parlour hotel there, this being on the Macleod Trail, and I go in. It's about five o'clock and in a few minutes this guy from the office comes in. He sees me and I wave and he comes over, a nice guy, about twenty-five. I shove a beer at him and wave the waiter for four more. That's okay. I think I can get some information out of this guy when he's away from work.

We talk about what's going on and about myself and how I've come down and we talk some more and I'm going to leave to take Sally to dinner and he says, 'You really want a job?' I said, 'You're darn tooting I do.' He said, 'Give me a hundred dollars right now and show up at the office at eight tomorrow morning and I'll have you working on the job by nine.' Just like that. This nice guy, and he's saying, give me a hundred bucks and I'll give you a job. Just like that. Sitting there. Then, boom, bribe me, he says.

It took me about five seconds to decide what to do. I reached in my wallet and gave him five twenties, knowing I might never see it again. I didn't, naturally, but when I got to the office next morning, he was there. He filled in the form, put eight dollars down in the hourly-rate space, and said, 'That's what we're paying now. Not nine dollars. This town is crawling with carpenters from Vancouver. They'll work for anything.'

I drove out to the site and sure enough, the foreman told me I would be working on a framing crew. Old stuff to me. He said the job would last to Christmas, and that was winter work. I didn't mind taking another guy's job. Because that's what I was doing. The foreman had fired a guy just before I showed up, sort of accidentally on purpose. I guess he was a guy who had been making nine bucks an hour. I was cheaper, so that's how I got in.

You think that's a rotten story? Let me tell you this. After that, things got tougher. I still held on to my eight bucks an hour, but there was guys working along with me when we moved inside and they were making seven bucks and happy with it.

We got by. Sally got a job in a real estate office. Same thing. Nobody buying houses, so they fire their accountant. They hire

Sally, who you'd call a book-keeper, for $1,000. With my $1,400 and her money we're doing great, but we were lucky."

🕊 *Praying for a Job*

"Somebody's going to have to write a book about the depression we got these days. Give you an example. This cousin of mine about sixty, he owns this wood-working shop in Calgary and, well, you know, he's got maybe fifteen guys working for him. Door frames, French doors are big now, and tables and chairs and so on, and he's got it cut pretty close to the line and he tells me . . . Well, no, I'll tell you what I see with my own eyes when I wander over there. These kids come in. Sixteen, seventeen, eighteen, dropped out of school. School's just not for them. By Grade 8 or so they have got all they need to know out of school, enough to keep them going for the rest of their lives, and now the jobs they had, they're gone. So there they are, going door to door.

One afternoon I was there and five came in. Separately, naturally. Those kids weren't asking if there was a job. They were pleading. Absolutely doing everything but getting down on their knees and praying for a job. They'd do anything. I mean anything, and for any amount. Any amount, you understand. Three dollars an hour. Below the minimum wage. And my cousin would just have to say, sorry, but I can't. I felt sorry for him, too. He'd like to hire them, but he just couldn't.

You talk about the look in a man's eyes. I always thought that was something writers wrote about, storybook stuff. No, it ain't. It is true. I'm telling you that. I saw old men's eyes in these young kids, eyes that were defeated. Eyes, well, it just made me sick. I couldn't sleep that night. That's the truth."

Sixteen

Trouble on the Family Farm

🐦

Not News . . . Telling the Kids . . . Losing Farmers . . . Just Mum and Me
. . . A Crazy and Mad Business . . . Left Holding the Bag . . . Good
Farmers . . . Shut Down the Farms! . . . I'm Going to Fight . . . Working
Wives . . . Especially the Wife . . . The Wise Old Lawyer . . . Battering
. . . Suicides . . . Off to the Cities

I asked one farm wife, working hard at a job in town to keep some money coming in, "Is there any chance you might lose all this?" Looking at the neat bungalow, the yard, the farm, she said, "No. No way. But there's a chance we could lose our minds."

On the farm it's always the same old problem – money. The farm family is more in tune with city life, far more, than the city family understands the problems of the farmer, his family, and their life. Consolidated school districts, highways leading into cities only an hour or two away, television, even politics, have put the rural community on the city's doorstep. They all cheer for the same hockey teams, eat the same fast food, wear the same clothing styles – well, almost – and all are bombarded by the same print and electronic messages that life is good and can be better if you have money.

Well, most farm families do not have much money these days. Perhaps one-third have no money at all, hard money, a bank balance, because wealth in terms of land and equipment does not count when buying groceries. Most think the situation for the farmers, mainly the straight grain producers, is going to get worse. The family farm is threatened, meaning their very way of life is in jeopardy.

This one looming factor, this threatened loss, produces anxieties which often lead to tragedy. There is every indication more drinking is taking place, and certainly more drug use among the young. Wife-beating, that point where the farmer's control snaps under financial pressure, is much more prevalent. More and more farm women must find outside employment – which sometimes is all that keeps the farm afloat. The old and true values are under siege. Farmers have often advised their sons never to be like them, the life is too hard. But now they are not saying, "You should go." They are saying, "You must go."

And the real tragedy is that the families who are giving up, sadly sending their

*young people off the land, are all too often the same families whose grandparents
went through hell to homestead that same land. The circle has been joined.*

🐌 *Not News*

"Here we have the worst financial crisis to hit this country since
the Depression and what do we read about it in the newspapers?
Very little. Boom all.

There are people in Calgary, and I guess in every city on the
Prairies, that have a daily newspaper and not one-tenth of them
probably realize that if they went half an hour out of town they
could drive into any farm and find those people are hanging on by
a thin edge. They are just not making it any more. The bottom
has been cut out from under them. I've got two brothers and a
flock of nephews and cousins farming, and the things they tell me,
you just wouldn't believe.

One of my neighbours has a son working in a radio station here
in Calgary and one day I asked him why there was nothing on the
radio about what is going on. I guess I asked him something like,
'Jimmie, what about the destruction of western agriculture?'

Oh, sure he knew what was going on, but he said it wasn't news.
Well, I say it is news, and it should be on the front page every day
and twice on Sundays. Because, if you're in a business like Bob and
me are, a family business, TV sales and repair, you'll know that
what is bad for the farmers is bad for every businessman in this
town and every place in Alberta and on the Prairies. It has the
percolator effect, if you know it. When he's flush, the farmer pours
in the water at the top. The water is money, what he buys from
all of us. It percolates down and we all get a bit of moisture. We
count on it."

🐌 *Telling the Kids*

"We got the kids around the table after supper this one night and
told them we were giving up the place. We just said we couldn't
carry the load of debt and interest any more and that we just
weren't taking enough off the farm to pay for it. Harry said we
were going deeper into debt, the last three years anyway, which

they could understand. We didn't use the word 'bankruptcy' because that really wasn't our situation. When we sold the six quarters and our equipment and paid off all the debts, we had quite a bit of money left. About $52,000, but that's not much to show for eighteen years on the farm. But buying those other three quarters when prices were so high back in 1980, that kind of killed us. If land prices had held up we would have been fine, but what we bought for $650 an acre we had to hustle around and get $400 for, so you can see that it was an awful big cut. Anyway, with the money we got, it got us out and up to Saskatoon and we bought a nice house, an old one, lots of work on it to be done, but it was a roof over our heads. I am forty-five and Harry is forty-two. My goodness, we're still young.

But it was the children. Now they're here in Saskatoon and we like it, and they like it. It is a nice city, you know. Right, Harry? You won't find a nicer place on the Prairies but, of course, it's certainly not like the farm. That was the best.

The children miss it. Terribly, I think sometimes. Moving away from all their friends, the clubs they belonged to, the 4-H and their calves. And the whole family curled, and every spring after seeding we'd take a nice long trip. Yank the kids out of school. That didn't bother me. I was a teacher before I married and I figure children learn nothing after Easter anyway. So we'd take these trips, fishing up north or out to visit my sister in Winnipeg or Harry's relations around Lethbridge and Pincher Creek. We can't do that now.

There's the money thing in the city too. We didn't think too much of it on the farm. The last two years Randy was on the family payroll. He was doing a man's job on the machinery and when he's doing that and you can prove it, you pay him instead of hiring someone, and he files an income tax. So he had money. The girls would do some baby-sitting because we were only a mile from town, so they got jobs, and two dollars an hour isn't bad for a thirteen-year-old. They had the money from their calves when they sold them, so they had money.

Now, in the city, that's out the window. Any money they get we have to give them, and it isn't much. This, I think, puts some kind of peer pressure on them at school because they don't dress well. Some of the children in the high school, they wear high fashion. Not at school, mind you. They look like tramps still. But at parties or going out, and my girls just can't do that. Every time you turn around it's another five dollars, ten dollars. So the girls tend to withdraw, or I mean they don't take part. They never were in a position to withdraw, because they were never in. And they don't want to ask us for more money and they don't know how to earn it. What was more than enough on the farm is only half enough in Saskatoon. Harry can tell you that. Right, Harry? We don't want them to feel guilty, but we don't have that much to give them.

Randy has been looking for a job after school and on Saturdays now for six months, but it's the old business. Not what you know but who you know. I thought it would be easy, cutting lawns, doing some painting, that sort of thing, but the people around here, they just don't seem to want to trust a young boy with anything. Here's a boy who could handle an expensive piece of machinery on the farm as good as any man, and they'll pay an adult nine dollars an hour to paint a garage when he'd be happy as a lark to do it for four dollars. Too bad, but I guess there's the other side. That man who gets nine dollars needs the money to feed his family. You've got to look at both sides of everything.

No baby-sitting jobs. I just don't know what city people do with their children when they go out. I suspect they leave an older one to look after the young ones. Now I don't approve of that. So much can go wrong that an eleven-year-old can't hope to cope with, but that's the way it seems to be. And there really isn't much work around the house, so there's nothing for me to tell them to do. So, after school, Saturdays, it's television. The cable came with the house and it's cheap, but Lord, I've never been convinced there is a real value in television. I really don't call what I see healthy entertainment and I really don't want my children watching it, but what can you do?

I know they feel the loss of their life on the farm. They don't talk about it much. I think they are afraid to, in some ways, thinking it will make Harry and me feel bad. No, it wouldn't. I think it would be good to talk about it, but I don't think we're the ones to start it all. Wouldn't you think this might stir up resentment that, well, if they thought about it too much they'd see Harry and me as the bad guys? The ones who gave up the place, that lovely home they had, and all the things they loved about it so much. I think so. But I think I'll have to start talking about it more.

You see, I think they think that we were the only people who did this to their children. Like we betrayed them. That just isn't so. It is happening right across Western Canada. Five or six hundred families a year are quitting the farm, and through circumstances just like ours. Like, if we kept on the way we were going, we would lose everything. I think they should know that the bravest and most courageous act my husband and I have ever done was to decide we could no longer survive. Harry is a good farmer. I was a good farm wife. But it was all these masses of forces beyond our control, and beyond anybody's control. That's what did us in. Will do everybody in, if it doesn't stop now. And it won't. You just have to read the papers to get the story. It's there, but people are not reading it. And that is very sad.

We're going well now, thanks to Harry's brother. He's a foreman in a machine shop and he got Harry this mechanic's job. I don't think we would have dared move into town if it hadn't been the offer of that job, but he got it and he's worked steadily for eleven months now, and his brother says he could work forever. The big boss likes him.

You see, back to our children. They have never had to go through a crisis before. A farm child's life is very smooth. Nothing happens and nothing is expected to happen, and there is one thing I don't know. I still don't know just how devastating it was to each one of them when we told them that night. They showed something, but not as much as I expected. I mean, they didn't cry or go into a deep depression, and now that worries me. Maybe that has yet to come. Maybe one day there'll be an explosion in this house and we'll have more than we can handle with Monica or Dale. Maybe both. One might trigger off the other. It is a thing I dread, but I don't think I know how to handle this.

I mean, I've explained it all to them. 'Yes,' they say, 'we understand.' But deep down, there may be a little bomb ticking away. The truth is, I live in a certain amount of fear that it is there. In the meantime, we've just got to be the best parents in the world, care for them, love them, and do our very best for them. Cross our fingers. Hope for luck. Hope it will all turn out all right down the road. Amen."

❧ Losing Farmers

"One day the farm kid makes up his mind. He's going to the city,

Regina, Saskatoon, to look for a job in a factory or driving truck or get on in a warehouse. That's worse than a farm, by a long shot. Much worse. There is no escape from that box he's putting himself in. The sand just keeps running in faster than he can shovel it out. So, he's like his old man.

But away he goes, and, okay, he gets a job and we lose one more farmer. By that, I mean he won't be back. He's not a farmer yet, not by a long shot, but his old man loses his good right arm, his farmhand. Now he can't farm as much and as well, and that just tips things over a little more, and under this set-up, it can be the old man just goes down, down, down, because he can't afford to hire a hand, and soon he's in more trouble than a pup in the tiger cage.

The government, they see this. It's right there in front of their eyes. They should pay the farmer to keep that boy on the farm. If the old man can't do it, then the boys in Regina and Ottawa should get together and work something out with him. It would help everybody. If the kid can help pull the farm out of trouble, then you listen to me, that is one more farm that is being saved. Two families kept on the land. That's important to Canada. You better believe it.

Okay. Okay. Nothing happens. The kid goes off to town to a job he hates and he's always thinking of the farm, how good it was, but he can't go back. There's no money there. But he still loves it. It kind of breaks his heart to go in at eight o'clock into that factory every darn day. The farm is in that boy's heart. But we've lost him. He's gone forever. That is a darn shame. You kind of destroy that boy, because if he wants to farm and knows he can't, doesn't that eat into his heart? I think it does.

I see them come back at Thanksgiving for some duck-shooting, or at Christmas, and they're at the curling club or the beer parlour with their dad, and I can see it in their eyes.

We are losing farmers and we can't afford to do that. The other thing, and this is worse, I really do think you are destroying people."

👐 *Just Mum and Me*

"Farmers like me, it's us who are being forced off the land, and this is land that my father homesteaded back in 1912 and I'm not feeling too good about it, no sir, and I'm sixty-seven and these guys are saying that's too old to be a farmer but I don't feel that old, not all that old.

It's not that I can't farm, but it's just that I can't handle it all myself. I could say, oh, I'll just sell these two sections and we'd go into town and live, but I'm not sure Mum and I could stand that, a little bungalow or one of those town houses and me still getting up at five in the morning, and you see, that makes a long day with nothing to do.

I say to her, if we had a good man around here, then it would be better and I wouldn't have to go out when my arthritis was too bad. And she can't help much except around the house, and not even in the garden which we don't have now. Just her flowers, and all the garden stuff comes from town now. And isn't that something awful when you think of how it was not even twenty years ago, like when the kids was growing up. Now it's just Mum and me."

❦ *A Crazy and Mad Business*

"From where I sit, I can perhaps see twenty miles to the horizon on a clear day, just wheat and grain flowing away in front of me. All good farms. All run by men who could be classified as the best farmers in the world – and one hell of a lot of them are deep in trouble now.

First, I should say that most of the farmers who are in trouble are the ambitious ones. Usually the younger ones, under forty. They usually have much better educations, and so do their wives and kids. They have been to university, quite a few of them. They know something about economics and the world and they've travelled and they are not afraid of the friendly banker in their town. They go to Arizona or Brownsville or California or Hawaii for a few weeks in January.

Another thing. They're grain farmers, all the way. You won't find many farms out there that has a cow. A cow means getting up at six on a rainy morning, or when a blizzard is raging. No cows. No chickens. No livestock. No gophers, either. I wonder what happened to those millions of gophers we've read about? A pony, maybe, for the kids, or a light horse. That's it. No mixed farming, which always was the farmer's lifeline in hard times, selling cream or eggs in town and eating off the big family vegetable garden. No more.

Okay, and things were humming right along in the mid-seventies. Crops were good. Prices were high. The wheat board was selling about everything a farmer could grow, and he was growing a lot. I'd say that except for the odd drought year or one near it, there had been an unbroken string of good years since about 1940. That is an awful long time. And every economist and deep thinker was telling the farmers that it would never end. The Third World was growing and they would take everything they could produce.

With this kind of thinking, that there would be a never-ending succession of good crops to be sold at good prices, the farmers started thinking they should expand. They can only expand one way, and that is by buying somebody out. There aren't too many small farmers around here, but when a few of the bigger farmers went after them, they thought, aha! Everybody wants my land, so I'll ask more for it. And they did. And they got it. You can call this land inflation or anything you like, but it was the old law of supply and demand. They just weren't making land any more. To expand, you had to bid. An auction, and the price just keeps going up, say ten per cent, twelve per cent, every year.

Suddenly people were sitting up and looking around and saying that land they could have bought for $180 an acre was now $380, and next year it would be $450, and so on. I can tell you that when it finally hit the top, you couldn't buy land around here for less than $700.

Do you know what that meant? Simple. Let's take a guy and his wife who've got 640 acres, a section, say thirty miles northwest of here. They're making a living, but not much more. Suddenly Ma and Pa wake up and open their eyes, and they're looking at an offer of $600 an acre, and that is awfully close to $400,000. Why, they never cleared more than $20,000 on that farm in all their lives and they never will, and here is some real estate slicker with an offer for $400,000, and at ten-per-cent interest they can pick up $40,000 a year for just doing nothing.

I know cases where they were even allowed to keep the house and sheds because all the farmer wanted was the other 638 acres. So they had the old farmhouse to live in, and a lot of money to have fun with, like going into town twice a week to curl and have a cup of coffee and a doughnut after the game.

That's the happy part of the whole business.

Now, here's a younger farmer and he's already got a section and a half and he wants more. Boy, does he ever want more! He looks at his earnings for the year, or his accountant in town here figures out one of those total-assets statements and shows Billy-boy that his assets have risen about $130,000 in one year. Sure they have, but about $100,000 of that is in the inflated value of his land. More land, more assets, more land, more assets. Those assets are collateral, and he can go to the bank and borrow a huge chunk of a floating interest rate and, next thing you know, he's bought the old boy's farm I've just told you about. Now he's big and getting bigger.

You see what's happening here? It's all inflationary. I don't care whether land is worth one hundred bucks an acre or seven hundred bucks an acre. It's only going to produce so many bushels of Number One wheat an acre. So that's what they all forgot, or just didn't want to be reminded about.

They could live with it when interest rates were low, but when inflation comes along, in farmland, then there is that old devil, the interest rates, just sneaking in along there too. Up, up, and up. At float rates, and these guys were borrowing against their land. The land was theirs, and it was their collateral, but it was a losing game for the farmers.

Hand in hand with all this, here are these bankers who've dealt with farmers all their careers, and they are going along with this dumb thinking that the good times will just keep rolling along, and the money will keep rolling in. The banks and trust companies were saying, 'Borrow, borrow, as much as you want, you've got the collateral and we're here to back you up!'

Then a bunch of bankers in Toronto must have been sitting around the club and one said he was wondering about his farm loans of two billion dollars out there. Another banker says he'll look into his. A third says he will, too.

They do some phoning around and they find their farm loans aren't in good shape, and they go a little farther and they suddenly discover that all these inflated values were just not supported by the economics of farming – and they wonder what would happen if interest went high again, or wheat prices dropped, or if there was dry spells, even drought, and on and on. In other words, what about my own ass?

So, they did what bankers have done for centuries. They tightened up credit. They called in existing loans, saying, 'Sorry, my boy, we thought you could make it, but now we've decided you can't, so it's game over. Pay up your $200,000 loan. You've got until next Wednesday.'

The young farmer can't make it, so they take his land and put it on the market. They try to find a buyer but everyone is looking at what happened to our friend. The bank drops the price. That automatically drops the value, the inflated value, of every farm in miles, and down it goes again. Twenty-five bucks an acre. Fifty. A hundred. The thing like a crazed beast is feeding on itself. Any farmer can figure it out one day that his two sections aren't worth $800,000 but are now worth only $400,000 and he's got loans out for $500,000 that he used to buy all that wonderful land that wasn't producing any more wheat last year than it was fifteen years ago.

You see, it was a crazy and mad business. Some farmers have been destroyed, and a lot of them had the old original homestead of 160 acres in them, going back into the eighties. The banks took a real kicking, too, but they've gone through all this time after time, and they can just sit and wait it out.

It is all greed, you know. Some will call it progress, that you get bigger and bigger. Some will call it the economics of sound farming. Call it anything. Call it human nature, if you want a polite name for plain old greed."

✌ Left Holding the Bag

"About three miles down our road there's a farm couple, wonderful people, and he came into this district in the late twenties and went through all the bad times and the good times like everybody else. For years he's been farming four quarters, one section. Mixed farming. Grain, cattle, and the usual. A good farmer, and he did pretty darn well.

He's got this one kid, Bobbie, kind of a late baby. He's about twenty-eight or so and they're getting up towards seventy. The boy comes out of agricultural school and works for the government for two years, so he knows everything there is to know about farming, and he decides to go out on his own, and he gets a line on a section right across the road from his folks' place – and this is about 1980, high prices and high interest – and he's just got to have that place. With his smooth talk and some help from the banker, he talks the old man into backing his note for that section. The old couple put everything in behind the kid and they plan to retire to town in a couple of years and the boy will farm the old man's section, too. So the old man signs the note, at $750 an acre. You're looking at about half a million and the old man's place is clear title, free and clear, so it seems like a good enough deal.

Comes closing time, the kid looks at the old man's equipment and says that stuff is too old for him to share, so he buys in deep, and I'd guess he's in for another $250,000 or $300,000. This takes another note signed by the old man. It was one of those wacky deals a lot of young guys seemed to be making because the price of wheat would stay high.

Then our Trudeau Recession hit us with a wallop. The rest doesn't take much figuring. The kid's got these sky-high payments on land and interest and machinery and he's got this floating rate, but even that doesn't help because the price of what he grows has gone down like a dropped hammer.

Now there's big trouble and all sorts of talk between the kid and the bank. He can't make the payments and he thinks he'll lose the land, but the section is worth only about $225,000 now. The machinery is second-hand now, and he'll get a third of what he paid. They'll take the kid's land, sure as shooting they will, but now there's a big difference between what everything was bought for and what the bank sold it for, a difference of maybe $350,000.

You know where that money comes from? The old man, this nice guy who wanted to help his son with the college degree, he's left holding the bag. He signed the notes. The bank can seize the old man's farm, everything, the good land and the beat-up machinery, and that might just pay off the bank. No, I don't know what bank it is, but they're all the same.

So? The kid Bobbie high-tails it off to the city, back to work for the government, and the old man is left high and dry. Selling that land would have been his retirement pension. Now he won't have it. He won't even have a farm. He can't pay off the kid's debt in five years of Sundays. He just doesn't have that kind of operation, and besides, he's near seventy and too old.

The old folk will have nothing except their old age pensions and that's about it, after all those years. And that's what I call tragedy."

🐦 *Good Farmers*

"I say this, the good ones will survive. They always do. I say that the good farmers today are those who are farming, and still have their heads above water and looking around for my truck coming down the road, and they can pay for a fill-up of diesel and invite me in for dinner and give me a good shot of Scotch and right then and there write me a cheque. Good farmer. He's surviving.

But I'd say twenty per cent of my customers are in trouble, another ten in real trouble, and another ten, I'd say, should just pack up now because there's not one damned bit of use fighting, working hard, trying to make it. They have had it. Beaten. The system, it's beaten them. And, of course, they made the system go. They were part of it.

Yep, I agree with you, it is sad. In the past three, four years I guess I've seen thirty of my accounts go down the tube. Farmers for a long time, three times it being the home farm taken up by a grandfather, and now she's gone. A lot of it just being leased out or rented out by the banks. At least the fellows who are farming that land, they're not responsible for the debt. They make it this year, fine, the bank gets its cut, they get theirs, and that's fine.

But when you think of these people in the towns now, in Lethbridge, Calgary, Red Deer, on up the line, and they've been farming all their lives and now they haven't got much more than a dime, looking for a job, not knowing anything but farming. What are they to do? On the trash heap, amd it's a sad day for this country when good farmers wind up on the trash heap, because they'll never leave it. All wasted. Too bad. There's something really wrong with the system."

🐦 *Shut Down the Farms!*

"There are guys with five university degrees sitting in their offices in Ottawa and they are actually saying, 'Maybe we should shut down the farm economy.' Don't laugh. I am serious. At the wheat-pool office we get enough material coming out of Ottawa and these here think-tanks to know that's what they are thinking. Now, have you ever heard anything so damned stupid in your life? I mean, in your whole damned life?

Now look, I'm not going into all the reasons they give, that maybe this country of ours could get along without farmers. Maybe they could. They could get along, too, without an army, a navy, and an air force, and you could throw half the civil servants into the drink and still run the country just fine.

But look, you shut down the farms – and I don't care if they are in Newfoundland or Vancouver Island or right here in Saskatchewan, right here at Rosetown – and if you do that, you are tearing the heart and the guts out of this country. This country is agriculture. I'll say that again, just in case they are listening in Ottawa. This country is agriculture. This country is farmers. This country is people whose folks came up from the States or over from France or Germany or Scotland, Russia, the Ukraine, Poland, the works, and they worked their bloody guts out for peanuts, year after year, and their kids did the same. And their kids, that's me, we worked our guts out, and when I pack it in, my kids are going to get this farm, I hope, and the two boys will work it out on how they share it, and they'll work their asses off.

Them, me, the boys, we'll still be building Canada, buying seed and planting and taking off the crop and selling and hoping next year will be better. Next-year country. Call it that. That's it.

I'll make this short. How would you shut down 300,000 farms? That's just for starters. There are a thousand complications when you even say that sentence, so there is not much point in even going on. But say you shut down this farm. No more subsidies for me, so, I go broke. Okay, so do most of the farms within a hundred miles of here. Not an elevator working. Not a doctor. Not a storekeeper. Not a guy selling second-hand machinery, even. Not a newspaper, like the one we've got in town. Or the little Rosetown bulk plant. Or anybody working the roads or even working in the municipal office. Christ, I could go on forever, and I'm just starting, or not even a town of Rosetown. Just a store here and there, a gas station, and the lumber yard, and maybe a café, and I'd say that would be it.

Go over to Regina, you know what you'd find? Grass in the streets. We don't have the manufacturing worth a hoot. Not much oil. Potash, she's just about finished. All that city has, or would have, is civil servants, and without the farmers there would be no money coming in, and they would be out on their asses pretty damned quick.

You would have, my friend, a dead province. Because the one and only thing old Saskatchewan has going for it is guys like me. Me and nothing more. You drive me out, you kill the place.

This is foolish, ain't it? Talking about this just because a few economists in Ottawa have these figures and computers and they've got nothing better to do with themselves. Go skate on the Rideau Canal. It must be 79 or 80 degrees Fahrenheit back there now – and none of Trudeau's Celsius bullshit for me – and let's see if they can skate on the Rideau Canal. It makes as much sense as this.

But here is this clipping from the *Globe and Mail* my eldest kid sent me, and it seriously asks if Canada should stay in the farming business. I mean, we know how things are. Real tough. It's never been this tough since the Depression, and my dad's still alive, and he can tell you that. But to start talking in print, quoting all these guys in Ottawa, about shutting down the farmers, well, you start to wonder what they're putting in the drinking-water down there.

Okay, shut us down. Say we can't compete. But listen, do you think those farmers in France and the European Economic Community, do you think they aren't subsidized? Right up to their belly-buttons. And those farmers in Iowa? Right up to their asses. And those Chinese? They are subsidized with people. It would take 360 Chinese using their methods to take off what me and my two younger boys can do in fourteen or fifteen days, weather permitting. Everybody in this whole damned world is subsidized. That's the truth.

I'm getting away from myself. Answer me this! What are you going to do with 300,000 farmers and their 300,000 wives, and their 600,000 kids, and their dogs and cats and cars and pickups and trucks and self-propelleds, combines and tractors and houses and sheds and barns? And here's the stickler, buddy. If everybody wants to sell out, then everything is worth nothing. So we got to stick on the farm and live anyway. Where's the money coming from to keep us going, and I don't mean welfare, because this is different than welfare. I'm talking about your living wage.

And here's the biggest cruncher of all. Who's going to maintain our bank debts? On this farm I've got more than $240,000 and I'm not in very deep. Okay, the government says, boys, we've decided. You got to stop farming. We've decided we can't afford you any more. So they got to do something about our debts. So they say, okay, we'll declare a moratorium on all your debts. You don't have to pay interest, and nobody can take your land and farms away from you.

The people across the country who blame the farmer for everything, they all jump up from the television sets and they cheer and say, 'None of them farmers any more, getting all that free money and all that.'

But you're forgetting somebody. The presidents of the five big banks, the Royal, Montreal, and so on. They haven't been consulted by these guys who smoke pipes, and feed stuff into computers down there in Ottawa, and then tell the government what to do. They get up from their television at the Six O'Clock News and they say, 'Bullshit, and bullshit again,' and they get on the phone to each other. In two hours they've got it all settled, and next morning they're in Ottawa.

That's it! In this country, out here, you scratch a banker and draw a little blood and soon you're bleeding from a dozen big holes yourself. The bankers wouldn't put up with all this, and they run the country, always have. They'd be down the tubes before you could count up to sixteen-per-cent interest and spell the word 'foreclosure'. So there would be no shutting down the farmers and shutting down the province and no shutting down the Royal and the Montreal and all those other friendly banks.

What I'm getting to is this. I don't think anybody on God's green earth hates the banks more than the Western Canadian farmer does. No, it is not possible. They have shafted us and bled us and screwed and blued and tattooed us since the days of Louis Riel, and there's never been a damned thing we could do about it, and there never will be.

But here's the big joke. Who would be our saviour so we could keep on losing money as long as we wanted to? Who'd save our skins? The goddamned big banks, the banking system, all the guys who've made life miserable for us for a hundred years. That's who, and you better believe it, eh?

So who is our best friends? Those goddamned bankers. Yeah!"

🐦 *I'm Going to Fight*

"When I quit in '78 and Mother and me moved into town here, I gave my only boy the farm, six miles south of here, and I said, 'Dick, she's all yours.' I taught him everything I knew and he was twenty-eight then and married and three kiddies. He'd tried the city and they didn't like it and I thought, good, this will keep it in the family.

There was three quarters then and a good house and buildings, and that really wasn't enough land to make a living, or that's what the farm experts from the college said. Mother and me, I think we did pretty well. My line of machinery was old but I kept it in top repair, and old as I was, I'd read those pamphlets put out by the government and I was always picking up a tip here and one there. Through the years, well, I can say we did pretty well. One thing is, we owned that land.

The first three years were good years for them, and he went out and bought half a section of a widow's farm and another quarter, so he ended up with six and some pasture, and that's close to 900 acres. Times were good. They were getting good crops, fifty-sixty to the acre, and that is awful good. But he paid too much for the land and he got loans from the bank for it. My equipment wasn't good enough for him, so he bought new machinery, and that was more loans – and that was when interest was higher than I thought it could ever go.

The upshot of it was, Dickie came in here in February of '85 and he told me he was going under. This is my farm he's talking about. My father pre-empted that farm, homesteader's ten-dollar fee for the first 160 acres, and he sits right there and just tells me that he's going under. It made me sick. It's not only him, it's Mother and me. He's buying that land from me on a twice-yearly payment, and if that goes, where do we go? We don't own this house. There's a mortgage on it like every other house. And he sits there and says he's going under.

I mean, if he'd sounded sorry about it, maybe that would have helped. He can't meet the mortgage payments, so he's behind on the widow's land and the machinery, and I know for a fact he's not maintaining it. He's behind on the mortgage because of the drought. We had it bad here last year and the year before that. All of this South Country got hit hard by drought.

I asked him what he was going to do, and that boy sits there on his ass and says there is nothing to do. I said, hadn't he ever heard of the word 'fight'? Like a soldier does in the war. Nothing he could do, he keeps saying. He'd lost hope.

I said, well, I'm going to fight. Your mother is going to fight. I'm going to get Marilyn to fight. That's his wife, a real spunky little girl. And I told him that if he didn't want to fight, then he was to stand off way over there and not meddle. And I told him that when I was finished, there would still be a Mason farm, and if he wanted to farm it, fine, but if he didn't, then I'd go back to it.

I told him to get in his truck and go back home and bring Marilyn in, and when he left I phoned her and told her what happened and she said yes, she knew. She was sick to death about it. I told her to get together every paper, receipts, mortgages, everything that had anything to do with the farm and them and us, and I told her there wasn't a minute to lose.

They came back and we spent the rest of the afternoon and a break for supper and that night going over the papers, the bank books, the mortgages. When it was all done, I told them what I was going to do. They'd sign everything over to me. The widow's land, the other quarter, the equipment and the bills and everything. I was taking charge and that was the way it was gonna be, and make no mistake about that. Maybe I didn't bring Dickie up right, favoured him too much. I would have liked to see him put up a fight of some sort, but he didn't. Marilyn, she did all the asking, and she was satisfied with my way of thinking.

Two days later I owned the whole lot, but remember, I still owned the first three quarters of the section. I owned the rest, so I also took over its debts and the mortgages. From now on they were working for me.

I'm gonna have to make this simple. I sold the widow's half section and I refinanced the loan and paid it off with a penalty through a trust company, so we were left with about one-tenth of the debt and at a lot lower interest. I did the same with the other quarter, and don't ask me to explain but it worked out and it took a week of meetings with accountants, and everybody saying, 'Bob, you can't do this. It doesn't make sense.'

I'd say, damn it all, don't you see? This makes perfect sense. We're getting down, back to the original 480 acres. All free and clear. There's a house and good buildings on it and we're going to be paying just a whittle of what the interest was before.

You can't farm three quarters and survive in this district in these times, they'd say. I'd say I did it for a long, long time and did pretty well. They'd say, times were different. I'd say, you tell that to the judge when he signs the foreclosure papers and you've lost every damn thing.

I was stuck with that $85,000 combine with the stereo radio and the air-conditioning, and I sold it for $35,000. Just like that. Sold the bugger. I bought one that would do the job, a '76 John Deere, in good shape because I knew the fellow who owned it, and I grabbed it at auction, about $6,000. With $20,000 of the money I got for the combine I went to the bank and I said, here's $20,000 and let's make a deal, otherwise, you don't get it. And I bought back the loan and paid a penalty and we were clear. You think they weren't doing things like that? Let me tell you. Those banks were so happy to clear some of those loans they'd eat some of the paper. They were digesting paper all over the country if you knew how to feed it to them. Managers were all scared because of these big loans they had out, and they weren't getting nothing for them. A little money will go a long way these days, if you know how.

Then I said to Marilyn, okay, here's your farm again, just like it was back in '78, when Mother and me moved into town. I said, I'm not going to be mean about this but I want to know everything you're doing. What you're cropping, and I told her I didn't want any more of this Canola and lentils and soy-beans business. I wanted wheat. This country was built on wheat, and this is the best land in the world for wheat and our land is going to grow wheat. I told her, you tell that boy of mine that the only way he's going to be able to buy this farm is to stick to doing what I know, and that is wheat. I asked her if she understood. She said yes, and she got up and came around the table and kissed me. That was nice of her.

Dickie? Ah, he was off up around Rocky Mountain House getting his moose when that happened. But that Marilyn, she gave him the message. I know that.

Things are a bit better with them. They had a damn good crop under their belt last year, '86. Things clicked, and she's keeping him close to the grindstone and they're not spending foolishly. I go out there about twice a week for lunch and I don't try and be pushy. That wouldn't be right. But we're working over all the machinery, giving it all a good fix-up, and they've got a big garden ready to go for next year, and they're cutting corners right, left, and centre. I got this feeling, and Mother has too, they're gonna make it.

You know, I could be taken out and hanged for this, but I got this deep suspicion that women, like Marilyn who was brought up on a farm, well, just this deep feeling I should have put Marilyn in charge of the thinking end of it, the money, the buying, back when they took over in '78. Let Dickie do all the work. I do not think they would have gotten themselves into the fix they got into. Maybe it's the women who had the brains all along and we was just too pig-headed to understand that."

❧ Working Wives

"City people seem to think the farmer is self-sufficient. He's no more self-sufficient these days than the city guy, like my brother working for an insurance company. Except the city guy is much better off. The net pay of the average farmer, and you're looking at him right now, the average income in one year, taking off everything, is about $9,500.

The answer is, the wife works. Maybe full-time, maybe part-time. It's something you didn't see fifteen years ago. I'm continually amazed at the number of women around here who suddenly popped up as nurses' aides or real nurses or teachers' aides or real teachers. If you knew them before, you'd forgotten that when they married they'd been teachers or nurses or stenographers. Now the crunch is on, and they've got jobs, and they're off to town in the morning. Some of them drive a long way. There's quite a few towns within thirty or forty miles of here each way and the businessmen hire them as clerks and secretaries. I'm not sure if all the money they bring home after taxes means all that much, but they do it, so it must.

So we've got all these women high-tailing it off every morning to town or the city to work, and that's getting to be a fact of life.

They're doing other things, too. Hell, our school district has forty-four buses. That's forty-four jobs, and six spares and mechanics and a couple of managers, and not all those buses are driven by farmers for extra money. Women can drive a school bus just as good as any man, and a lot of them do.

There's a woman around here who sells those Amway products. Done it for years. Twice a year, there she is knocking at your door. My brother's niece, she's the queen of Tupperware around here. She makes a little bit of a living at it too. Two other women, they run a day-care centre for the kids of these women. Drop 'em off at eight and pick them up at six, and that's taken care of. Down the road there's a woman with a hairdressing sign right out on the road. Every Friday night and all day Saturday she's open for business and there's always cars and trucks in the yard. There's another woman over towards Isabella, I think, who has goats, and she sells the milk. The milk is good for ulcers, and when you think of all the guys around here with big money problems, then you can see why she makes a buck.

Dress-making. Income tax returns. Catering. They got more damned gimmicks to make money than I ever saw. I don't know whether most of them are serious or not. But the women who work in town, nursing, teaching, clerking, and doing double duty, as it were, farm and town, they're serious. They're keeping the old family farm afloat.

Now take me. Sure, I've got a second-hand back-hoe and a second-hand Cat and I call myself a construction company, and I'm out there chasing down every two-bit job I can. If you're lucky you get a week here and two days there, and by the time you figure your diesel and your time and renting a low bed and hiring a kid and breakdowns, you're not making much. But I figure I pretty well got to, just to stay in the farming business. It's not easy, I tell you. You do it to just damn well survive.

My wife? Sure, she works. Part-time. She's one of those nurses I was telling you about."

🐦 Especially the Wife

"Some of these families around here, they'd be eating day-old bread and beans and drinking powdered skim milk if it wasn't for the wives working. I can tell you that. No other way. They've got some income coming in when they sell their quota, get their first payment, but more's going out than coming in. Stands to reason. These young fellows are producing a product they can't sell at a profit. That's the long and short of it.

Wives, they finally say, well, I've got to get a job. Some of them driving forty, fifty miles into Regina every day, both ways, maybe ninety miles, and doing a job in a hospital or some government office, an office or maybe substitute teaching, and then home again.

That $1,000 or $1,200 a month they get, that's what's keeping the
farm afloat. After income tax and paying the gas and expenses it's
a lot less than that, but every little bit helps.

And remember, it's not a case of them wanting to do it. They
gotta do it – every day, every week and month – and that's the way
it is. Tough on everybody. The hubby, the kids, but especially the
wife."

_____

❧ The Wise Old Lawyer

"Everybody talks about stress in the city. The fast lane and all that
business. Don't you believe it isn't right here in the farms around
the little towns and little cities of the Prairies. These guys are being
eaten up by insecurity, and that is just a nice fancy name for fear.
F-e-a-r.

It brings on medical problems. You've heard of ulcers? Heart
attacks? Biliousness? Bad headaches? Can't sleep. Can't eat. Yep!
All these things. And you don't think that man isn't sick? He's
real sick and he needs help. That may be the physical side, but
there is also the mental side, and that is what worries me the most.

They'd knock you down if you mentioned they should see a
psychiatrist, and if you mentioned that you know they've devel-
oped a pretty bad drinking problem in the past few years, they'd
deny it. If you went all the way and said you knew they were
beating up their wives, well, I don't know what would happen.
For a couple, maybe, that would be the last straw, and they might
break down and cry right in front of you.

All because they tried to bite off more than they can chew. They
wanted everything, and in a hurry. No steady and slow wins the
race. If I don't grab it, then somebody else will grab it. They want
that double-wide in some park in Arizona, and that ten-thousand-
dollar boat to truck over to Lake Diefenbaker for a week, and big
parties with lots of booze, and that super-duper John Deere combine and everything. Well, they can't have it, and it is the banks
and the trust companies that are saying no, and they are telling
these young bucks what to do. They don't like that. It makes them
insecure. Boy, does it ever. And they can't handle it.

I see it in this office, my clients, at least once a week. The guy
comes in to get something notarized, and in an hour he walks out.

Maybe he feels better. I don't know. Five minutes for business, and maybe it's this kind old face of mine, but he wants to talk to somebody. Like me, the wise old lawyer. When he walks out that door he might feel a bit better, but I know that he is one young fellow in one big load of trouble.

You never read about this, you know. Perhaps it is part of our strange Canadian culture that the only people who go to psychiatrists are wealthy people in the city, or child-molesters who are ordered to take psychiatric treatment by a Supreme Court judge.

I'm not saying these farmers are sick. I am just saying they are troubled. It's like they're paddling down a wild river, but they haven't got a paddle any more. They're watching the cliffs go zipping by and they're heading for a big whirlpool and they're saying, 'Hey, I didn't lose the paddle. I didn't throw it away. It was yanked out of my hand by someone I don't even know and didn't even see.' I really feel sorry for them."

✥ Battering

"When we say wife-abuse, people think it is verbal – swearing, cursing a lot – but what it boils down to is wife-battering. And I do mean battering. Assault with the fists, by the husband. The women we find who have broken cheekbones, and that's no laughing matter, they'll tell us they've been punched so many times, black eyes, cuts and bruises, and all that goes with it.

I never thought I'd live to see the day when these things happened in our community. This is crime. A man can be charged with it, although the police are reluctant to do it. It takes a great deal of will on the part of the wife to go through with it, and I'm sometimes of the opinion that nothing is really resolved.

We know what's happening. In four out of five cases you could blame the economy. The husband is laid off, or his job just disappears, and the guy has worked hard and long all his life. Maybe twenty-five years. Now here he is, out on the streets there, so to speak, no job, no money, can't support his family. Can't live with himself is one way to look at it. Pride wrecked. Manhood challenged, and you would be surprised how many feel they are impotent, and maybe they are. Even the fact they can't go out with the boys for a few drinks some night, that is important to them. They can't buy decent clothes for their kids. Some of these battering cases have occurred around Christmas, and you could put your own label on that. Christmas, and the husband and wage-earner can't even buy presents. And so it goes.

The wife, the long-suffering wife, she is the victim of it, and I'd like to say we're not just dealing with city people. Brandon is a nice and quiet city, nothing much happens here, and the farmers around consider it their second home, and so we get these cases. Oh, yes, a goodly number are farm wives. The frustration of a farmer is no different from a city man. None at all. The farmer works harder than the city worker and worries more and has so much more to lose, and these days so little to gain, and so he is tested so much more.

Let me tell you something, the one call the police hate to respond to the most is one called a family dispute. They never know what might meet them on the other side of that door. A dying woman. Maybe a drunk with a gun. The number-two cause of deaths of policemen are those very family trouble calls. They are very cautious, but now they see that this is becoming an epidemic, this wife-punching, kid-kicking, house-wrecking, and they are more inclined to lay charges. But it goes on more and more, and often close to home. It could be your neighbour, and you might never know."

🦑 *Suicides*

"There was this little item in the paper some time ago and it was the word 'suicidologist' that caught my eye. They've got a doctor up there in Edmonton and he specializes in . . . right, you got it, suicides.

He was saying that suicides among farmers in Alberta were way up, since '81 when the high interest rates and the National Energy Program hit us. Not a big story, but it should have got better publicity. Have you ever heard of an economy measuring their prosperity in suicides?

The figures were 15 suicides in every 100,000 for farmers in 1981 when everything was still going along pretty good. Then we come up to '84, and that figure has gone from 15 suicides to 40. Now you just think about that, from 15 to 40 is one helluva jump, and all among farmers. Not city and town people. Farmers.

Now right around here, like from Taber going out fifteen or so miles, I've heard of two. Didn't know them but, yep, both farmers. Just two, but this isn't that kind of area. We got a lot of immigrants, pretty stable people, and we're chock full of Mormons, and I can't see them doing that, and there's Hutterites in colonies around and about, and I doubt if they know what the word means. The rest, just like any mix you'd find anywhere. Good and bad, big and small. Folks, I'd call them.

One guy, he just drove into Lethbridge and got a bottle of vodka and drove down by the river one day and hooked a hose to his exhaust pipe and into the cab and started her up, and I'll bet he didn't even have time to have more than a couple of good drinks. That stuff is fast and deadly. Some kids found him, playing down there after school. And the other, he told his wife he was going deer-hunting and went out to the equipment shed and she heard a shot and ran out, and there he was. That was messy, I heard. Both were in deep trouble with bills and the bank, and there they go and do this stupid thing. The wife gets to clean up. If she can.

There must be more. A guy coming home from town slams at 70 right into a highway transport truck. That's it for him. The trucker don't get hurt, but I bet he thinks about it for a long time. Not his fault. I figure some of those kinds of smashes on straight roads, they're suicide, too. What else can you figure? You can't.

It's not a pretty thing to talk about, but it's all part and parcel of the times the farmers are going through, and I guess it has mostly to do with their land. Look, maybe their grandfather homesteaded that land way back when, and they grew up on it when their father worked it through thick and thin, and then they got it. Okay, the way things were going in the sixties and seventies, they probably doubled or even tripled the size of the family farm. That's not impossible. You had to. Bigger is best. Bigger, more grain to sell, more profits. Like every other damn fool in this country from one end to the other, they thought the good times would never stop. Well, I guess all you have to do is look at our history. Good times end. Bad times sure as living hell come right in behind. That's always. Nothing so sure as death and taxes, and that bad times always come. This time it's the Americans doing it to us and the Europeans doing it to the Americans, so we wind up on the short end.

Then comes the banks and they say, 'We want your land. You're way behind and you'll never catch up. We can't do anything with your land because we can't sell it, but we want you and your wife and kids off it, and we don't mean maybe. Okay, mister, off in thirty days.' He goes to his lawyer and he says, 'Sorry, I can't do anything about it, and that will be fifty bucks please. Pay my secretary on the way out.' So, something just cracks in the poor bastard. Just snaps. He doesn't know what he's doing, but he knows he just can't hang in there any longer. He goes to the liquor store and he buys a bottle of vodka and he goes to Sears and he buys a length of hose. Not even so much as a 'So long, wife, so long, kids, I'm sorry and I love you.' It's very sad.

Does the government give some kind of counselling to these guys who are on the brink? I never heard of it. Something they should think about. In the long run, hell, it's always the government's fault, even in this kind of thing. Oh, I know we can't hook up every farmer with some apparatus to a big computer that will blink a red light when he goes over the line. No way.

But now that I'm on the subject, so the guy's gone. But there's his wife, and what can she do? The kids, if they're young. Under eighteen, say. He's not only destroyed his own life, but he's destroyed her life for a while and left the kids with something they'll never forget for as long as they live. 'Oh, yeah,' people will say, 'her father blew his brains out with his deer rifle.' "

❧ *Off to the Cities*

"Look, I had four boys and three girls, a good-sized family. My youngest boy is on my farm, the one I sold him. My second girl is a farmer's wife and they live at Melfort. I've got another boy who is manager of an implement company at Yorkton and the other four are gone, off to the cities, and one even living in Halifax. I'm doing better than most. At least three of mine are still in agriculture. In the old days, different, far different. The Prairies today just won't support their children on the land. Those days are gone."

Seventeen

People Will Never Know

🕊 ═══════════════════════════════════════

Going East ... Something More to Life ... A Grade Six Education ...
A Weekend on the Farm ... Antiques and Butter ... Quiet Mary and
the Premier ... No Sense of History ... What Farming Should Be All
About ... Prairieness ... Live and Let Live ... Nobodies ... Arabian
Farmer ... A Factory Hand on the Land ... Sunsets, Sunrises ... No
More Prairie Winters ... Prairie People ... People Will Never Know

═══════════════════════════════════════

Back in 1930, wheat was our biggest export commodity–but in 1986 the export of Canadian-made trucks was more than double the value of our export of wheat. Does it matter that the Western agricultural economy really is irrelevant to Canada's wealth? In Canadian political life, does it matter that most federal elections are decided before the polls close in Manitoba?

Yes, it may seem that the agricultural economy of the West and its political presence don't carry much weight. But this book has not concerned itself with this, because it has dealt with the most important factor Canada has–its people. Nobody on the Prairies considers the region irrelevant, and you won't find Prairie people who consider themselves irrelevant.

They are strong and strong-minded, independent in a nation where personal independence often seems curiously lacking. The farmers and the ranchers are their own bosses. They can say, "To hell with it," or "To hell with you." They are proud of their heritage, proud that their grandparents survived and their parents weathered the storms of life so distinctive to the Prairies. Now they are fighting their own battles–Westerners versus Ottawa, the politicians, the bureaucrats, international agricultural policies, protectionism, the Bay Street bankers, the East, and, above all, kindly old Mother Nature, and terrible drought, possibly the worst in history in 1988. Anybody else but Westerners – farmers and city people alike–would say it was a no-win situation.

But they've seen a lot of it before, and their grandchildren will see it too, probably. But they remain tough, resilient, cheery, confident, neighbourly, hard-working, and long-suffering, which produces a very special kind of Canadian. Now they are fighting another major battle, for the preservation of their way of life, and they're fighting back with the weapons they have, which aren't many.

There has been no academic attempt in this book to dig into the fundamental economic problems of the West. *I have only tried to pass on the stories of the people I met, and I hope that they show how the people of the Prairies have come to grips with their own problems, the how-when-what-where-why of their survival down the long decades since 1900.*

They have one bright and noble badge of honour – a lesser breed would not have survived.

🐛 Going East

"When I graduate I'll load up everything in the trunk, my clothes, my books, my stereo, my everything, and get out on Number One and keep going east until I hit Toronto. I'm not going to wait for graduation. They can send the diploma to my folks. I just want to get out of this province, out of Regina, out of this place.

There's nothing here, and there never was. Its first name was Pile of Bones. It still is. There's no damned reason to stay here, even if you can go into your old man's law firm or his business, because all that will happen is that you might get as rich as they are, but it's damned certain you'll soon become as dull as them.

When I hit the Ontario border, I'm going to stop the heap and get out and kiss the ground, just like those American astronauts did the first time they went to the moon . They did it on an aircraft carrier, I think, but I'll do it on the blacktop. 'I'm free!' I'm gonna yell that. 'Damn it, I'm free!' "

🐛 Something More to Life

"My son and I drove out from Toronto to Vancouver and then back to Calgary and spent a couple of days there, and then we took some roads back in the foothills and the mountains, not going anywhere, just sleeping in the camper and doing some fishing and talking about things in general. We had a good time. The first time we'd talked as father and son in a long, long time. I found out he was a good guy and he felt the same about me.

Everywhere we went we met people, just ordinary people, like us. We'd be in a camp-ground or a park and there we'd be, talking away around a fire and nipping on a bottle, and it was like we'd known these people for a long time. In the cafés, the stores, I noticed you could talk to anybody. It was nagging me back in my mind that this was the way it should be. Not the way I'd lived my life in Toronto, working as a printer and then as a superintendent of a big shop, and in at eight in the morning, deadlines, paperwork, hiring and firing, the two things I hated to do, and not knowing many people. It was getting to me after just a week roaming about that there was something more to life, something more like this.

It happened like this. Allen and I, we'd taken a motel room in Pincher Creek and after dinner we went to the beer parlour. In Toronto, you sit and drink and stare at the TV or just look at your glass and pay through the nose for what you're drinking. In this place, we hadn't sat down for more than five minutes when a big farmer came over and said we looked kind of lonely. Why not join him and his wife and some other folks at a big table. Just like that, you know. 'Come on over, you're welcome.' Just like that.

Nice people. Fine people. Out to enjoy themselves and we did too, and about eleven o'clock the farmer said we'd all go to a party, and I think I had more fun that night than any time since my wife died. I guess I was a pretty unhappy guy those two years, and the walls were too tight around me. Too much work, missing Catherine, not feeling part of our old life. Then getting back with my son and he had just got his divorce, no kids, and getting to know him again. Anyway, we had a wonderful time at the party, and lots of good people.

Anyway, the party broke up about four in the morning and Allen said no point in sleeping and so we went back to the motel and showered and fixed up and threw everything into the camper and headed down south. As we drove, the sun came up and we hit Waterton and turned east, and that was it – heading home, and we were going to drive straight through.

About ten miles down the road there was a little gravel road turning off, and I thought, well, one last look, and I turned up it and went for about a mile and stopped on a ridge. The whole country was around us, lock, stock, and barrel. There were the mountains with the snow and the foothills coming green and some farmland and a lot of ranches and smoke coming out of some chimneys, and away off we saw a couple of cowboys moving some cattle along. There was no sound, just the wind in our faces and the clean and clear air and the mountains out there.

Allen got a couple of beer out of the cooler and we sat on two rocks and we didn't say anything. It hadn't been the kind of party where you got drunk, just a good fun party, and the beer felt good. It just felt good and cold and just right. It felt just right to be sitting there, like we were the only people in the world. I'm not religious, but I felt that the whole world had been created by God for us, just on that morning about seven o'clock.

I remember Allen going to the truck for two more bottles and when he sat down he was quiet for a time and then he said, 'Dad, I'm coming back. I'm going to live around here somewhere. Start things over. Maybe it's a mistake right now, saying this, but it might be the best mistake I'll ever make.'

It didn't seem at all funny him saying that, and what I said next, well, it didn't seem funny either and I just said, off-hand, 'Me too.'

Just like that. I mean everything came together. It was like it wasn't me talking. It was my soul talking, taking over from my mind, I guess, or something. You've seen those movie tricks where a magician throws out a deck of cards any which way and then the film is reversed and they all come flinging themselves in from nowhere and end up in his hand in a neat and nice deck of cards. That was it. Everything came in, whoosh, and that was it.

Allen laughed and leaned over and gave me a hug and shook my hand.

'Partners,' he said, 'we'll make out.'

That was five years ago. We went back and I quit two months later, arranged for my pension and severance, benefits, everything, and sold the house, the cottage up north, the furniture, everything. That was it. I was sixty-one. Didn't know what I was going to do. Didn't care.

I came out in August, and I spent a month just goofing around, first down to Pincher Creek and you should have heard my new friends when I told them. No, they weren't surprised. You'd think it happened all the time. This was the Alberta spirit talking. Kind of big in the chest, you know, and howdy, friend, glad to have you.

I went all over the province and I decided to spend the winter in Lethbridge, and I got a little apartment for $175 a month, with all the trimmings, and picked up odd jobs in the printing trade. There was enough to keep me busy. I didn't need the work, but I wanted to do it and there was enough. The word got around, and I didn't play the hot-shot Toronto superintendent with two hundred men and women working for me. I was just one of the boys.

I thought I'd miss certain Toronto things and I found I had to even think hard to remember what maybe I should be missing. No deadlines and no hassles. Looking back then, it seemed Toronto was just one big hassle.

I liked the people and Lethbridge the first year and then I moved to Calgary and I spent the summer and fall in my camper, just going everywhere. I've enjoyed every minute of it. I guess you'd say it is what I want to do for the rest of my life. I can't see anything wrong with it. If I find something wrong, I'll let you know."

🕊 *A Grade Six Education*

"My father, now there's a story. No education to speak of, Grade 6, but that meant he could read and write and do arithmetic, and at twelve or thirteen he was doing a man's work. Starting off on the hayrake, then the mower, then four horses and the harrows and so on, and absorbing everything. The war came along in '39 and he held off for two years and then did his three or four years with the army and then home. The song goes, the farmer takes a wife, old McDonald and all that, and he did, and he bought his first farm from the Veterans' Land Act, half a section. The usual. Cows, beef cattle, grain, what they called mixed farming. He was always slow and steady, and as he tells it, he survived drought and low prices and wheat gluts and high interest and he and Mother just kept plugging away.

I can still see him, at the big table in the kitchen after supper reading those pamphlets the government used to send him. How to be a better farmer, that sort of thing. He never missed a Farmers' Field Day, no matter how far away, and he was active in the Co-op and he was known as a good neighbour.

All this time he was buying land. A quarter would come up and he'd bid and get it, at sixty dollars an acre. You laugh at that price now, but that's the way it was. One day, I guess it was at Christmas and I was home from university, fourth-year Economics, he asked me to sit down at the table and he had all these lists and sheets full of figures. He said something like, 'Well, you're the financial expert now, how am I doing?'

It took me about half an hour to go over them, and he sat there smoking that pipe of his, and I was amazed. Why, he had nearly four sections. My old man was a big farmer. All those years, my brothers and I growing up, we just hadn't realized. He had about

2,200 acres, and he was handling it with just himself, my brother Bill, my mother, and the hired man, another Bill, who looked after about a hundred head of beef cattle the old man had.

He had a full line of good equipment, none of it new because he always bought second-hand. He had a perfect eye for a good piece of equipment and he bought right, and he maintained everything himself. Most of his land was free and clear and his payment schedules were letter-perfect. He was a big farmer for those days, the mid-sixties.

I remember him saying, 'Land, it's getting too expensive,' and here he's talking about it way up to two hundred dollars an acre. 'That's as far as she should go,' he said. He'd seen boom and bust before, but he didn't know what was coming. Nobody did, although we should have known. Anyway, he picked up two more quarters and rounded it off at sixteen quarters, four sections, and he'd played it cool. Most of it was in a tight package.

Then came Dad's happy hunting-ground. Land prices started to go crazy in the late seventies, and Dad was getting on and Mom had a heart condition and Bill was getting old, and they must have been hypnotized by those prices going up. Like fifteen per cent a year, twenty per cent a year, and land was selling for seven hundred dollars an acre. These younger farmers, say, the ones under forty, they just had to have more land. By their reasoning, the only way to make it was to think big and be big.

The banks, well, let me tell you about the banks. They practically had open houses where you could get a loan just for the asking. If you had other land as collateral you were a cinch, and all with that lovely floating interest rate built in. Lovely but deadly.

In the meantime, my dad is selling off his land. A quarter here, cash from the bank in the hand. No holding mortgages for him. Then wait. Up it goes a little, from $650 to $675, say, and he'd deal out another little quarter, cash again, into mutual funds, and then a half section, more cash.

At Christmas of '81, big family dinner at the farm, Dad took Bill and me into the parlour and we sat around with a drink and he told us that he was retiring. At age sixty-two. We were flabbergasted. I asked what he was going to do with the farm. He said, with a grin, 'Boys, there isn't any farm to speak of. Just three quarters left and the deal is going through next month on that half section west of the house.' He was keeping one quarter, the home place, and everything else was going, going, gone.

I wasn't mad. Hell, I could see what he'd done. He'd acted like
all the textbooks say. Buy low and sell high. He couldn't lose, and
because he'd got rid of the beef-cattle operation years before, he
was scot-free. I mean, he was really retired and sitting on about
$2,000,000 in tax-free capital gains and I thought, you old bugger.
Me, the economist, and he doesn't let on a bit. He asked me what
I would have done. I said, if I had had your brains, Dad, I'd have
done the same thing. If I had used my own brains, I'd probably
have held on. I'd have lost the whole kit and caboodle, I guess, still
buying high, and when the bottom fell out, big surpluses, rock-
bottom prices, falling land values, and still that deadly floating
interest rate, why, I would have been busted."

🐦 *A Weekend on the Farm*

"We've got friends in Calgary, and they come up and see Old
McDonald's Farm, hee-haw, and see the animals and smell the fresh
air and go fishing in the creek or just walk about. One day Jilly
told them we were setting up a bed-and-breakfast. A weekend thing.
With meals, mind you. She told them, any of your city-slicker
friends want a weekend down on the old homestead, give us a
jingle. Well, that was on a Sunday when we had a picnic for some
buddies of ours, and damn it all if we didn't get a phone call on
Tuesday. A couple in Calgary, asking about it. That knocked us
for a loop. Jilly, sharp as a tack, said come Friday about eight
o'clock and we'll have a late dinner, then three meals on Saturday
and brunch on Sunday. I think she was figuring things out even
while she was talking to them. The woman asked how much, and
as easy as you please she said $200 and bring your own liquor. And
that Friday they come, an accountant and his wife. Both off the
farm, brought up as farm kids. They loved it, and no trouble for
us. What's two more extra people, and good talk, and they kept
out of our way when we were working. Just walked hand in hand
around the farm all Saturday, maybe thinking, why can't we be
like this?

That started it. We could have had three or four couples every
weekend but we only had one bedroom as a spare, and we fixed
that up nice, and anyway, it was just a place to lay their heads, if
you know what I mean. Good company and talk. We've never had

a bummer of a couple yet. Lots of singles, though. That surprised
me. They got good meals, we usually drank a bit on Saturday night
and sometimes I'd invite in a neighbour and his wife, and they'd
be gone by two on Sunday afternoon, back to Calgary to spread
the good word. We could make a business of it, but two nights is
enough because of Jilly's shift work.

We don't advertise. They do it for us. The third year we boosted
it to $225 and even the repeaters didn't bat an eye. A lot more
money flying around than you'd think. Well, look at it. Suppose
they go up to Lake Louise. There's $250 right there, for their room
in some motel or the hotel. Then their meals. Then all those people,
the tourists clogging up the works. At our farm, peace, peace and
more peace."

❧ *Antiques and Butter*

"I was scouting for a bit of film I needed of a pioneer house, you
know, logs all silvered and rotting, and windows gaping open, and
weeds growing through the cracks in the floor. Real atmosphere.

One morning I just drove east out of Edmonton and I turned
south and began to drive slowly over those gravel roads. A farm
here, one there, but mostly bush and what looked like land that
had been cleared and then abandoned a long time ago.

Then, damn it all, I got a flat. You don't think you can get flats
any more but I did, and damn it all again, I found out that the
spare had gone flat too. I'm in trouble, because there's not a farmhouse in sight. Not even telephone poles to indicate there are any
farms along this road.

So I lock it up and start hiking up ahead where I know there's a
crossroad, and before I get there, yes, there is a farm. I can't see
the house but there's a road and tracks going in and so in I go.

About an eighth of a mile in I come on a grain field, and on the
other side there is a pasture with maybe twenty cattle in it. But it
still mostly is bush. Then I come out in this big clearing, and there
is broken and rusty machinery every damned place and an old, old,
old barn just ready to sag over and die in a heap.

And the house, it was a real Old West calendar bit of artwork,
typical prairie architecture. You couldn't miss it anywhere in the
world. Front porch. Side hall, and living-room, dining-room, and

kitchen all in a line. Upstairs, front bedroom and two behind. Right out of the 1910 era. It probably got a coat of paint when they built it, and that was it. The house was on its own, house versus the elements, after that.

About four dogs came bee-lining at me, all howling. Chickens scattering everywhere, dogs howling, but they soon stopped. God, is there anything more cowardly than a farm mongrel when you yell at it? And I noticed the smell of lilacs. This being late June there was a huge bush by the front door, and the smell was everywhere.

There was a woman standing by the door. She had bare feet and an old dress and she looked about eighty years old. Right out of some late-night television movie about the Depression. And she was eighty-six, she told me. I won't mention her name but she was a character. Educated. A cultured English gentlewoman in bare feet out there on a farm you wouldn't use to graze your scrub cattle. Very gracious. You just can't disguise that kind of character. You can't acquire it. You have to be born with it.

She invited me in, and, well, I just didn't know what to expect because I hadn't really talked to her yet. But that house. Wowser! It was immaculate. The yard may have been a junkyard but not inside. Spotless, everything shining. And the living-room and the dining-room were loaded with these wonderful old antiques of another way of life. I'm no good at describing them, but go into one of these heritage villages where they've got these rooms fixed up. Okay, then this house made those places look pretty sick. This was the real thing.

She said she had just taken some scones out of the oven, and yes, it was a real old wood-stove, and she laid out two places at this fabulous dining-room table and we had scones and her home-made raspberry jam and she told me the butter was from her Guernsey cows. It was the real stuff, too, and I wondered where you could buy that in Edmonton now.

I told her about the flat tires and she said no problem. Her husband was out somewhere but he'd be back soon and he'd dig an air pump out for me, and we talked. They were from England. They'd come out in 1912 when they were both twenty-two and just married, and she didn't say anything else about her early life. I didn't have to guess. The landed gentry, or I miss my guess.

Her name was Rebecca, and somehow that seemed to fit nicely, and about forty years ago she and her husband had decided that they would get out of the rat race. None of this newfangled stuff like telephones and electricity when it was coming in. They just went along in their own way and lived off their land and paid their taxes, and that was their obligation to society, I guess. A big Stromberg-Carlson radio about fifty years old was sitting there, run by their Delco plant, and no television, but plenty of books. You can tell a lot about people by the books they read. I scanned the shelf behind me and they read the right things.

They had the old age pension, of course, and she mentioned the interest off some inheritance her husband had gotten years before, and then she mentioned the antiques. Well, the house was loaded with these beauties and she asked if I would like to see them. I said yes, they are very nice, and she said no, not these. She took me out and past a huge garden and into a very large shed you couldn't see from the front of the house. It looked fairly new, maybe twenty years old, and we went in–and this place, insulated and well heated, was just jammed with every kind of antiques of the 1900s you've ever seen.

She was smiling, as if saying, pretty neat, eh?

It appeared that way back after the war when everyone was getting high prices for big crops, she and her husband used to go to auction sales for miles around. They'd buy this stuff. This for a dollar, that for two dollars, that wardrobe for five dollars. People then were building new houses on their farms and they just wanted to get all this wonderful old stuff out of the house. She said she and her husband could see a long way down the road, and they just bought it.

I asked her how they sold it, and get this. They sold stuff from their garden and from their cows. In fact, she showed me one upstairs bedroom they'd converted into a greenhouse, with the glass roof and ventilation and heating and everything, and they started their bedding-plants and fruits and vegetables and then planted it. It was a bit early then, but she said people would start driving out from Edmonton and towns around next month. I liked her. She was honest, honest with a chuckle, telling me she was putting one over on the city slickers.

She said, 'We've got a few friends in Edmonton who come out here in the evening or weekend and they just love to buy this stuff, right out of the ground. I say, here's a bag or here's a pail or a basket. Go and pick your radishes or onions. Dig your own potatoes, choose your own corn.'

Of course, they loved it, and this little old lady in the bare feet, she said she knew what city prices in the supermarket were, and she charged fifteen per cent more and nobody complained. After all, who would? Pick your own stuff right out of the ground. So they made money that way, and no income tax or whatever, and how she kept her yard from being jammed with cars I don't know.

Then she'd invite them in for tea and scones, some food and a chat, and they'd be looking at some priceless old piece of furniture, something they'd picked up for a few dollars, and somehow it was mentioned that some of this stuff was for sale. But she'd say something like, 'Oh, we could use the money, but I don't think I could sell that. It's been with us too long and it's like an old friend.' Rather a classic kind of salesmanship. We really don't want to sell, but . . .

Then, maybe the next time, the visitor would come back and say, 'Rebecca, I know you don't want to sell that chair but we would like to buy it off you, so why don't you set your price? If we don't think it's our limit, then we'll just forget it and eat your lovely scones and come back another time.'

Bright as a shiny button, Rebecca said she'd say, 'Well, I've been offered $150 for it, but that was last year. I just don't know.'

Bang, they'd offer $175 and, the way she said it to me, she'd say, 'Well, I guess that would be all right, and I hope Will won't shoot me.'

And everybody was happy and when they'd left, proudly bearing their prize, Will would go out to the shed and haul in another one, and she'd give it a fast polish and wait for another customer from the big and wicked city.

Those people were doing very well. They weren't running any scam or anything, everything was on the up-and-up. They just had a different way of selling antiques. Bring people in to choose their own farm produce and eggs – sell at their own price, don't come down a cent, and send them away happy, with a pound of their own fabulous Guernsey-cow butter, which she'd made and boxed herself. You just can't beat it.

And besides, they were as genuine as genuine could be. Nothing phoney about them. This is the way they lived, and she was eighty-six and going strong, and I'm sure that well-bred and well-educated English manner had something to do with it, too."

🕊 *Quiet Mary and the Premier*

"A few years ago we had our anniversary dinner in the community hall and Mr. Lougheed was there. I was running the program part of the dinner and before I introduced the entertainers, the dancers and singers, I told the premier this. I said he should take a little bit out of our Heritage Fund every year and use it to pay old people to go around to the schools and the villages and the churches and they'd tell the young people what it was like in the old times. Before tractors. Before combines. Before everything but horses and the sixteen-inch plough, and about slopping pigs and milking twelve cows morning and night, and the bitter cold, the dust storms, the way people helped each other. All working together. Hard times. Good times. Every kind of times. How we made this province.

Send the old people out, and let them tell of our history. Alberta is such a young province, only eighty years old. So all these old people, a lot of them have the memories of what it was like when it was nothing. You know, I mean nothing. A shack here. A sod house over there. No roads. No schools. Nothing everywhere.

That's what I said in my five minutes of little talk.

Everybody cheered. They stood up and clapped and cheered. They thought it was the great idea of the century. Here was Mary Pruse, quiet Mary, here she was standing up and giving the premier of Alberta such a wonderful plan. They cheered a long time.

It was so loud the premier had to stand up, and he said he thought it was a wonderful idea and that he would pass it on to the people in his government who handled these kinds of things. But it was all political baloney. Two years went by and nothing happened, and I just thought, more political baloney we just heard. End of my story."

🕊 *No Sense of History*

"When I finished my degree at the University of Manitoba in 1943 I thought, oh, well, I have a bit of money. My father had died several years back and my mother died the year I graduated and I had the estate money, which was certainly enough then to go for my Master's in Education. I talked it over with my favourite professor, a man I really admired, and I said I wanted to do my thesis on the cohesion of the families of the West. The glue that held the communities together, the little villages that were the life and the spirit and the heartbeat of the West.

I told him you could take your cities of Winnipeg and Regina and Saskatoon and blow them away with a strong wind. I didn't think they really had much to do with the life and style and depth and breadth of what we know as Western living, or prairie living. They were trading-centres, educational centres, government centres, but in all the things that really mattered, they really had little to do with it.

I remember all this, sitting in his little office on the campus that warm afternoon in May. The university closed down for the summer and the infantry troops were stationed there and I looked out the window while he was on the phone and I thought, you know, the only real stability about this whole campus, the only thing that makes it worth while to the province of Manitoba, is the agricultural college.

This professor was from Ontario, Toronto, and a very good teacher, but I should have known he would not see it my way. He was an Easterner, for one thing. He was a city man, that's point number two. Thirdly, he was a history teacher, and more concerned with battles won or lost a long time ago than the effects of the just-past Depression on the West, or what the Prairies would be like after the war. He just laughed at my suggestion. I think he represented a type of thinking in those days that Western Canada didn't matter. It would always be there, and there would always be farmers and their families, but what really mattered, what only mattered, was what went on in Winnipeg.

I tried to get across my feelings, about the Scots settlers, and I could see him thinking, 'Oh, yes, the Selkirk Settlers,' as if they were yesterday. Or the Ukrainian and German and Polish and Russian immigrants of the years after 1900, and I could see him thinking, 'Oh, yes, the Men in the Big Sheepskin Coats.' These two mythologies. If it wasn't to be about the Selkirk Settlers being rained out or flooded out in 1817, or about Doukhobor women pulling the ploughs in 1911, he didn't want it. You'd have thought he was a newspaper editor looking for a headline for the front page that day.

I tried to explain the importance of the family, the family tradition, the very strong tendency for families and generations following to stay in the same district, within maybe twenty miles of where they were born. And the strong tendency for Scot to marry Scot and Ukrainian to marry Ukrainian, until whole districts were, well, some could almost be called the Total Ukraine. Of course, religion and language and the old ways played a very strong part in all this, but there was also the old-country feeling that the blood is strong. We've got to stick together. We can't intermarry, as if a Scottish girl marrying a Swedish boy was diluting the blood. Or a Ukrainian boy not marrying an English girl he'd met in the city because the community back home would frown on it. Very fiercely, I might add.

And yet they all got together, in business and to some degree in their social life. They mixed, but they did not mix where it was considered important. Religion, language, old ways, a way of thinking. But you'd have a district, all white in the early 1900s and by 1920 it was half English and half Slavic, farms interspersed, the school boards half and half, a few of the town's businesses owned by the newcomers, a mix on the volunteer fire department and the town's baseball team. That kind of thing.

And did you catch what I just said? I said a district would be all white. I don't do that very often. You can see, I am a product of my community too. Today that is not done. But when I was a child, the Slavic people were utter strangers from a faraway foreign land, and the pioneers and their descendants, us, we were the whites, and they were the foreigners. A slip of the tongue, but really a slip of the mind. Sorry.

What I am saying is that there was no sense of history in the West about the West. A few, but very few, were labouring away at this thankless task, and receiving no credit. The books didn't sell.

Summing up, I got nowhere. I'm not blaming this professor. He was just the start of it. I went further. I knew, however, that it would be the same. They just couldn't grasp the concept. I went over to a professor at United College, a man who had his roots deep in the part of Manitoba I came from, and do you know what he said? He said, almost his very words, 'You could do better in the marks department for your thesis if you did something about the CPR.' The CPR! It had been done to death then, and it's been done to death ever since, and what can you write about that bunch of thugs who bled and milked the West dry and are still doing it, and that is the scandal of it all. When I think of the several professors I went to with my idea for the thesis, I thought, is there any hope for any of us? It turned me off the academic community.

Of course, look at today. Everybody out there is writing of some aspect of what I was talking about. But I could have got them when the real thing was there. Now, it seems, they are just interviewing grandchildren and their children. None of the original stuff left. What a sad thing, a pity, really.

It is all still there, though, just the tales and the tall tales are missing. There are districts populated or pioneered by three or four families seven decades, nine decades, ago, and these families are still dominant, although there has been a strong ethnic mix. Good! Good! I say that is very good. Mix it up. We were never the melting-pot that some people seem to think we were. But the family and the family tradition and the communities they formed, that is still important.

The museums, like the Western Development Museums and others, and the books and the plays, they can tell some of it. But it is still a lot of what people have in their brains, their minds, their hearts, their souls, and yes, oh yes, in their likes and dislikes and prejudices, that's where you find the true story. Maybe it can't be put down on paper for a book any more, but I wish they had let me try."

ꙮ *What Farming Should Be All About*

"I'd like to be farming today like my dad did thirty years ago, and that's for sure. He had a section, just 640 acres, and that was okay. He had a good line of machinery and it was paid for. He had 450 acres of good cropland and the rest was pasture and bush, and on the pasture he had twenty cows and a bunch of calves, so he fed about sixteen to twenty steers and sold some of them every fall. He could sell every bushel of wheat he took off, and none of this quota business.

He and Mom had a nice house for us kids, and the school bus ran right by the door and we had a good sedan, a Chev, and a pickup truck and neither of them was new, just like the equipment, and we didn't owe a cent. No Visa card, no MasterCard, and he paid cash.

Mom had chickens and ducks and turkeys and she was a real

farm wife, and my brothers and sisters and myself, we worked in
the big garden and she canned and preserved and we had a root
cellar. We went to town or into Saskatoon quite a lot to the pictures
or to have a big meal, a dinner for a birthday, and we went to
church on Sundays, too.

That was farming, and my father did not owe one cent. Not one
damned penny.

Now look at us. My brother is on that farm, Dad dead and
Mother in the old folks' home in town and happy as she ever was.
And my brother is up to his ears in debt, owes on everything, has
2,300 acres, and is going broke. The rest of us, we're scraping away
too, all in the city now. And I look back on those days when I was
a kid, no TV then, our own land, our own ponies, playing ball
half the summer nights, and damn it, that was good. And I think,
that's what farming should be all about. Not this rat race we're in
now."

🕊 *Prairieness*

"Like they say now, farmers live poor and die rich. Well, I'll tell
you, my wife and I didn't. We walked away with about $325,000
plus what we got for the machinery and all that, so you're looking
at nearly $400,000 and that looks pretty good, doesn't it? You bet
it does.

But look at it this way. I put forty years into that land, and so
did my wife and my kids, growing up. That's forty years, and
divide it and you've got $10,000 a year. I don't think there are
many businessmen who would say they were doing good if they
only put $10,000 a year away in profits. So we didn't get much of
a price when you think of it that way, but it was the only price we
could get, the way we were thinking.

That was in the spring of '85. We thought, where will we go?
We could live in the house until fall when the new owner would
move his family in, but we decided we'd move out as soon as we
could. That was a gut-wrencher in some ways. Not leaving farming,
no, that wasn't hard. Leaving the place was hard. Like saying
goodbye to an old friend and knowing we would never see him
again. I didn't figure we had any right to come back, poking around.

We thought of Red Deer. They've got that great Legion there, and I could have fit in okay and so could Marg. Lots of activities, and the town is full of retired farmers like ourselves. It would have been okay. And then we thought of the Coast. Vancouver Island somewhere, Nanaimo or Parksville or Courtenay, one of those smaller places than Victoria. We'd been out there. Good climate. No winters to speak of. That part of the country seemed okay, but somehow, well, to this day I'm not sure why we didn't go. Might as well be miserable in a place where it's warm as in a place like Calgary where it's cold half the year.

I guess we chose Calgary for a reason I can't explain. Couldn't then, anyway. It was just that I didn't want to lose my prairieness, if there's such a word. A part of which is me, and my wife. That part that says you're prairie folk. And all those high cedar trees and high mountains and the sea, the ocean, that's fine, but I guess what it all boils down to was the sunrises and the sunsets. And the wind. Sun and wind. Our house, in the morning at home when I'd be having breakfast, say at 5:30 in the summer and 8 in winter, there would be the sun coming up, just a-burning in the sky, and I'd finish and go outside and there would be the wind. Sometimes soft from the west, sometimes hard. Always there, it seemed, kind of like an old friend.

When we were out on the Coast that couple of times I remembered I'd missed the wind, kind of like that nature was all around us but something important was missing. That wind. Like the high clouds in the west, coming in on you, and you knew the wind was there driving them along. And the sunsets. All different kinds. Rosy right across the sky, kind of a nice way to end each day, and each one was different. We're supposed to be a kind of unsentimental bunch, not all that much education, and our noses to the grindstones all the time, well, that is not so. I could get pretty sentimental about that sunrise and those sunsets and the wind.

So, like the damn fools we were, we decided not to go to the Coast, but I'm not sure Calgary was the right place. Too big. Now this is an unfriendly place. Even in the downtown Legion, there is people, guys sitting alone at a table or a couple, talking a bit but not much, and nobody has the idea of ringing a big bell at the bar and the bartender yelling, 'Okay, everybody, join the people at the next table. They're lonely too.' "

🕊 *Live and Let Live*

"This town hasn't changed much. Still three stores but not the same owners. The Co-op too. The hotel, two cafés, the bakery, same family for forty years, and our little newspaper, and new things like a jewellery store and, would you believe it, a florist shop, and the young woman seems to be making some sort of a go of it.

I'm eighty-eight and I've seen a lot and I'd say not much has changed except the young people. Or their morals is what I'm talking about. Or lack of them. The girl across the street, not more than sixteen, got pregnant and went off to Winnipeg. Had it, came back without it, waltzed right back into the school here, just as merry as you please. A cheery smile for me when I see her on the street, and no shame. No shame at all. Can you believe it? I'm showing my age, aren't I? You don't seem shocked. Oh well.

You hear the gossip at the club, or downstairs at dinner. This girl is pregnant, or that one went off to Winnipeg or Brandon and had an abortion. Why, it never seems to stop. Who are these girls and who are these boys that are getting them that way? Well, I'll just tell you. Right in our own local high school.

So, little May across the street, no last name please, she has her baby and somebody adopts it. Let's hope it is a doctor or a lawyer's wife who can't have any. The child is in better hands than in May's. She's just a little small-town girl. Why ruin her life with a baby she thinks is a toy more than her own flesh and blood? Just hope all the Mays in Canada get over it, because it must be a great pain to her, too. Just accept her as she is. Really she is a very nice girl. Let her go back to her high school classes and laugh and play like the other kids and hope she has learned a lesson.

Forget we're a small town and everybody knows, and everybody sees her. Just let her live her life up until she gets married and has babies of her own, and let's not criticize. Five years ago I wouldn't be talking this way. Live and let live, I mean. But I've changed. The children, their parents, us grandparents, we all live in different worlds, but we all live in the same world, too, and it's time we realized it. It still is wrong in my heart, but I've lived eighty-eight years and should be big enough now to accept these things. You're not doing yourself or anybody else any good in trying to think otherwise, or change things."

🐦 *Nobodies*

"This unemployment we've got now among the young people – everybody wants to go to university. I mean it. You ask a nine-year-old what he wants to do, and he doesn't want to be a fireman or a locomotive engineer. The kid wants to be a computer engineer. And they're teaching him computers at his age, right there in the schools. Christ, the kid is only nine years old. He should be out playing, kicking a soccer ball around and playing cowboys and Indians and going fishing in the polluted creek and diving off the railway bridge and breaking his neck. No, they all want to be doctors and lawyers and God knows what. They've got so many lawyers around now that soon they'll start cheating each other instead of the public. Everyone wants to be somebody.

Well, I say, somebody has got to be nobodies like myself. We make the world go round. Working on back-hoes, framing houses, driving truck, working the midnight shift in the bakeries and the dairies. I tell you, I don't know where it's all going to end. Aren't there going to be any welders or guys who drive Cat or do surveying up north or, well, hell, who's going to do the Joe jobs around this country?"

🐦 *Arabian Farmer*

"I'm going to tell you about the goddamnedest farmer I've ever heard of in all my life, and I know this because he's my sister's oldest kid.

Cathie scraped and sweated to send that boy to college, and when he got his degree he worked around for a while. This was back about twelve years ago and he got on with an oil outfit and was doing fine, and then he got this offer to work in Saudi Arabia. He did that for five years, no income tax to pay here, nothing, all gravy.

Now this is where it gets crazy. Because he came back about three years ago and he got one hell of a bargain on a section of good land around Didsbury. Put a big pile of his huge savings on it and that year put in winter wheat, which is kind of far north for that, but he did it. He had this month's holiday and he worked it over and seeded about five hundred acres and hired a guy from town to kind of keep an eye on the place a couple of times a week.

Off he goes to Saudi Arabia again and next July he comes back on his vacation again, company paying it, and hires another farmer with good equipment and they take off the crop, and it is a good one, believe you me. Back to the desert and the Arabs again and this time his father keeps an eye on the seeding, again by this neighbour, and the winter wheat gets sold this way or that way or stays in the bins. I know it's pretty complicated, but it works.

This nephew of mine, he's been doing this for three years and he's doing it again, and he's paying off that land with the money from the crop. A little for hired help and his lawyer, and the deal he's got with the farmer, this neighbour, to seed and take it off whether he's there or not, and boy, if that is not a sweet deal I don't know what is.

I guess I'm the only one that thinks it's a bit unusual, but I might be prejudiced. I'm just his uncle, and I remember that fellow when I thought he was just about the dumbest relative I had. And there he was, farming from ten thousand miles away."

✒ *A Factory Hand on the Land*

"Some day, maybe in ten years if things keep up, parts of Saskatchewan are just going to be these huge corporate farms, like 150,000 acres and more. If you lived in Russia you'd call them state farms.

The lads who are farming today, those caught with their pants down with land bought at seven hundred dollars an acre and high interest over twenty years and a yardful of expensive machinery, a $120,000 combine, they'll be working for the corporates.

They'll live in town and get up, drive to a place where there's a room with computers in it, and they'll be handed a slip of paper and they'll drive to work, discing, harrowing, combining, whatever, and when six o'clock rolls around they'll drive home for supper, and that's what farming will be all about. Half the farmers you see today won't own their farms. They'll be working for the corporates, for so much an hour and such and such benefits, and it will be not much different than working in a factory. A lot more fresh air to breathe, but not much more.

You take the ownership of land away from a farmer, then you

take the love of the land away, too. And that's what farming is all about. Love of the land. It's deep in us. Our roots. What our daddy's genes gave us. Take away that love, and all you've got is a factory hand.

To me that's awful sad. It's a crying shame, and I don't know how it came about. I'd like to blame the government, but no, that's not right this time. Blame the farmers. No. Who do you blame? Nobody. Everybody. That's what's so sad about the whole thing."

🕊 *Sunsets, Sunrises*

"I miss the farm. You can love the farm and you can hate it, but I think you'll always miss it. Oh, yes, even after all these years, normal school, teaching five years, marriage, five babies, Edmonton and then Calgary, and even now, when I'm up and about the kitchen early and I see the sun rising, I think, oh, it's just like it was back on the farm.

Fifty years since the Depression and I still remember the awful times, but then I think of the good things, like the sunrises in winter and so cold out and that big orange ball coming up, red and then orange, and then I see it from my kitchen in the mornings now, and I don't think of the bad times of the thirties. I think of the good times. School. Friends. Our little Christmas parties. Gopher-hunting. Going to town with my family on Saturday night in the buggy. Sunsets. Sunrises."

🕊 *No More Prairie Winters*

"We were in Victoria, in this motel, we'd driven all the way from our place near Brandon. And one night we'd been to a darn good Chinese restaurant with the Carters from Wetaskiwin and the Kolnyks from near Battleford and we've had a few drinks. We get back and we settle down and I pour us a good drink of rye and I'm thinking and then I say, 'Meg, old girl, why don't we take off one more crop and sell out and live here?'

Just popped out, kind of like when a young fellow proposes marriage and doesn't know he's ready to pop the question but he's been thinking about it and he gets the idea his girl is ready.

Quick as a slick, she says, 'Why take off another crop? Why not sell out next month, or in April? Why waste another year taking off a crop, and it could be drought or we'll get hailed?'

I hope it just wasn't the drinks I'd had, but you know I got up and I stood in the middle of the floor and I said I was gonna make a speech. I said, 'I ain't gonna put up with no more prairie winters ever again, and you can bet your life on that.'

That's all it was. You know, some people who have just made the biggest decision of their lives, selling out, they'd be most likely to talk about it, jawing back and forth, like what about this and what about that. We didn't. No sir. No sirree. We made up our minds for good right then and there. In that room we were renting.

She only said one thing. She said, 'I'm worried about my lilacs.' I told her, 'Look outside, they could grow bananas here, why can't you have lilacs? I'll buy a house with a yardful of them.'

A couple of more drinks out of that bottle and it was finished, but we sipped and talked and, darn it all, it was all settled. I'd lived sixty-four years more or less on that home place, and built it up by seven quarters, all good land and paying good, too, and it was like walking away from a hotel room after staying the night.

Well, I'm putting you on there. Not quite as easy."

❧ Prairie People

"My wife and I moved to Duncan and boy, nobody talked to us for a long time, months, people we'd see every day, and I said to my wife, what's wrong here? We just had been running up against the wrong kind of people, people not from the Prairies. Then one day I'm in the fast check-out at our supermarket, and there's this woman ahead of me with a pretty big bag of potatoes, the net-string kind of bag, and it had come loose, and spuds were going to start spilling. She noticed it and quick as a wink she grabbed the loose end and gave it a twist and a fast knot to it and I said, 'Boy, you must have sacked a lot of spuds in your life.' She smiled and said, 'Thousands, tens of thousands,' and then she went through and I bought my tin of tobacco and caught up with her outside the door. I hoisted this bag and said I'd take it to her car and she said her husband was supposed to drive up but he hadn't, so we walked to the car and there he was, having a little snooze. The three of us got talking and they were from Taber and I was from near Brandon and we talked the same talk and the upshot was, we went for coffee. Yep, you guessed it. They were as lonely as the wife and I were, and what happened was this. We got together for a beer in the Legion that Friday night and went on from there, a game of bridge a week later, and we met a couple of couples they had met, and in about a year there were a lot of couples from the Prairies we knew. Life started to get better then.

The prairie people, when you had them for friends you didn't need any British Columbians. There is just something about living on the Prairies that binds people together. It is like being in a war, I'd say. Hardship, surviving, that's it in a nutshell. It brings people together."

🕊 *People Will Never Know*

"Every spring just about this time, late in May I get in the car and drive out to the old home place. It's all these huge farms now, those huge tractors going across the fields and the houses far apart, and I really don't think of it as my part of the country, where I was born and raised, until I get to the farm.

It's not our farm any more. It used to be known as the Davidson Place, the way they identified farms in those days. The Rushton Place, the McKay Place, and so on. It's down this road, not a good road any more but still better than I remembered it when it was dirt, mud in spring and dusty in summer, and at least they put some gravel on it.

I've often asked myself why I go back. There's nothing there but the old buildings and a lot of my memories. There should be–after all, I spent seventeen years of my life there on that farm. Old house, old sheds, old trees, it's a picture that you often see in the galleries at high prices, but they don't get into the painting what you feel when you see it, or you've lived it. It's a shame, really, because in that painting could be the hopes and dreams and the loving and the hating and the disappointments and the happy successes of one family. I'm sure you know what I mean. You see these old home-steads all over the country. A city person would say, why don't they burn that eyesore down? It would just take a few minutes. One can of gas and three matches and it would be gone. But they don't, not even the new farmers who take over the land.

I suppose, in one way, the new farmer thinks like I do, that these so-called eyesores are the monuments to the people who came west in the early days, and struggled like nobody today would believe. Terrible odds. No sane gambler would go up against those odds. But the homesteaders didn't know, of course. And one year followed the next, summer into winter into summer, and they carried on. They raised their children, and they grew old and died on the farm or they moved into town. And the children, some went off to the city or died in the two wars, and farming changed, and it just wasn't possible to make a living off a small farm. There are times I doubt whether it ever was possible, remembering how we lived.

Now I go back, and my daughter tells me that at sixty-nine I'm too old to be driving all that way, but I want to be alone. I take a little lunch and I sit on one of the rock piles and eat my lunch and I wander around the home place. Me and my memories. The place is unsafe and I dare not go in, but there's where my mother slaved over that big Empress stove, and slaved is the word. I think now she was never more than four steps from it the whole day. Always something on it, simmering or bubbling away, and she was a marvellous cook.

The kitchen table, with the oilcloth on it. Everything was done at that table. You made your bread on it, cut your vegetables, ate off it, did your homework at it, read stories there, and when people came to visit, if they were friends you sat around it and talked or played cards. If it was business, of course that was done in the parlour. That was off limits to us kids.

Upstairs the bedrooms, three of them, and no bathroom, of course. That was out at the back, about fifty steps beyond the garden and off to the side where my dad had his pigs.

I walk around and sit on a rock pile in the Big Field, as we called it, and the smooth rocks are warm and I sit there and look off to the west. The day I go the sun is always just right with a few clouds, a kind of calendar-art day, and I think about those rocks. I wonder how many I picked, just a little kid and throwing them on to the stone-boat? Mickey and Jack were our horses for that kind of work, and they'd drag that stone-boat over and we'd throw the rocks on. Summer and fall, day after day when there was nothing to do.

'We're picking rocks today, kids,' my father used to say at breakfast. Oh, dreaded words. Those rocks could tell a story. Tens of thousands of them. Every spring the earth would push them up everywhere, and they had to be moved.

The old trees are there, the ones planted by my grandfather and my father. Some are so gnarled and old and withered you could hardly call them trees any more, but the brave leaves come out, and there are the birds' nests. Many generations of young ones hatched there, you know, and for years there has been a family of coyotes somewhere in there. She's got a den, and if you're quiet the pups will finally get tired of the dark and come out, looking around, and then they start fooling around. I know the mother is somewhere keeping an eye on me, but if she's the same mother of the past four or five years she should be used to me. Foxes, too. Down near where the two granaries used to be there is a fox den, but we're not on speaking terms. And an old owl. It's been there as long as I can remember, and, of course, the hawks. You never see a mouse anywhere, but they must be around.

It is so quiet. The sound of a truck on the highway three miles north, you can hear it sometimes, and the cry of the hawk, but most of all it is the wind. That old wind has been around since I was a little girl so long ago. Strong sometimes, and you can see the dust devils twirling around on the summer fallow and the seeded land, but mostly it is just there. Always there. From the west. It always reminds me of that line out of one of Pauline Johnson's poems, remember her? She was a heroine to all us girls in those days. It went, 'Oh, wind of the West, I wait for you. . . .'

I feel so comfortable when it is blowing gently on my face, and I'll sit on one of those smooth, warm rocks and eat my little lunch and drink my coffee and think, and this is what I think, you know. This is the land. If everything crumbles into nothing in some huge nuclear blast, but people who have fled from the city have survived, they will have nothing. Nothing of what they think is important in the city. But they will have this land. Always there and always ready and willing and happy to feed you. The land. It's deep in my heart, just like it is in the heart of any person who was born on it, and it is something they can't take away from you. It is part of you. I'm not trying to be dramatic or sentimental in telling you this. I'm too old for that. But the feeling is there, and it is such a strong feeling.

My oldest grandson, the Genius of the Computer as I call him, he'd say, 'It's just dirt. It can be explained, Grandma. Nothing mysterious or magical about it.' I don't argue with him. Let him explain everything with his computer. But it is mysterious and magical because it affects us. You can pick up a handful, look at it, rub it together with your other hand, let it fall, and yes, it is just dirt. Just soil. But if you didn't have that, mankind would not survive. It is as simple as that. There would be no world without that handful of what he calls just dirt.

I sit there, an old woman living alone, feeling poetic in a way, and the sun is warm on me and I hear the skirling cry that the hawks make and I just sit there and remember the good days our family had here. Never the bad days. Thinking about the bad days is for another place and another time, not with the sun coming down on you. I think of when I left the place to go to normal school, and when we all got together many years later and decided to sell the farm after my father died, and the last supper we had in the house before the new owner moved in, a real farm supper. I think of all these things and how it was for me as a child, such a happy time, so happy, and then it is time to go.

I think each time will be my last visiting the old home place, my last kick at the can, so to speak. I treat it as such, not morbidly, not with sadness. I enjoy myself thoroughly with my memories.

Then it is time to go, and that is it for another year with my memories. People will never know.' "